THE P

OF

EUGENE FIELD

COMPLETE EDITION

WILDSIDE PRESS

www.wildsidepress.com

Published November, 1910
Reprinted January, March, December, 1911; August, 1912; December, 1913; May, 1915; September, 1916; May, 1917; December, 1918; May, 1919.

CONTENTS

WESTERN AND OTHER VERSE

vi

CONTENTS

POEMS OF CHILDHOOD

ECHOES FROM THE SABINE FARM

By Eugene and Roswell Martin Field

VARIOUS TRANSLATIONS

SHARPS AND FLATS

THE POEMS
OF
EUGENE FIELD

WESTERN AND OTHER VERSE

TO MARY FIELD FRENCH

A DYING mother gave to you
   Her child a many years ago;
How in your gracious love he grew,
   You know, dear, patient heart, you know.

The mother's child you fostered then
   Salutes you now and bids you take
These little children of his pen
   And love them for the author's sake.

To you I dedicate this book,
   And, as you read it line by line,
Upon its faults as kindly look
   As you have always looked on mine.

Tardy the offering is and weak;—
   Yet were I happy if I knew
These children had the power to speak
   My love and gratitude to you.

CASEY'S TABLE D'HÔTE

OH, them days on Red Hoss Mountain, when the skies wuz fair
      'nd blue,
When the money flowed like likker, 'nd the folks wuz brave 'nd
      true!
When the nights wuz crisp 'nd balmy, 'nd the camp wuz all astir,
With the joints all throwed wide open 'nd no sheriff to demur!
Oh, them times on Red Hoss Mountain in the Rockies fur away,—

There 's no sich place nor times like them as I kin find to-day!
What though the camp *hez* busted? I seem to see it still
A-lyin', like it loved it, on that big 'nd warty hill;
And I feel a sort of yearnin' 'nd a chokin' in my throat
When I think of Red Hoss Mountain 'nd of Casey's tabble dote!

Wal, yes; it's true I struck it rich, but that don't cut a show
When one is old 'nd feeble 'nd it 's nigh his time to go;
The money that he 's got in bonds or carries to invest
Don't figger with a codger who has lived a life out West;
Us old chaps like to set around, away from folks 'nd noise,
'Nd think about the sights we seen and things we done when boys;
The which is why *I* love to set 'nd think of them old days
When all us Western fellers got the Colorado craze,—
And *that* is why I love to set around all day 'nd gloat
On thoughts of Red Hoss Mountain 'nd of Casey's tabble dote.

This Casey wuz an Irishman,—you 'd know it by his name
And by the facial features appertainin' to the same.
He 'd lived in many places 'nd had done a thousand things,
From the noble art of actin' to the work of dealin' kings,
But, somehow, had n't caught on; so, driftin' with the rest,
He drifted for a fortune to the undeveloped West,
And he come to Red Hoss Mountain when the little camp wuz
    new,
When the money flowed like likker, 'nd the folks wuz brave 'nd
    true;
And, havin' been a stewart on a Mississippi boat,
He opened up a caffy 'nd he run a tabble dote.

The bar wuz long 'nd rangy, with a mirrer on the shelf,
'Nd a pistol, so that Casey, when required, could help himself;
Down underneath there wuz a row of bottled beer 'nd wine,
'Nd a kag of Burbun whiskey of the run of '59;
Upon the walls wuz pictures of hosses 'nd of girls,—
Not much on dress, perhaps, but strong on records 'nd on curls!
The which had been identified with Casey in the past,—
The hosses 'nd the girls, I mean,—and both wuz mighty fast!
But all these fine attractions wuz of precious little note
By the side of what wuz offered at Casey's tabble dote.

There wuz half-a-dozen tables altogether in the place,
And the tax you had to pay upon your vittles wuz a case;
The boardin'-houses in the camp protested 't wuz a shame
To patronize a robber, which this Casey wuz the same!
They said a case was robbery to tax for ary meal;
But Casey tended strictly to his biz, 'nd let 'em squeal;
And presently the boardin'-houses all began to bust,
While Casey kept on sawin' wood 'nd layin' in the dust;
And oncet a trav'lin' editor from Denver City wrote
A piece back to his paper, puffin' Casey's tabble dote.

A tabble dote is different from orderin' aller cart:
In *one* case you git all there is, in *t' other*, only *part!*
And Casey's tabble dote began in French,—as all begin,—
And Casey's ended with the same, which is to say, with "vin";
But in between wuz every kind of reptile, bird, 'nd beast,
The same like you can git in high-toned restauraws down East;
'Nd windin' up wuz cake or pie, with coffee demy tass,
Or, sometimes, floatin' Ireland in a soothin' kind of sass
That left a sort of pleasant ticklin' in a feller's throat,
'Nd made him hanker after more of Casey's tabble dote.

The very recollection of them puddin's 'nd them pies
Brings a yearnin' to my buzzum 'nd the water to my eyes;
'Nd seems like cookin' nowadays ain't what it used to be
In camp on Red Hoss Mountain in that year of '63;
But, maybe, it is better, 'nd, maybe, I'm to blame—
I'd like to be a-livin' in the mountains jest the same—
I'd like to live that life again when skies wuz fair 'nd blue,
When things wuz run wide open 'nd men wuz brave 'nd true;
When brawny arms the flinty ribs of Red Hoss Mountain smote
For wherewithal to pay the price of Casey's tabble dote.

And you, O cherished brother, a-sleepin' 'way out West,
With Red Hoss Mountain huggin' you close to its lovin' breast,—
Oh, do you dream in your last sleep of how we used to do,
Of how we worked our little claims together, me 'nd you?
Why, when I saw you last a smile wuz restin' on your face,
Like you wuz glad to sleep forever in that lonely place;

And so you wuz, 'nd I 'd be, too, if I wuz sleepin' so.
But, bein' how a brother's love ain't for the world to know,
Whenever I 've this heartache 'nd this chokin' in my throat,
I lay it all to thinkin' of Casey's tabble dote.

THE CONVERSAZZHYONY

WHAT conversazzhyonies wuz I really did not know,
For that, you must remember, wuz a powerful spell ago;
The camp wuz new 'nd noisy, 'nd only modrit sized,
So fashionable sossiety wuz hardly crystallized.
There had n't been no grand events to interest the men,
But a lynchin', or a inquest, or a jackpot now an' then.
The wimmin-folks wuz mighty scarce, for wimmin, ez a rool,
Don't go to Colorado much, excep' for teachin' school,
An' bein' scarce an' chipper and pretty (like as not),
The bachelors perpose, 'nd air acepted on the spot.

Now Sorry Tom wuz owner uv the Gosh-all-Hemlock mine,
The wich allowed his better haff to dress all-fired fine;
For Sorry Tom wuz mighty proud uv her, an' she uv him,
Though *she* wuz short an' tacky, an' *he* wuz tall an' slim,
An' *she* wuz edjicated, an' Sorry Tom wuz *not*,
Yet, for *her* sake, he 'd whack up every cussid cent he 'd got!
Waal, jest by way uv celebratin' matrimonial joys,
She thought she 'd give a conversazzhyony to the boys,—
A peert an' likely lady, 'nd ez full uv 'cute idees
'Nd uv etiquettish notions ez a fyste is full uv fleas.

Three-Fingered Hoover kind uv kicked, an' said they might be
    durned
So far ez any conversazzhyony was concerned;
He 'd come to Red Hoss Mountain to tunnel for the ore,
An' *not* to go to parties,—quite another kind uv bore!
But, bein' he wuz candidate for marshal uv the camp,
I rayther had the upper holts in arguin' with the scamp;

Sez I, "Three-Fingered Hoover, can't ye see it is yer game
To go for all the votes ye kin an' collar uv the same?"
The wich perceivin', Hoover sez, "Waal, ef I *must,* I *must;*
So I'll frequent that conversazzhyony, ef I bust!"

Three-Fingered Hoover wuz a trump! Ez fine a man wuz he
Ez ever caused a inquest or blossomed on a tree!—
A big, broad man, whose face bespoke a honest heart within,—
With a bunch uv yaller whiskers appertainin' to his chin,
'Nd a fierce mustache turnt up so fur that both his ears wuz hid,
Like the picture that you always see in the "Life uv Cap'n Kidd."
His hair wuz long an' wavy an' fine as Southdown fleece,—
Oh, it shone an' smelt like Eden when he slicked it down with
    grease!
I 'll bet there wuz n't anywhere a man, all round, ez fine
Ez wuz Three-Fingered Hoover in the spring uv '69!

The conversazzhyony wuz a notable affair,
The bong tong deckolett 'nd en regaly bein' there;
The ranch where Sorry Tom hung out wuz fitted up immense,—
The Denver papers called it a "palashal residence."
There wuz mountain pines an' fern an' flowers a-hangin' on the
    walls,
An' cheers an' hoss-hair sofies wuz a-settin' in the halls;
An' there wuz heaps uv pictures uv folks that lived down East,
Sech ez poets an' perfessers, an' last, but not the least,
Wuz a chromo uv old Frémont,—we liked that best, you bet,
For there 's lots uv us old miners that is votin' for him yet!

When Sorry Tom received the gang perlitely at the door,
He said that keerds would be allowed upon the second floor;
And then he asked us would we like a drop uv ody vee.
Connivin' at his meanin', we responded promptly, "Wee."
A conversazzhyony is a thing where people speak
The langwidge in the wich they air partickulerly weak:
"I see," sez Sorry Tom, "you grasp what that 'ere lingo means."
"You bet yer boots," sez Hoover; "I've lived at Noo Orleens,
An', though I ain't no Frenchie, nor kin unto the same,
I kin parly voo, an' git there, too, like Eli, toot lee mane!"

As speakin' French wuz not my forte,- -not even oovry poo,—
I stuck to keerds ez played by them ez did not parly voo,
An' bein' how that poker wuz my most perficient game,
I ponyed up for 20 blues an' set into the same.
Three-Fingered Hoover stayed behind an' parly-vood so well
That all the kramy delly krame allowed he wuz *the* belle.
The other candidate for marshal did n't have a show;
For, while Three-Fingered Hoover parlyed, ez they said, tray bow,
Bill Goslin did n't know enough uv French to git along,
'Nd I reckon that he had what folks might call a movy tong.

From Denver they had freighted up a real pianny-fort
Uv the warty-leg and pearl-around-the-keys-an'-kivver sort,
An', later in the evenin', Perfesser Vere de Blaw
Performed on that pianny, with considerable eclaw,
Sech high-toned opry airs ez one is apt to hear, you know,
When he rounds up down to Denver at a Emmy Abbitt show;
An' Barber Jim (a talented but ornery galoot)
Discoursed a obligatter, conny mory, on the floot,
Till we, ez sot up-stairs indulgin' in a quiet game,
Conveyed to Barber Jim our wish to compromise the same.

The maynoo that wuz spread that night wuz mighty hard to beat,—
Though somewhat awkward to pernounce, it was not so to eat:
There wuz puddin's, pies, an' sandwidges, an' forty kinds uv sass,
An' floatin' Irelands, custards, tarts, an' patty dee foy grass;
An' millions uv cove oysters wuz a-settin' round in pans,
'Nd other native fruits an' things that grow out West in cans.
But I wuz all kufflummuxed when Hoover said he 'd choose
"Oon peety morso, see voo play, de la cette Charlotte Rooze;"
I 'd knowed Three-Fingered Hoover for fifteen years or more,
'Nd I 'd never heern him speak so light uv wimmin folks before!

Bill Goslin heern him say it, 'nd uv course *he* spread the news
Uv how Three-Fingered Hoover had insulted Charlotte Rooze
At the conversazzhyony down at Sorry Tom's that night,
An' when they asked me, I allowed that Bill for once wuz right:
Although it broke my heart to see my friend go up the fluke,
We all opined his treatment uv the girl deserved rebuke.
It war n't no use for Sorry Tom to nail it for a lie,—

When it come to sassin' wimmin, there wuz blood in every eye;
The boom for Charlotte Rooze swep' on an' took the polls by storm,
An' so Three-Fingered Hoover fell a martyr to reform!

Three-Fingered Hoover said it was a terrible mistake,
An' when the votes wuz in, he cried ez if his heart would break.
We never knew who Charlotte wuz, but Goslin's brother Dick
Allowed she wuz the teacher from the camp on Roarin' Crick,
That had come to pass some foreign tongue with them uv our alite
Ez wuz at the high-toned party down at Sorry Tom's that night.
We let it drop—this matter uv the lady—there an' then,
An' we never heerd, nor wanted to, of Charlotte Rooze again,
An' the Colorado wimmin-folks, ez like ez not, don't know
How we vindicated all their sex a twenty year ago.

For in these wondrous twenty years has come a mighty change,
An' most of them old pioneers have gone acrost the range,
Way out into the silver land beyond the peaks uv snow,—
The land uv rest an' sunshine, where all good miners go.
I reckon they love to look, from out the silver haze,
Upon that God's own country where they spent sech happy days;
Upon the noble cities that have risen since they went;
Upon the camps an' ranches that are prosperous an' content;
An' best uv all, upon those hills that reach into the air,
Ez if to clasp the loved ones that are waitin' over there.

PROF. VERE DE BLAW

Achievin' sech distinction with his moddel tabble dote
Ez to make his Red Hoss Mountain restauraw a place uv note,
Our old friend Casey innovated somewhat round the place,
In hopes he would ameliorate the sufferin's uv the race;
'Nd uv the many features Casey managed to import
The most important wuz a Steenway gran' pianny-fort,
An' bein' there wuz nobody could play upon the same,
He telegraffed to Denver, 'nd a real perfesser came,—
The last an' crownin' glory uv the Casey restauraw
Wuz that tenderfoot musicianer, Perfesser Vere de Blaw!

His hair wuz long an' dishybill, an' he had a yaller skin,
An' the absence uv a collar made his neck look powerful thin:
A sorry man he wuz to see, ez mebby you 'd surmise,
But the fire uv inspiration wuz a-blazin' in his eyes!
His name wuz Blanc, wich same is Blaw (for that 's what Casey
      said,
An' Casey passed the French ez well ez any Frenchie bred);
But no one ever reckoned that it really wuz his name,
An' no one ever asked him how or why or whence he came,—
Your ancient history is a thing the Coloradan hates,
An' no one asks another what his name wuz in the States!

At evenin', when the work wuz done, an' the miners rounded up
At Casey's, to indulge in keerds or linger with the cup,
Or dally with the tabble dote in all its native glory,
Perfesser Vere de Blaw discoursed his music repertory
Upon the Steenway gran' pianny-fort, the wich wuz sot
In the hallway near the kitchen (a warm but quiet spot),
An' when De Blaw's environments induced the proper pride,—
Wich gen'rally wuz whiskey straight, with seltzer on the side,—
He throwed his soulful bein' into opry airs 'nd things
Wich bounded to the ceilin' like he 'd mesmerized the strings.

Oh, you that live in cities where the gran' piannies grow,
An' primy donnies round up, it 's little that you know
Uv the hungerin' an' the yearnin' wich us miners an' the rest
Feel for the songs we used to hear before we moved out West.
Yes, memory is a pleasant thing, but it weakens mighty quick;
It kind uv dries an' withers, like the windin' mountain crick,
That, beautiful, an' singin' songs, goes dancin' to the plains,
So long ez it is fed by snows an' watered by the rains;
But, uv that grace uv lovin' rains 'nd mountain snows bereft,
Its breachin' rocks, like dummy ghosts, is all its memory left.

The toons wich the perfesser would perform with sech eclaw
Would melt the toughest mountain gentleman I ever saw,—
Sech touchin' opry music ez the Trovytory sort,
The sollum "Mizer Reery," an' the thrillin' "Keely Mort";
Or, sometimes, from "Lee Grond Dooshess" a trifle he would play,
Or morsoze from a' opry boof, to drive dull care away;

Or, feelin' kind uv serious, he 'd discourse somewhat in C,—
The wich he called a' opus (whatever that may be);
But the toons that fetched the likker from the critics in the crowd
Wuz *not* the high-toned ones, Perfesser Vere de Blaw allowed.

'T wuz "Dearest May," an' "Bonnie Doon," an' the ballard
    uv "Ben Bolt,"
Ez wuz regarded by all odds ez Vere de Blaw's best holt;
Then there wuz "Darlin' Nellie Gray," an' "Settin' on the Stile,"
An' "Seein' Nellie Home," an' "Nancy Lee," 'nd "Annie Lisle,"
An' "Silver Threads among the Gold," an' "The Gal that Winked
    at Me,"
An' "Gentle Annie," "Nancy Till," an' "The Cot beside the Sea."
Your opry airs is good enough for them ez likes to pay
Their money for the truck ez can't be got no other way;
But opry to a miner is a thin an' holler thing,—
The music that he pines for is the songs he used to sing.

One evenin' down at Casey's De Blaw wuz at his best,
With four-fingers uv old Willer-run concealed beneath his vest;
The boys wuz settin' all around, discussin' folks an' things,
'Nd I had drawed the necessary keerds to fill on kings;
Three-Fingered Hoover kind uv leaned acrost the bar to say
If Casey 'd liquidate right off, *he 'd* liquidate next day;
A sperrit uv contentment wuz a-broodin' all around
(Onlike the other sperrits wich in restauraws abound),
When, suddenly, we heerd from yonder kitchen-entry rise
A toon each ornery galoot appeared to recognize.

Perfesser Vere de Blaw for once eschewed his opry ways,
An' the remnants uv his mind went back to earlier, happier days,
An' grappled like an' wrassled with a' old familiar air
The wich we all uv us had heern, ez you have, everywhere!
Stock still we stopped,—some in their talk uv politics an' things,
I in my unobtrusive attempt to fill on kings,
'Nd Hoover leanin' on the bar, an' Casey at the till,—
We all stopped short an' held our breaths (ez a feller sometimes
    will),
An' sot there more like bumps on logs than healthy, husky men,
Ez the memories uv that old, old toon come sneakin' back again.

You 've guessed it? No, you hav n't; for it wuzn 't that there song
Uv the home we 'd been away from an' had hankered for so
long,—
No, sir; it wuz n't "Home, Sweet Home," though it 's always
heard around
Sech neighborhoods in wich the home that *is* "sweet home" is
found.
And, ez for me, I seemed to see the past come back again,
And hear the deep-drawed sigh my sister Lucy uttered when
Her mother asked her if she 'd practised her two hours that day,
Wich, if she had n't she must go an' do it right away!
The homestead in the States 'nd all its memories seemed to come
A-floatin' round about me with that magic lumty-tum.

And then uprose a stranger wich had struck the camp that night;
His eyes wuz sot an' fireless, 'nd his face wuz spookish white,
'Nd he sez: "Oh, how I suffer there is nobody kin say,
Onless, like me, he 's wrenched himself from home an' friends away
To seek surcease from sorrer in a fur, seclooded spot,
Only to find—alars, too late!—the wich surcease is not!
Only to find that there air things that, somehow, seem to live
For nothin' in the world but jest the misery they give!
I 've travelled eighteen hundred miles, but that toon has got here
first;
I 'm done,—I 'm blowed,—I welcome death, an' bid it do its
worst!"

Then, like a man whose mind wuz sot on yieldin' to his fate,
He waltzed up to the counter an' demanded whiskey straight,
Wich havin' got outside uv,—both the likker and the door,—
We never seen that stranger in the bloom uv health no more!
But some months later, what the birds had left uv him wuz found
Associated with a tree, some distance from the ground;
And Husky Sam, the coroner, that set upon him, said
That two things wuz apparent, namely: first, deceast wuz dead;
And, second, previously had got involved beyond all hope
In a knotty complication with a yard or two uv rope!

OUR LADY OF THE MINE

THE Blue Horizon wuz a mine us fellers all thought well uv,
And there befell the episode I now perpose to tell uv;
'T wuz in the year uv sixty-nine,—somewhere along in summer,—
There hove in sight one afternoon a new and curious comer;
His name wuz Silas Pettibone,—a' artist by perfession,—
With a kit of tools and a big mustache and a pipe in his possession.
He told us, by our leave, he 'd kind uv like to make some sketches
Uv the snowy peaks, 'nd the foamin' crick, 'nd the distant mountain
  stretches;
"You 're welkim, sir," sez we, although this scenery dodge seemed
  to us
A waste uv time where scenery wuz already sooper-*floo*-us.

All through the summer Pettibone kep' busy at his sketchin',—
At daybreak off for Eagle Pass, and home at nightfall, fetchin'
That everlastin' book uv his with spider-lines all through it;
Three-Fingered Hoover used to say there war n't no meanin' to it.
"Gol durn a man," sez he to him, "whose shif'less hand is sot at
A-drawin' hills that 's full uv quartz that's pinin' to be got at!"
"Go on," sez Pettibone, "go on, if joshin' gratifies ye;
But one uv these fine times I 'll show ye sumthin' will surprise ye!"
The which remark led us to think—although he did n't say it—
That Pettibone wuz owin' us a gredge 'nd meant to pay it.

One evenin' as we sat around the Restauraw de Casey,
A-singin' songs 'nd tellin' yarns the which wuz sumwhat racy,
In come that feller Pettibone, 'nd sez, "With your permission,
I 'd like to put a picture I have made on exhibition."
He sot the picture on the bar 'nd drew aside its curtain,
Sayin', "I reckon you 'll allow as how *that* 's art, f'r certain!"
And then we looked, with jaws agape, but nary word wuz spoken,
And f'r a likely spell the charm uv silence wuz unbroken—
Till presently, as in a dream, remarked Three-Fingered Hoover:
"Onless I am mistaken, this is Pettibone's shef doover!"

It wuz a face—a human face—a woman's, fair 'nd tender—
Sot gracefully upon a neck white as a swan's, and slender;

The hair wuz kind uv sunny, 'nd the eyes wuz sort uv dreamy,
The mouth wuz half a-smilin', 'nd the cheeks wuz soft 'nd creamy;
It seemed like she wuz lookin' off into the west out yonder,
And seemed like, while she looked, we saw her eyes grow softer,
    fonder,—
Like, lookin' off into the west, where mountain mists wuz fallin',
She saw the face she longed to see and heerd his voice a-callin';
"Hooray!" we cried,—"a woman in the camp uv Blue Horizon!
Step right up, Colonel Pettibone, 'nd nominate your pizen!"

A curious situation,—one deservin' uv your pity,—
No human, livin', female thing this side of Denver City!
But jest a lot uv husky men that lived on sand 'nd bitters,—
Do you wonder that that woman's face consoled the lonesome
    critters?
And not a one but what it served in some way to remind him
Of a mother or a sister or a sweetheart left behind him;
And some looked back on happier days, and saw the old-time faces
And heerd the dear familiar sounds in old familiar places,—
A gracious touch of home. "Look here," sez Hoover, "ever'body
Quit thinkin' 'nd perceed at oncet to name his favorite toddy!"

It wuz n't long afore the news had spread the country over,
And miners come a-flockin' in like honey-bees to clover;
It kind uv did 'em good, they said, to feast their hungry eyes on
That picture uv Our Lady in the camp uv Blue Horizon.
But one mean cuss from Nigger Crick passed criticisms on 'er,—
Leastwise we overheerd him call her Pettibone's madonner,
The which we did not take to be respectful to a lady,
So we hung him in a quiet spot that wuz cool 'nd dry 'nd shady;
Which same might not have been good law, but it *wuz* the right
    manœuvre
To give the critics due respect for Pettibone's shef doover.

Gone is the camp,—yes, years ago the Blue Horizon busted,
And every mother's son uv us got up one day 'nd dusted,
While Pettibone perceeded East with wealth in his possession,
And went to Yurrup, as I heered, to study his perfession;
So, like as not, you'll find him now a-paintin' heads 'nd faces
At Venus, Billy Florence, and the like I-talyun places.

But no sech face he 'll paint again as at old Blue Horizon,
For I 'll allow no sweeter face no human soul sot eyes on;
And when the critics talk so grand uv Paris 'nd the Loover,
I say, "Oh, but you orter seen the Pettibone shef doover!"

MODJESKY AS CAMEEL

AFORE we went to Denver we had heerd the Tabor Grand,
Allowed by critics ez the finest opry in the land;
And, roundin' up at Denver in the fall of '81,
Well heeled in p'int uv looker 'nd a-pinin' for some fun,
We told Bill Bush that we wuz fixed quite comf'table for wealth,
And had n't struck that altitood entirely for our health.
You see we knew Bill Bush at Central City years ago;
(An' a whiter man than that same Bill you could not wish to
    know!)
Bill run the Grand for Tabor, 'nd he gin us two a deal
Ez how we really otter see Modjesky ez Cameel.

Three-Fingered Hoover stated that he'd great deal ruther go
To call on Charley Simpson than frequent a' opry show.
"The queen uv tragedy," sez he, "is wot I 've never seen,
And I reckon there is more for *me* in some other kind uv queen."
"Git out!" sez Bill, disgusted-like, "and can't you never find
A pleasure in the things uv life wich ellervates the mind?
You 've set around in Casey's restauraw a year or more,
An' heerd ol' Vere de Blaw perform shef doovers by the score,
Only to come down here among us *tong* an' say you feel
You 'd ruther take in faro than a' opry like 'Cameel'!"

But it seems it wur n't no opry, but a sort uv foreign play,
With a heap uv talk an' dressin' that wuz both de*kolly*tay.
A young chap sparks a gal, who 's caught a dook that 's old an'
    wealthy,—
She has a cold 'nd faintin' fits, and is gin'rally onhealthy.
She says she has a record; but the young chap does n't mind,
And it looks ez if the feller wuz a proper likely kind

Until his old man sneaks around 'nd makes a dirty break,
And the young one plays the sucker 'nd gives the girl the shake.
"Armo! Armo!" she hollers; but he flings her on the floor,
And says he ain'ter goin' to have no truck with her no more.

At that Three-Fingered Hoover says, "I ll chip into this game,
And see if Red Hoss Mountain cannot reconstruct the same.
I won't set by an' see the feelin's uv a lady hurt,—
Gol durn a critter, anyhow, that does a woman dirt!"
He riz up like a giant in that little painted pen,
And stepped upon the platform with the women-folks 'nd men;
Across the trough of gaslights he bounded like a deer,
An' grabbed Armo an' hove him through the landscape in the
     rear;
And then we seen him shed his hat an' reverently kneel,
An' put his strong arms tenderly around the gal Cameel.

A-standin' in his stockin' feet, his height wuz siz foot three,
And a huskier man than Hoover wuz you could not hope to see.
He downed Lafe Dawson wrasslin'; and one night I seen him lick
Three Cornish miners that come into camp from Roarin' Crick
To clean out Casey's restauraw an' do the town, they said.
He could whip his weight in wildcats, an' paint whole townships red,
But good to helpless folks and weak,—a brave and manly heart
A cyclone could n't phase, but any child could rend apart;
Jest like the mountain pine, wich dares the storm that howls
     along,
But rocks the winds uv summer-time, an' sings a soothin' song.

"Cameel," sez he, "your record is ag'in you, I 'll allow,
But, bein' you 're a woman, you 'll git justice anyhow;
So, if you say you're sorry, and intend to travel straight,—
Why, never mind that other chap with which you meant to mate,—
I'll marry you myself, and take you back to-morrow night
To the camp on Red Hoss Mountain, where the boys 'll treat you
     white,
Where Casey runs a tabble dote, and folks are brave 'nd true,
Where there ain't no ancient history to bother me or you,
Where there ain't no law but honesty, no evidence but facts,
Where between the verdick and the rope there ain't no *onter acts*."

I wuz mighty proud of Hoover; but the folks began to shout
That the feller was intrudin', and would some one put him out.
"Well, no; I reckon not," says I, or words to that effect,
Ez I perduced a' argument I thought they might respect,—
A long an' harnsome weepon I 'd pre-empted when I come
Out West (its cartridges wuz big an' juicy ez a plum),
Wich, when persented properly, wuz very apt to sway
The popular opinion in a most persuasive way.
"Well, no; I reckon not," says I; but I did n't say no more,
Observin' that there wuz a gin'ral movement towards the door.

First Dr. Lemen he allowed that he had got to go
And see a patient he jest heerd wuz lyin' very low;
An' Charlie Toll riz up an' said he guessed he 'd jine the Dock,
An' go to see a client wich wuz waitin' round the block;
John Arkins reckollected he had interviews to write,
And previous engagements hurried Cooper from our sight;
Cal Cole went out to buy a hoss, Fred Skiff and Belford too;
And Stapleton remembered he had heaps uv work to do.
Somehow or other every one wuz full uv business then;
Leastwise, they all vamoosed, and did n't bother us again.

I reckollect that Willard Morse an' Bush come runnin' in,
A-hollerin', "Oh, wot two idiots you durned fools have been!"
I reckollect that they allowed we 'd made a big mistake,—
They otter knowed us tenderfoots wuz sure to make a break!
An', while Modjesky stated we wuz somewhat off our base,
I half opined she liked it, by the look upon her face.
I reckollect that Hoover regretted he done wrong
In throwin' that there actor through a vista ten miles long.
I reckollect we all shuck hands, and ordered vin frappay,—
And I never shall forget the head I had on me next day!

I have n't seen Modjesky since; I 'm hopin' to again.
She 's goin' to show in Denver soon; I 'll go to see her then.
An' may be I shall speak to her, wich if I do 't will be
About the old friend restin' by the mighty Western sea,—
A simple man, perhaps, but good ez gold and true ez steel;
He could whip his weight in wildcats, and you never heerd him
    squeal;

Good to the helpless an' the weak; a brave an' manly heart
A cyclone could n't phase, but any child could rend apart;
So like the mountain pine, that dares the storm wich sweeps along,
But rocks the winds uv summer-time, an' sings a soothin' song.

MARTHY'S YOUNKIT

THE mountain brook sung lonesomelike, and loitered on its way
Ez if it waited for a child to jine it in its play;
The wild-flowers uv the hillside bent down their heads to hear
The music uv the little feet that had somehow grown so dear;
The magpies, like winged shadders, wuz a-flutterin' to an' fro
Among the rocks an' holler stumps in the ragged gulch below;
The pines an' hemlocks tosst their boughs (like they wuz arms) and
    made
Soft, sollum music on the slope where he had often played;
But for these lonesome, sollum voices on the mountain-side,
There wuz no sound the summer day that Marthy's younkit died.

We called him Marthy's younkit, for Marthy wuz the name
Uv her ez wuz his mar, the wife uv Sorry Tom,—the same
Ez taught the school-house on the hill, way back in '69,
When she marr'd Sorry Tom, wich owned the Gosh-all-Hemlock
    mine!
And Marthy's younkit wuz their first, wich, bein' how it meant
The first on Red Hoss Mountain, wuz truly a' event!
The miners sawed off short on work ez soon ez they got word
That Dock Devine allowed to Casey what had just occurred;
We loaded up an' whooped around until we all wuz hoarse
Salutin' the arrival, wich weighed ten pounds, uv course!

Three years, and sech a pretty child!—his mother's counterpart!
Three years, an' sech a holt ez he had got on every heart:—
A peert an' likely little tyke with hair ez red ez gold,
A-laughin', toddlin' everywhere,—'nd only three years old!
Up yonder, sometimes, to the store, an' sometimes down the hill
He kited (boys is boys, you know,—you could n't keep him still!)

An' there he 'd play beside the brook where purpul wild-flowers
    grew,
An' the mountain pines an' hemlocks a kindly shadder threw,
An' sung soft, sollum toons to him, while in the gulch below
The magpies, like strange sperrits, went flutterin' to an' fro.

Three years, an' then the fever come,—it wuz n't right, you know,
With all us old ones in the camp, for that little child to go;
It 's right the old should die, but that a harmless little child
Should miss the joy uv life an' love,—that can't be reconciled!
That 's what we thought that summer day, an' that is what we
    said
Ez we looked upon the piteous face uv Marthy's younkit dead.
But for his mother's sobbin', the house wuz very still,
An' Sorry Tom wuz lookin', through the winder, down the hill,
To the patch beneath the hemlocks where his darlin' used to play,
An' the mountain brook sung lonesomelike an' loitered on its way.

A preacher come from Roarin' Crick to comfort 'em an' pray,
'Nd all the camp wuz present at the obsequies next day;
A female teacher staged it twenty miles to sing a hymn,
An' we jined her in the chorus,—big, husky men an' grim
Sung "Jesus, Lover uv my Soul," an' then the preacher prayed,
An' preacht a sermon on the death uv that fair blossom laid
Among them other flowers he loved,—wich sermon set sech
    weight
On sinners bein' always heeled against the future state,
That, though it had been fashionable to swear a perfec' streak,
There war n't no swearin' in the camp for pretty nigh a week!

Last thing uv all, four strappin' men took up the little load
An' bore it tenderly along the windin', rocky road,
To where the coroner had dug a grave beside the brook,
In sight uv Marthy's winder, where the same could set an' look
An' wonder if his cradle in that green patch, long an' wide,
Wuz ez soothin' ez the cradle that wuz empty at her side;
An' wonder if the mournful songs the pines wuz singin' then
Wuz ez tender ez the lullabies she 'd never sing again,
'Nd if the bosom of the earth in wich he lay at rest
Wuz half ez lovin' 'nd ez warm ez wuz his mother's breast.

The camp is gone; but Red Hoss Mountain rears its kindly
    head,
An' looks down, sort uv tenderly, upon its cherished dead;
'Nd I reckon that, through all the years, that little boy wich
    died
Sleeps sweetly an' contentedly upon the mountain-side;
That the wild-flowers uv the summer-time bend down their heads
    to hear
The footfall uv a little friend they know not slumbers near;
That the magpies on the sollum rocks strange flutterin' shadders
    make,
An' the pines an' hemlocks wonder that the sleeper does n't wake;
That the mountain brook sings lonesomelike an' loiters on its
    way
Ez if it waited for a child to jine it in its play.

MADGE: YE HOYDEN

I

At Madge, ye hoyden, gossips scofft,
    Ffor that a romping wench was shee—
"Now marke this rede," they bade her oft,
    "Forsooken sholde your folly bee!"
But Madge, ye hoyden, laught & cried,
    "Oho, oho," in girlish glee,
And noe thing mo replied.

II

No griffe she had nor knew no care,
    But gayly rompit all daies long,
And, like ye brooke that everywhere
    Goes jinking with a gladsome song,
Shee danct and songe from morn till night,—
    Her gentil harte did know no wrong,
Nor did she none despight.

III

Sir Tomas from his noblesse halle
   Did trend his path a somer's daye,
And to ye hoyden he did call
   And these ffull evill words did say:
"O wolde you weare a silken gown
   And binde your haire with ribands gay?
Then come with me to town!"

IV

But Madge, ye hoyden, shoke her head,—
   "Ile be no lemman unto thee
For all your golde and gownes," shee said,
   "ffor Robin hath bespoken mee."
Then ben Sir Tomas sore despight,
   And back unto his hall went hee
With face as ashen white.

V

"O Robin, wilt thou wed this girl,
   Whenas she is so vaine a sprite?"
So spak ffull many an envious churle
   Unto that curteyse countrie wight.
But Robin did not pay no heede;
   And they ben wed a somer night
& danct upon ye meade.

VI

Then scarse ben past a yeare & daye
   Whan Robin toke unto his bed,
And long, long time therein he lay,
   Nor colde not work to earn his bread;
in soche an houre, whan times ben sore,
   Sr. Tomas came with haughtie tread
& knockit at ye doore.

VII

Saies: "Madge, ye hoyden, do you know
   how that you once despighted me?
But Ile forgiff an you will go
   my swete harte lady ffor to bee!"
But Madge, ye hoyden, heard noe more,—
   straightway upon her heele turnt shee,
& shote ye cottage doore.

VIII

Soe Madge, ye hoyden, did her parte
   whiles that ye years did come and go;
't was somer allwais in her harte,
   tho' winter strewed her head with snowe.
She toilt and span thro' all those years
   nor bid repine that it ben soe,
nor never shad noe teares.

IX

Whiles Robin lay within his bed,
   A divell came and whispered lowe,—
"Giff you will doe my will," he said,
   "None more of sickness you shall knowe!"
Ye which gave joy to Robin's soul—
   Saies Robin: "Divell, be it soe,
an that you make me whoale!"

X

That day, upp rising ffrom his bed,
   Quoth Robin: "I am well again!"
& backe he came as from ye dead,
   & he ben mickle blithe as when
he wooed his doxy long ago;
   & Madge did make ado & then
Her teares ffor joy did flowe.

XI

Then came that hell-born cloven thing—
  Saies: "Robin, I do claim your life,
and I hencefoorth shall be your king,
  and you shall do my evill strife.
Look round about and you shall see
  sr. Tomas' young and ffoolish wiffe—
a comely dame is shee!"

XII

Ye divell had him in his power,
  and not colde Robin say thereto:
Soe Robin from that very houre
  did what that divell bade him do;
He wooed and clipt, and on a daye
  sr. Tomas' wife and Robin flewe
a many leagues away.

XIII

Sir Tomas ben wood wroth and swore,
  And sometime strode thro' leaf & brake
and knockit at ye cottage door
  and thus to Madge, ye hoyden, spake:
Saies, "I wolde have you ffor mine own,
  So come with mee & bee my make,
syn tother birds ben flown."

XIV

But Madge, ye hoyden, bade him noe;
  Saies: "Robin is my swete harte still,
And, tho' he doth despight me soe,
  I mean to do him good for ill.
So goe, Sir Tomas, goe your way;
  ffor whiles I bee on live I will
ffor Robin's coming pray!"

XV

Soe Madge, ye hoyden, kneelt & prayed
　　that Godde sholde send her Robin backe.
And tho' ye folke vast scoffing made,
　　and tho' ye worlde ben colde and blacke,
And tho', as moneths dragged away,
　　ye hoyden's harte ben like to crack
With griff, she still did praye.

XVI

Sicke of that divell's damnèd charmes,
　　Aback did Robin come at last,
And Madge, ye hoyden, sprad her arms
　　and gave a cry and held him fast;
And as she clong to him and cried,
　　her patient harte with joy did brast,
& Madge, ye hoyden, died.

THE BIBLIOMANIAC'S PRAYER

KEEP me, I pray, in wisdom's way
　　That I may truths eternal seek;
I need protecting care to-day,—
　　My purse is light, my flesh is weak.
So banish from my erring heart
　　All baleful appetites and hints
Of Satan's fascinating art,
　　Of first editions, and of prints.
Direct me in some godly walk
　　Which leads away from bookish strife,
That I with pious deed and talk
　　May extra-illustrate my life.

But if, O Lord, it pleaseth Thee
　　To keep me in temptation's way.
I humbly ask that I may be
　　Most notably beset to-day;

Let my temptation be a book,
  Which I shall purchase, hold, and keep,
Whereon when other men shall look,
  They 'll wail to know I got it cheap.
Oh, let it such a volume be
  As in rare copperplates abounds,
Large paper, clean, and fair to see,
  Uncut, unique, unknown to Lowndes.

THE TRUTH ABOUT HORACE

It is very aggravating
To hear the solemn prating
Of the fossils who are stating
    That old Horace was a prude;
When we know that with the ladies
He was always raising Hades,
And with many an escapade his
    Best productions are imbued.

There 's really not much harm in a
Large number of his carmina,
But these people find alarm in a
    Few records of his acts;
So they 'd squelch the muse caloric,
And to students sophomoric
They 'd present as metaphoric
    What old Horace meant for facts.

We have always thought 'em lazy;
Now we adjudge 'em crazy!
Why, Horace was a daisy
    That was very much alive!
And the wisest of us know him
As his Lydia verses show him,—
Go, read that virile poem,—
    It is No. 25.

He was a very owl, sir,
And starting out to prowl, sir,
You bet he made Rome howl, sir,
 Until he filled his date;
With a massic-laden ditty
And a classic maiden pretty
He painted up the city,
 And Mæcenas paid the freight!

———

OUR TWO OPINIONS

Us two wuz boys when we fell out,—
 Nigh to the age uv my youngest now;
Don't rec'lect what 't wuz about,
 Some small deeff'rence, I 'll allow.
Lived next neighbors twenty years,
 A-hatin' each other, me 'nd Jim,—
He havin' *his* opinyin uv *me*,
 'Nd *I* havin' *my* opinyin uv *him*.

Grew up together 'nd would n't speak,
 Courted sisters, 'nd marr'd 'em, too;
'Tended same meetin'-house oncet a week,
 A-hatin' each other through 'nd through!
But when Abe Linkern asked the West
 F'r soldiers, we answered,—me 'nd Jim,—
He havin' *his* opinyin uv *me*,
 'Nd *I* havin' *my* opinyin uv *him*.

But down in Tennessee one night
 Ther' wuz sound uv firin' fur away,
'Nd the sergeant allowed ther' 'd be a fight
 With the Johnnie Rebs some time nex' day;
'Nd as I wuz thinkin' uv Lizzie 'nd home
 Jim stood afore me, long 'nd slim,—
He havin' *his* opinyin uv *me*,
 'Nd *I* havin' *my* opinyin uv *him*.

Seemed like we knew there wuz goin' to be
   Serious trouble f'r me 'nd him;
Us two shuck hands, did Jim 'nd me,
   But never a word from me or Jim!
He went *his* way 'nd *I* went *mine*,
   'Nd into the battle's roar went we,—
I havin' *my* opinyin uv Jim,
   'Nd *he* havin' *his* opinyin uv *me*.

Jim never come back from the war again,
   But I hain't forgot that last, last night
When, waitin' f'r orders, us two men
   Made up 'nd shuck hands, afore the fight.
'Nd, after it all, it's soothin' to know
   That here *I* be 'nd yonder's Jim,—
He havin' *his* opinyin uv *me*,
   'Nd *I* havin' *my* opinyin uv *him*.

LITTLE MACK

THIS talk about the journalists that run the East is bosh,
We've got a Western editor that's little, but, O gosh!
He lives here in Mizzoora where the people are so set
In ante-bellum notions that they vote for Jackson yet;
But the paper he is running makes the rusty fossils swear,—
The smartest, likeliest paper that is printed anywhere!
And, best of all, the paragraphs are pointed as a tack,
     And that's because they emanate
       From little Mack.

In architecture he is what you'd call a chunky man,
As if he'd been constructed on the summer cottage plan;
He has a nose like Bonaparte; and round his mobile mouth
Lies all the sensuous languor of the children of the South;
His dealings with reporters who affect a weekly bust
Have given to his violet eyes a shadow of distrust;
In glorious abandon his brown hair wanders back
     From the grand Websterian forehead
      Of little Mack.

No matter what the item is, if there 's an item in it,
You bet your life he 's on to it and nips it in a minute!
From multifarious nations, countries, monarchies, and lands,
From Afric's sunny fountains and India's coral strands,
From Greenland's icy mountains and Siloam's shady rills,
He gathers in his telegrams, and Houser pays the bills;
What though there be a dearth of news, he has a happy knack
        Of scraping up a lot of scoops,
            Does little Mack.

And learning? Well he knows the folks of every tribe and age
That ever played a part upon this fleeting human stage;
His intellectual system 's so extensive and so greedy
That, when it comes to records, he 's a walkin' cyclopedy;
For having studied (and digested) all the books a-goin',
It stands to reason he must know about all 's worth a-knowin'!
So when a politician with a record 's on the track,
        We 're apt to hear some history
            From little Mack.

And when a fellow-journalist is broke and needs a twenty,
Who 's allus ready to whack up a portion of his plenty?
Who 's allus got a wallet that 's as full of sordid gain
As his heart is full of kindness and his head is full of brain?
Whose bowels of compassion will in-va-ri-a-bly move
Their owner to those courtesies which plainly, surely prove
That he 's the kind of person that never does go back
        On a fellow that 's in trouble?
            Why, little Mack!

I've heard 'em tell of Dana, and of Bonner, and of Reid,
Of Johnnie Cockerill, who, I 'll own, is very smart indeed;
Yet I don't care what their renown or influence may be,
One metropolitan exchange is quite enough for me!
So keep your Danas, Bonners, Reids, your Cockerills, and the
    rest,
The woods is full of better men all through this woolly West;
For all that sleek, pretentious, Eastern editorial pack
        We would n't swap the shadow of
            Our little Mack!

TO ROBIN GOODFELLOW

I SEE you, Maister Bawsy-brown,
  Through yonder lattice creepin';
You come for cream and to gar me dream,
  But you dinna find me sleepin'.
The moonbeam, that upon the floor
  Wi' crickets ben a-jinkin',
Now steals away fra' her bonnie play—
  Wi' a rosier blie, I 'm thinkin'.

I saw you, Maister Bawsy-brown,
  When the blue bells went a-ringin'
For the merrie fays o' the banks an' braes,
  And I kenned your bonnie singin';
The gowans gave you honey sweets,
  And the posies on the heather
Dript draughts o' dew for the faery crew
  That danct and sang together.

But posie-bloom an' simmer-dew
  And ither sweets o' faery
C'u'd na gae down wi' Bawsy-brown,
  Sae nigh to Maggie's dairy!
My pantry shelves, sae clean and white,
  Are set wi' cream and cheeses,—
Gae, gin you will, an' take your fill
  Of whatsoever pleases.

Then wave your wand aboon my een
  Until they close awearie,
And the night be past sae sweet and fast
  Wi' dreamings o' my dearie.
But pinch the wench in yonder room,
  For she 's na gude nor bonnie,—
Her shelves be dust and her pans be rust,
  And she winkit at my Johnnie!

APPLE–PIE AND CHEESE

FULL many a sinful notion
  Conceived of foreign powers
Has come across the ocean
  To harm this land of ours;
And heresies called fashions
  Have modesty effaced,
And baleful, morbid passions
  Corrupt our native taste.
O tempora! O mores!
  What profanations these
That seek to dim the glories
  Of apple-pie and cheese!

I 'm glad my education
  Enables me to stand
Against the vile temptation
  Held out on every hand;
Eschewing all the tittles
  With vanity replete,
I 'm loyal to the victuals
  Our grandsires used to eat!
I 'm glad I 've got three willing boys
  To hang around and tease
Their mother for the filling joys
  Of apple-pie and cheese!

Your flavored creams and ices
  And your dainty angel-food
Are mighty fine devices
  To regale the dainty dude;
Your terrapin and oysters,
  With wine to wash 'em down,
Are just the thing for roisters
  When painting of the town;
No flippant, sugared notion
  Shall *my* appetite appease,
Or bate my soul's devotion
  To apple-pie and cheese!

The pie my Julia makes me
   (God bless her Yankee ways!)
On memory's pinions takes me
   To dear Green Mountain days;
And seems like I see Mother
   Lean on the window-sill,
A-handin' me and brother
   What she knows 'll keep us still;
And these feelings are so grateful,
   Says I, "Julia, if you please,
I 'll take another plateful
   Of that apple-pie and cheese!"

And cheese! No alien it, sir,
   That 's brought across the sea,—
No Dutch antique, nor Switzer,
   Nor glutinous de Brie;
There 's nothing I abhor so
   As mawmets of this ilk—
Give *me* the harmless morceau
   That 's made of true-blue milk!
No matter what conditions
   Dyspeptic come to feaze,
The best of all physicians
   Is apple-pie and cheese!

Though ribalds may decry 'em,
   For these twin boons we stand,
Partaking thrice per diem
   Of their fulness out of hand;
No enervating fashion
   Shall cheat us of our right
To gratify our passion
   With a mouthful at a bite!
We 'll cut it square or bias,
   Or any way we please,
And faith shall justify us
   When we carve our pie and cheese!

De gustibus, 't is stated,
  Non disputandum est.
Which meaneth, when translated.
  That all is for the best.
So let the foolish choose 'em
  The vapid sweets of sin,
I will not disabuse 'em
  Of the heresy they 're in;
But I, when I undress me
  Each night, upon my knees
Will ask the Lord to bless me
  With apple-pie and cheese!

THE LITTLE PEACH

A LITTLE peach in the orchard grew,—
  A little peach of emerald hue;
Warmed by the sun and wet by the dew,
      It grew.

One day, passing that orchard through,
That little peach dawned on the view
Of Johnny Jones and his sister Sue—
      Them two.

Up at that peach a club they threw—
Down from the stem on which it grew
Fell that peach of emerald hue.
      Mon Dieu!

John took a bite and Sue a chew,
And then the trouble began to brew,—
Trouble the doctor could n't subdue.
      Too true!

Under the turf where the daisies grew
They planted John and his sister Sue,
And their little souls to the angels flew,—
      Boo hoo!

What of that peach of the emerald hue,
Warmed by the sun, and wet by the dew?
Ah, well, its mission on earth is through.
               Adieu!
1880

THE DIVINE LULLABY

I HEAR Thy voice, dear Lord;
I hear it by the stormy sea
   When winter nights are black and wild,
And when, affright, I call to Thee;
It calms my fears and whispers me,
   "Sleep well, my child."

I hear Thy voice, dear Lord,
In singing winds, in falling snow,
   The curfew chimes, the midnight bell.
"Sleep well, my child," it murmurs low;
"The guardian angels come and go,—
   O child, sleep well!"

I hear Thy voice, dear Lord,
Ay, though the singing winds be stilled,
   Though hushed the tumult of the deep,
My fainting heart with anguish chilled
By Thy assuring tone is thrilled,—
   "Fear not, and sleep!"

Speak on—speak on, dear Lord!
And when the last dread night is near,
   With doubts and fears and terrors wild,
Oh, let my soul expiring hear
Only these words of heavenly cheer,
   "Sleep well, my child!"

DE AMICITIIS

Though care and strife
Elsewhere be rife,
Upon my word I do not heed 'em;
In bed I lie
With books hard by,
And with increasing zest I read 'em

Propped up in bed,
So much I 've read
Of musty tomes that I 've a headful
Of tales and rhymes
Of ancient times,
Which, wife declares, are "simply dreadfull"

They give me joy
Without alloy;
And is n't that what books are made for?
And yet—and yet—
(Ah, vain regret!)
I would to God they all were paid for!

No festooned cup
Filled foaming up
Can lure me elsewhere to confound me;
Sweeter than wine
This love of mine
For these old books I see around me!

A plague, I say,
On maidens gay;
I 'll weave no compliments to tell 'em!
Vain fool I were,
Did I prefer
Those dolls to these old friends in vellum!

At dead of night
My chamber's bright
Not only with the gas that's burning,
But with the glow
Of long ago,—
Of beauty back from eld returning.

Fair women's looks
I see in books,
I see *them*, and I hear their laughter,—
Proud, high-born maids,
Unlike the jades
Which men-folk now go chasing after!

Herein again
Speak valiant men
Of all nativities and ages;
I hear and smile
With rapture while
I turn these musty, magic pages.

The sword, the lance,
The morris dance,
The highland song, the greenwood ditty,
Of these I read,
Or, when the need,
My Miller grinds me grist that's gritty!

When of such stuff
We've had enough,
Why, there be other friends to greet us;
We'll moralize
In solemn wise
With Plato or with Epictetus.

Sneer as you may,
I'm proud to say
That I, for one, am very grateful

To Heaven, that sends
These genial friends
To banish other friendships hateful!

And when I 'm done,
I 'd have no son
Pounce on these treasures like a vulture;
Nay, give them half
My epitaph,
And let them share in my sepulture.

Then, when the crack
Of doom rolls back
The marble and the earth that hide me,
I 'll smuggle home
Each precious tome,
Without a fear my wife shall chide me!

THE WANDERER

Upon a mountain height, far from the sea,
I found a shell,
And to my listening ear the lonely thing
Ever a song of ocean seemed to sing,
Ever a tale of ocean seemed to tell.

How came the shell upon that mountain height?
Ah, who can say
Whether there dropped by some too careless hand,
Or whether there cast when Ocean swept the Land,
Ere the Eternal had ordained the Day?

Strange, was it not? Far from its native deep,
One song it sang,—
Sang of the awful mysteries of the tide,
Sang of the misty sea, profound and wide,—
Ever with echoes of the ocean rang.

And as the shell upon the mountain height
 Sings of the sea,
So do I ever, leagues and leagues away,—
So do I ever, wandering where I may,—
 Sing, O my home! sing, O my home! of thee.

1883.

SOLDIER, MAIDEN, AND FLOWER

"Sweetheart, take this," a soldier said,
 "And bid me brave good-by;
It may befall we ne'er shall wed,
 But love can never die.
Be steadfast in thy troth to me,
 And then, whate'er my lot,
'My soul to God, my heart to thee,'—
 Sweetheart, forget me not!"

The maiden took the tiny flower
 And nursed it with her tears:
Lo! he who left her in that hour
 Came not in after years.
Unto a hero's death he rode
 'Mid shower of fire and shot;
But in the maiden's heart abode
 The flower, forget-me-not.

And when *he* came not with the rest
 From out the years of blood,
Closely unto her widowed breast
 She pressed a faded bud;
Oh, there is love and there is pain,
 And there is peace, God wot,—
And these dear three do live again
 In sweet forget-me-not.

'T is to an unmarked grave to-day
  That I should love to go,—
Whether he wore the blue or gray,
  What need that we should know?
"He loved a woman," let us say,
  And on that sacred spot,
To woman's love, that lives for aye,
  We 'll strew forget-me-not.

1887.

AILSIE, MY BAIRN

Lie in my arms, Ailsie, my bairn,—
  Lie in my arms and dinna greit;
Long time been past syn I kenned you last,
  But my harte been allwais the same, my swete.

Ailsie, I colde not say you ill,
  For out of the mist of your bitter tears,
And the prayers that rise from your bonnie eyes,
  Cometh a promise of oder yeres.

I mind the time when we lost our bairn,—
  Do you ken that time? A wambling tot,
You wandered away ane simmer day,
  And we hunted and called, and found you not.

I promised God, if He 'd send you back,
  Alwaies to keepe and to love you, childe;
And I 'm thinking again of that promise when
  I see you creep out of the storm sae wild.

You came back then as you come back now,—
  Your kirtle torn and your face all white;
And you stood outside and knockit and cried,
  Just as you, dearie, did to-night.

Oh, never a word of the cruel wrang,
    That has faded your cheek and dimmed your ee,
And never a word of the fause, fause lord,—
    Only a smile and a kiss for me.

Lie in my arms, as long, long syne,
    And sleepe on my bosom, deere wounded thing,—
I 'm nae sae glee as I used to be,
    Or I 'd sing you the songs I used to sing.

But Ile kemb my fingers thro' y'r haire,
    And nane shall know, but you and I,
Of the love and the faith that came to us baith
    When Ailsie, my bairn, came home to die.

MR. DANA, OF THE NEW YORK SUN

THAR showed up out'n Denver in the spring uv '81
A man who 'd worked with Dana on the Noo York Sun.
His name wuz Cantell Whoppers, 'nd he wuz a sight ter view
Ez he walked inter the orfice 'nd inquired fer work ter do.
Thar war n't no places vacant then,—fer be it understood,
That wuz the time when talent flourished at that altitood;
But thar the stranger lingered, tellin' Raymond 'nd the rest
Uv what perdigious wonders he could do when at his best,
Till finally he stated (quite by chance) that he hed done
A heap uv work with Dana on the Noo York Sun.

Wall, that wuz quite another thing; we owned that ary cuss
Who 'd worked f'r Mr. Dana *must* be good enough fer *us!*
And so we tuk the stranger's word 'nd nipped him while we could,
For if *we* *did n't* take him we knew John Arkins *would;*
And Cooper, too, wuz mouzin' round fer enterprise 'nd brains,
Whenever them commodities blew in across the plains.
At any rate we nailed him, which made ol' Cooper swear
And Arkins tear out handfuls uv his copious curly hair;
But *we* set back and cackled, 'nd hed a power uv fun
With our man who 'd worked with Dana on the Noo York Sun.

It made our eyes hang on our cheeks 'nd lower jaws ter drop,
Ter hear that feller tellin' how ol' Dana run his shop:
It seems that Dana wuz the biggest man you ever saw,—
He lived on human bein's, 'nd preferred to eat 'em raw!
If he hed Democratic drugs ter take, before he took 'em,
As good old allopathic laws prescribe, he allus shook 'em.
The man that could set down 'nd write like Dany never grew,
And the sum of human knowledge wuz n't half what Dana knew;
The consequence appeared to be that nearly every one
Concurred with Mr. Dana of the Noo York Sun.

This feller, Cantell Whoppers, never brought an item in,—
He spent his time at Perrin's shakin' poker dice f'r gin.
Whatever the assignment, he wuz allus sure to shirk,
He wuz very long on likker and all-fired short on work!
If any other cuss had played the tricks he dared ter play,
The daisies would be bloomin' over his remains to-day;
But somehow folks respected him and stood him to the last,
Considerin' his superior connections in the past.
So, when he bilked at poker, not a sucker drew a gun
On the man who 'd worked with Dana on the Noo York Sun.

Wall, Dana came ter Denver in the fall uv '83,
A very different party from the man we thought ter see,—
A nice 'nd clean old gentleman, so dignerfied 'nd calm,
You bet yer life he never did no human bein' harm!
A certain hearty manner 'nd a fulness uv the vest
Betokened that his sperrits 'nd his victuals wuz the best;
His face wuz so benevolent, his smile so sweet 'nd kind,
That they seemed to be the reflex uv an honest, healthy mind;
And God had set upon his head a crown uv silver hair
In promise uv the golden crown He meaneth him to wear.
So, uv us boys that met him out'n Denver, there wuz none
But fell in love with Dana uv the Noo York Sun.

But when he came to Denver in that fall uv '83,
His old friend Cantell Whoppers disappeared upon a spree;
The very thought uv seein' Dana worked upon him so
(They had n't been together fer a year or two, you know),

That he borrered all the stuff he could and started on a bat,
And, strange as it may seem, we did n't see him after that.
So, when ol' Dana hove in sight, we could n't understand
Why he did n't seem to notice that his crony wa'n't on hand;
No casual allusion, not a question, no, not one,
For the man who 'd "worked with Dana on the Noo York Sun!"

We broke it gently to him, but he did n't seem surprised,
Thar wuz no big burst uv passion as we fellers had surmised.
He said that Whoppers wuz a man he 'd never heerd about,
But he mought have carried papers on a Jarsey City route;
And then he recollected hearin' Mr. Laffan say
That he 'd fired a man named Whoppers fur bein' drunk one day,
Which, with more likker *underneath* than money *in* his vest,
Had started on a freight-train fur the great 'nd boundin' West,
But further information or statistics he had none
Uv the man who 'd "worked with Dana on the Noo York Sun."

We dropped the matter quietly 'nd never made no fuss,—
When we get played for suckers, why, that's a horse on us!—
But every now 'nd then we Denver fellers have to laff
To hear some other paper boast uv havin' on its staff
A man who 's "worked with Dana," 'nd then we fellers wink
And pull our hats down on our eyes 'nd set around 'nd think.
It seems like Dana could n't be as smart as people say,
If he educates so many folks 'nd lets 'em get away;
And, as for us, in future we 'll be very apt to shun
The man who "worked with Dana on the Noo York Sun."

But bless ye, Mr. Dana! may you live a thousan' years,
To sort o' keep things lively in this vale of human tears;
An' may *I* live a thousan', too,—a thousan' less a day,
For I should n't like to be on earth to hear you 'd passed away.
And when it comes your time to go you 'll need no Latin chaff
Nor biographic data put in your epitaph;
But one straight line of English and of truth will let folks know
The homage 'nd the gratitude 'nd reverence they owe;
You 'll need no epitaph but this: "Here sleeps the man who run
That best 'nd brightest paper, the Noo York Sun."

THE TWENTY–THIRD PSALM

My Shepherd is the Lord my God,—
　There is no want I know;
His flock He leads in verdant meads,
　Where tranquil waters flow.

He doth restore my fainting soul
　With His divine caress,
And, when I stray, He points the way
　To paths of righteousness.

Yea, though I walk the vale of death,
　What evil shall I fear?
Thy staff and rod are mine, O God,
　And Thou, my Shepherd, near!

Mine enemies behold the feast
　Which my dear Lord hath spread;
And, lo! my cup He filleth up,
　With oil anoints my head!

Goodness and mercy shall be mine
　Unto my dying day;
Then will I bide at His dear side
　Forever and for aye!

THE BIBLIOMANIAC'S BRIDE

The women-folk are like to books,—
　Most pleasing to the eye,
Whereon if anybody looks
　He feels disposed to buy.

I hear that many are for sale,—
　Those that record no dates,
And such editions as regale
　The view with colored plates.

Of every quality and grade
　And size they may be found,—
Quite often beautifully made,
　As often poorly bound.

Now, as for me, had I my choice,
　I 'd choose no folio tall,
But some octavo to rejoice
　My sight and heart withal,—

As plump and pudgy as a snipe;
　Well worth her weight in gold;
Of honest, clean, conspicuous type,
　And *just* the size to hold!

With such a volume for my wife
　How should I keep and con!
How like a dream should run my life
　Unto its colophon!

Her frontispiece should be more fair
　Than any colored plate;
Blooming with health, she would not care
　To extra-illustrate.

And in her pages there should be
　A wealth of prose and verse,
With now and then a *jeu d'esprit,*—
　But nothing ever worse!

Prose for me when I wished for prose,
　Verse when to verse inclined,—
Forever bringing sweet repose
　To body, heart, and mind.

Oh, I should bind this priceless prize
  In bindings full and fine,
And keep her where no human eyes
  Should see her charms, but mine!

With such a fair unique as this
  What happiness abounds!
Who—who could paint my rapturous bliss,
  My joy unknown to Lowndes!

CHRISTMAS HYMN

SING, Christmas bells!
  Say to the earth this is the morn
Whereon our Saviour-King is born;
  Sing to all men,—the bond, the free,
The rich, the poor, the high, the low,
  The little child that sports in glee,
The aged folk that tottering go,—
  Proclaim the morn
  That Christ is born,
That saveth them and saveth me!

Sing, angel host!
Sing of the star that God has placed
Above the manger in the east;
  Sing of the glories of the night,
The virgin's sweet humility,
  The Babe with kingly robes bedight,—
Sing to all men where'er they be
  This Christmas morn;
  For Christ is born,
That saveth them and saveth me!

Sing, sons of earth!
O ransomed seed of Adam, sing!
God liveth, and we have a king!
  The curse is gone, the bond are free,—

By Bethlehem's star that brightly beamed,
  By all the heavenly signs that be,
We know that Israel is redeemed;
      That on this morn
      The Christ is born
  That saveth you and saveth me!

      Sing, O my heart!
Sing thou in rapture this dear morn
Whereon the blessed Prince is born!
  And as thy songs shall be of love,
So let my deeds be charity,—
  By the dear Lord that reigns above,
By Him that died upon the tree,
      By this fair morn
      Whereon is born
  The Christ that saveth all and me!

———

"GOOD-BY—GOD BLESS YOU!"

I LIKE the Anglo-Saxon speech
  With its direct revealings; ·
It takes a hold, and seems to reach
  'Way down into your feelings;
That some folk deem it rude, I know,
  And therefore they abuse it;
But I have never found it so,—
  Before all else I choose it.
I don't object that men should air
  The Gallic they have paid for,
With "Au revoir," "Adieu, ma chère,"
  For that 's what French was made for.
But when a crony takes your hand
  At parting, to address you,
He drops all foreign lingo and
  He says, "Good-by—God bless you!"

This seems to me a sacred phrase,
    With reverence impassioned,—
A thing come down from righteous days,
    Quaintly but nobly fashioned;
It well becomes an honest face,
    A voice that's round and cheerful;
It stays the sturdy in his place,
    And soothes the weak and fearful.
Into the porches of the ears
    It steals with subtle unction,
And in your heart of hearts appears
    To work its gracious function;
And all day long with pleasing song
    It lingers to caress you,—
I'm sure no human heart goes wrong
    That's told "Good-by—God bless you!"

I love the words,—perhaps because,
    When I was leaving Mother,
Standing at last in solemn pause
    We looked at one another,
And I—I saw in Mother's eyes
    The love she could not tell me,—
A love eternal as the skies,
    Whatever fate befell me;
She put her arms about my neck
    And soothed the pain of leaving,
And though her heart was like to break,
    She spoke no word of grieving;
She let no tear bedim her eye,
    For fear *that* might distress me,
But, kissing me, she said good-by,
    And asked our God to bless me.

CHRYSTMASSE OF OLDE

God rest you, Chrysten gentil men,
   Wherever you may be,—
God rest you all in fielde or hall,
   Or on ye stormy sea;
For on this morn oure Chryst is born
   That saveth you and me.

Last night ye shepherds in ye east
   Saw many a wondrous thing;
Ye sky last night flamed passing bright
   Whiles that ye stars did sing,
And angels came to bless ye name
   Of Jesus Chryst, oure Kyng.

God rest you, Chrysten gentil men,
   Faring where'er you may;
In noblesse court do thou no sport,
   In tournament no playe,
In paynim lands hold thou thy hands
   From bloudy works this daye.

But thinking on ye gentil Lord
   That died upon ye tree,
Let troublings cease and deeds of peace
   Abound in Chrystantie;
For on this morn ye Chryst is born
   That saveth you and me.

A PROPER TREWE IDYLL OF CAMELOT

Whenas ye plaisaunt Aperille shoures have washed and purged
   awaye
Ye poysons and ye rheums of earth to make a merrie May,
Ye shraddy boscage of ye woods ben full of birds that syng
Right merrilie a madrigal unto ye waking spring,

Ye whiles that when ye face of earth ben washed and wiped
    ycleane
Her peeping posies blink and stare like they had ben her een;
Then, wit ye well, ye harte of man ben turned to thoughts of
    love,
And, tho' it ben a lyon erst, it now ben like a dove!
And many a goodly damosel in innocence beguiles
Her owne trewe love with sweet discourse and divers plaisaunt
    wiles.
In soche a time ye noblesse liege that ben Kyng Arthure hight
Let cry a joust and tournament for evereche errant knyght,
And, lo! from distant Joyous-garde and eche adjacent spot
A company of noblesse lords fared unto Camelot,
Wherein were mighty feastings and passing merrie cheere,
And eke a deale of dismal dole, as you shall quickly heare.

It so befell upon a daye when jousts ben had and while
Sir Launcelot did ramp around ye ring in gallaunt style,
There came an horseman shriking sore and rashing wildly home,—
A mediæval horseman with ye usual flecks of foame;
And he did brast into ye ring, wherein his horse did drop,
Upon ye which ye rider did with like abruptness stop,
And with fatigue and fearfulness continued in a swound
Ye space of half an hour or more before a leech was founde.
"Now tell me straight," quod Launcelot, "what varlet knyght
    you be,
Ere that I chine you with my sworde and cleave your harte in
    three!"
Then rolled that knyght his bloudy een, and answered with a
    groane,—
"By worthy God that hath me made and shope ye sun and
    mone,
There fareth hence an evil thing whose like ben never seene,
And tho' he sayeth nony worde, he bodethe ill, I ween.
So take your parting, evereche one, and gird you for ye fraye,—
By all that 's pure, ye Divell sure doth trend his path this
    way!"
Ye which he quoth and fell again into a deadly swound,
And on that spot, perchance (God wot), his bones mought yet
    be founde.

Then evereche knyght girt on his sworde and shield and hied him
    straight
To meet ye straunger sarasen hard by ye city gate;
Full sorely moaned ye damosels and tore their beautyse haire
For that they feared an hippogriff wolde come to eate them
    there;
But as they moaned and swounded there too numerous to relate,
Kyng Arthure and Sir Launcelot stode at ye city gate,
And at eche side and round about stode many a noblesse knyght
With helm and speare and sworde and shield and mickle valor
    dight.

Anon there came a straunger, but not a gyaunt grim,
Nor yet a draggon,—but a person gangling, long, and slim;
Yclad he was in guise that ill-beseemed those knyghtly days,
And there ben nony etiquette in his uplandish ways;
His raiment was of dusty gray, and perched above his lugs
There ben the very latest style of blacke and shiny pluggs;
His nose ben like a vulture beake, his blie ben swart of hue,
And curly ben ye whiskers through ye which ye zephyrs blewe;
Of all ye een that ben yseene in countries far or nigh,
None nonywhere colde hold compare unto that straunger's eye;
It was an eye of soche a kind as never ben on sleepe,
Nor did it gleam with kindly beame, nor did not use to weepe;
But soche an eye ye widdow hath,—an hongrey eye and wan,
That spyeth for an oder chaunce whereby she may catch on;
An eye that winketh of itself, and sayeth by that winke
Ye which a maiden sholde not knowe nor never even thinke;
Which winke ben more exceeding swift nor human thought ben
    thunk,
And leaveth doubting if so be that winke ben really wunke;
And soche an eye ye catte-fysshe hath when that he ben on dead
And boyled a goodly time and served with capers on his head;
A rayless eye, a bead-like eye, whose famisht aspect shows
It hungereth for ye verdant banks whereon ye wild time grows;
An eye that hawketh up and down for evereche kind of game,
And, when he doth espy ye which, he tumbleth to ye same.

Now when he kenned Sir Launcelot in armor clad, he quod,
"Another put-a-nickel-in-and-see-me-work, be god!"

But when that he was ware a man ben standing in that suit,
Ye straunger threw up both his hands, and asked him not to
    shoote.

Then spake Kyng Arthure: "If soe be you mind to do no ill,
Come, enter into Camelot, and eat and drink your fill;
But say me first what you are hight, and what mought be your
    quest."
Ye straunger quod, "I 'm five feet ten, and fare me from ye West!"
"Sir Fivefeetten," Kyng Arthure said, "I bid you welcome here;
So make you merrie as you list with plaisaunt wine and cheere;
This very night shall be a feast soche like ben never seene,
And you shall be ye honored guest of Arthure and his queene.
Now take him, good sir Maligraunce, and entertain him well
Until soche time as he becomes our guest, as I you tell."
That night Kyng Arthure's table round with mighty care ben
    spread,
Ye oder knyghts sate all about, and Arthure at ye heade:
Oh, 't was a goodly spectacle to ken that noblesse liege
Dispensing hospitality from his commanding siege!
Ye pheasant and ye meate of boare, ye haunch of velvet doe,
Ye canvass hamme he them did serve, and many good things
    moe.
Until at last Kyng Arthure cried: "Let bring my wassail cup,
And let ye sound of joy go round,—I 'm going to set 'em up!
I 've pipes of Malmsey, May-wine, sack, metheglon, mead, and
    sherry,
Canary, Malvoisie, and Port, swete Muscadelle and perry;
Rochelle, Osey, and Romenay, Tyre, Rhenish, posset too,
With kags and pails of foaming ales of brown October brew.
To wine and beer and other cheere I pray you now despatch ye,
And for ensample, wit ye well, sweet sirs, I 'm looking at ye!"

Unto which toast of their liege lord ye oders in ye party
Did lout them low in humble wise and bid ye same drink hearty.
So then ben merrisome discourse and passing plaisaunt cheere,
And Arthure's tales of hippogriffs ben mervaillous to heare;
But straunger far than any tale told of those knyghts of old
Ben those facetious narratives ye Western straunger told.
He told them of a country many leagues beyond ye sea

Where evereche forraine nuisance but ye Chinese man ben free,
And whiles he span his monstrous yarns, ye ladies of ye court
Did deem ye listening thereunto to be right plaisaunt sport;
And whiles they listened, often he did squeeze a lily hande,—
Ye which proceeding ne'er before ben done in Arthure's lande;
And often wank a sidelong wink with either roving eye,
Whereat ye ladies laughen so that they had like to die.
But of ye damosels that sat around Kyng Arthure's table
He liked not her that sometime ben ron over by ye cable,
Ye which full evil hap had harmed and marked her person so
That in a passing wittie jest he dubbeth her ye crow.

But all ye oders of ye girls did please him passing well
And they did own him for to be a proper seeming swell;
And in especial Guinevere esteemed him wondrous faire,
Which had made Arthure and his friend, Sir Launcelot, to sware
But that they both ben so far gone with posset, wine, and beer,
They colde not see ye carrying-on, nor neither colde not heare;
For of eche liquor Arthure quafft, and so did all ye rest,
Save only and excepting that smooth straunger from the West.
When as these oders drank a toast, he let them have their fun
With divers godless mixings, but *he* stock to willow run,
Ye which (and all that reade these words sholde profit by ye
    warning)
Doth never make ye head to feel like it ben swelled next morning.
Now, wit ye well, it so befell that when the night grew dim,
Ye Kyng was carried from ye hall with a howling jag on him,
Whiles Launcelot and all ye rest that to his highness toadied
Withdrew them from ye banquet-hall and sought their couches
    loaded.

Now, lithe and listen, lordings all, whiles I do call it shame
That, making cheer with wine and beer, men do abuse ye same;
Though eche be well enow alone, ye mixing of ye two
Ben soche a piece of foolishness as only ejiots do.
Ye wine is plaisaunt bibbing whenas ye gentles dine,
And beer will do if one hath not ye wherewithal for wine,
But in ye drinking of ye same ye wise are never floored
By taking what ye tipplers call too big a jag on board.
Right hejeous isit for to see soche dronkonness of wine

Whereby some men are used to make themselves to be like swine;
And sorely it repenteth them, for when they wake next day
Ye fearful paynes they suffer ben soche as none mought say,
And soche ye brenning in ye throat and brasting of ye head
And soche ye taste within ye mouth like one had ben on dead,—
Soche be ye foul condicions that these unhappy men
Sware they will never drink no drop of nony drinke again.
Yet all so frail and vain a thing and weak withal is man
That he goeth on an oder tear whenever that he can.
And like ye evil quatern or ye hills that skirt ye skies,
Ye jag is reproductive and jags on jags arise.

Whenas Aurora from ye east in dewy splendor hied
Kyng Arthure dreemed he saw a snaix and ben on fire inside,
And waking from this hejeous dreeme he sate him up in bed,—
"What, ho! an absynthe cocktail, knave! and make it strong!" he
    said;
Then, looking down beside him, lo! his lady was not there—
He called, he searched, but, Goddis wounds! he found her nony-
    where;
And whiles he searched, Sir Maligraunce rashed in, wood wroth,
    and cried,
"Methinketh that ye straunger knyght hath snuck away my bride!"
And whiles *he* spake a motley score of other knyghts brast in
And filled ye royall chamber with a mickle fearful din,
For evereche one had lost his wiffe nor colde nor spye ye same,
Nor colde not spye ye straunger knyght, Sir Fivefeetten of name.

Oh, then and there was grevious lamentation all arounde,
For nony dame nor damosel in Camelot ben found,—
Gone, like ye forest leaves that speed afore ye autumn wind.
Of all ye ladies of that court not one ben left behind
Save only that same damosel ye straunger called ye crow,
And she allowed with moche regret she ben too lame to go;
And when that she had wept full sore, to Arthure she confess'd
That Guinevere had left this word for Arthure and ye rest:
"Tell them," she quod, "we shall return to them whenas we've
    made
This little deal we have with ye Chicago Bourde of Trade."

IN FLANDERS

THROUGH sleet and fogs to the saline bogs
  Where the herring fish meanders,
An army sped, and then, 't is said,
  Swore terribly in Flanders:
          "＿＿ ＿＿ ＿＿ ＿＿!"
          "＿＿ ＿＿ ＿＿ ＿＿!"
A hideous store of oaths they swore,
  Did the army over in Flanders!

At this distant day we 're unable to say
  What so aroused their danders;
But it 's doubtless the case, to their lasting disgrace,
  That the army swore in Flanders:
          "＿＿ ＿＿ ＿＿ ＿＿!"
          "＿＿ ＿＿ ＿＿ ＿＿!"
And many more such oaths they swore,
  Did that impious horde in Flanders!

Some folks contend that these oaths without end
  Began among the commanders,
That, taking this cue, the subordinates, too,
  Swore terribly in Flanders:
      'T was "＿＿ ＿＿ ＿＿!"
          "＿＿ ＿＿ ＿＿ ＿＿!"
Why, the air was blue with the hullaballoo
  Of those wicked men in Flanders!

But some suppose that the trouble arose
  With a certain Corporal Sanders,
Who sought to abuse the wooden shoes
  That the natives wore in Flanders.
      Saying: "＿＿ ＿＿ ＿＿!"
          "＿＿ ＿＿ ＿＿ ＿＿!"
What marvel then, that the other men
  Felt encouraged to swear in Flanders!

At any rate, as I grieve to state,
  Since these soldiers vented their danders
Conjectures obtain that for language profane
  There is no such place as Flanders.
       "———— ———— ———— ————!"
       "———— ———— ———— ————!"
This is the kind of talk you 'll find
  If you ever go to Flanders.

How wretched is he, wherever he be,
  That unto this habit panders!
And how glad am I that my interests lie
  In Chicago, and not in Flanders!
       "———— ———— ———— ————!"
       "———— ———— ———— ————!"
Would never go down in this circumspect town
  However it might in Flanders.

OUR BIGGEST FISH

WHEN in the halcyon days of eld, I was a little tyke,
I used to fish in pickerel ponds for minnows and the like;
And oh, the bitter sadness with which my soul was fraught
When I rambled home at nightfall with the puny string I 'd
    caught!
And, oh, the indignation and the valor I 'd display
When I claimed that all the biggest fish I 'd caught had got away!

Sometimes it was the rusty hooks, sometimes the fragile lines,
And many times the treacherous reeds would foil my just designs;
But whether hooks or lines or reeds were actually to blame,
I kept right on at losing all the monsters just the same—
I never lost a *little* fish—yes, I am free to say
It always was the *biggest* fish I caught that got away.

And so it was, when later on, I felt ambition pass
From callow minnow joys to nobler greed for pike and bass;
I found it quite convenient, when the beauties would n't bite

And I returned all bootless from the watery chase at night,
To feign a cheery aspect and recount in accents gay
How the biggest fish that I had caught had somehow got away.

And really, fish look bigger than they are before they 're caught—
When the pole is bent into a bow and the slender line is taut,
When a fellow feels his heart rise up like a doughnut in his throat
And he lunges in a frenzy up and down the leaky boat!
Oh, you who've been a-fishing will indorse me when I say
That it always *is* the biggest fish you catch that gets away!

'T 'is even so in other things—yes, in our greedy eyes
The biggest boon is some elusive, never-captured prize;
We angle for the honors and the sweets of human life—
Like fishermen we brave the seas that roll in endless strife;
And then at last, when all is done and we are spent and gray,
We own the biggest fish we 've caught are those that got away.

I would not have it otherwise; 't is better there should be
Much bigger fish than I have caught a-swimming in the sea;
For now some worthier one than I may angle for that game—
May by his arts entice, entrap, and comprehend the same;
Which, having done, perchance he 'll bless the man who 's proud
    to say
That the biggest fish he ever caught were those that got away.

THIRTY-NINE

O HAPLESS day! O wretched day!
    I hoped you 'd pass me by—
Alas, the years have sneaked away
    And all is changed but I!
Had I the power, I would remand
    You to a gloom condign,
But here you 've crept upon me and
    I—I am thirty-nine!

Now, were I thirty-five, I could
    Assume a flippant guise;
Or, were I forty years, I should
    Undoubtedly look wise;
For forty years are said to bring
    Sedateness superfine;
But thirty-nine don't mean a thing—
    À bas with thirty-nine!

You healthy, hulking girls and boys,—
    What makes you grow so fast?
Oh, I'll survive your lusty noise—
    I'm tough and bound to last!
No, no—I'm old and withered too—
    I feel my powers decline
(Yet none believes this can be true
    Of one at thirty-nine).

And you, dear girl with velvet eyes,
    I wonder what you mean
Through all our keen anxieties
    By keeping sweet sixteen.
With your dear love to warm my heart,
    Wretch were I to repine;
I was but jesting at the start—
    I'm glad I'm thirty-nine!

So, little children, roar and race
    As blithely as you can,
And, sweetheart, let your tender grace
    Exalt the Day and Man;
For then these factors (I'll engage)
    All subtly shall combine
To make both juvenile and sage
    The one who's thirty-nine!

Yes, after all, I'm free to say
    I would much rather be
Standing as I do stand to-day,
    'Twixt devil and deep sea;

For though my face be dark with care
  Or with a grimace shine,
Each haply falls unto my share,
  For I am thirty-nine!

'T is passing meet to make good cheer
  And lord it like a king,
Since only once we catch the year
  That does n't mean a thing.
O happy day! O gracious day!
  I pledge thee in this wine—
Come, let us journey on our way
  A year, good Thirty-Nine!

Sept. 2, 1889

YVYTOT

Where wail the waters in their flow
A spectre wanders to and fro,
  And evermore that ghostly shore
Bemoans the heir of Yvytot.

Sometimes, when, like a fleecy pall,
  The mists upon the waters fall,
Across the main float shadows twain
  That do not heed the spectre's call.

The king his son of Yvytot
Stood once and saw the waters go
  Boiling around with hissing sound
The sullen phantom rocks below.

And suddenly he saw a face
Lift from that black and seething place—
  Lift up and gaze in mute amaze
And tenderly a little space,

A mighty cry of love made he—
No answ'ring word to him gave she,
  But looked, and then sunk back again
Into the dark and depthless sea.

And ever afterward that face,
That he beheld such little space,
  Like wraith would rise within his eyes
And in his heart find biding place.

So oft from castle hall he crept
Where mid the rocks grim shadows slept,
  And where the mist reached down and kissed
The waters as they wailed and wept.

The king it was of Yvytot
That vaunted, many years ago,
  There was no coast his valiant host
Had not subdued with spears and bow.

For once to him the sea-king cried:
  "In safety all thy ships shall ride
An thou but swear thy princely heir
  Shall take my daughter to his bride.

"And lo, these winds that rove the sea
Unto our pact shall witness be,
  And of the oath which binds us both
Shall be the judge 'twixt me and thee!"

Then swore the king of Yvytot
Unto the sea-king years ago,
  And with great cheer for many a year
His ships went harrying to and fro.

Unto this mighty king his throne
Was born a prince, and one alone—
  Fairer than he in form and blee
And knightly grace was never known.

But once he saw a maiden face
Lift from a haunted ocean place—
   Lift up and gaze in mute amaze
And tenderly a little space.

Wroth was the king of Yvytot,
For that his son would never go
   Sailing the sea, but liefer be
Where wailed the waters in their flow,

Where winds in clamorous anger swept,
Where to and fro grim shadows crept,
   And where the mist reached down and kissed
The waters as they wailed and wept.

So sped the years, till came a day
The haughty king was old and gray,
   And in his hold were spoils untold
That he had wrenched from Norroway.

Then once again the sea-king cried:
"Thy ships have harried far and wide;
   My part is done—now let thy son
Require my daughter to his bride!"

Loud laughed the king of Yvytot,
And by his soul he bade him no—
   "I heed no more what oath I swore,
For I was mad to bargain so!"

Then spake the sea-king in his wrath:
"Thy ships lie broken in my path!
   Go now and wring thy hands, false king!
Nor ship nor heir thy kingdom hath!

"And thou shalt wander evermore
All up and down this ghostly shore,
   And call in vain upon the twain
That keep what oath a dastard swore!"

The king his son of Yvytot
Stood even then where to and fro
   The breakers swelled—and there beheld
A maiden face lift from below.

"Be thou or truth or dream," he cried,
"Or spirit of the restless tide,
   It booteth not to me, God wot!
But I would have thee to my bride."

Then spake the maiden: "Come with me
Unto a palace in the sea,
   For there my sire in kingly ire
Requires thy king his oath of thee!"

Gayly he fared him down the sands
And took the maiden's outstretched hands;
   And so went they upon their way
To do the sea-king his commands.

The winds went riding to and fro
And scourged the waves that crouched below,
   And bade them sing to a childless king
The bridal song of Yvytot.

So fell the curse upon that shore,
And hopeless wailing evermore
   Was the righteous dole of the craven soul
That heeded not what oath he swore.

An hundred ships went down that day
All off the coast of Norroway,
   And the ruthless sea made mighty glee
Over the spoil that drifting lay.

The winds went calling far and wide
To the dead that tossed in the mocking tide:
   "Come forth, ye slaves! from your fleeting graves
And drink a health to your prince his bride!"

Where wail the waters in their flow
A spectre wanders to and fro,
　But nevermore that ghostly shore
Shall claim the heir of Yvytot.

Sometimes, when, like a fleecy pall,
The mists upon the waters fall,
　Across the main flit shadows twain
That do not heed the spectre's call.

TO A SOUBRETTE

'TIS years, soubrette, since last we met;
　And yet—ah, yet, how swift and tender
My thoughts go back in time's dull track
　To you, sweet pink of female gender!
I shall not say—though others may—
　That time all human joy enhances;
But the same old thrill comes to me still
　With memories of your songs and dances.

Soubrettish ways these latter days
　Invite my praise, but never get it;
I still am true to yours and you—
　My record's made, I 'll not upset it!
The pranks they play, the things they say—
　I 'd blush to put the like on paper,
And I 'll avow they don't know how
　To dance, so awkwardly they caper!

I used to sit down in the pit
　And see you flit like elf or fairy
Across the stage, and I 'll engage
　No moonbeam sprite was half so airy;
Lo, everywhere about me there
　Were rivals reeking with pomatum,
And if, perchance, they caught your glance
　In song or dance, how did I hate 'em!

At half-past ten came rapture—then
  Of all those men was I most happy,
For bottled beer and royal cheer
  And têtes-à-têtes were on the tapis.
Do you forget, my fair soubrette,
  Those suppers at the Café Rector,—
The cosey nook where we partook
  Of sweeter cheer than fabled nectar?

Oh, happy days, when youth's wild ways
  Knew every phase of harmless folly!
Oh, blissful nights, whose fierce delights
  Defied gaunt-featured Melancholy!
Gone are they all beyond recall,
  And I—a shade, a mere reflection—
Am forced to feed my spirit's greed
  Upon the husks of retrospection!

And lo! to-night, the phantom light,
  That, as a sprite, flits on the fender,
Reveals a face whose girlish grace
  Brings back the feeling, warm and tender;
And, all the while, the old-time smile
  Plays on my visage, grim and wrinkled,—
As though, soubrette, your footfalls yet
  Upon my rusty heart-strings tinkled!

DEDICATION TO "SECOND BOOK OF VERSE"

A LITTLE bit of a woman came
  Athwart my path one day;
So tiny was she that she seemed to be
A pixy strayed from the misty sea,
  Or a wandering greenwood fay.

"Oho, you little elf!" I cried,
  "And what are you doing here?

So tiny as you will never do
For the brutal rush and hullaballoo
    Of this practical world, I fear."

"Voice have I, good sir," said she.—
    " 'T is soft as an Angel's sigh,
But to fancy a word of yours were heard
In all the din of this world 's absurd!"
    Smiling, I made reply.

"Hands have I, good sir," she quoth.—
    "Marry, and that have you!
But amid the strife and the tumult rife
In all the struggle and battle for life,
    What can those wee hands do?"

"Eyes have I, good sir," she said.—
    "Sooth, you have," quoth I,
"And tears shall flow therefrom, I trow,
And they betimes shall dim with woe,
    As the hard, hard years go by!"

That little bit of a woman cast
    Her two eyes full on me,
And they smote me sore to my inmost core,
And they hold me slaved forevermore,—
    Yet would I not be free!

That little bit of a woman's hands
    Reached up into my breast,
And rent apart my scoffing heart,—
And they buffet it still with such sweet art
    As cannot be expressed.

That little bit of a woman's voice
    Hath grown most wondrous dear;
Above the blare of all elsewhere
(An inspiration that mocks at care)
    It riseth full and clear.

Dear one, I bless the subtle power
That makes me wholly thine;
And I 'm proud to say that I bless the day
When a little woman wrought her way
Into this life of mine!

FATHER'S WAY

My father was no pessimist; he loved the things of earth,—
Its cheerfulness and sunshine, its music and its mirth.
He never sighed or moped around whenever things went wrong,—
I warrant me he 'd mocked at fate with some defiant song;
But, being he war n't much on tune, when times looked sort o'
    blue,
He 'd whistle softly to himself this only tune he knew,—

Now mother, when she heard that tune which father whistled so,
Would say, "There 's something wrong to-day with Ephraim,
    I know;
He never tries to make believe he 's happy that 'ere way
But that I 'm certain as can be there 's somethin' wrong to pay."
And so betimes, quite natural-like, to us observant youth
There seemed suggestion in that tune of deep, pathetic truth.

When Brother William joined the war, a lot of us went down
To see the gallant soldier boys right gayly out of town.
A-comin' home, poor mother cried as if her heart would break,
And all us children, too,—for *hers*, and *not* for *William's* sake!
But father, trudgin' on ahead, his hands behind him so,
Kept whistlin' to himself, so sort of solemn-like and low.

And when my oldest sister, Sue, was married and went West,
Seemed like it took the tuck right out of mother and the rest.
She was the sunlight in our home,—why, father used to say

It would n't seem like home at all if Sue should go away;
But when she went, a-leavin' us all sorrer and all tears,
Poor father whistled lonesome-like—and went to feed the steers.

When crops were bad, and other ills befell our homely lot,
He'd set of nights and try to act as if he minded not;
And when came death and bore away the one he worshipped so,
How vainly did his lips belie the heart benumbed with woe!
You see the telltale whistle told a mood he'd not admit,—
He'd always stopped his whistlin' when he thought we noticed it.

I 'd like to see that stooping form and hoary head again,—
To see the honest, hearty smile that cheered his fellow-men.
Oh, could I kiss the kindly lips that spake no creature wrong,
And share the rapture of the heart that overflowed with song!
Oh, could I hear the little tune he whistled long ago,
When he did battle with the griefs he would not have *us* know!

TO MY MOTHER

How fair you are, my mother!
　Ah, though ' tis many a year
　Since you were here,
Still do I see your beauteous face,
　And with the glow
Of your dark eyes cometh a grace
　Of long ago.
So gentle, too, my mother!
　Just as of old, upon my brow,
　Like benedictions now,
Falleth your dear hand's touch;
　And still, as then,
A voice that glads me overmuch
　Cometh again,
My fair and gentle mother!

How you have loved me, mother,
  I have not power to tell,
    Knowing full well
That even in the rest above
    It is your will
To watch and guard me with your love,
  Loving me still.
And, as of old, my mother,
  I am content to be a child,
    By mother's love beguiled
From all these other charms;
    So to the last
Within thy dear, protecting arms
  Hold thou me fast,
My guardian angel, mother!

A VALENTINE TO MY WIFE

ACCEPT, dear girl, this little token,
  And if between the lines you seek,
You 'll find the love I 've often spoken—
  The love my dying lips shall speak.

Our little ones are making merry
  O'er am'rous ditties rhymed in jest,
But in *these* words (though awkward—very,
  The genuine article 's expressed.

You are as fair and sweet and tender,
  Dear brown-eyed little sweetheart mine,
As when, a callow youth and slender,
  I asked to be your Valentine.

What though these years of ours be fleeting?
  What though the years of youth be flown?
I 'll mock old Tempus with repeating,
  "I love my love and her alone!"

And when I fall before his reaping,
    And when my stuttering speech is dumb,
Think not my love is dead or sleeping,
    But that it waits for you to come.

So take, dear love, this little token,
    And if there speaks in any line
The sentiment I 'd fain have spoken,
    Say, will you kiss your Valentine?

GOSLING STEW

In Oberhausen, on a time,
    I fared as might a king;
And now I feel the muse sublime
Inspire me to embalm in rhyme
    That succulent and sapid thing
Behight of gentile and of Jew
    A gosling stew!

The good Herr Schmitz brought out his best,—
    Soup, cutlet, salad, roast,—
And I partook with hearty zest,
And fervently anon I blessed
    That generous and benignant host,
When suddenly dawned on my view
    A gosling stew!

I sniffed it coming on apace,
    And as its odors filled
The curious little dining-place,
I felt a glow suffuse my face,
    I felt my very marrow thrilled
With rapture altogether new,—
    'T was gosling stew!

These callow birds had never played
    In yonder village pond;·
Had never through the gateway strayed,
And plaintive spissant music made
    Upon the grassy green beyond:
Cooped up, they simply ate and grew
    For gosling stew!

My doctor said I must n't eat
    High food and seasoned game;
But surely gosling is a meat
With tender nourishment replete.
    Leastwise I gayly ate this same;
I braved dyspepsy—would n't you
    For gosling stew?

I 've feasted where the possums grow,
    Roast turkey have I tried,
The joys of canvasbacks I know,
And frequently I 've eaten crow
    In bleak and chill Novembertide;
I 'd barter all that native crew
    For gosling stew!

And when from Rhineland I adjourn
    To seek my Yankee shore,
Back shall my memory often turn,
And fiercely shall my palate burn
    For sweets I 'll taste, alas! no more,—
Oh, that mein kleine frau could brew
    A gosling stew!

Vain are these keen regrets of mine,
    And vain the song I sing;
Yet would I quaff a stoup of wine
To Oberhausen auf der Rhine,
    Where fared I like a very king:
And here 's a last and fond adieu
    To gosling stew!

JOHN SMITH

To-day I strayed in Charing Cross, as wretched as could be,
With thinking of my home and friends across the tumbling sea;
There was no water in my eyes, but my spirits were depressed,
And my heart lay like a sodden, soggy doughnut in my breast.
This way and that streamed multitudes, that gayly passed me by;
Not one in all the crowd knew me, and not a one knew I.
"Oh for a touch of home!" I sighed; "oh for a friendly face!
Oh for a hearty hand-clasp in this teeming, desert place!"
And so soliloquizing, as a homesick creature will,
Incontinent, I wandered down the noisy, bustling hill,
And drifted, automatic-like and vaguely, into Lowe's,
Where Fortune had in store a panacea for my woes.
The register was open, and there dawned upon my sight
A name that filled and thrilled me with a cyclone of delight,—
The name that I shall venerate unto my dying day,
The proud, immortal signature: "John Smith, U. S. A."

Wildly I clutched the register, and brooded on that name;
I knew John Smith, yet could not well identify the same.
I knew him North, I knew him South, I knew him East and West:
I knew him all so well I knew not which I knew the best.
His eyes, I recollect, were gray, and black, and brown, and blue;
And when he was not bald, his hair was of chameleon hue;
Lean, fat, tall, short, rich, poor, grave, gay, a blonde and a bru-
    nette,—
Aha, amid this London fog, John Smith, I see you yet!
I see you yet; and yet the sight is all so blurred I seem
To see you in composite, or as in a waking dream.
Which are you, John? I'd like to know, that I might weave a
    rhyme
Appropriate to your character, your politics, and clime.
So tell me, were you "raised" or "reared"? your pedigree confess
In some such treacherous ism as "I reckon" or "I guess."
Let fall your telltale dialect, that instantly I may
Identify my countryman, "John Smith, U. S. A."

It 's like as not you air the John that lived a spell ago
Deown East, where codfish, beans, 'nd *bona-fide* schoolma'ams
    grow;
Where the dear old homestead nestles like among the Hampshire
    hills,
And where the robin hops about the cherry-boughs, 'nd trills;
Where Hubbard squash 'nd huckleberries grow to powerful size,
And everything is orthodox from preachers down to pies;
Where the red-wing blackbirds swing 'nd call beside the pick'rÎl
    pond,
And the crows air cawin' in the pines uv the pasture lot beyond;
Where folks complain uv bein' poor, because their money's lent
Out West on farms 'nd railroads at the rate uv ten per cent;
Where we ust to spark the Baker girls a-comin' home from
    choir,
Or a-settin' namin' apples round the roarin, kitchen fire;
Where we had to go to meetin' at least three times a week,
And our mothers learnt us good religious Dr. Watts to speak;
And where our grandmas sleep their sleep—God rest their souls,
    I say;
And God bless yours, ef you 're that John, "John Smith, U. S. A."

Or, mebbe, Col. Smith, yo' are the gentleman I know
In the country whar the finest Democrats 'nd hosses grow;
Whar the ladies are all beautiful, an' whar the crap of cawn
Is utilized for Burbon, and true awters are bawn.
You 've ren for jedge, and killed yore man, and bet on Proctor
    Knott;
Yore heart is full of chivalry, yore skin is full of shot;
And I disremember whar I 've met with gentlemen so true
As yo' all in Kaintucky, whar blood an' grass are blue,
Whar a niggah with a ballot is the signal fo' a fight,
Whar the yaller dawg pursues the coon throughout the bammy
    night,
Whar blooms the furtive possum,—pride an' glory of the South!
And aunty makes a hoe-cake, sah, that melts within yo' mouth,
Whar all night long the mockin'-birds are warblin' in the trees,
And black-eyed Susans nod and blink at every passing breeze,
Whar in a hallowed soil repose the ashes of our Clay,—
H'yar 's lookin' at yo', Col. "John Smith. U. S. A."

Or wuz you that John Smith I knew out yonder in the West,—
That part of our Republic I shall always love the best!
Wuz you him that went prospectin' in the spring of '69
In the Red Hoss Mountain country for the Gosh-all-Hemlock
    mine?
Oh, how I 'd liked to clasped your hand, an' set down by your side,
And talked about the good old days beyond the Big Divide,—
Of the rackaboar, the snaix, the bear, the Rocky Mountain goat,
Of the conversazzhyony, 'nd of Casey's tabble dote,
And a word of them old pardners that stood by us long ago,—
Three-fingered Hoover, Sorry Tom, and Parson Jim, you know!
Old times, old friends, John Smith, would make our hearts beat
    high again,
And we 'd see the snow-top mountains like we used to see 'em then;
The magpies would go flutterin' like strange sperrits to 'nd fro,
And we 'd hear the pines a-singin' in the ragged gulch below;
And the mountain brook would loiter like upon its windin' way,
Ez if it waited for a child to jine it in its play.

You see, John Smith, just which you are I cannot well recall;
And, really, I am pleased to think you somehow must be all!
For when a man sojourns abroad awhile, as I have done,
He likes to think of all the folks he left at home as one.
And so they are,—for well you know there 's nothing in a name;
Our Browns, our Joneses, and our Smiths are happily the same,—
All represent the spirit of the land across the sea;
All stand for one high purpose in our country of the free.
Whether John Smith be from the South, the North, the West, the
    East,
So long as he 's American, it mattereth not the least;
Whether his crest be badger, bear, palmetto, sword, or pine,
His is the glory of the stars that with the stripes combine.
Where'er he be, whate'er his lot, he 's eager to be known,
Not by his mortal name, but by his country's name alone;
And so, compatriot, I am proud you wrote your name to-day
Upon the register at Lowe's, "John Smith, U. S. A."

ST. MARTIN'S LANE

St. Martin's Lane winds up the hill
  And trends a devious way;
I walk therein amid the din
  Of busy London day:
I walk where wealth and squalor meet,
  And think upon a time
When others trod this saintly sod,
  And heard St. Martin's chime.

But when those solemn bells invoke
  The midnight's slumbrous grace,
The ghosts of men come back again
  To haunt that curious place:
The ghosts of sages, poets, wits,
  Come back in goodly train;
And all night long, with mirth and song,
  They walk St. Martin's Lane.

There 's Jerrold paired with Thackeray,
  Maginn and Thomas Moore,
And here and there and everywhere
  Fraserians by the score;
And one wee ghost that climbs the hill
  Is welcomed with a shout,—
No king could be revered as he,—
  The *padre*, Father Prout!

They banter up and down the street,
  And clamor at the door
Of yonder inn, which once has been
  The scene of mirth galore:
'T is now a lonely, musty shell,
  Deserted, like to fall;
And Echo mocks their ghostly knocks,
  And iterates their call.

Come back, thou ghost of ruddy host,
  From Pluto's misty shore;
Renew to-night the keen delight
  Of by-gone years once more;
Brew for this merry, motley horde,
  And serve the steaming cheer;
And grant that I may lurk hard by,
  To see the mirth, and hear.

Ah, me! I dream what things may seem
  To others childish vain,
And yet at night 't is my delight
  To walk St. Martin's Lane;
For, in the light of other days,
  I walk with those I love,
And all the time St. Martin's chime
  Makes piteous moan above.

DEAR OLD LONDON

WHEN I was broke in London in the fall of '89,
I chanced to spy in Oxford Street this tantalizing sign—
"A Splendid Horace cheap for Cash!" Of course I had to look
Upon the vaunted bargain, and it was a noble book!
A finer one I 've never seen, nor can I hope to see,—
The first edition, richly bound, and clean as clean can be,
And, just to think, for three-pounds-ten I might have had that Pine,
When I was broke in London in the fall of '89!

Down at Noseda's, in the Strand, I found, one fateful day,
A portrait that I pined for as only maniac may,—
A print of Madame Vestris (she flourished years ago,
Was Bartolozzi's daughter and a thoroughbred, you know).
A clean and handsome print it was, and cheap at thirty bob,—
That 's what I told the salesman, as I choked a rising sob;
But I hung around Noseda's as it were a holy shrine,
When I was broke in London in the fall of '89!

At Davey's, in Great Russell Street, were autographs galore,
And Mr. Davey used to let me con that precious store.
Sometimes I read what warriors wrote, sometimes a king's command,
But oftener still a poet's verse, writ in a meagre hand.
Lamb, Byron, Addison, and Burns, Pope, Johnson, Swift, and
    Scott,—
It needed but a paltry sum to comprehend the lot;
Yet, though Friend Davey marked 'em down, what could I but
    decline?
For I was broke in London in the fall of '89.

Of antique swords and spears I saw a vast and dazzling heap
That Curio Fenton offered me at prices passing cheap;
And, oh, the quaint old bureaus, and the warming-pans of brass,
And the lovely hideous freaks I found in pewter and in glass!
And, oh, the sideboards, candlesticks, the cracked old china plates,
The clocks and spoons from Amsterdam that antedate all dates!
Of such superb monstrosities I found an endless mine
When I was broke in London in the fall of '89.

O ye that hanker after boons that others idle by,—
The battered things that please the soul, though they may vex
    the eye,—
The silver plate and crockery all sanctified with grime,
The oaken stuff that has defiled the tooth of envious Time,
The musty tomes, the speckled prints, the mildewed bills of play,
And other costly relics of malodorous decay,—
Ye only can appreciate what agony was mine
When I was broke in London in the fall of '89.

When, in the course of natural things, I go to my reward,
Let no imposing epitaph my martyrdoms record;
Neither in Hebrew, Latin, Greek, nor any classic tongue,
Let my ten thousand triumphs over human griefs be sung;
But in plain Anglo-Saxon—that he may know who seeks
What agonizing pangs I've had while on the hunt for freaks—
Let there be writ upon the slab that marks my grave this line:
"Deceased was broke in London in the fall of '89."

THE CLINK OF THE ICE

NOTABLY fond of music, I dote on a sweeter tone
Than ever the harp has uttered or ever the lute has known.
When I wake at five in the morning with a feeling in my head
Suggestive of mild excesses before I retired to bed;
When a small but fierce volcano vexes me sore inside,
And my throat and mouth are furred with a fur that seemeth a
    buffalo hide,—
How gracious those dews of solace that over my senses fall
At the clink of the ice in the pitcher the boy brings up the
    hall!

Oh, is it the gaudy ballet, with features I cannot name,
That kindles in virile bosoms that slow but devouring flame?
Or is it the midnight supper, eaten before we retire,
That presently by combustion setteth us all afire?
Or is it the cheery magnum?—nay, I'll not chide the cup
That makes the meekest mortal anxious to whoop things up:
Yet, what the cause soever, relief comes when we call,—
Relief with that rapturous clinkety-clink that clinketh alike for all.

I 've dreamt of the fiery furnace that was one vast bulk of
    flame,
And that I was Abednego a-wallowing in that same;
And I 've dreamt I was a crater, possessed of a mad desire
To vomit molten lava, and to snort big gobs of fire;
I 've dreamt I was Roman candles and rockets that fizzed and
    screamed,—
In short, I have dreamt the cussedest dreams that ever a human
    dreamed:
But all the red-hot fancies were scattered quick as a wink
When the spirit within that pitcher went clinking its clinkety-clink.

Boy, why so slow in coming with that gracious, saving cup?
Oh, haste thee to the succor of the man who is burning up!
See how the ice bobs up and down, as if it wildly strove
To reach its grace to the wretch who feels like a red-hot kitchen
    stove!

The piteous clinks it clinks methinks should thrill you through
    and through:
An erring soul is wanting drink, and he wants it p. d. q.!
And, lo! the honest pitcher, too, falls in so dire a fret
That its pallid form is presently bedewed with a chilly sweat.

May blessings be showered upon the man who first devised this
    drink
That happens along at five A. M. with its rapturous clinkety-clink!
I never have felt the cooling flood go sizzling down my throat
But what I vowed to hymn a hymn to that clinkety-clink devote;
So now, in the prime of my manhood, I polish this lyric gem
For the uses of all good fellows who are thirsty at five A. M.,
But specially for those fellows who have known the pleasing thrall
Of the clink of the ice in the pitcher the boy brings up the hall.

THE BELLS OF NOTRE DAME

WHAT though the radiant thoroughfare
    Teems with a noisy throng?
What though men bandy everywhere
    The ribald jest and song?
Over the din of oaths and cries
    Broodeth a wondrous calm,
And 'mid that solemn stillness rise
    The bells of Notre Dame.

"Heed not, dear Lord," they seem to say,
    "Thy weak and erring child;
And thou, O gentle Mother, pray
    That God be reconciled;
And on mankind, O Christ, our King,
    Pour out Thy gracious balm,"—
'T is thus they plead and thus they sing,
    Those bells of Notre Dame.

And so, methinks, God, bending down
　To ken the things of earth,
Heeds not the mockery of the town
　Or cries of ribald mirth;
For ever soundeth in His ears
　A penitential psalm,—
'T is thy angelic voice He hears,
　O bells of Notre Dame!

Plead on, O bells, that thy sweet voice
　May still forever be
An intercession to rejoice
　Benign divinity;
And that thy tuneful grace may fall
　Like dew, a quickening balm,
Upon the arid hearts of all,
　O bells of Notre Dame!

LOVER'S LANE, SAINT JO

Saint Jo, Buchanan County,
　Is leagues and leagues away;
And I sit in the gloom of this rented room,
　And pine to be there to-day.
Yes, with London fog around me
　And the bustling to and fro,
I am fretting to be across the sea
　In Lover's Lane, Saint Jo.

I would have a brown-eyed maiden
　Go driving once again;
And I 'd sing the song, as we snailed along,
　That I sung to that maiden then:
I purposely say, "as we *snailed* along,"
　For a proper horse goes slow
In those leafy aisles, where Cupid smiles,
　In Lover's Lane, Saint Jo.

From her boudoir in the alders
   Would peep a lynx-eyed thrush,
And we 'd hear her say, in a furtive way,
   To the noisy cricket, "Hush!"
To think that the curious creature
   Should crane her neck to know
The various things one says and sings
   In Lover's Lane, Saint Jo.

But the maples they should shield us
   From the gossips of the place;
Nor should the sun, except by pun,
   Profane the maiden's face;
And the girl should do the driving,
   For a fellow can't, you know,
Unless he 's neglectful of what 's quite respectful
   In Lover's Lane, Saint Jo.

Ah! sweet the hours of springtime,
   When the heart inclines to woo,
And it 's deemed all right for the callow wight
   To do what he wants to do;
But cruel the age of winter,
   When the way of the world says no
To the hoary men who would woo again
   In Lover's Lane, Saint Jo!

In the Union Bank of London
   Are forty pounds or more,
Which I 'm like to spend, ere the month shall end,
   In an antiquarian store;
But I 'd give it all, and gladly,
   If for an hour or so
I could feel the grace of a distant place,—
   Of Lover's Lane, Saint Jo.

Let us sit awhile, beloved,
   And dream of the good old days,—
Of the kindly shade which the maples made
   Round the stanch but squeaky chaise;

With your head upon my shoulder,
And my arm about you so,
Though exiles, we shall seem to be
In Lover's Lane, Saint Jo.

CRUMPETS AND TEA

THERE are happenings in life that are destined to rise
Like dear, hallowed visions before a man's eyes;
And the passage of years shall not dim in the least
The glory and joy of our Sabbath-day feast,—
The Sabbath-day luncheon that's spread for us three,—
My worthy companions, Teresa and Leigh,
And me, all so hungry for crumpets and tea.

There are cynics who say with invidious zest
That a crumpet's a thing that will never digest;
But I happen to *know* that a crumpet is prime
For digestion, if only you give it its time.
Or if, by a chance, it should *not* quite agree,
Why, who would begrudge a physician his fee
For plying his trade upon crumpets and tea?

To toast crumpets quite *à la mode*, I require
A proper long fork and a proper quick fire;
And when they are browned, without further ado,
I put on the butter, that soaks through and through.
And meantime Teresa, directed by Leigh,
Compounds and pours out a rich brew for us three;
And so we sit down to our crumpets—and tea.

A hand-organ grinds in the street a weird bit,—
Confound those Italians! I wish they would quit
Interrupting our feast with their dolorous airs,
Suggestive of climbing the heavenly stairs.
(It's thoughts of the future, as all will agree,
That we fain would dismiss from our bosoms when we
Sit down to discussion of crumpets and tea!)

The Sabbath-day luncheon whereof I now speak
Quite answers its purpose the rest of the week;
Yet with the next Sabbath I wait for the bell
Announcing the man who has crumpets to sell;
Then I scuttle downstairs in a frenzy of glee,
And purchase for sixpence enough for us three,
Who hunger and hanker for crumpets and tea.

But soon—ah! too soon—I must bid a farewell
To joys that succeed to the sound of that bell,
Must hie me away from the dank, foggy shore
That's filled me with colic and—yearnings for more!
Then the cruel, the heartless, the conscienceless sea
Shall bear me afar from Teresa and Leigh
And the other twin friendships of crumpets and tea.

Yet often, ay, ever, before my wan eyes
That Sabbath-day luncheon of old shall arise.
My stomach, perhaps, shall improve by the change,
Since crumpets it seems to prefer at long range;
But, oh, how my palate will hanker to be
In London again with Teresa and Leigh,
Enjoying the rapture of crumpets and tea!

AN IMITATION OF DR. WATTS

THROUGH all my life the poor shall find
    In me a constant friend;
And on the meek of every kind
    My mercy shall attend.

The dumb shall never call on me
    In vain for kindly aid;
And in my hands the blind shall see
    A bounteous alms displayed.

In all their walks the lame shall know
    And feel my goodness near;
And on the deaf will I bestow
    My gentlest words of cheer.

'T is by such pious works as these,
    Which I delight to do,
That men their fellow-creatures please,
    And please their Maker too.

———

THE TEA-GOWN

My lady has a tea-gown
    That is wondrous fair to see,—
It is flounced and ruffed and plaited and puffed,
    As a tea-gown ought to be;
And I thought she must be jesting
    Last night at supper when
She remarked, by chance, that it came from France,
    And had cost but two pounds ten.

Had she told me fifty shillings,
    I might (and would n't you?)
Have referred to that dress in a way folks express
    By an eloquent dash or two;
But the guileful little creature
    Knew well her tactics when
She casually said that that dream in red
    Had cost but two pounds ten.

Yet our home is all the brighter
    For that dainty, sentient thing,
That floats away where it properly may,
    And clings where it ought to cling;
And I count myself the luckiest
    Of all us married men
That I have a wife whose joy in life
    Is a gown at two pounds ten.

It is n't the gown compels me
  Condone this venial sin;
It 's the pretty face above the lace,
  And the gentle heart within.
And with her arms about me
  I say, and say again,
" 'T was wondrous cheap,"—and I think a heap
  Of that gown at two pounds ten!

DOCTORS

'T is quite the thing to say and sing
  Gross libels on the doctor,—
To picture him an ogre grim
  Or humbug-pill concocter;
Yet it 's in quite another light
  My friendly pen would show him,
Glad that it may with verse repay
  Some part of what I owe him.

When one 's all right, he 's prone to spite
  The doctor's peaceful mission;
But when he 's sick, it 's loud and quick
  He bawls for a physician.
With other things, the doctor brings
  Sweet babes, our hearts to soften:
Though I have four, I pine for more,—
  Good doctor, pray come often!

What though he sees death and disease
  Run riot all around him?
Patient and true, and valorous too,
  Such have I always found him.
Where'er he goes, he soothes our woes;
  And when skill 's unavailing,
And death is near, his words of cheer
  Support our courage failing.

In ancient days they used to praise
  The godlike art of healing,—
An art that then engaged all men
  Possessed of sense and feeling.
Why, Raleigh, he was glad to be
  Famed for a quack elixir;
And Digby sold, as we are told,
  A charm for folk lovesick, sir.

Napoleon knew a thing or two,
  And clearly *he* was partial
To doctors, for in time of war
  He chose one for a marshal.
In our great cause a doctor was
  The first to pass death's portal,
And Warren's name at once became
  A beacon and immortal.

A heap, indeed, of what we read
  By doctors is provided;
For to those groves Apollo loves
  Their leaning is decided.
Deny who may that Rabelais
  Is first in wit and learning,
And yet all smile and marvel while
  His brilliant leaves they're turning.

How Lever's pen has charmed all men!
  How touching Rab's short story!
And I will stake my all that Drake
  Is still the school-boy's glory.
A doctor-man it was began
  Great Britain's great museum,—
The treasures there are all so rare,
  It drives me wild to see 'em!

There's Cuvier, Parr, and Rush; they are
  Big monuments to learning.
To Mitchell's prose (how smooth it flows!)
  We all are fondly turning.

Tomes might be writ of that keen wit
  Which Abernethy's famed for;
With bread-crumb pills he cured the ills
  Most doctors now get blamed for.

In modern times the noble rhymes
  Of Holmes, a great physician,
Have solace brought and wisdom taught
  To hearts of all condition.
The sailor, bound for Puget Sound,
  Finds pleasure still unfailing,
If he but troll the barcarole
  Old Osborne wrote on Whaling.

If there were need, I could proceed
  Ad naus. with this prescription,
But, *inter nos,* a larger dose
  Might give you fits conniption;
Yet, ere I end, there's one dear friend
  I 'd hold before these others,
For he and I in years gone by
  Have chummed around like brothers.

Together we have sung in glee
  The song old Horace made for
Our genial craft, together quaffed
  What bowls that doctor paid for!
I love the rest, but love him best;
  And, were not times so pressing,
I 'd buy and send—you smile, old friend?
  Well, then, here goes my blessing.

BARBARA

BLITHE was the youth that summer day
  As he smote at the ribs of earth,
And he plied his pick with a merry click,
  And he whistled anon in mirth;
And the constant thought of his dear one's face
Seemed to illumine that ghostly place.

The gaunt earth envied the lover's joy,
  And she moved, and closed on his head:
With no one nigh and with never a cry
  The beautiful boy lay dead;
And the treasure he sought for his sweetheart fair
Crumbled, and clung to his glorious hair.

Fifty years is a mighty space
  In the human toil for bread;
But to Love and to Death 't is merely a breath,
  A dream that is quickly sped,—
Fifty years, and the fair lad lay
Just as he fell that summer day.

At last came others in quest of gold,
  And hewed in that mountain place;
And deep in the ground one time they found
  The boy with the smiling face:
All uncorrupt by the pitiless air,
He lay, with his crown of golden hair.

They bore him up to the sun again,
  And laid him beside the brook,
And the folk came down from the busy town
  To wonder and prate and look;
And so, to a world that knew him not,
The boy came back to the old-time spot.

Old Barbara hobbled among the rest,—
  Wrinkled and bowed was she,—

And she gave a cry, as she fared anigh,
  "At last he is come to me!"
And she kneeled by the side of the dead boy there,
And she kissed his lips, and she stroked his hair.

"Thine eyes are sealed, O dearest one!
  And better it is 't is so,
Else thou might 'st see how harsh with me
  Dealt Life thou couldst not know·
Kindlier Death has kept *thee* fair;
The sorrow of Life hath been *my* share."

Barbara bowed her aged face,
  And fell on the breast of her dead;
And the golden hair of her dear one there
  Caressed her snow-white head.
Oh, Life is sweet, with its touch of pain;
But sweeter the Death that joined those twain.

THE CAFÉ MOLINEAU

THE Café Molineau is where
  A dainty little minx
Serves God and men as best she can
By serving meats and drinks.
Oh, such an air the creature has,
  And such a pretty face!
I took delight that autumn night
  In hanging round the place.

I know but very little French
  (I have not long been here);
But when she spoke, her meaning broke
  Full sweetly on my ear.
Then, too, she seemed to understand
  Whatever I 'd to say,
Though most I knew was "oony poo,"
  "Bong zhoor," and "see voo play."

The female wit is always quick,
    And of all womankind
'T is here in France that you, perchance,
    The keenest wits shall find; .
And here you 'll find that subtle gift,
    That rare, distinctive touch,
Combined with grace of form and face,
    That glads men overmuch.

"Our girls at home," I mused aloud,
    "Lack either that or this;
They don't combine the arts divine
    As does the Gallic miss.
Far be it from me to malign
    Our belles across the sea,
And yet I 'll swear none can compare
    With this ideal She."

And then I praised her dainty foot
    In very awful French,
And parleywood in guileful mood
    Until the saucy wench
Tossed back her haughty auburn head,
    And froze me with disdain:
"There are on me no flies," said she,
    "For I come from Bangor, Maine!"

HOLLY AND IVY

HOLLY standeth in ye house
    When that Noel draweth near;
Evermore at ye door
Standeth Ivy, shivering sore
    In ye night wind bleak and drear;
And, as weary hours go by,
Doth ye one to other cry.

"Sister Holly," Ivy quoth,
    "What is that within you see?
To and fro doth ye glow
Of ye yule-log flickering go;
        Would its warmth did cherish me!
Where thou bidest is it warm;
I am shaken of ye storm."

"Sister Ivy," Holly quoth,
    "Brightly burns the yule-log here,
And love brings beauteous things,
While a guardian angel sings
        To the babes that slumber near;
But, O Ivy! tell me now,
What without there seest thou?"

"Sister Holly," Ivy quoth,
    "With fair music comes ye Morn,
And afar burns ye Star
Where ye wondering shepherds are
        And the Shepherd King is born:
'Peace on earth, good-will to men,'
Angels cry, and cry again."

Holly standeth in ye house
        When that Noel draweth near;
Clambering o'er yonder door,
Ivy standeth evermore;
        And to them that rightly hear
Each one speaketh of ye love
That outpoureth from Above.

THE BOLTONS, 22

WHEN winter nights are grewsome, and the heavy, yellow fog
Gives to Piccadilly semblance of a dank, malarious bog;
When a demon, with companion in similitude of bell,
Goes round informing people he has crumpets for to sell;

When a weird, asthmatic minstrel haunts your door for hours along,
Until you've paid him tu'pence for the thing he calls a song,—
When, in short, the world's against you, and you'd give that
  world, and more,
To lay your weary heart at rest upon your native shore,
There's happily one saving thing for you and yours to do:
Go call on Isaac Henderson, The Boltons, 22.

The place is all so cheery and so warm, I love to spend
My evenings in communion with the genial host, my friend.
One sees *chefs d'œuvre* of masters in profusion on the walls,
And a monster canine swaggers up and down the spacious halls;
There are divers things of beauty to astound, instruct, and please,
And everywhere assurance of contentment and of ease:
But best of all the gentle hearts I meet with in the place,—
The host's good-fellowship, his wife's sincere and modest grace;
Why, if there be cordiality that warms you through and through,
It's found at Isaac Henderson's, The Boltons, 22.

My favorite room's the study that is on the second floor;
And there we sit in judgment on men and things galore.
The fire burns briskly in the grate, and sheds a genial glare
On me, who most discreetly have pre-empted Isaac's chair,—
A big, low chair, with grateful springs, and curious device
To keep a fellow's cerebellum comf'table and nice.
A shade obscures the functions of the stately lamp, in spite
Of Mrs. Henderson's demands for somewhat more of light;
But he and I demur, and say a mystic gloom will do
For winter-night communion at the Boltons, 22.

Sometimes he reads me Browning, or from Bryant culls a bit,
And sometimes plucks a gem from Hood's philosophy and wit;
And oftentimes I tell him yarns, and (what I fear is worse)
Recite him sundry specimens of woolly Western verse.
And while his muse and mine transcend the bright Horatian's stars,
He smokes his modest pipe, and I—I smoke his choice cigars!
For best of mild Havanas this considerate host supplies,—
The proper brand, the proper shade, and quite the proper size;
And so I buckle down and smoke and smoke,—and so will you,
If ever you're invited to the Boltons, 22.

But, oh! the best of worldly joys is as a dream short-lived:
'T is twelve o'clock, and Robinson reports our cab arrived.
A last libation ere we part, and hands all round, and then
A cordial invitation to us both to come again.
So home through Piccadilly and through Oxford Street we jog,
On slippery, noisy pavements and in blinding, choking fog,—
The same old route through Circus, Square, and Quadrant we
        retrace,
Till we reach the princely mansion known as 20 Alfred Place;
And then we seek our feathery beds of cotton to renew
In dreams the sweet distractions of the Boltons, 22.

God bless you, good friend Isaac, and your lovely, gracious wife;
May health and wealth attend you, and happiness, through life;
And as you sit of evenings that quiet room within,
Know that in spirit I shall be your guest as I have been.
So fill and place beside that chair that dainty claret-cup;
Methinks that ghostly hands shall take the tempting offering up,
That ghostly lips shall touch the bowl and quaff the ruby wine,
Pledging in true affection this toast to thee and thine:
"May God's best blessings fall as falls the gentle, gracious dew
Upon the kindly household at the Boltons, 22!"

———

DIBDIN'S GHOST

DEAR wife, last midnight, whilst I read
    The tomes you so despise,
A spectre rose beside the bed,
    And spake in this true wise:
"From Canaan's beatific coast
    I 've come to visit thee,
For I am Frognall Dibdin's ghost,"
    Says Dibdin's ghost to me.

I bade him welcome, and we twain
    Discussed with buoyant hearts
The various things that appertain
    To bibliomaniac arts.

"Since you are fresh from t' other side,
  Pray tell me of that host
That treasured books before they died,"
  Says I to Dibdin's ghost.

"They 've entered into perfect rest;
  For in the life they 've won
There are no auctions to molest,
  No creditors to dun.
Their heavenly rapture has no bounds
  Beside that jasper sea;
It is a joy unknown to Lowndes,"
  Says Dibdin's ghost to me.

Much I rejoiced to hear him speak
  Of biblio-bliss above,
For I am one of those who seek
  What bibliomaniacs love.
"But tell me, for I long to hear
  What doth concern me most,
Are wives admitted to that sphere?"
  Says I to Dibdin's ghost.

"The women folk are few up there;
  For 't were not fair, you know,
That they our heavenly joy should share
  Who vex us here below.
The few are those who have been kind
  To husbands such as we;
They knew our fads, and did n't mind,"
  Says Dibdin's ghost to me.

"But what of those who scold at us
  When we would read in bed?
Or, wanting victuals, make a fuss
  If we buy books instead?
And what of those who 've dusted not
  Our motley pride and boast,—
Shall they profane that sacred spot?"
  Says I to Dibdin's ghost.

"Oh, no! they tread that other path,
　Which leads where torments roll,
And worms, yes, bookworms, vent their wrath
　Upon the guilty soul.
Untouched of bibliomaniac grace,
　That saveth such as we,
They wallow in that dreadful place,"
　Says Dibdin's ghost to me.

"To my dear wife will I recite
　What things I 've heard you say;
She 'll let me read the books by night,
　She 's let me buy by day.
For we together by and by
　Would join that heavenly host;
She 's earned a rest as well as I,"
　Says I to Dibdin's ghost.

THE BOTTLE AND THE BIRD

ONCE on a time a friend of mine prevailed on me to go
To see the dazzling splendors of a sinful ballet show;
And after we had revelled in the saltatory sights,
We sought a neighboring *café* for more tangible delights.
When I demanded of my friend what viands he preferred,
He quoth:　"A large cold bottle, and a small hot bird!"

Fool that I was, I did not know what anguish hidden lies
Within the morceau that allures the nostrils and the eyes!
There is a glorious candor in an honest quart of wine,
A certain inspiration which I cannot well define!
How it bubbles, how it sparkles, how its gurgling seems to say:
"Come! on a tide of rapture let me float your soul away!"

But the crispy, steaming mouthful that is spread upon your plate,—
How it discounts human sapience and satirizes fate!
You wouldn't think a thing so small could cause the pains and aches

That certainly accrue to him that of that thing partakes;
To me, at least (a guileless wight!), it never once occurred
What horror was encompassed in that small hot bird.

Oh! what a head I had on me when I awoke next day
And what a firm conviction of intestinal decay!
What seas of mineral water and of bromide I applied
To quench those fierce volcanic fires that rioted inside!
And, oh, the thousand solemn, awful vows I plighted then
Never to tax my system with a small hot bird again!

The doctor seemed to doubt that birds could worry people so,
But, bless him! since I ate the bird, I guess I ought to know!
The acidous condition of my stomach, so he said,
Bespoke a vinous irritant that amplified my head,
And, ergo, the causation of the thing, as he inferred,
Was the large cold bottle,—*not* the small hot bird.

Of course I know it was n't, and I 'm sure you 'll say I 'm right
If ever it has been your wont to train around at night.
How sweet is retrospection when one's heart is bathed in wine,
And before its balmy breath how do the ills of life decline!
How the gracious juices drown what griefs would vex a mortal
        breast,
And float the flattered soul into the port of dreamless rest!

But you, O noxious, pigmy bird! whether it be you fly,
Or paddle in the stagnant pools that sweltering, festering lie,—
I curse you and your evil kind for that you do me wrong,
Engendering poisons that corrupt my petted muse of song;
Go, get thee hence! and never more discomfit me and mine,—
I fain would barter all thy brood for one sweet draught of wine!

So hither come, O sportive youth! when fades the telltale day,—
Come hither, with your fillets and your wreaths of posies gay;
We shall unloose the fragrant seas of seething, frothing wine
Which now the cobwebbed glass and envious wire and corks
        confine,
And midst the pleasing revelry the praises shall be heard
Of the large cold bottle,—*not* the small hot bird!

CARLSBAD

DEAR Palmer, just a year ago we did the Carlsbad cure,
Which, though it be exceeding slow, is as exceeding sure;
To corpulency you were prone, dyspepsia bothered me,—
You tipped the beam at twenty stone and I at ten stone three!
The cure, they told us, works both ways: it makes the fat man lean;
The thin man, after many days, achieves a portly mien;
And though it's true you still are fat, while I am like a crow,—
All skin and feathers,—what of that? The cure takes time, you
    know.

The Carlsbad scenery is sublime,—that's what the guide-books say;
We did not think so at that time, nor think *I* so to-day!
The bluffs that squeeze the panting town permit no pleasing views,
But weigh the mortal spirits down and give a chap the blues.
With nothing to amuse us then or mitigate our spleen,
We rose and went to bed again, with three bad meals between;
And constantly we made our moan,—ah, none so drear as we,
When you were weighing twenty stone and I but ten stone three!

We never scaled the mountain-side, for walking was my bane,
And you were much too big to ride the mules that there obtain;
And so we loitered in the shade, with Israel out in force,
Or through the Pupp'sche allee strayed and heard the band dis-
    course.
Sometimes it pleased us to recline upon the Tepl's brink,
Or watch the bilious human line file round to get a drink;
Anon the portier's piping tone embittered you and me,
When you were weighing twenty stone and I but ten stone three!

And oh! those awful things to eat! No pudding, cake, or pie,
But just a little dab of meat, and crusts absurdly dry;
Then, too, that water twice a day,—one swallow was enough
To take one's appetite away,—the tepid, awful stuff!
Tortured by hunger's cruel stings, I'd little else to do
Than feast my eyes upon the things prescribed and cooked for you.
The goodies went to you alone, the husks all fell to me,
When you were weighing twenty stone and I weighed ten stone three.

Yet happy days! and rapturous ills! and sweetly dismal date!
When, sandwiched in between those hills, we twain bemoaned
  our fate.
The little woes we suffered then like mists have sped away,
And I were glad to share again those ills with you to-day,—
To flounder in those rains of June that flood that Austrian vale,
To quaff that tepid Kaiserbrunn and starve on victuals stale!
And often, leagues and leagues away from where we suffered then,
With envious yearnings I survey what cannot be again!

And often in my quiet home, through dim and misty eyes,
I seem to see that curhaus dome blink at the radiant skies;
I seem to hear that Wiener band above the Tepl's roar,—
To feel the pressure of your hand and hear your voice once more;
And, better yet, my heart is warm with thoughts of you and yours,
For friendship hath a sweeter charm than thrice ten thousand cures!
So I am happy to have known that time across the sea
When you were weighing twenty stone and I weighed ten stone three.

RED

Any color, so long as it 's red,
  Is the color that suits me best,
Though I will allow there is much to be said
  For yellow and green and the rest;
But the feeble tints which some affect
  In the things they make or buy
Have never—I say it with all respect—
  Appealed to my critical eye.

There 's that in red that warmeth the blood,
  And quickeneth a man within,
And bringeth to speedy and perfect bud
  The germs of original sin;
So, though I 'm properly born and bred,
  I 'll own, with a certain zest,
That any color, so long as it 's red,
  Is the color that suits me best.

For where is the color that can compare
  With the blush of a buxom lass;
Or where such warmth as of the hair
  Of the genuine white horse class˄
And, lo! reflected within this cup
  Of cheery Bordeaux I see
What inspiration girdeth me up,—
  Yes, red is the color for me!

Through acres and acres of art I 've strayed
  In Italy, Germany, France;
On many a picture a master has made
  I 've squandered a passing glance:
Marines I hate, madonnas and
  Those Dutch freaks I detest;
But the peerless daubs of my native land,—
  They 're red, and I like them best.

'T is little I care how folk deride,—
  I 'm backed by the West, at least;
And we are free to say that we can't abide
  The tastes that obtain down East;
And we 're mighty proud to have it said
  That here in the versatile West
Most any color, so long as it 's red,
  Is the color that suits us best.

———

AT CHEYENNE

Young Lochinvar came in from the West,
With fringe on his trousers and fur on his vest;
The width of his hat-brim could nowhere be beat,
His No. 10 brogans were chuck full of feet,
His girdle was horrent with pistols and things,
And he flourished a handful of aces on kings.

The fair Mariana sate watching a star,
When who should turn up but the young Lochinvar!
Her pulchritude gave him a pectoral glow,
And he reined up his hoss with stentorian "Whoa!"
Then turned on the maiden a rapturous grin,
And modestly asked if he might n't step in.

With presence of mind that was marvellous quite,
The fair Mariana replied that he might;
So in through the portal rode young Lochinvar,
Pre-empted the claim, and cleaned out the bar.
Though the justice allowed he wa'n't wholly to blame,
He taxed him ten dollars and costs, just the same.

THE PNEUMOGASTRIC NERVE

Upon an average, twice a week,
  When anguish clouds my brow,
My good physician friend I seek
  To know "what ails me now."
He taps me on the back and chest,
  And scans my tongue for bile,
And lays an ear against my breast
  And listens there awhile;
Then is he ready to admit
  That all he can observe
Is something wrong inside, to wit:
  My pneumogastric nerve!

Now, when these Latin names within
  Dyspeptic hulks like mine
Go wrong, a fellow should begin
  To draw what's called the line.
It seems, however, that this same,
  Which in my hulks abounds,
Is not, despite its awful name,
  So fatal as it sounds;

Yet of all torments known to me,
  I 'll say without reserve,
There is no torment like to thee,
  Thou pneumogastric nerve!

This subtle, envious nerve appears
  To be a patient foe,—
It waited nearly forty years
  Its chance to lay me low;
Then, like some blithering blast of hell,
  It struck this guileless bard,
And in that evil hour I fell
  Prodigious far and hard.
Alas! what things I dearly love—
  Pies, puddings, and preserves—
Are sure to rouse the vengeance of
  All pneumogastric nerves!

Oh that I could remodel man!
  I 'd end these cruel pains
By hitting on a different plan
  From that which now obtains.
The stomach, greatly amplified,
  Anon should occupy
The all of that domain inside
  Where heart and lungs now lie.
But, first of all, I should depose
  That diabolic curve
And author of my thousand woes,
  The pneumogastric nerve!

TELKA

Through those golden summer days
Our twin flocks were wont to graze
On the hillside, which the sun
Rested lovingly upon,—
Telka's flock and mine; and we

Sung our songs in rapturous glee,
Idling in the pleasant shade
Which the solemn Yew-tree made,
While the Brook anear us played,
And a white Rose, ghost-like, grew
In the shadow of the Yew.

Telka loved me passing well;
How I loved her none can tell!
How I love her none may know,—
Oh, that man loves woman so!
When she was not at my side,
Loud my heart in anguish cried,
And my lips, till she replied.
Yet they think to silence me,—
As if love could silenced be!
Fool were I, and fools were they!
Still I wend my lonely way,
"Telka," evermore I cry;
Answer me the woods and sky,
And the weary years go by.

Telka, she was passing fair;
And the glory of her hair
Was such glory as the sun
With his blessing casts upon
Yonder lonely mountain height,
Lifting up to bid good-night
To her sovereign in the west,
Sinking wearily to rest,
Drowsing in that golden sea
Where the realms of Dreamland be.

So our love to fulness grew,
Whilst beneath the solemn Yew
Ghost-like paled the Rose of white,
As it were some fancied sight
Blanched it with a dread affright.
Telka, she was passing fair;
And our peace was perfect there

Till, enchanted by her smile,
Lurked the South Wind there awhile.
Underneath that hillside tree
Where with singing idled we,
And I heard the South Wind say
Flattering words to her that day
Of a city far away.
But the Yew-tree crouched as though
It were like to whisper No
To the words the South wind said
As he smoothed my Telka's head.
And the Brook, all pleading, cried
To the dear one at my side:
"Linger always where I am;
Stray not thence, O cosset lamb!
Wander not where shadows deep
On the treacherous quicksands sleep,
And the haunted waters leap;
Be thou ware the waves that flow
Toward the prison pool below,
Where, beguiled from yonder sky,
Captive moonbeams shivering lie,
And at dawn of morrow die."
So the Brook to Telka cried,
But my Telka naught replied;
And, as in a strange affright,
Paled the Rose a ghostlier white.

When anon the North Wind came,—
Rudely blustering Telka's name,
And he kissed the leaves that grew
Round about the trembling Yew,—
Kissed and romped till, blushing red,
All one day in terror fled,
And the white Rose hung her head;
Coming to our trysting spot,
Long I called; she answered not.
"Telka!" pleadingly I cried
Up and down the mountain-side
Where we twain were wont to bide.

There were those who thought that **I**
Could be silenced with a lie,
And they told me Telka's name
Should be spoken now with shame;
"She is lost to us and thee,"—
That is what they said to me.

"Is my Telka lost?" quoth I.
"On this hilltop shall I cry,
So that she may hear and then
Find her way to me again.
The South Wind spoke a lie that **day;**
All deceived, she lost her way;
Yonder where the shadows sleep
'Mongst the haunted waves that **leap**
Over treacherous quicksands deep,
And where captive moonbeams lie
Doomed at morrow's dawn to **die,**
She is lost, and that is all;
I will search for her, and call."

Summer comes and winter goes,
Buds the Yew and blooms the Rose;
All the others are anear,—
Only Telka is not here!
Gone the peace and love I knew
Sometime 'neath the hillside Yew;
And the Rose, that mocks me so,
I had crushed it long ago
But that Telka loved it then,
And shall soothe its terror when
She comes back to me again.
Call I, seek I everywhere
For my Telka, passing fair.

It is, oh, so many a year
I have called! She does not hear,
Yet nor feared nor worn am I;
For I know that if I cry
She shall sometime hear my call.

She is lost, and that is all,—
She is lost in some far spot;
I have searched, and found it not.
Could she hear me calling, then
Would she come to me again;
For she loved me passing well,—
How I love her none can tell!
That is why these years I 've cried
"Telka!" on this mountain-side.
"Telka!" still I, pleading, cry;
Answer me the woods and sky,
And the lonely years go by.

On an evening dark and chill
Came a shadow up the hill,—
Came a spectre, grim and white
As a ghost that walks the night,
Grim and bowed, and with the cry
Of a wretch about to die,—
Came and fell and cried to me:
"It is Telka come!" said she.
So she fell and so she cried
On that lonely mountain-side
Where was Telka wont to bide.

"Who hath bribed those lips to lie?
Telka's face was fair," quoth I;
"Thine is furrowed with despair.
There is winter in thy hair;
But upon her beauteous head
Was there summer glory shed,—
Such a glory as the sun,
When his daily course is run,
Smiles upon this mountain height
As he kisses it good-night.
There was music in her tone,
Misery in thy voice alone.
They have bid thee lie to me.
Let me pass!   Thou art not she!
Let my sorrow sacred be
Underneath this trysting tree!"

So in wrath I went my way,
And they came another day,—
Came another day, and said:
"Hush thy cry, for she is dead.
Yonder on the mountain-side
She is buried where she died,
Where you twain were wont to bide.
Where she came and fell and cried
Pardon that thy wrath denied;
And above her bosom grows
As in mockery the Rose:
It was white; but now 't is red,
And in shame it bows its head
Over sinful Telka dead."

So they thought to silence me,—
As if love could silenced be!
Fool were I, and fools were they!
Scornfully I went my way,
And upon the mountain-side
"Telka!" evermore I cried.
"Telka!" evermore I cry;
Answer me the woods and sky:
So the lonely years go by.

She is lost, and that is all;
Sometime she shall hear my call,
Hear my pleading call, and then
Find her way to me again.

PLAINT OF THE MISSOURI 'COON IN THE BERLIN ZOOLOGICAL GARDENS

Friend, by the way you hump yourself you 're from the States, I
    know,
And born in old Mizzoorah, where the 'coons in plenty grow.
I, too, am native of that clime; but harsh, relentless fate
Has doomed me to an exile far from that noble State;

And I, who used to climb around, and swing from tree to tree,
Now lead a life of ignominious ease, as you can see.
Have pity, O compatriot mine! and bide a season near,
While I unfurl a dismal tale to catch your friendly ear.

My pedigree is noble: they used my grandsire's skin
To piece a coat for Patterson to warm himself within,—
Tom Patterson, of Denver; no ermine can compare
With the grizzled robe that Democratic statesman loves to wear.
Of such a grandsire I am come; and in the County Cole
All up an ancient cottonwood our family had its hole.
We envied not the liveried pomp nor proud estate of kings,
As we hustled round from day to day in search of bugs and things.

And when the darkness fell around, a mocking-bird was nigh,
Inviting pleasant, soothing dreams with his sweet lullaby;
And sometimes came the yellow dog to brag around all night
That nary 'coon could wallop him in a stand-up barrel fight.
We simply smiled and let him howl, for all Mizzoorians know
That ary 'coon can best a dog, if the coon gets half a show;
But we 'd nestle close and shiver when the mellow moon had ris'n,
And the hungry nigger sought our lair in hopes to make us his'n.

Raised as I was, it 's hardly strange I pine for those old days;
I cannot get acclimated, or used to German ways.
The victuals that they give me here may all be very fine
For vulgar, common palates, but they will not do for mine.
The 'coon that 's been accustomed to stanch Democratic cheer
Will not put up with onion tarts and sausage steeped in beer!
No; let the rest, for meat and drink, accede to slavish terms,
But send *me* back from whence I came, and let me grub for worms!

They come, these gaping Teutons do, on Sunday afternoons,
And wonder what I am,—alas, there are no German 'coons!
For if there were, I still might swing at home from tree to tree,
The symbol of Democracy, that 's woolly, blithe, and free.
And yet for what my captors are I would not change my lot,
For *I* have tasted liberty, these others, *they* have not;
So, even caged, the Democratic 'coon more glory feels
Than the conscript German puppets with their swords about their
    heels.

Well, give my love to Crittenden, to Clardy, and O'Neill,
To Jasper Burke and Colonel Jones, and tell 'em how I feel;
My compliments to Cockrill, Stephens, Switzler, Francis, Vest,
Bill Nelson, J. West Goodwin, Jedge Broadhead, and the rest.
Bid them be steadfast in the faith, and pay no heed at all
To Joe McCullagh's badinage or Chauncey Filley's gall;
And urge them to retaliate for what I 'm suffering here
By cinching all the alien class that wants its Sunday beer.

THE PARTRIDGE

As beats the sun from mountain crest,
    With "Pretty, pretty,"
Cometh the partridge from her nest.
The flowers threw kisses sweet to her
(For all the flowers that bloomed knew her);
Yet hasteneth she to mine and me,—
    Ah, pretty, pretty!
    Ah, dear little partridge!

And when I hear the partridge cry
    So pretty, pretty,
Upon the house-top breakfast I.
She comes a-chirping far and wide.
And swinging from the mountain-side
I see and hear the dainty dear,—
    Ah, pretty, pretty!
    Ah, dear little partridge!

Thy nest 's inlaid with posies rare,
    And pretty, pretty,
Bloom violet, rose, and lily there;
The place is full of balmy dew
(The tears of flowers in love with you!);
And one and all, impassioned, call,
    "O pretty, pretty!
    O dear little partridge!"

Thy feathers they are soft and sleek,—
    So pretty, pretty!
Long is thy neck, and small thy beak,
The color of thy plumage far
More bright than rainbow colors are.
Sweeter than dove is she I love,—
    My pretty, pretty!
    My dear little partridge!

When comes the partridge from the tree,
    So pretty, pretty,
And sings her little hymn to me,
Why, all the world is cheered thereby,
The heart leaps up into the eye,
And Echo then gives back again
    Our "Pretty, pretty!"
    Our "Dear little partridge!"

Admitting thee most blest of all,
    And pretty, pretty,
The birds come with thee at thy call,
In flocks they come, and round thee play,
And this is what they seem to say:—
They say, and sing, each feathered thing,
    "Ah, pretty, pretty!
    Ah, dear little partridge!"

CORINTHIAN HALL

CORINTHIAN HALL is a tumble-down place,
Which some finical folks have pronounced a disgrace
But once was a time when Corinthian Hall
Excited the rapture and plaudits of all,
    With its carpeted stairs,
    And its new yellow chairs,
And its stunning *ensemble* of citified airs.
Why, the Atchison Champion said 't was the best
Of Thespian temples extant in the West.

It was new, and was ours,—that was ages ago,
Before opry had spoiled the legitimate show,—
It was new, and was ours! We could toss back the jeers
Our rivals had launched at our city for years.
         Corinthian Hall,
         Why, it discounted all
Other halls in the Valley, and well I recall
The night of the opening; from near and afar
Came the crowd to see Toodles performed by De Bar.

Oh, those days they were palmy, and never again
Shall earth see such genius as gladdened us then;
For actors were actors, and each one knew how
To whoop up his art in the sweat of his brow.
He'd a tragedy air, and wore copious hair;
And when he ate victuals, he ordered 'em rare.
Dame Fortune ne'er feazed him,—in fact, never could
When liquor was handy and walking was good.

And the shows in those days! Ah, how well I recall
The shows that I saw in Corinthian Hall!
Maggie Mitchell and Lotty were then in their prime;
And as for Jane Coombs, she was simply sublime;
And I'm ready to swear there is none could compare
With Breslau in Borgia, supported by Fair;
While in passionate rôles it was patent to us
That the great John A. Stevens was *ne ultra plus.*

And was there demand for the tribute of tears,
We had sweet Charlotte Thompson those halcyon years,
And wee Katie Putnam. The savants allow
That the like of Kate Fisher ain't visible now.
What artist to-day have we equal to Rae,
Or to sturdy Jack Langrishe? God rest 'em, I say!
And when died Buchanan, the "St. Jo Gazette"
Opined that the sun of our drama had set.

Corinthian Hall was devoted to song
When the Barnabee concert troupe happened along,

Or Ossian E. Dodge, or the Comical Brown,
Or the Holmans with William H. Crane struck our town;
    But the one special card
    That hit us all hard
Was Caroline Richings and Peter Bernard;
And the bells of the Bergers still ring in my ears;
And, oh, how I laughed at Sol Russell those years!

The Haverly Minstrels were boss in those days,
And our critics accorded them columns of praise;
They'd handsome mustaches and big cluster rings,
And their shirt fronts were blazing with diamonds and things;
They gave a parade, and sweet music they made
Every evening in front of the house where they played.
'Twixt posters and hand-bills the town was agog
For Primrose and West in their great statue clog.

Many years intervene, yet I 'm free to maintain
That I doted on Chanfrau, McWade, and Frank Frayne;
Tom Stivers, the local, declared for a truth
That Mayo as Hamlet was better than Booth:
While in rôles that were thrillin', involving much killin',
Jim Wallick loomed up our ideal of a villain;
Mrs. Bowers, Alvin Joslin, Frank Aiken,—they all
Earned their titles to fame in Corinthian Hall.

But Time, as begrudging the glory that fell
On the spot I revere and remember so well,
Spent his spite on the timbers, the plaster, and paint,
And breathed on them all his morbiferous taint;
So the trappings of gold and the gear manifold
Got gangrened with rust and rheumatic with mould,
And we saw dank decay and oblivion fall,
Like vapors of night, on Corinthian Hall.

When the gas is ablaze in the opry at night,
And the music goes floating on billows of light,
Why, I often regret that I 'm grown to a man,
And I pine to be back where my mission began,

And I 'm fain to recall
Reminiscences all
That come with the thought of Corinthian Hall,—
To hear and to see what delighted me then,
And to revel in raptures of boyhood again.

Though Corinthian Hall is a tumble-down place,
Which some finical folks have pronounced a disgrace,
There is one young old boy, quite as worthy as they,
Who, aweary of art as expounded to-day,
Would surrender what gold
He 's amassed to behold
A tithe of the wonderful doings of old,
A glimpse of the glories that used to enthrall
Our *crème de la crème* in Corinthian Hall.

THE RED, RED WEST

I 've travelled in heaps of countries, and studied all kinds of art,
Till there is n't a critic or connoisseur who 's properly deemed so
smart;
And I 'm free to say that the grand results of my explorations show
That somehow paint gets redder the farther out West I go.

I 've sipped the voluptuous sherbet that the Orientals serve,
And I 've felt the glow of red Bordeaux tingling each separate
nerve;
I 've sampled your classic Massic under an arbor green,
And I 've reeked with song a whole night long over a brown poteen.

The stalwart brew of the land o' cakes, the schnapps of the fru-
gal Dutch,
The much-praised wine of the distant Rhine, and the beer praised
overmuch,
The ale of dear old London, and the port of Southern climes,—
All, *ad infin.*, have I taken in a hundred thousand times.

Yet, as I afore-mentioned, these other charms are naught
Compared with the paramount gorgeousness with which the West
    is fraught;
For Art and Nature are just the same in the land where the porker
    grows,
And the paint keeps getting redder the farther out West one goes.

Our savants have never discovered the reason why this is so,
And ninety per cent. of the laymen care less than the savants know;
It answers every purpose that this is manifest:
The paint keeps getting redder the farther you go out West.

Give me no home 'neath the pale pink dome of European skies,
No cot for me by the salmon sea that far to the southward lies;
But away out West I would build my nest on top of a carmine hill,
Where I can paint, without restraint, creation redder still!

THE THREE KINGS OF COLOGNE

From out Cologne there came three kings
    To worship Jesus Christ, their King.
To Him they sought fine herbs they brought,
    And many a beauteous golden thing;
They brought their gifts to Bethlehem town,
And in that manger set them down.

Then spake the first king, and he said:
    "O Child, most heavenly, bright, and fair!
I bring this crown to Bethlehem town
    For Thee, and only Thee, to wear;
So give a heavenly crown to me
When I shall come at last to Thee!"

The second, then. "I bring Thee here
    This royal robe, O Child!" he cried;
"Of silk 't is spun, and such an one
    There is not in the world beside;
So in the day of doom requite
Me with a heavenly robe of white!"

The third king gave his gift, and quoth:
  "Spikenard and myrrh to Thee I bring,
And with these twain would I most fain
  Anoint the body of my King;
So may their incense sometime rise
To plead for me in yonder skies!'

Thus spake the three kings of Cologne,
  That gave their gifts, and went their way;
And now kneel I in prayer hard by
  The cradle of the Child to-day;
Nor crown, nor robe, nor spice I bring
As offering unto Christ, my King.

Yet have I brought a gift the Child
  May not despise, however small;
For here I lay my heart to-day,
  And it is full of love to all.
Take Thou the poor but loyal thing,
My only tribute, Christ, my King!

———

IPSWICH

In Ipswich nights are cool and fair,
  And the voice that comes from the yonder sea
Sings to the quaint old mansions there
  Of "the time, the time that used to be";
And the quaint old mansions rock and groan,
And they seem to say in an undertone,
With half a sigh and with half a moan:
  "It was, but it never again will be."

In Ipswich witches weave at night
  Their magic spells with impish glee;
They shriek and laugh in their demon flight
  From the old Main House to the frightened sea.

And ghosts of eld come out to weep
Over the town that is fast asleep;
And they sob and they wail, as on they creep:
    "It was, but it never again will be."

In Ipswich riseth Heart-Break Hill
    Over against the calling sea;
And through the nights so deep and chill
    Watcheth a maiden constantly,—
Watcheth alone, nor seems to hear
Over the roar of the waves anear
The pitiful cry of a far-off year:
    "It was, but it never again will be."

In Ipswich once a witch I knew,—
    An artless Saxon witch was she;
By that flaxen hair and those eyes of blue,
    Sweet was the spell she cast on me.
Alas! but the years have wrought me ill,
And the heart that is old and battered and chill
Seeketh again on Heart-Break Hill
    What was, but never again can be.

Dear Anna, I would not conjure down
    The ghost that cometh to solace me;
I love to think of old Ipswich town,
    Where somewhat better than friends were we;
For with every thought of the dear old place
Cometh again the tender grace
Of a Saxon witch's pretty face,
    As it was, and is, and ever shall be.

BILL'S TENOR AND MY BASS

BILL was short and dapper, while I was thin and tall;
I had flowin' whiskers, but Bill had none at all;
    Clothes would never seem to set so nice on *me* as *him*,—
    Folks used to laugh, and say I was too powerful slim,—

But Bill's clothes fit him like the paper on the wall;
And we were the sparkin'est beaus in all the place
When Bill sung tenor and I sung bass.

Cyrus Baker's oldest girl was member of the choir,—
Eyes as black as Kelsey's cat, and cheeks as red as fire!
She had the best sopranner voice I think I ever heard,—
Sung "Coronation," "Burlington," and "Chiny" like a bird;
Never done better than with Bill a-standin' nigh 'er,
A-holdin' of her hymn-book so she would n't lose the place,
When Bill sung tenor and I sung bass.

Then there was Prudence Hubbard, so cosey-like and fat,—
She sung alto, and wore a pee-wee hat;
Beaued her around one winter, and, first thing I knew,
One evenin' on the portico I up and called her "Prue"!
But, sakes alive! she did n't mind a little thing like that;
On all the works of Providence she set a cheerful face
When Bill was singin' tenor and I was singin' bass.

Bill, nevermore we two shall share the fun we used to then,
Nor know the comfort and the peace we had together when
We lived in Massachusetts in the good old courtin' days,
And lifted up our voices in psalms and hymns of praise.
Oh, how I wisht that I could live them happy times again!
For life, as we boys knew it, had a sweet, peculiar grace
When you was singin' tenor and I was singin' bass.

The music folks have nowadays ain't what it used to be,
Because there ain't no singers now on earth like Bill and me.
Why, Lemuel Bangs, who used to go to Springfield twice a year,
Admitted that for singin' Bill and me had not a peer
When Bill went soarin' up to A and I dropped down to D!
The old bull-fiddle Beza Dimmitt played war n't in the race
'Longside of Bill's high tenor and my sonorious bass.

Bill moved to Californy in the spring of '54,
And we folks that used to know him never knew him any more;
Then Cyrus Baker's oldest girl, she kind o' pined a spell,
And, hankerin' after sympathy, it naterally befell

That she married Deacon Pitkin's boy, who kep' the general store;
    And so the years, the changeful years, have rattled on apace
    Since Bill sung tenor and I sung bass.

As I was settin' by the stove this evenin' after tea,
I noticed wife kep' hitchin' close and closer up to me;
    And as she patched the gingham frock our gran'child wore to-day,
    I heerd her gin a sigh that seemed to come from fur away.
Could n't help inquirin' what the trouble might be;
    "Was thinkin' of the time," says Prue, a-breshin' at her face,
    "When Bill sung tenor and you sung bass."

THE "ST. JO GAZETTE"

WHEN I helped 'em run the local on the "St. Jo Gazette,"
I was upon familiar terms with every one I met;
For "items" were my stock in trade in that my callow time,
Before the muses tempted me to try my hand at rhyme,—
    Before I found in verses
    Those soothing, gracious mercies,
Less practical, but much more glorious than a well-filled purse is.
A votary of Mammon, I hustled round and sweat,
And helped 'em run the local on the "St. Jo Gazette."

The labors of the day began at half-past eight A. M.,
For the farmers came in early, and I had to tackle them;
And many a noble bit of news I managed to acquire
By those discreet attentions which all farmer-folk admire,
    With my daily commentary
    On affairs of farm and dairy,
The tone of which anon with subtle pufferies I 'd vary,—
Oh, many a peck of apples and of peaches did I get
When I helped 'em run the local on the "St. Jo Gazette."

Dramatic news was scarce, but when a minstrel show was due,
Why, Milton Tootle's opera house was then my rendezvous;
Judge Grubb would give me points about the latest legal case.
And Dr. Runcie let me print his sermons when I 'd space;

Of fevers, fractures, humors,
Contusions, fits, and tumors,
Would Dr. Hall or Dr. Baines confirm or nail the rumors;
From Colonel Dawes what railroad news there was I used to
get,—
When I helped 'em run the local on the "St. Jo Gazette."

For "personals" the old Pacific House was just the place,—
Pap Abell knew the pedigrees of all the human race;
And when he 'd gi'n up all he had, he 'd drop a subtle wink,
And lead the way where one might wet one's whistle with a drink.
Those drinks at the Pacific,
When days were sudorific,
Were what Parisians (pray excuse my French!) would call "mag-
nifique";
And frequently an invitation to a meal I 'd get
When I helped 'em run the local on the "St. Jo Gazette."

And when in rainy weather news was scarce as well as slow,
To Saxton's bank of Hopkins' store for items would I go.
The jokes which Colonel Saxton told were old, but good enough
For local application in lieu of better stuff;
And when the ducks were flying,
Or the fishing well worth trying—
Gosh! but those "sports" at Hopkins' store could beat the world
at lying!
And I—I printed all their yarns, though not without regret,
When I helped 'em run the local on the "St. Jo Gazette."

For squibs political I 'd go to Colonel Waller Young,
Or Colonel James N. Burnes, the "statesman with the silver
tongue";
Should some old pioneer take sick and die, why, then I 'd call
On Frank M. Posegate for the "life," and Posegate knew 'em all.
Lon Tullar used to pony
Up descriptions that were tony
Of toilets worn at party, ball, or conversazione;
For the ladies were addicted to the style called "deckolett"
When I helped 'em run the local on the "St. Jo Gazette."

So was I wont my daily round of labor to pursue;
And when came night I found that there was still more work to do,—
The telegraph to edit, yards and yards of proof to read,
And reprint to be gathered to supply the printers' greed.
        Oh, but it takes agility,
        Combined with versatility,
To run a country daily with appropriate ability!
There never were a smarter lot of editors, I 'll bet,
Than we who whooped up local on the "St. Jo Gazette."

Yes, maybe it was irksome; maybe a discontent
Rebellious rose amid the toil I daily underwent.
If so, I don't remember; this only do I know,—
My thoughts turn ever fondly to that time in old St. Jo.
        The years that speed so fleetly
        Have blotted out completely
All else than that which still remains to solace me so sweetly;
The friendships of that time,—ah, me! they are as precious yet
As when I was a local on the "St. Jo Gazette."

IN AMSTERDAM

MEYNHEER Hans Von Der Bloom has got
A majazin in Kalverstraat,
Where one may buy for sordid gold
Wares quaint and curious, new and old.
Here are antiquities galore,—
The jewels which Dutch monarchs wore,
Swords, teacups, helmets, platters, clocks,
Bright Dresden jars, dull Holland crocks,
And all those joys I might rehearse
That please the eye, but wreck the purse.

I most admired an ancient bed,
With ornate carvings at its head,—
A massive frame of dingy oak,
Whose curious size and mould bespoke
Prodigious age. "How much?" I cried.

"Ein tousand gildens," Hans replied;
And then the honest Dutchman said
A king once owned that glorious bed,—
King Fritz der Foorst, of blessed fame,
Had owned and slept within the same!

Then long I stood and mutely gazed,
By reminiscent splendors dazed,
And I had bought it right away
Had I the wherewithal to pay.
But, lacking of the needed pelf,
I thus discoursed within myself:
"O happy Holland! where 's the bliss
That can approximate to this
Possession of the rare antique
Which maniacs hanker for and seek?
My native land is full of stuff
That 's good, but is not old enough.
Alas! it has no oaken beds
Wherein have slumbered royal heads,
No relic on whose face we see
The proof of grand antiquity."

Thus reasoned I a goodly spell
Until, perchance, my vision fell
Upon a trademark at the head
Of Fritz der Foorst's old oaken bed,—
A rampant wolverine, and round
This strange device these words I found:
"Patent Antique. Birkey & Gay,
Grand Rapids, Michigan, U. S. A."

At present I 'm not saying much
About the simple, guileless Dutch;
And as it were a loathsome spot
I keep away from Kalverstraat,
Determined when I want a bed
In which hath slept a royal head
I 'll patronize no middleman,
But deal direct with Michigan.

TO THE PASSING SAINT

As to-night you came your way,
  Bearing earthward heavenly joy,
Tell me, O dear saint, I pray,
  Did you see my little boy?

By some fairer voice beguiled,
  Once he wandered from my sight;
He is such a little child,
  He should have my love this night.

It has been so many a year,—
  Oh, so many a year since then!
Yet he was so very dear,
  Surely he will come again.

If upon your way you see
  One whose beauty is divine,
Will you send him back to me?
  He is lost, and he is mine.

Tell him that his little chair
  Nestles where the sunbeams meet,
That the shoes he used to wear
  Yearn to kiss his dimpled feet.

Tell him of each pretty toy
  That was wont to share his glee;
Maybe that will bring my boy
  Back to them and back to me.

O dear saint, as on you go
  Through the glad and sparkling frost,
Bid those bells ring high and low
  For a little child that's lost!

O dear saint, that blessest men
  With the grace of Christmas joy,
Soothe this heart with love again,—
  Give me back my little boy!

———

THE FISHERMAN'S FEAST

OF all the gracious gifts of Spring,
  Is there another can surpass
This delicate, voluptuous thing,—
  This dapple-green, plump-shouldered bass?
Upon a damask napkin laid,
  What exhalations superfine
Our gustatory nerves pervade,
  Provoking quenchless thirsts for wine!

The ancients loved this noble fish;
  And, coming from the kitchen fire
All piping hot upon a dish,
  What raptures did he not inspire?
"Fish should swim twice," they used to say,—
  Once in their native, vapid brine,
And then again, a better way—
  You understand; fetch on the wine!

Ah, dainty monarch of the flood,
  How often have I cast for you,
How often sadly seen you scud
  Where weeds and water-lilies grew!
How often have you filched my bait,
  How often snapped my treacherous line!
Yet here I have you on this plate,—
  You *shall* swim twice, and *now* in *wine*.

And harkee, garçon! let the blood
  Of cobwebbed years be spilled for him,—
Ay, in a rich Burgundian flood
  This piscatorial pride should swim;

So, were he living, he would say
    He gladly died for me and mine,
And, as it were his native spray,
    He 'd lash the sauce—what, ho! the wine!

I would it were ordained for me
    To share your fate, O finny friend!
I surely were not loath to be
    Reserved for such a noble end;
For when old Chronos, gaunt and grim,
    At last reels in his ruthless line,
What were my ecstasy to swim
    In wine, in wine, in glorious wine!

Well, here 's a health to you, sweet Spring!
    And, prithee, whilst I stick to earth,
Come hither every year and bring
    The boons provocative of mirth;
And should your stock of bass run low,
    However much I might repine,
I think I might survive the blow,
    If plied with wine and still more wine!

THE ONION TART

Of tarts there be a thousand kinds,
    So versatile the art,
And, as we all have different minds,
    Each has his favorite tart;
But those which most delight the rest
    Methinks should suit me not:
The onion tart doth please me best,—
    Ach, Gott! mein lieber Gott!

Where but in Deutschland can be found
    This boon of which I sing?
Who but a Teuton could compound
    This *sui generis* thing?

None with the German frau can vie
   In arts cuisine, I wot,
Whose *summum bonum* breeds the sigh,
   "Ach, Gott! mein lieber Gott!"

You slice the fruit upon the dough,
   And season to the taste,
Then in an oven (not too slow)
   The viand should be placed;
And when 't is done, upon a plate
   You serve it piping hot,
Your nostrils and your eyes dilate,—
   Ach, Gott! mein lieber Gott!

It sweeps upon the sight and smell
   In overwhelming tide,
And then the sense of taste as well
   Betimes is gratified:
Three noble senses drowned in bliss!
   I prithee tell me, what
Is there beside compares with this?
   Ach, Gott! mein lieber Gott!

For if the fruit be proper young,
   And if the crust be good,
How shall they melt upon the tongue
   Into a savory flood!
How seek the Mecca down below,
   And linger round that spot,
Entailing weeks and months of woe,—
   Ach, Gott! mein lieber Gott!

If Nature gives men appetites
   For things that won't digest,
Why, let *them* eat whatso delights,
   And let *her* stand the rest;
And though the sin involve the cost
   Of Carlsbad, like as not
'T is better to have loved and lost,—
   Ach, Gott! mein lieber Gott!

Beyond the vast, the billowy tide,
　　Where my compatriots dwell,
All kinds of victuals have I tried,
　　All kinds of drinks, as well;
But nothing known to Yankee art
　　Appears to reach *the spot*
Like this Teutonic onion tart,—
　　Ach, Gott! mein lieber Gott!

So, though I quaff of Carlsbad's tide
　　As full as I can hold,
And for complete reform inside
　　Plank down my hoard of gold,
Remorse shall not consume my heart,
　　Nor sorrow vex my lot,
For I have eaten onion tart,—
　　Ach, Gott! mein lieber Gott!

GRANDMA'S BOMBAZINE

It 's everywhere that women fair invite and please my eye,
And that on dress I lay much stress I can't and sha' n't deny:
The English dame who 's all aflame with divers colors bright,
The Teuton belle, the ma'moiselle,—all give me keen delight;
And yet I 'll say, go where I may, I never yet have seen
A dress that 's quite as grand a sight as was that bombazine.

Now, you must know 't was years ago this quaint but noble gowr
Flashed in one day, the usual way, upon our solemn town.
'T was Fisk who sold for sordid gold that gravely scrumptious
　　thing,—
Jim Fisk, the man who drove a span that would have joyed a
　　king,—
And grandma's eye fell with a sigh upon that sombre sheen,
And grandpa's purse looked much the worse for grandma's bom-
　　bazine.

Though ten years old, I never told the neighbors of the gown;
For grandma said, "This secret, Ned, must not be breathed in
   town."
The sitting-room for days of gloom was in a dreadful mess
When that quaint dame, Miss Kelsey, came to make the wondrous
   dress:
To fit and baste and stitch a waist, with whalebones in between,
Is precious slow, as all folks know who 've made a bombazine.

With fortitude dear grandma stood the trial to the end
(The nerve we find in womankind I cannot comprehend!);
And when 't was done, resolved that none should guess at the
   surprise,
Within the press she hid that dress, secure from prying eyes;
For grandma knew a thing or two,—by which remark I mean
That Sundays were the days for her to wear that bombazine.

I need not state she got there late; and, sailing up the aisle
With regal grace, on grandma's face reposed a conscious smile.
It fitted so, above, below, and hung so well all round,
That there was not one faulty spot a critic could have found.
How proud I was of her, because she looked so like a queen!
And that was why, perhaps, that I admired the bombazine.

But there *were* those, as you 'd suppose, who scorned that per-
   fect gown;
For ugly-grained old cats obtained in that New England town:
The Widow White spat out her spite in one: "It does n't fit!"
The Packard girls (they wore false curls) all giggled like to split;
Sophronia Wade, the sour old maid, *she* turned a bilious green,
When she descried that joy and pride, my grandma's bomba-
   zine.

But grandma knew, and I did too, that gown was wondrous fine,—
The envious sneers and jaundiced jeers were a conclusive sign.
Why, grandpa said it went ahead of all the girls in town,
And, saying this, he snatched a kiss that like to burst that gown;
But, blushing red, my grandma said, "Oh, is n't grandpa mean!"
Yet evermore my grandma wore *his* favorite bombazine.

And, when she died that sombre pride passed down to heedless
    heirs,—
Alas, the day 't was hung away beneath the kitchen stairs!
Thence in due time, with dust and grime, came foes on foot and
    wing,
And made their nests and sped their guests in that once beauteous
    thing.
'T is so, forsooth! Time 's envious tooth corrodes each human scene;
And so, at last, to ruin passed my grandma's bombazine.

Yet to this day, I 'm proud to say, it plays a grateful part,—
The thoughts it brings are of such things as touch and warm my
    heart.
This gown, my dear, you show me here I 'll own is passing fair,
Though I 'll confess it 's no such dress as grandma used to wear.
Yet wear it, *do;* perchance when you and I are off the scene,
Our boy shall sing *this* comely thing as *I* the bombazine.

RARE ROAST BEEF

When the numerous distempers to which all flesh is heir
Torment us till our very souls are reeking with despair;
When that monster fiend, Dyspepsy, rears its spectral hydra head,
Filling *bon vivants* and epicures with certain nameless dread;
When *any* ill of body or of intellect abounds,
Be it sickness known to Galen or disease unknown to Lowndes,—
In such a dire emergency it is my firm belief
That there is no diet quite so good as rare roast beef.

And even when the body 's in the very prime of health,
When sweet contentment spreads upon the cheeks her rosy wealth,
And when a man devours three meals per day and pines for more,
And growls because instead of three square meals there are not
    four,—
Well, even then, though cake and pie do service on the side,
And coffee is a luxury that may not be denied,
Still of the many viands there is one that 's hailed as chief,
And that, as you are well aware, is rare roast beef.

Some like the sirloin, but I think the porterhouse is best,—
'T is juicier and tenderer and meatier than the rest;
Put on this roast a dash of salt, and then of water pour
Into the sizzling dripping-pan a cupful, and no more;
The oven being hot, the roast will cook in half an hour;
Then to the juices in the pan you add a little flour,
And so you get a gravy that is called the cap sheaf
Of that glorious *summum bonum,* rare roast beef.

Served on a platter that is hot, and carved with thin, keen knife,
How does this savory viand enhance the worth of life!
Give me no thin and shadowy slice, but a thick and steaming slab,—
Who would not choose a generous hunk to a bloodless little dab?
Upon a nice hot plate how does the juicy morceau steam,
A symphony in scarlet or a red incarnate dream!
Take from me eyes and ears and all, O Time, thou ruthless thief!
Except these teeth werewith to deal with rare roast beef.

Most every kind and rôle of modern victuals have I tried,
Including roasted, fricasseed, broiled, toasted, stewed, and fried,
Your canvasbacks and papa-bottes and mutton-chops subese,
Your patties *à la* Turkey and your doughnuts *à la* grease;
I 've whiled away dyspeptic hours with crabs in marble halls,
And in the lowly cottage I 've experienced codfish balls;
But I 've never found a viand that could so allay all grief
And soothe the cockles of the heart as rare roast beef.

I honor that sagacious king who, in a grateful mood,
Knighted the savory loin that on the royal table stood;
And as for me I 'd ask no better friend than this good roast,
Which is my squeamish stomach's fortress (*feste Burg*) and host;
For with this ally with me I can mock Dyspepsy's wrath,
Can I pursue the joy of Wisdom's pleasant, peaceful path.
So I do off my vest and let my waistband out a reef
When I soever set me down to rare roast beef.

OLD TIMES, OLD FRIENDS, OLD LOVE

THERE are no days like the good old days,—
    The days when we were youthful!
When humankind were pure of mind,
    And speech and deeds were truthful;
Before a love for sordid gold
    Became man's ruling passion,
And before each dame and maid became
    Slave to the tyrant fashion!

There are no girls like the good old girls,—
    Against the world I 'd stake 'em!
As buxom and smart and clean of heart
    As the Lord knew how to make 'em!
They were rich in spirit and common-sense,
    And piety all supportin';
They could bake and brew, and had taught school, too,
    And they made such likely courtin'!

There are no boys like the good old boys,—
    When *we* were boys together!
When the grass was sweet to the brown bare feet
    That dimpled the laughing heather;
When the pewee sung to the summer dawn
    Of the bee in the billowy clover,
Or down by the mill the whip-poor-will
    Echoed his night song over.

There is no love like the good old love,—
    The love that mother gave us!
We are old, old men, yet we pine again
    For that precious grace, —God save us!
So we dream and dream of the good old times,
    And our hearts grow tenderer, fonder,
As those dear old dreams bring soothing gleams
    Of heaven away off yonder.

MR. BILLINGS OF LOUISVILLE

THERE are times in one's life which one cannot forget;
And the time I remember 's the evening I met
A haughty young scion of bluegrass renown
Who made my acquaintance while painting the town
A handshake, a cocktail, a smoker, and then
Mr. Billings of Louisville touched me for ten.

There flowed in his veins the blue blood of the South,
And a cynical smile curled his sensuous mouth;
He quoted from Lanier and Poe by the yard,
But his purse had been hit by the war, and hit hard:
I felt that he honored and flattered me when
Mr. Billings of Louisville touched me for ten.

I wonder that never again since that night
A vision of Billings has hallowed my sight;
I pine for the sound of his voice and the thrill
That comes with the touch of a ten-dollar bill:
I wonder and pine; for—I say it again—
Mr. Billings of Louisville touched me for ten.

I 've heard what old Whittier sung of Miss Maud;
But all such philosophy 's nothing but fraud;
To one who 's a bear in Chicago to-day,
With wheat going up, and the devil to pay,
These words are the saddest of tongue or of pen:
"Mr. Billings of Louisville touched me for ten."

POET AND KING

THOUGH I am king, I have no throne
Save this rough wooden siege alone;
I have no empire, yet my sway
Extends a myriad leagues away;

No servile vassal bends his knee
In grovelling reverence to me,
Yet at my word all hearts beat high,
And there is fire in every eye,
And love and gratitude they bring
As tribute unto me, a king.

The folk that throng the busy street
Know not it is a king they meet;
And I am glad there is not seen
The monarch in my face and mien.
I should not choose to be the cause
Of fawning or of coarse applause:
I am content to know the arts
Wherewith to lord it o'er their hearts;
For when unto their hearts I sing,
I am a king, I am a king!

My sceptre,—see, it is a pen!
Wherewith I rule these hearts of men.
Sometime it pleaseth to beguile
Its monarch fancy with a smile;
Sometime it is athirst for tears:
And so adown the laurelled years
I walk, the noblest lord on earth,
Dispensing sympathy and mirth.
Aha! it is a magic thing
That makes me what I am,—a king!

Let empires crumble as they may,
Proudly I hold imperial sway;
The sunshine and the rain of years
Are human smiles and human tears
That come or vanish at my call,—
I am the monarch of them all!
Mindful alone of this am I:
The songs I sing shall never die;
Not even envious Death can wring
His glory from so great a king.

Come, brother, be a king with me,
And rule mankind eternally;
Lift up the weak, and cheer the strong,
Defend the truth, combat the wrong!
You'll find no sceptre like the pen
To hold and sway the hearts of men;
Its edicts flow in blood and tears
That will outwash the flood of years:
So, brother, sing your songs, oh, sing!
And be with me a king, a king!

LIZZIE

I WONDER ef all wimmin air
  Like Lizzie is when we go out
To theatres an' concerts where
  Is things the papers talk about.
Do other wimmin fret an' stew
  Like they wuz bein' crucified,—
Frettin' a show or concert through,
  With wonderin' ef the baby cried?

Now Lizzie knows that gran'ma 's there
  To see that everything is right;
Yet Lizzie thinks that gran'ma's care
  Ain't good enuff f'r baby, quite.
Yet what am I to answer when
  She kind uv fidgets at my side,
An' asks me every now an' then,
  "I wonder ef the baby cried?"

Seems like she seen two little eyes
  A-pinin' f'r their mother's smile;
Seems like she heern the pleadin' cries
  Uv one she thinks uv all the while;
An' so she 's sorry that she come.
  An' though she allus tries to hide

The truth, she 'd ruther stay to hum
　　Than wonder ef the baby cried.

Yes, wimmin folks is all alike—
　　By Lizzie you kin jedge the rest;
There never wuz a little tyke,
　　But that his mother loved him best.
And nex' to bein' what I be—
　　The husband uv my gentle bride—
I 'd wisht I wuz that croodlin' wee,
　　With Lizzie wonderin' ef I cried.

ALWAYS RIGHT

Don't take on so, Hiram,
　　But do what you're told to do;
It 's fair to suppose that yer mother knows
　　A heap sight more than you.
I 'll allow that sometimes *her* way
　　Don't seem the wisest, quite;
But the *easiest* way,
When she 's had her say,
　　Is to reckon yer mother is right.

Courted her ten long winters,
　　Saw her to singin'-school;
When she went down one spell to town,
　　I cried like a durned ol' fool;
Got mad at the boys for callin'
　　When I sparked her Sunday night:
But she said she knew
A thing or two,—
　　An' I reckoned yer mother wuz right.

I courted till I wuz aging,
　　And she wuz past her prime,—
I 'd have died, I guess, if she had n't said yes
　　When I popped f'r the hundredth time.

Said she 'd never have took me
  If I had n't stuck so tight;
Opined that we
Could never agree,—
  And I reckon yer mother wuz right!

PROVIDENCE AND THE DOG

WHEN I was young and callow, which was many years ago,
Within me the afflatus went surging to and fro;
And so I wrote a tragedy that fairly reeked with gore,
With every act concluding with the dead piled on the floor,—
A mighty effort, by the gods! and after I had read
The manuscript to Daly, that dramatic censor said:
"The plot is most exciting, and I like the dialogue;
You should take the thing to Providence, and try it on a dog."

McCambridge organized a troupe, including many a name
Unknown alike to guileless me, to riches, and to fame.
A pompous man whose name was Rae was Nestor of this troupe,—
Amphibious, he was quite at home outside or in the soup!
The way McCambridge billed him! Why, such dreams in red
    and green
Had ne'er before upon the boards of Yankeedom been seen;
And my proud name was heralded,—oh, that I'd gone incog.,
When we took that play to Providence to try it on a dog!

Shall I forget the awful day we struck that wretched town?
Yet in what melting irony the treacherous sun beamed down!
The sale of seats had not been large; but then McCambridge
    said
The factory people seldom bought their seats so far ahead,
And Rae indorsed McCambridge. So they partly set at rest
The natural misgivings that perturbed my youthful breast;
For I wondered and lamented that the town was not agog
When I took my play to Providence to try it on a dog.

They never came at all,—aha! I knew it all the time,—
They never came to see and hear my tragedy sublime.
Oh, fateful moment when the curtain rose on act the first!
Oh, moment fateful to the soul for wealth and fame athirst!
But lucky factory girls and boys to stay away that night,
When the author's fervid soul was touched by disappointment's
    blight,—
When desolation settled down on me like some dense fog
For having tempted Providence, and tried it on a dog!

Those actors did n't know their parts; they maundered to and fro,
Ejaculating platitudes that were quite *mal à propos;*
And when I sought to reprimand the graceless scamps, the lot
Turned fiercely on me, and denounced my charming play as rot.
I might have stood their bitter taunts without a passing grunt,
If I 'd had a word of solace from the people out in front;
But that chilly corporal's guard sat round like bumps upon a log
When I played that play at Providence with designs upon the dog.

We went with lots of baggage, but we did n't bring it back,—
For who would be so hampered as he walks a railway track?
"Oh, ruthless muse of tragedy! what prodigies of shame,
What marvels of injustice are committed in thy name!"
Thus groaned I in the spirit, as I strode what stretch of ties
'Twixt Providence, Rhode Island, and my native Gotham lies;
But Rae, McCambridge, and the rest kept up a steady jog,—
T' was not the first time they had plied their arts upon the dog.

So much for my first battle with the fickle goddess, Fame,—
And I hear that some folks nowadays are faring just the same.
Oh, hapless he that on the graceless Yankee dog relies!
The dog fares stout and hearty, and the play it is that dies.
So ye with tragedies to try, I beg of you, beware!
Put not your trust in Providence, that most delusive snare;
Cast, if you will, your pearls of thought before the Western hog,
But never go to Providence to try it on a dog.

GETTIN' ON

WHEN I wuz somewhat younger,
  I wuz reckoned purty gay;
I had my fling at everything
  In a rollickin', coltish way.
But times have strangely altered
  Since sixty years ago—
This age of steam an' things don't seem
  Like the age I used to know.
Your modern innovations
  Don't suit me, I confess,
As did the ways of the good ol' days,—
  But I 'm gettin' on, I guess.

I set on the piazza,
  An' hitch round with the sun;
Sometimes, mayhap, I take a nap,
  Waitin' till school is done.
An' then I tell the children
  The things I done in youth,—
An' near as I can, as a vener'ble man,
  I stick to the honest truth,—
But the looks of them 'at listen
  Seem sometimes to express
The remote idee that I 'm gone—you see?—
  An' I *am* gettin' on, I guess.

I get up in the mornin',
  An', nothin' else to do,
Before the rest are up an' dressed,
  I read the papers through.
I hang round with the women
  All day an' hear 'em talk;
An' while they sew or knit I show
  The baby how to walk.
An', somehow, I feel sorry
  When they put away his dress
An' cut his curls ('cause they 're like a girl's!)—
  I 'm gettin' on, I guess.

Sometimes, with twilight round me,
   I see, or seem to see,
A distant shore where friends of yore
   Linger an' watch for me.
Sometimes I 've heered 'em callin'
   So tender-like 'nd low
That it almost seemed like a dream I dreamed,
   Or an echo of long ago;
An' sometimes on my forehead
   There falls a soft caress,
Or the touch of a hand,—you understand,—
   I 'm gettin' on, I guess.

THE SCHNELLEST ZUG

From Hano.er to Leipzig is but a little way,
Yet the journey by the so-called schnellest zug consumes a day,
You start at half-past ten or so, and not till nearly night
Do the double towers of Magdeburg loom up before your sight;
From thence to Leipzig's quick enough,—of that I 'll not com-
   plain,—
But from Hanover to Magdeburg—confound that schnellest train!

The Germans say, that "schnell" means fast, and "schnellest"
   faster yet,—
In all my life no grimmer bit of humor have I met!
Why, thirteen miles an hour 's the greatest speed they ever go,
While on the engine piston-rods do moss and lichens grow;
And yet the average Teuton will presumptuously maintain
That one *can't* know what swiftness is till he 's tried das schnel-
   lest train!

Fool that I was! I should have walked,—I had no time to waste;
The little journey I had planned I had to do in haste,—
The quaint old town of Leipzig with its literary mart,
And Dresden with its crockery-shops and wondrous wealth of art,
The Saxon Alps, the Carlsbad cure for all dyspeptic pain,—
These were the ends I had in view when I took that schnellest train.

THE SCHNELLEST ZUG 133

The natives dozed around me, yet none too deep to hear
The guard's sporadic shout of "funf minuten" (meaning beer);
I counted forty times at least that voice announce the stops
Required of those fat natives to glut their greed for hops,
Whilst *I* crouched in a corner, a monument to woe,
And thought unholy, awful things, and felt my whiskers grow!

And then, the wretched sights one sees while travelling by that
    train,—
The women doing men-folks' work at harvesting the grain,
Or sometimes grubbing in the soil, or hitched to heavy carts
Beside the family cow or dog, doing their slavish parts!
The husbands strut in soldier garb,—indeed *they* were too vain
To let creation see *them* work from that creeping schnellest train!

I found the German language all too feeble to convey
The sentiments that surged through my dyspeptic hulk that day;
I had recourse to English, and exploded without stint
Such virile Anglo-Saxon as would never do in print,
But which assuaged my rising gorge and cooled my seething brain
While snailing on to Magdeburg upon that schnellest train.

The typical New England freight that maunders to and fro,
The upper Mississippi boats, the bumptious B. & O.,
The creeping Southern railroads with their other creeping things,
The Philadelphy cable that is run out West for rings,
The Piccadilly 'buses with their constant roll and shake,—
All have I tried, and yet I 'd give the "schnellest zug" the cake!

My countrymen, if ever you should seek the German clime,
Put not your trust in Baedeker if you are pressed for time;
From Hanover to Magdeburg is many a weary mile
By "schnellest zug," but done afoot it seems a tiny while;
Walk, swim, or skate, and then the task will not appear in vain,
But you 'll break the third commandment if you take the schnell-
    est train!

BETHLEHEM–TOWN

As I was going to Bethlehem-town,
Upon the earth I cast me down
All underneath a little tree
That whispered in this wise to me:
"Oh, I shall stand on Calvary
And bear what burthen saveth thee!"

As up I fared to Bethlehem-town,
I met a shepherd coming down,
And thus he quoth: "A wondrous sight
Hath spread before mine eyes this night,—
An angel host most fair to see,
That sung full sweetly of a tree
That shall uplift on Calvary
What burthen saveth you and me!"

And as I gat to Bethlehem-town,
Lo! wise men came that bore a crown.
"Is there," cried I, "in Bethlehem
A King shall wear this diadem?"
"Good sooth," they quoth, "and it is He
That shall be lifted on the tree
And freely shed on Calvary
What blood redeemeth us and thee!"

Unto a Child in Bethlehem-town
The wise men came and brought the crown;
And while the infant smiling slept,
Upon their knees they fell and wept;
But, with her babe upon her knee,
Naught recked that Mother of the tree,
That should uplift on Calvary
What burthen saveth all and me.

Again I walk in Bethlehem-town
And think on Him that wears the crown
I may not kiss His feet again,

Nor worship Him as did I then,
My King hath died upon the tree,
And hath outpoured on Calvary
What blood redeemeth you and me!

THE DOINGS OF DELSARTE

In former times my numerous rhymes excited general mirth,
And I was then of all good men the merriest man on earth;
        And my career
        From year to year
          Was full of cheer
           And things,
Despite a few regrets, perdieu! which grim dyspepsia brings;
But now how strange and harsh a change has come upon the
    scene!
Horrors appall the life where all was formerly so serene:
Yes, wasting care hath cast its snare about my honest heart,
Because, alas! it hath come to pass my daughter's learned Delsarte.

In flesh and joint and every point the counterpart of me,
She grew so fast she grew at last a marvellous thing to see,—
Long, gaunt, and slim, each gangling limb played stumbling-
    block to t' other,
The which excess of awkwardness quite mortified her mother.
Now, as for me, I like to see the carriages uncouth
Which certify to all the shy, unconscious age of youth.
If maidenkind be pure of mind, industrious, tidy, smart,
What need that they should fool away their youth upon Delsarte?

In good old times my numerous rhymes occasioned general mirth,
But now you see
        Revealed in me
          The gloomiest bard on earth.
I sing no more of the joys of yore that marked my happy life,
But rather those depressing woes with which the present's rife.

Unreconciled to that gaunt child, who 's now a fashion-plate,
One song I raise in Art's dispraise, and so do I fight with Fate:
This gangling bard has found it hard to see his counterpart
Long, loose, and slim, divorced from him by that hectic dude,
    Delsarte.

        Where'er she goes,
          She loves to pose,
      In classic attitudes,
And droop her eyes in languid wise, and feign abstracted moods;
         And she, my child,
          Who all so wild,
      So helpless and so sweet,
That once she knew not what to do with those great big hands
    and feet,
Now comes and goes with such repose, so calmly sits or stands,
Is so discreet with both her feet, so deft with both her hands.
Why, when I see that satire on me, I give an angry start,
And I utter one word—it is commonly heard—derogatory to
    Delsarte.

In years gone by 't was said that I was quite a scrumptious man,
Conceit galore had I before this Delsarte craze began;
But now these wise
        Folks criticise
           My figure and my face,
And I opine they even incline to sneer at my musical bass.
Why, sometimes they presume to say this wart upon my cheek
Is not refined, and remarks unkind they pass on that antique.
With lusty bass and charms of face and figure will I part
Ere they extort this grand old wart to placate their Delsarte.

Oh, wretched day! as all shall say who 've known my Muse be-
    fore,
When by this rhyme you see that I 'm not in it any more.
Good-by the mirth that over earth diffused such keen delight;
The old-time bard
        Of pork and lard
           Is plainly out of sight.

All withered now about his brow the laurel fillets droop,
While Lachesis brews
  For the poor old Muse
   A portion of scalding soup.
Engrave this line, O friends of mine! over my broken heart:
"He hustled and strove, and fancied he throve, till his daughter
 learned Delsarte."

THE SINGING IN GOD'S ACRE

Out yonder in the moonlight, wherein God's Acre lies,
Go angels walking to and fro, singing their lullabies.
Their radiant wings are folded, and their eyes are bended low,
As they sing among the beds whereon the flowers delight to grow,—

   "Sleep, oh, sleep!
   The Shepherd guardeth His sheep.
  Fast speedeth the night away,
  Soon cometh the glorious day;
  Sleep, weary ones, while ye may,
   Sleep, oh, sleep!"

The flowers within God's Acre see that fair and wondrous sight,
And hear the angels singing to the sleepers through the night;
And, lo! throughout the hours of day those gentle flowers prolong
The music of the angels in that tender slumber-song,—

   "Sleep, oh, sleep!
   The Shepherd loveth His sheep.
  He that guardeth His flock the best
  Hath folded them to His loving breast;
  So sleep ye now, and take your rest,—
   Sleep, oh, sleep!"

From angel and from flower the years have learned that soothing
 song,
And with its heavenly music speed the days and nights along;
So through all time, whose flight the Shepherd's vigils glorify,
God's Acre slumbereth in the grace of that sweet lullaby,—

"Sleep, oh, sleep!
The Shepherd loveth His sheep.
Fast speedeth the night away,
Soon cometh the glorious day;
Sleep, weary ones, while ye may,—
Sleep, oh, sleep!"

———

THE DREAM-SHIP

WHEN the world is fast asleep,
  Along the midnight skies—
As though it were a wandering cloud—
  The ghostly dream-ship flies.

An angel stands at the dream-ship's helm,
  An angel stands at the prow,
And an angel stands at the dream-ship's side
  With a rue-wreath on her brow.

The other angels, silver-crowned,
  Pilot and helmsman are,
And the angel with the wreath of rue
  Tosseth the dreams afar.

The dreams they fall on rich and poor;
  They fall on young and old;
And some are dreams of poverty,
  And some are dreams of gold.

And some are dreams that thrill with joy,
  And some that melt to tears;
Some are dreams of the dawn of love,
  And some of the old dead years.

On rich and poor alike they fall,
  Alike on young and old,
Bringing to slumbering earth their joys
  And sorrows manifold.

The friendless youth in them shall do
  The deeds of mighty men,
And drooping age shall feel the grace
  Of buoyant youth again.

The king shall be a beggarman—
  The pauper be a king—
In that revenge or recompense
  The dream-ship dreams do bring.

So ever downward float the dreams
  That are for all and me,
And there is never mortal man
  Can solve that mystery.

But ever onward in its course
  Along the haunted skies—
As though it were a cloud astray—
  The ghostly dream-ship flies.

Two angels with their silver crowns
  Pilot and helmsman are,
And an angel with a wreath of rue
  Tosseth the dreams afar.

BALLAD OF WOMEN I LOVE

PRUDENCE MEARS hath an old blue plate
  Hid away in an oaken chest,
And a Franklin platter of ancient date
  Beareth Amandy Baker's crest;
What times soever I 've been their guest,
  Says I to myself in an undertone:
"Of womenfolk, it must be confessed,
  These do I love, and these alone."

Well, again, in the Nutmeg State,
  Dorothy Pratt is richly blest

With a relic of art and a land effete—
  A pitcher of glass that's cut, not pressed.
And a Washington teapot is possessed
  Down in Pelham by Marthy Stone—
Think ye now that I say in jest
  "These do I love, and these alone?"

Were Hepsy Higgins inclined to mate,
  Or Dorcas Eastman prone to invest
In Cupid's bonds, they could find their fate
  In the bootless bard of Crockery Quest.
For they've heaps of trumpery—so have the rest
  Of those spinsters whose ware I'd like to own;
You can see why I say with such certain zest,
  "These do I love, and these alone."

ENVOY

Prince, show me the quickest way and best
  To gain the subject of my moan;
We've neither spinsters nor relics out West—
  These do I love, and these alone.

SUPPOSE

Suppose, my dear, that you were I
  And by your side your sweetheart sate;
Suppose you noticed by and by
  The distance 'twixt you were too great;
Now tell me, dear, what would you do?
  I know—and so do you.

And when (so comfortably placed)
  Suppose you only grew aware
That that dear, dainty little waist
  Of hers looked very lonely there;
Pray tell me sooth—what would you do?
  I know, and so do you.

When, having done what I just did
  With not a frown to check or chill,
Suppose her red lips seemed to bid
  Defiance to your lordly will;
Oh, tell me, sweet, what would you **do?**
  I know, and so do you.

MYSTERIOUS DOINGS

As once I rambled in the woods
  I chanced to spy amid the brake
A huntsman ride his way beside
  A fair and passing tranquil lake;
Though velvet bucks sped here and there,
  He let them scamper through the green—
Not one smote he, but lustily
  He blew his horn—what could it mean?

As on I strolled beside that lake,
  A pretty maid I chanced to see
Fishing away for finny prey,
  Yet not a single one caught she;
All round her boat the fishes leapt
  And gambolled to their hearts' content,
Yet never a thing did the maid but sing—
  I wonder what on earth it meant.

As later yet I roamed my way,
  A lovely steed neighed loud and long,
And an empty boat sped all afloat
  Where sang a fishermaid her song;
All underneath the prudent shade,
  Which yonder kindly willows threw,
Together strayed a youth and maid—
  I can't explain it all, can you?

WITH TWO SPOONS FOR TWO SPOONS

How trifling shall these gifts appear
   Among the splendid many
That loving friends now send to cheer
   Harvey and Ellen Jenney.

And yet these baubles symbolize
   A certain fond relation
That well beseems, as I surmise,
   This festive celebration.

Sweet friends of mine, be spoons once more,
   And with your tender cooing
Renew the keen delights of yore—
   The rapturous bliss of wooing.

What though that silver in your hair
   Tells of the years aflying?
'T is yours to mock at Time and Care
   With love that is undying.

In memory of this Day, dear friends,
   Accept the modest token
From one who with the bauble sends
   A love that can't be spoken.

MARY SMITH

AWAY down East where I was reared amongst my Yankee kith,
There used to live a pretty girl whose name was Mary Smith;
And though it's many years since last I saw that pretty girl,
And though I feel I'm sadly worn by Western strife and whirl;
Still, oftentimes, I think about the old familiar place,
Which, someway, seemed the brighter for Miss Mary's pretty face,
And in my heart I feel once more revivified the glow
I used to feel in those old times when I was Mary's beau.

I saw her home from singing school—she warbled like a bird.
A sweeter voice than hers for song or speech I never heard.
She was soprano in the choir, and I a solemn bass,
And when we unisoned our voices filled that holy place;
The tenor and the alto never had the slightest chance,
For Mary's upper register made every heartstring dance;
And, as for me, I shall not brag, and yet I'd have you know
I sung a very likely bass when I was Mary's beau.

On Friday nights I'd drop around to make my weekly call,
And though I came to visit her, I'd have to see 'em all.
With Mary's mother sitting here and Mary's father there,
The conversation never flagged so far as I'm aware;
Sometimes I'd hold her worsted, sometimes we'd play at games,
Sometimes dissect the apples which we'd named each other's
    names.
Oh how I loathed the shrill-toned clock that told me when to go—
'T was ten o'clock at half-past eight when I was Mary's beau.

Now there was Luther Baker—because he'd come of age
And thought himself some pumpkins because he drove the stage—
He fancied he could cut me out; but Mary was my friend—
Elsewise I'm sure the issue had had a tragic end.
For Luther Baker was a man I never could abide,
And, when it came to Mary, either he or I had died.
I merely cite this instance incidentally to show
That I was quite in earnest when I was Mary's beau.

How often now those sights, those pleasant sights, recur again:
The little township that was all the world I knew of then—
The meeting-house upon the hill, the tavern just beyond,
Old deacon Packard's general store, the sawmill by the pond,
The village elms I vainly sought to conquer in my quest
Of that surpassing trophy, the golden oriole's nest.
And, last of all those visions that come back from long ago,
The pretty face that thrilled my soul when I was Mary's beau.

Hush, gentle wife, there is no need a pang should vex your heart—
'T is many years since fate ordained that she and I should part;
To each a true, maturer love came in good time, and yet

It brought not with its nobler grace the power to forget.
And would you fain begrudge me now the sentimental joy
That comes of recollections of my sparkings when a boy?
I warrant me that, were your heart put to the rack, 't would show
That it had predilections when I was Mary's beau.

And, Mary, should these lines of mine seek out your biding place,
God grant they bring the old sweet smile back to your pretty face—
God grant they bring you thoughts of me, not as I am to-day,
With faltering step and brimming eyes and aspect grimly gray;
But thoughts that picture me as fair and full of life and glee
As *we* were in the olden times—as *you* shall always be.
Think of me ever, Mary, as the boy you used to know
When time was fleet, and life was sweet, and I was Mary's beau.

Dear hills of old New England, look down with tender eyes
Upon one little lonely grave that in your bosom lies;
For in that cradle sleeps a child who was so fair to see
God yearned to have unto Himself the joy she brought to me;
And bid your winds sing soft and low the song of other days,
When, hand in hand and heart to heart, we went our pleasant
    ways—
Ah me! but could I sing again that song of long ago,
Instead of this poor idle song of being Mary's beau.

———

JESSIE

WHEN I remark her golden hair
    Swoon on her glorious shoulders,
I marvel not that sight so rare
    Doth ravish all beholders;
For summon hence all pretty girls
    Renowned for beauteous tresses,
And you shall find among their curls
    There's none so fair as Jessie's.

And Jessie's eyes are, oh, so blue
    And full of sweet revealings—
They seem to look you through and through
    And read your inmost feelings;
Nor black emits such ardent fires,
    Nor brown such truth expresses—
Admit it, all ye gallant squires—
    There are no eyes like Jessie's.

Her voice (like liquid beams that roll
    From moonland to the river)
Steals subtly to the raptured soul,
    Therein to lie and quiver;
Or falls upon the grateful ear
    With chaste and warm caresses—
Ah, all concede the truth (who hear):
    There 's no such voice as Jessie's.

Of other charms she hath such store
    All rivalry excelling,
Though I used adjectives galore,
    They 'd fail me in the telling;
But now discretion stays my hand—
    Adieu, eyes, voice, and tresses.
Of all the husbands in the land
    There 's none so fierce as Jessie's.

TO EMMA ABBOTT

There—let thy hands be folded
    Awhile in sleep's repose;
The patient hands that wearied not,
But earnestly and nobly wrought
        In charity and faith;
    And let thy dear eyes close—
The eyes that looked alway to God,
Nor quailed beneath the chastening rod
        Of sorrow;

Fold thou thy hands and eyes
            For just a little while,
        And with a smile
            Dream of the morrow.

And, O white voiceless flower,
        The dream which thou shalt dream
Should be a glimpse of heavenly things,
        For yonder like a seraph sings
            The sweetness of a life
        With faith alway its theme;
While speedeth from those realms above
The messenger of that dear love
            That healeth sorrow.
        So sleep a little while,
            For thou shalt wake and sing
            Before thy King
                When cometh the morrow.

THE GREAT JOURNALIST IN SPAIN

Good editor Dana—God bless him, we say—
        Will soon be afloat on the main,
            Will be steaming away
            Through the mist and the spray
        To the sensuous climate of Spain.

Strange sights shall he see in that beautiful land
        Which is famed for its soap and its Moor,
            For, as we understand,
            The scenery is grand
        Though the system of railways is poor.

For moonlight of silver and sunlight of gold
        Glint the orchards of lemons and mangoes,
            And the ladies, we 're told,
            Are a joy to behold
        As they twine in their lissome fandangoes.

What though our friend Dana shall twang a guitar
   And murmur a passionate strain;
      Oh, fairer by far
      Than those ravishments are
   The castles abounding in Spain.

These castles are built as the builder may list—
   They are sometimes of marble or stone,
      But they mostly consist
      Of east wind and mist
   With an ivy of froth overgrown.

A beautiful castle our Dana shall raise
   On a futile foundation of hope,
      And its glories shall blaze
      In the somnolent haze
   Of the mythical lake del y Soap.

The fragrance of sunflowers shall swoon on the air
   And the visions of Dreamland obtain,
      And the song of "World's Fair"
      Shall be heard everywhere
   Through that beautiful castle in Spain.

THE STODDARDS

When I am in New York, I like to drop around at night,
To visit with my honest, genial friends, the Stoddards hight;
Their home in Fifteenth street is all so snug, and furnished so,
That, when I once get planted there, I don't know when to go;
A cosey cheerful refuge for the weary homesick guest,
Combining Yankee comforts with the freedom of the West.

The first thing you discover, as you maunder through the hall,
Is a curious little clock upon a bracket on the wall;

'T was made by Stoddard's father, and it 's very, very old—
The connoisseurs assure me it is worth its weight in gold;
And I, who 've bought all kinds of clocks, 'twixt Denver and the
 Rhine,
Cast envious eyes upon that clock, and wish that it were mine.

But in the parlor. Oh, the gems on tables, walls, and floor—
Rare first editions, etchings, and old crockery galore.
Why, talk about the Indies and the wealth of Orient things—
They couldn't hold a candle to these quaint and sumptuous
 things;
In such profusion, too—Ah me! how dearly I recall
How I have sat and watched 'em and wished I had 'em all.

Now, Mr. Stoddard's study is on the second floor,
A wee blind dog barks at me as I enter through the door;
The Cerberus would fain begrudge what sights it cannot see,
The rapture of that visual feast it cannot share with me;
A miniature edition this—this most absurd of hounds—
A genuine unique, I 'm sure, and one unknown to Lowndes.

Books—always books—are piled around; some musty, and all old;
Tall, solemn folios such as Lamb declared he loved to hold;
Large paper copies with their virgin margins white and wide,
And presentation volumes with the author's comps. inside;
I break the tenth commandment with a wild impassioned cry:
Oh, how came Stoddard by these things? Why Stoddard, and
 not I?

From yonder wall looks Thackeray upon his poet friend,
And underneath the genial face appear the lines he penned;
And here, gadzooks, ben honge ye prynte of marvaillous renowne
Yt shameth Chaucers gallaunt knyghtes in Canterbury towne;
And still more books and pictures. I 'm dazed, bewildered, vexed;
Since I 've broke the tenth commandment, why not break the eighth
 one next?

And, furthermore, in confidence inviolate be it said
Friend Stoddard owns a lock of hair that grew on Milton's head:

Now I have Gladstone axes and a lot of curious things,
Such as pimply Dresden teacups and old German wedding-rings;
But nothing like that saintly lock have I on wall or shelf,
And, being somewhat short of hair, I should like that lock myself.

But Stoddard has a soothing way, as though he grieved to see
Invidious torments prey upon a nice young chap like me.
He waves me to an easy chair and hands me out a weed
And pumps me full of that advice he seems to know I need;
So sweet the tap of his philosophy and knowledge flows
That I can't help wishing that I knew a half what Stoddard knows.

And so we sit for hours and hours, praising without restraint
The people who are thoroughbreds, and roasting the ones that ain't;
Happy, thrice happy, is the man we happen to admire,
But wretched, oh, how wretched he that hath provoked our ire;
For I speak emphatic English when I once get fairly r'iled,
And Stoddard's wrath 's an Ossa upon a Pelion piled.

Out yonder, in the alcove, a lady sits and darns,
And interjects remarks that always serve to spice our yarns;
She 's Mrs. Stoddard; there 's a dame that 's truly to my heart:
A tiny little woman, but so quaint, and good, and smart
That, if you asked me to suggest which one I should prefer
Of all the Stoddard treasures, I should promptly mention her.

O dear old man, how I should like to be with you this night,
Down in your home in Fifteenth street, where all is snug and bright;
Where the shaggy little Cerberus dreams in its cushioned place,
And the books and pictures all around smile in their old friend's face;
Where the dainty little sweetheart, whom you still were proud to woo,
Charms back the tender memories so dear to her and you.

THE THREE TAILORS

I SHALL tell you in rhyme how, once on a time,
Three tailors tramped up to the inn Ingleheim,
      On the Rhine, lovely Rhine;
They were broke, but the worst of it all, they were curst
With that malady common to tailors—a thirst
      For wine, lots of wine.

"Sweet host," quoth the three, "we 're hard up as can be,
Yet skilled in the practice of cunning are we,
      On the Rhine, genial Rhine;
And we pledge you we will impart you that skill
Right quickly and fully, providing you 'll fill
      Us with wine, cooling wine."

But that host shook his head, and he warily said:
"Though cunning be good, we take money instead,
      On the Rhine, thrifty Rhine;
If ye fancy ye may without pelf have your way
You 'll find there 's both host and the devil to pay
      For your wine, costly wine."

Then the first knavish wight took his needle so bright
And threaded its eye with a wee ray of light
      From the Rhine, sunny Rhine;
And, in such a deft way, patched a mirror that day
That where it was mended no expert could say—
      Done so fine 't was for wine.

The second thereat spied a poor little gnat
Go toiling along on his nose broad and flat
      Towards the Rhine, pleasant Rhine;
"Aha, tiny friend, I should hate to offend,
But your stockings need darning"—which same did he mend,
      All for wine, soothing wine.

And next there occurred what you 'll deem quite absurd—
His needle a space in the wall thrust the third.
      By the Rhine, wondrous Rhine;

And then all so spry, he leapt through the eye
Of that thin cambric needle—nay, think you I 'd lie
   About wine—not for wine.

The landlord allowed (with a smile) he was proud
To do the fair thing by that talented crowd
   On the Rhine, generous Rhine.
So a thimble filled he as full as could be—
"Drink long and drink hearty, my jolly friends three,
   Of my wine, filling wine."

———

THE JAFFA AND JERUSALEM RAILWAY

A TORTUOUS double iron track; a station here, a station there;
A locomotive, tender, tanks; a coach with stiff reclining chair;
Some postal cars, and baggage, too; a vestibule of patent make;
With buffers, duffers, switches, and the soughing automatic brake—
This is the Orient's novel pride, and Syria's gaudiest modern gem:
The railway scheme that is to ply 'twixt Jaffa and Jerusalem.

Beware, O sacred Mooley cow, the engine when you hear its bell;
Beware, O camel, when resounds the whistle's shrill, unholy swell;
And, native of that guileless land, unused to modern travel's snare,
Beware the fiend that peddles books—the awful peanut-boy beware.
Else, trusting in their specious arts, you may have reason to con-
   demn
The traffic which the knavish ply 'twixt Jaffa and Jerusalem.

And when, ah, when the bonds fall due, how passing wroth will
   wax the state
From Nebo's mount to Nazareth will spread the cry "Repudiate"!
From Hebron to Tiberius, from Jordan's banks unto the sea,
Will rise profuse anathemas against "that —— monopoly!"
And F. M. B. A. shepherd-folk, with Sockless Jerry leading them,
Will swamp that corporation line 'twixt Jaffa and Jerusalem.

THE WOOING OF THE SOUTHLAND

(ALASKAN BALLAD)

THE Northland reared his hoary head
  And spied the Southland leagues away—
"Fairest of all fair brides," he said,
  "Be thou my bride, I pray!"

Whereat the Southland laughed and cried:
  "I'll bide beside my native sea,
And I shall never be thy bride
  Till thou com'st wooing me!"

The Northland's heart was a heart of ice,
  A diamond glacier, mountain high—
Oh, love is sweet at any price,
  As well know you and I!

So gayly the Northland took his heart
  And cast it in the wailing sea—
"Go, thou, with all thy cunning art.
  And woo my bride for me!"

For many a night and for many a day,
  And over the leagues that rolled between,
The true-heart messenger sped away
  To woo the Southland queen.

But the sea wailed loud, and the sea wailed long,
  While ever the Northland cried in glee:
"Oh, thou shalt sing us our bridal song,
  When comes my bride, O sea!"

At the foot of the Southland's golden throne
  The heart of the Northland ever throbs—
For that true-heart speaks in the waves that moan,
  The songs that it sings are sobs.

Ever the Southland spurns the cries
   Of the messenger pleading the Northland's part;
The summer shines in the Southland's eyes—
   The winter bides in her heart!

And ever unto that far-off place
   Which love doth render a hallowed spot,
The Northland turneth his honest face
   And wonders she cometh not.

The sea wails loud, and the sea wails long,
   As the ages of waiting drift slowly by
But the sea shall sing no bridal song—
   As well know you and I!

STAR OF THE EAST

Star of the East, that long ago
   Brought wise men on their way
Where, angels singing to and fro,
   The Child of Bethlehem lay—
Above that Syrian hill afar
Thou shinest out to-night, O Star!

Star of the East, the night were drear
   But for the tender grace
That with thy glory comes to cheer
   Earth's loneliest, darkest place;
For by that charity we see
Where there is hope for all and me.

Star of the East! show us the way
   In wisdom undefiled
To seek that manger out and lay
   Our gifts before the child—
To bring our hearts and offer them
Unto our King in Bethlehem!

TWIN IDOLS

THERE are two phrases, you must know,
   So potent (yet so small)
That wheresoe'er a man may go
   He needs none else at all;
No servile guide to lead the way
   Nor lackey at his heel,
If he be learned enough to say
   "Comme bien" and "Wie viel."

The sleek, pomaded Parleyvoo
   Will air his sweetest airs
And quote the highest rates when you
   "Comme bien" for his wares;
And, though the German stolid be,
   His so-called heart of steel
Becomes as soft as wax when he
   Detects the words "Wie viel."

Go, search the boulevards and rues
   From Havre to Marseilles—
You'll find all eloquence you use
   Except "Comme bien" fails;
Or in the country auf der Rhine
   Essay a business deal
And all your art is good fuhr nein
   Beyond the point—"Wie viel."

It matters not what game or prey
   Attracts your greedy eyes—
You must pursue the good old way
   If you would win the prize;
It is to get a titled mate
   All run down at the heel,
If you inquire of stock effete,
   "Comme bien" or "Wie viel."

So he is wise who envieth not
   A wealth of foreign speech,
Since with two phrases may be got
   Whatever 's in his reach;
For Europe is a soulless shrine
   In which all classes kneel
Before twin idols, deemed divine—
   "Comme bien" and "Wie viel."

BEN APFELGARTEN

THERE was a certain gentleman, Ben Apfelgarten called,
  Who lived way off in Germany a many years ago,
And he was very fortunate in being very bald
  And so was very happy he was so.
      He warbled all the day
      Such songs as only they
Who are very, very circumspect and very happy may;
      The people wondered why,
      As the years went gliding by,
They never heard him once complain or even heave a sigh!

The women of the province fell in love with genial Ben,
  Till (maybe you can fancy it) the dickens was to pay
Among the callow students and the sober-minded men—
  With the women-folk a-cuttin' up that way!
      Why, they gave him turbans red
      To adorn his hairless head,
And knitted jaunty nightcaps to protect him when abed!
      In vain the rest demurred—
      Not a single chiding word
Those ladies deigned to tolerate—remonstrance was absurd!

Things finally got into such a very dreadful way
  That the others (oh, how artful) formed the politic design
To send him to the reichstag; so, one dull November day,
  They elected him a member from the Rhine!

Then the other members said:
    "Gott im Himmel! what a head!"
But they marvelled when his speeches they listened to or read;
    And presently they cried:
    "There must be heaps inside
Of the smooth and shiny cranium his constituents deride!"

Well, when at last he up 'nd died—long past his ninetieth year—
    The strangest and the most lugubrious funeral he had,
For women came in multitudes to weep upon his bier—
    The men all wond'ring why on earth the women had gone
        mad!
            And this wonderment increased
            Till the sympathetic priest
Inquired of those same ladies: "Why this fuss about deceased?"
            Whereupon were they appalled,
            For, as one, those women squalled:
"We doted on deceased for being bald—bald—bald!"

He was bald because his genius burnt that shock of hair away
    Which, elsewise, clogs one's keenness and activity of mind;
And (barring present company, of course) I'm free to say
    That, after all, it's intellect that captures womankind.
            At any rate, since then
            (With a precedent in Ben),
The women-folk have been in love with us bald-headed men!

THE DREAMS

Two dreams came down to earth one night
    From the realm of mist and dew;
One was a dream of the old, old days,
    And one was a dream of the new.

One was a dream of a shady lane
    That led to the pickerel pond
Where the willows and rushes bowed themselves
    To the brown old hills beyond.

And the people that peopled the old-time dream
    Were pleasant and fair to see,
And the dreamer he walked with them again
    As often of old walked he.

Oh, cool was the wind in the shady lane
    That tangled his curly hair!
Oh, sweet was the music the robins made
    To the springtime everywhere!

Was it the dew the dream had brought
    From yonder midnight skies,
Or was it tears from the dear, dead years
    That lay in the dreamer's eyes?

The *other* dream ran fast and free,
    As the moon benignly shed
Her golden grace on the smiling face
    In the little trundle-bed.

For 't was a dream of times to come—
    Of the glorious noon of day—
Of the summer that follows the careless spring
    When the child is done with play.

And 't was a dream of the busy world
    Where valorous deeds are done;
Of battles fought in the cause of right,
    And of victories nobly won.

It breathed no breath of the dear old home
    And the quiet joys of youth;
It gave no glimpse of the good old friends
    Or the old-time faith and truth.

But 't was a dream of youthful hopes,
    And fast and free it ran,
And it told to a little sleeping child
    Of a boy become a man!

These were the dreams that came one night
  To earth from yonder sky;
These were the dreams two dreamers dreamed—
  My little boy and and I.

And in our hearts my boy and I
  Were glad that it was so;
He loved to dream of days to come,
  And *I* of long ago.

So from our dreams my boy and I
  Unwillingly awoke,
But neither of his precious dream
  Unto the other spoke.

Yet of the love we bore those dreams
Gave each his tender sign;
For there was triumph in *his* eyes—
  And there were tears in *mine!*

IN NEW ORLEANS

'Twas in the Crescent City not long ago befell
The tear-compelling incident I now propose to tell;
So come, my sweet collector friends, and listen while I sing
Unto your delectation this brief, pathetic thing—
No lyric pitched in vaunting key, but just a requiem
Of blowing twenty dollars in by nine o'clock a. m.

Let critic folk the poet's use of vulgar slang upbraid,
But, when I 'm speaking by the card, I call a spade a spade;
And I, who have been touched of that same mania, myself,
Am well aware that, when it comes to parting with his pelf,
The curio collector is so blindly lost in sin
That he doesn't spend his money—he simply blows it in!

In Royal street (near Conti) there's a lovely curio-shop,
And there, one balmy, fateful morn, it was my chance to stop;
To stop was hesitation—in a moment I was lost—
That kind of hesitation does not hesitate at cost!
I spied a pewter tankard there, and, my! it was a gem—
And the clock in old St. Louis told the hour of eight a. m.!

Three quaint Bohemian bottles, too, of yellow and of green,
Cut in archaic fashion that I ne'er before had seen;
A lovely, hideous platter wreathed about with pink and rose,
With its curious depression into which the gravy flows;
Two dainty silver salts—oh, there was no resisting *them*—
And I'd blown in twenty dollars by nine o'clock a. m.

With twenty dollars, one who is a prudent man, indeed,
Can buy the wealth of useful things his wife and children need;
Shoes, stockings, knickerbockers, gloves, bibs, nursing-bottles, caps,
A gown—*the* gown for which his spouse too long has pined, per-
    haps!
These and ten thousand other spectres harrow and condemn
The man who's blown in twenty by nine o'clock a. m.

Oh, mean advantage conscience takes (and one that I abhor!)
In asking one this question: "What *did* you buy it for?"
Why doesn't conscience ply its blessed trade *before* the act,
Before one's cussedness becomes a bald, accomplished fact—
Before one's fallen victim to the Tempter's stratagem
And blown in twenty dollars by nine o'clock a. m.?

Ah me! now that the deed is done, how penitent I am!
I *was* a roaring lion—behold a bleating lamb!
I've packed and shipped those precious things to that more pre-
    cious wife
Who shares with our sweet babes the strange vicissitudes of life,
While he who, in his folly, gave up his store of wealth
Is far away, and means to keep his distance—for his health!

MY PLAYMATES

THE wind comes whispering to me of the country green and cool-
Of redwing blackbirds chattering beside a reedy pool;
It brings me soothing fancies of the homestead on the hill,
And I hear the thrush's evening song and the robin's morning trill:
So I fall to thinking tenderly of those I used to know
Where the sassafras and snakeroot and checkerberries grow.

What has become of Ezra Marsh, who lived on Baker's hill?
And what's become of Noble Pratt, whose father kept the mill?
And what's become of Lizzie Crum and Anastasia Snell,
And of Roxie Root, who 'tended school in Boston for a spell?
They were the boys and they the girls who shared my youthful
    play—
They do not answer to my call!   My playmates—where are they?

What has become of Levi and his little brother Joe,
Who lived next door to where we lived some forty years ago?
I'd like to see the Newton boys and Quincy Adams Brown,
And Hepsy Hall and Ella Cowles, who spelled the whole school
    down!
And Gracie Smith, the Cutler boys, Leander Snow, and all
Who I am sure would answer could they only hear my call!

I'd like to see Bill Warner and the Conkey boys again
And talk about the times we used to wish that we were men!
And one—I shall not name her—could I see her gentle face
And hear her girlish treble in this distant, lonely place!
The flowers and hopes of springtime—they perished long ago,
And the garden where they blossomed is white with winter snow.

O cottage 'neath the maples, have you seen those girls and boys
That but a little while ago made, oh! such pleasant noise?
O trees, and hills, and brooks, and lanes, and meadows, do you
    know
Where I shall find my little friends of forty years ago?
You see I'm old and weary, and I've travelled long and far;
I am looking for my playmates—I wonder where they are!

STOVES AND SUNSHINE

PRATE, ye who will, of so-called charms you find across the sea—
The land of stoves and sunshine is good enough for me!
I 've done the grand for fourteen months in every foreign clime,
And I 've learned a heap of learning, but I 've shivered all the time;
And the biggest bit of wisdom I 've acquired—as I can see—
Is that which teaches that this land 's the land of lands for me.

Now, I am of opinion that a person should get some
Warmth in this present life of ours, not all in that to come;
So when Boreas blows his blast, through country and through
    town,
Or when upon the muddy streets the stifling fog rolls down,
Go, guzzle in a pub, or plod some bleak malarious grove,
But let me toast my shrunken shanks beside some Yankee stove.

The British people say they "don't believe in stoves, y' know";
Perchance because we warmed 'em so completely years ago!
They talk of "drahfts" and "stuffiness" and "ill effects of heat,"
As they chatter in their barny rooms or shiver 'round the street;
With sunshine such a rarity, and stoves esteemed a sin,
What wonder they are wedded to their fads—catarrh and gin?

In Germany are stoves galore, and yet you seldom find
A fire within the stoves, for German stoves are not that kind;
The Germans say that fires make dirt, and dirt 's an odious
    thing,
But the truth is that the pfennig is the average Teuton's king,
And since the fire costs pfennigs, why, the thrifty soul denies
Himself all heat except what comes with beer and exercise.

The Frenchman builds a fire of cones, the Irishman of peat;
The frugal Dutchman buys a fire when he has need of heat—
That is to say, he pays so much each day to one who brings
The necessary living coals to warm his soup and things;
In Italy and Spain they have no need to heat the house—
Neath balmy skies the native picks the mandolin and louse.

Now, we 've no mouldy catacombs, no feudal castles grim,
No ruined monasteries, no abbeys ghostly dim;
Our ancient history is new, our future 's all ahead,
And we 've got a tariff bill that 's made all Europe sick abed—
But what is best, though short on tombs and academic groves,
We double discount Christendom on sunshine and on stoves.

Dear land of mine! I come to you from months of chill and
    storm,
Blessing the honest people whose hearts and hearths are warm;
A fairer, sweeter song than this I mean to weave to you
When I 've reached my lakeside 'dobe and once get heated through;
But, even then, the burthen of that fairer song shall be
That the land of stoves and sunshine is good enough for me.

A DRINKING SONG

Come, brothers, share the fellowship
    We celebrate to-night;
There 's grace of song on every lip
    And every heart is light!
But first, before our mentor chimes
    The hour of jubilee,
Let 's drink a health to good old times,
    And good times yet to be!
        Clink, clink, clink!
        Merrily let us drink!
            There 's store of wealth
            And more of health
        In every glass, we think.
        Clink, clink, clink!
        To fellowship we drink!
            And from the bowl
            No genial soul
        In such an hour can shrink.

And you, oh, friends from west and east
   And other foreign parts,
Come share the rapture of our feast,
   The love of loyal hearts;
And in the wassail that suspends
   All matters burthensome,
We 'll drink a health to good old friends
   And good friends yet to come.
        Clink, clink, clink!
        To fellowship we drink!
          And from the bowl
          No genial soul
        In such an hour will shrink.
        Clink, clink, clink!
        Merrily let us drink!
          There 's fellowship
          In every sip
        Of friendship's brew, we think.

THE STRAW PARLOR

WAY up at the top of a big stack of straw
Was the cunningest parlor that ever you saw!
And there could you lie when weary of play
And gossip or laze in the cosiest way;
No matter how careworn or sorry one's mood
No worldly distraction presumed to intrude.
As a refuge from onerous mundane ado
I think I approve of straw parlors, don't you?

A swallow with jewels aflame on her breast
On that straw parlor's ceiling had builded her nest;
And she flew in and out all the happy day long,
And twittered the soothingest lullaby song.
Now some might suppose that that beautiful bird
Performed for her babies the music they heard;
I reckon she twittered her répertoire through
For the folk in the little straw parlor, don't you?

And down from a rafter a spider had hung
Some swings upon which he incessantly swung.
He cut up such didoes—such antics he played
Way up in the air, and was never afraid!
He never made use of his horrid old sting,
But was just upon earth for the fun of the thing!
I deeply regret to observe that so few
Of these good-natured insects are met with, don't you?

And, down in the strawstack, a wee little mite
Of a cricket went chirping by day and by night;
And further down, still, a cunning blue mouse
In a snug little nook of that strawstack kept house!
When the cricket went "chirp," Miss Mousie would squeak
"Come in," and a blush would enkindle her cheek!
She thought—silly girl! 't was a beau come to woo,
But I guess it was only the cricket, don't you?

So the cricket, the mouse, and the motherly bird
Made as soothingsome music as ever you heard;
And, meanwhile, that spider by means of his swings
Achieved most astounding gyrations and things!
No wonder the little folk liked what they saw
And loved what they heard in that parlor of straw!
With the mercury up to 102
In the shade, I opine they just sizzled, don't you?

But once there invaded that Eden of straw
The evilest Feline that ever you saw!
She pounced on that cricket with rare promptitude
And she tucked him away where he'd do the most good
And then, reaching down to the nethermost house,
She deftly expiscated little Miss Mouse!
And, as for the Swallow, she shrieked and withdrew—
I rather admire her discretion, don't you?

Now listen: That evening a cyclone obtained,
And the mortgage was all on that farm that remained!
Barn, strawstack and spider—they all blew away,
And nobody knows where they're at to this day!

And, as for the little straw parlor, I fear
It was wafted clean off this sublunary sphere!
I really incline to a hearty "boo-hoo"
When I think of this tragical ending, don't you?

THE DISCREET COLLECTOR

Down south there is a curio-shop
   Unknown to many men;
Thereat do I intend to stop
   When I am South again;
The narrow street through which to go—
   Aha! I know it well!
And maybe you would like to know—
   But no—I will not tell!

'T is there to find the loveliest plates
   (The bluest of the blue!)
At such surprisingly low rates
   You 'd not believe it true!
And there is one Napoleon vase
   Of dainty Sèvres to sell—
I 'm sure you 'd like to know that place—
   But no—I will not tell!

Then, too, I know another shop
   Has old, old beds for sale,
With lovely testers up on top
   Carved in ornate detail;
And there are sideboards rich and rare,
   With fronts that proudly swell—
Oh, there are bargains waiting there,
   But where I will not tell!

And hark! I know a bottle-man
   Smiling and debonair,
And he has promised me I can
   Choose of his precious ware!

In age and shape and color, too,
  His dainty goods excel—
Aha, my friends, if you but knew—
  But no! I will not tell!

A thousand other shops I know
  Where bargains can be got—
Where other folk would like to go
  Who have what I have not.
I let them hunt; I hold my mouth—
  Yes, though I know full well
Where lie the treasures of the South,
  I 'm not a-going to tell!

———

THE WIND

(THE TALE)

Cometh the Wind from the garden, fragrant and full of sweet
    singing—
Under my tree where I sit cometh the Wind to confession.

"Out in the garden abides the Queen of the beautiful Roses—
Her do I love and to-night wooed her with passionate singing;
Told I my love in those songs, and answer she gave in her
    blushes—
She shall be bride of the Wind, and she is the Queen of the
    Roses!"

"Wind, there is spice in thy breath; thy rapture hath fragrance
    Sabæan!"

"Straight from my wooing I come—my lips are bedewed with her
    kisses—
My lips and my song and my heart are drunk with the rapture
    of loving!"

(THE SONG)

The Wind he loveth the red, red Rose,
  And he wooeth his love to wed:
     Sweet is his song
     The Summer long
  As he kisseth her lips so red;
And he recketh naught of the ruin wrought
  When the Summer of love is sped!

(AGAIN THE TALE)

Cometh the Wind from the garden, bitter with sorrow of winter.

"Wind, is thy love-song forgot? Wherefore thy dread lamenta-
    tions?"

Sigheth and moaneth the Wind: "Out of the desolate garden
Come I from vigils with ghosts over the grave of the Summer!"

"Thy breath that was fragrant anon with rapture of music and
    loving,
It grieveth all things with its sting and the frost of its wailing
    displeasure."

The Wind maketh evermore moan and ever it giveth this answer:
"My heart it is numb with the cold of the love that was born of
    the Summer—
I come from the garden all white with the wrath and the sorrow
    of Winter;
I have kissed the low, desolate tomb where my bride in her loveli-
    ness lieth
And the voice of the ghost in my heart is the voice that forever
    outcrieth!"

(AGAIN THE SONG)

The Wind he waileth the red, red Rose
  When the Summer of love is sped—

He waileth above
His lifeless love
With her shroud of snow o'erspread—
Crieth such things as a true heart brings
To the grave of its precious dead.

A PARAPHRASE

OUR Father who art in Heaven, hallowed be Thy name;
Thy Kingdom come, Thy will be done on earth, in Heaven tne
    same;
Give us this day our daily bread, and may our debts to Heaven—
As we our earthly debts forgive—by Thee be all forgiven;
When tempted or by evil vexed, restore Thou us again,
And Thine be the Kingdom, the Power, and the Glory, forever and
    ever; amen.

WITH BRUTUS IN ST. JO

OF all the opry-houses then obtaining in the West
The one which Milton Tootle owned was, by all odds, the best;
Milt, being rich, was much too proud to run the thing alone,
So he hired an "acting manager," a gruff old man named Krone—
A stern, commanding man with piercing eyes and flowing beard,
And his voice assumed a thunderous tone when Jack and I ap-
    peared;
He said that Julius Cæsar had been billed a week or so,
And would have to have some armies by the time he reached St. Jo!

O happy days, when Tragedy still winged an upward flight,
When actors wore tin helmets and cambric robes at night!
O happy days, when sounded in the public's rapturous ears
The creak of pasteboard armor and the clash of wooden spears!
O happy times for Jack and me and that one other supe
That then and there did constitute the noblest Roman's troop!
With togas, battle axes, shields, we made a dazzling show,
When we were Roman soldiers with Brutus in St. Jo!

We wheeled and filed and double-quicked wherever Brutus led,
The folks applauding what we did as much as what he said;
'T was work, indeed; yet Jack and I were willing to allow
'T was easier following Brutus than following father's plough;
And at each burst of cheering, our valor would increase—
We tramped a thousand miles that night, at fifty cents apiece!
For love of Art—not lust for gold—consumed us years ago,
When we were Roman soldiers with Brutus in St. Jo!

To-day, while walking in the Square, Jack Langrish says to me:
"My friend, the drama nowadays ain't what it used to be!
These farces and these comedies—how feebly they compare
With that mantle of the tragic art which Forrest used to wear!
My soul is warped with bitterness to think that you and I—
Co-heirs to immortality in seasons long gone by—
Now draw a paltry stipend from a Boston comic show,
We, who were Roman soldiers with Brutus in St. Jo!"

And so we talked and so we mused upon the whims of Fate
That had degraded Tragedy from its old, supreme estate;
And duly, at the Morton bar, we stigmatized the age
As sinfully subversive of the interests of the Stage!
For Jack and I were actors in the halcyon, palmy days
Long, long before the Hoyt school of farce became the craze;
Yet, as I now recall it, it was twenty years ago
That we were Roman soldiers with Brutus in St. Jo!

We were by birth descended from a race of farmer kings
Who had done eternal battle with grasshoppers and things;
But the Kansas farms grew tedious—we pined for that delight
We read of in the *Clipper* in the barber's shop by night!
We would be actors—Jack and I—and so we stole away
From our native spot, Wathena, one dull September day,
And started for Missouri—ah, little did we know
We were going to train as soldiers with Brutus in St. Jo!

Our army numbered three in all—Marc Antony's was four;
Our army hankered after fame, but Marc's was after gore!
And when we reached Philippi, at the outset we were met
With an inartistic gusto I can never quite forget.

For Antony's overwhelming force of thumpers seemed to be
Resolved to do "them Kansas jays"—and that meant Jack and me!
My lips were sealed but that it seems quite proper you should know
That Rome was nowhere in it at Philippi in St. Jo!

I've known the slow-consuming grief and ostentatious pain
Accruing from McKean Buchanan's melancholy Dane;
Away out West I've witnessed Bandmann's peerless hardihood,
With Arthur Cambridge have I wrought where walking was not
     good;
In every phase of horror have I bravely borne my part,
And even on my uppers have I proudly stood for Art!
And, after all my suffering, it were not hard to show
That I got my allopathic dose with Brutus at St. Jo!

That army fell upon me in a most bewildering rage
And scattered me and mine upon that histrionic stage;
My toga rent, my helmet gone and smashed to smithereens,
They picked me up and hove me through whole centuries of scenes!
I sailed through Christian eras and mediæval gloom
And fell from Arden forest into Juliet's painted tomb!
Oh, yes, I travelled far and fast that night, and I can show
The scars of honest wounds I got with Brutus in St. Jo!

Ah me, old Davenport is gone, of fickle fame forgot,
And Barrett sleeps forever in a much neglected spot;
Fred Warde, the papers tell me, in far woolly western lands
Still flaunts the banner of high Tragic Art at one-night stands;
And Jack and I, in Charley Hoyt's Bostonian dramas wreak
Our vengeance on creation at some eensty dolls. per week.
By which you see that public taste has fallen mighty low
Since we fought as Roman soldiers with Brutus in St. Jo!

PAN LIVETH

THEY told me once that Pan was dead,
  And so, in sooth, I thought him;
For vainly where the streamlets led
  Through flowery meads I sought him—
Nor in his dewy pasture bed
  Nor in the grove I caught him.
    "Tell me," 'twas so my clamor ran—
    "Tell me, oh, where is Pan?"

But, once, as on my pipe I played
  A requiem sad and tender,
Lo, thither came a shepherd-maid—
  Full comely she and slender!
I were indeed a churlish blade
  With wailings to offend 'er—
    For, surely, wooing's sweeter than
    A mourning over Pan!

So, presently, whiles I did scan
  That shepherd-maiden pretty,
And heard her accents, I began
  To pipe a cheerful ditty;
And so, betimes, forgot old Pan
  Whose death had waked my pity;
    So—so did Love undo the man
    Who sought and pined for Pan!

He was *not* dead! I found him there—
  The Pan that I was after!
Caught in that maiden's tangling hair,
  Drunk with her song and laughter!
I doubt if there be otherwhere
  A merrier god or dafter—
    Nay, nor a mortal kindlier than
    Is this same dear old Pan!

Beside me, as my pipe I play,
　My shepherdess is lying,
While here and there her lambkins stray
　As sunny hours go flying;
They look like me—those lambs—they say,
　And that I 'm not denying!
　　And for that sturdy, romping clan,
　　All glory be to Pan!

Pan is not dead, O sweetheart mine!
　It is to hear his voices
In every note and every line
　Wherein the heart rejoices!
He liveth in that sacred shrine
　That Love's first, holiest choice is!
　　So pipe, my pipe, while still you can,
　　Sweet songs in praise of Pan!

DR. SAM

TO MISS GRACE KING

Down in the old French quarter,
　Just out of Rampart street,
　　I went my way
　　At close of day
　Unto the quaint retreat
Where lives the Voodoo Doctor
　By some esteemed a sham,
Yet I 'll declare there 's none elsewhere
　So skilled as Doctor Sam
　　With the claws of a devilled crawfish,
　　The juice of the prickly prune,
　　And the quivering dew
　　From a yarb that grew
　　In the light of a midnight moon!

I never should have known him
  But for the colored folk
    That here obtain
    And ne'er in vain
  That wizard's art invoke;
For when the Eye that's Evi
  Would him and his'n damn,
The negro's grief gets quick relief
  Of Hoodoo-Doctor Sam.
    With the caul of an alligator,
      The plume of an unborn loon,
        And the poison wrung
        From a serpent's tongue
      By the light of the midnight moon!

In all neurotic ailments
  I hear that he excels,
    And he insures
    Immediate cures
  Of weird, uncanny spells;
The most unruly patient
  Gets docile as a lamb
And is freed from ill by the potent skill
  Of Hoodoo-Doctor Sam;
    Feathers of strangled chickens,
      Moss from the dank lagoon,
        And plasters wet
        With spider sweat
      In the light of a midnight moon!

They say when nights are grewsome
  And hours are, oh! so late,
    Old Sam steals out
    And hunts about
  For charms that hoodoos hate!
That from the moaning river
  And from the haunted glen
He silently brings what eerie things
  Give peace to hoodooed men:—

The tongue of a piebald 'possum,
The tooth of a senile 'coon,
The buzzard's breath that smells of death,
And the film that lies
On a lizard's eyes
In the light of a midnight moon!

———

WINFREDA

(A BALLAD IN THE ANGLO-SAXON TONGUE)

WHEN to the dreary greenwood gloam
  Winfreda's husband strode that day,
The fair Winfreda bode at home
  To toil the weary time away;
"While thou are gone to hunt," said she,
"I'll brew a goodly sop for thee."

Lo, from a further, gloomy wood,
  A hungry wolf all bristling hied
And on the cottage threshold stood
  And saw the dame at work inside;
And, as he saw the pleasing sight,
He licked his fangs so sharp and white.

Now when Winfreda saw the beast,
  Straight at the grinning wolf she ran,
And, not affrighted in the least,
  She hit him with her cooking pan,
And as she thwacked him on the head—
"Scat! scat!" the fair Winfreda said.

The hills gave answer to their din—
  The brook in fear beheld the sight,
And all that bloody field within
  Wore token of Winfreda's might.
The wolf was very loath to stay—
But, oh! he could not get away.

Winfreda swept him o'er the wold
  And choked him till his gums were blue,
And till, beneath her iron hold,
  His tongue hung out a yard or two,
And with his hair the riven ground
Was strewn for many leagues around.

They fought a weary time that day,
  And seas of purple blood were shed,
Till by Winfreda's cunning lay
  That awful wolf all limp and dead;
Winfreda saw him reel and drop—
Then back she went to brewing sop.

So when the husband came at night
  From bootless chase, cold, gaunt, and grim,
Great was that Saxon lord's delight
  To find the sop dished up for him;
And as he ate, Winfreda told
How she had laid the wolf out cold.

The good Winfreda of those days
  Is only "pretty Birdie" now—
Sickly her soul and weak her ways—
  And she, to whom we Saxons bow,
Leaps on a bench and screams with fright
If but a mouse creeps into sight.

LYMAN, FREDERICK, AND JIM

(FOR THE FELLOWSHIP CLUB)

LYMAN and Frederick and Jim, one day,
  Set out in a great big ship—
Steamed to the ocean adown the bay
  Out of a New York slip.
"Where are you going and what is your game?"
  The people asked those three.

"Darned if we know; but all the same
  Happy as larks are we;
And happier still we 're going to be!"
        Said Lyman
        And Frederick
        And Jim.

The people laughed "Aha, oho!
  Oho, aha!" laughed they;
And while those three went sailing so
  Some pirates steered that way.
The pirates they were laughing, too—
  The prospect made them glad;
But by the time the job was through
  Each of them pirates, bold and bad,
  Had been done out of all he had
        By Lyman
        And Frederick
        And Jim.

Days and weeks and months they sped,
  Painting that foreign clime
A beautiful, bright vermilion red—
  And having a —— of a time!
'T was all so gaudy a lark, it seemed
  As if it could not be,
And some folks thought it a dream they dreamed
  Of sailing that foreign sea,
  But I 'll identify you these three—
        Lyman
        And Frederick
        And Jim.

Lyman and Frederick are bankers and sich
  And Jim is an editor kind;
The first two named are awfully rich
  And Jim ain't far behind!
So keep your eyes open and mind your tricks,
  Or you are like to be
In quite as much of a Tartar fix

As the pirates that sailed the sea
And monkeyed with the pardners three,
     Lyman
     And Frederick
     And Jim!

BE MY SWEETHEART

SWEETHEART, be my sweetheart
  When birds are on the wing,
When bee and bud and babbling flood
  Bespeak the birth of spring,
Come, sweetheart, be my sweetheart
  And wear this posy-ring!

Sweetheart, be my sweetheart
  In the mellow golden glow
Of earth aflush with the gracious blush
  Which the ripening fields foreshow;
Dear sweetheart, be my sweetheart,
  As into the noon we go!

Sweetheart, be my sweetheart
  When falls the bounteous year,
When fruit and wine of tree and vine
  Give us their harvest cheer;
Oh, sweetheart, be my sweetheart,
  For winter it draweth near.

Sweetheart, be my sweetheart
  When the year is white and old,
When the fire of youth is spent, forsooth,
  And the hand of age is cold;
Yet, sweetheart, be my sweetheart
  Till the year of our love be told!

THE PETER-BIRD

Out of the woods by the creek cometh a calling for Peter,
And from the orchard a voice echoes and echoes it over;
Down in the pasture the sheep hear that strange crying for Peter,
Over the meadows that call is aye and forever repeated.
So let me tell you the tale, when, where, and how it all happened,
And, when the story is told, let us pay heed to the lesson.

Once on a time, long ago, lived in the State of Kentucky
One that was reckoned a witch—full of strange spells and devices;
Nightly she wandered the woods, searching for charms voodoo-
     istic—
Scorpions, lizards, and herbs, dormice, chameleons, and plantains!
Serpents and caw-caws and bats, screech-owls and crickets and
     adders—
These were the guides of that witch through the dank deeps of
     the forest.
Then, with her roots and her herbs, back to her cave in the morning
Ambled that hussy to brew spells of unspeakable evil;
And, when the people awoke, seeing that hillside and valley
Sweltered in swathes as of mist—"Look!" they would whisper in
     terror—
"Look! the old witch is at work brewing her spells of great evil!"
Then would they pray till the sun, darting his rays through the
     vapor,
Lifted the smoke from the earth and baffled the witch's intentions.

One of the boys at that time was a certain young person named
     Peter,
Given too little to work, given too largely to dreaming;
Fonder of books than of chores, you can imagine that Peter
Led a sad life on the farm, causing his parents much trouble.
"Peter!" his mother would call, "the cream is a'ready for
     churning!"
"Peter!" his father would cry, "go grub at the weeds in the
     garden!"
So it was "Peter!" all day—calling, reminding, and chiding—
Peter neglected his work; therefore that nagging at Peter!

Peter got hold of some books—how, I 'm unable to tell you;
Some have suspected the witch—this is no place for suspicions!
It is sufficient to stick close to the thread of the legend.
Nor is it stated or guessed what was the trend of those volumes;
What thing soever it was—done with a pen and a pencil,
Wrought with a brain, not a hoe—surely 't was hostile to farming!
"Fudge on all readin'!" they quoth; or "*that 's* what 's the ruin
    of Peter!"

So, when the mornings were hot, under the beech or the maple,
Cushioned in grass that was blue, breathing the breath of the blos-'
    soms,
Lulled by the hum of the bees, the coo of the ring-doves a-mating,
Peter would frivol his time at reading, or lazing, or dreaming.
"Peter!" his mother would call, "the cream is a' ready for
    churning!"
"Peter!" his father would cry, "go grub at the weeds in the
    garden!"
"Peter!" and "Peter!" all day—calling, reminding, and chiding—
Peter neglected his chores; therefore that outcry for Peter;
Therefore the neighbors allowed evil would surely befall him—
Yes, on account of these things, ruin would come upon Peter!

Surely enough, on a time, reading and lazing and dreaming
Wrought the calamitous ill all had predicted for Peter;
For, of a morning in spring when lay the mist in the valleys—
"See," quoth the folk, "how the witch breweth her evil decoctions!
See how the smoke from her fire broodeth on woodland and meadow!
Grant that the sun cometh out to smother the smudge of her
    caldron!
She hath been forth in the night, full of her spells and devices,
Roaming the marshes and dells for heathenish magical nostrums;
Digging in leaves and at stumps for centipedes, pismires, and
    spiders,
Grubbing in poisonous pools for hot salamanders and toadstools;
Charming the bats from the flues, snaring the lizards by twilight,
Sucking the scorpion's egg and milking the breast of the adder!"

Peter derided these things held in such faith by the farmer,
Scouted at magic and charms, hooted at Jonahs and hoodoos—

Thinking and reading of books must have unsettled his reason!
"There ain't no witches," he cried; "it is n't smoky, but foggy!
I will go out in the wet—you all can't hender me, nuther!"

Surely enough he went out into the damp of the morning,
Into the smudge that the witch spread over woodland and meadow,
Into the fleecy gray pall brooding on hillside and valley.
Laughing and scoffing, he strode into that hideous vapor;
Just as he said he would do, just as he bantered and threatened,
Ere they could fasten the door, Peter had done gone and done it!
Wasting his time over books, you see, had unsettled his reason—
Soddened his callow young brain with semipubescent paresis,
And his neglect of his chores hastened this evil condition.

Out of the woods by the creek cometh a calling for Peter
And from the orchard a voice echoes and echoes it over;
Down in the pasture the sheep hear that shrill crying for Peter,
Up from the spring house the wail stealeth anon like a whisper,
Over the meadows that call is aye and for ever repeated.
Such *were* the voices that whooped wildly and vainly for Peter
Decades and decades ago down in the State of Kentucky—
Such *are* the voices that cry now from the woodland and meadow,
"Peter—O Peter!" all day, calling, reminding, and chiding—
Taking us back to the time when Peter he done gone and done it!
These are the voices of those left by the boy in the farmhouse
When, with his laughter and scorn, hatless and bootless and
    sockless,
Clothed in his jeans and his pride, Peter sailed out in the weather,
Broke from the warmth of his home into that fog of the devil,
Into the smoke of that witch brewing her damnable porridge!

Lo, when he vanished from sight, knowing the evil that threatened
Forth with importunate cries hastened his father and mother.
"Peter!" they shrieked in alarm, "Peter!" and evermore
    "Peter!"—
Ran from the house to the barn, ran from the barn to the garden,
Ran to the corn-crib anon, then to the smoke-house proceeded;
Henhouse and woodpile they passed, calling and wailing and
    weeping,
Through the front gate to the road, braving the hideous vapor—

Sought him in lane and on pike, called him in orchard and meadow,
Clamoring "Peter!" in vain, vainly outcrying for Peter.
Joining the search came the rest, brothers and sisters and cousins,
Venting unspeakable fears in pitiful wailing for Peter!
And from the neighboring farms gathered the men and the women,
Who, upon hearing the news, swelled the loud chorus for Peter.

Farmers and hussifs and maids, bosses and field-hands and niggers,
Colonels and jedges galore from cornfields and mint-beds and
    thickets,
All that had voices to voice, all to those parts appertaining,
Came to engage in the search, gathered and bellowed for Peter.
The Taylors, the Dorseys, the Browns, the Wallers, the Mitchells,
    the Logans,
The Yenowines, Crittendens, Dukes, the Hickmans, the Hobbses,
    the Morgans;
The Ormsbys, the Thompsons, the Hikes, the Williamsons, Mur-
    rays, and Hardins,
The Beynroths, the Sherleys, the Hokes, the Haldermans, Harneys,
    and Slaughters—
All, famed in Kentucky of old for prowess prodigious at farming,
Now surged from their prosperous homes to join in that hunt for
    the truant,
To ascertain where he was at, to help out the chorus for Peter.

Still on those prosperous farms where heirs and assigns of the
    people
Specified hereinabove and proved by the records of probate—
Still on those farms shall you hear (and still on the turnpikes ad-
    jacent)
That pitiful, petulant call, that pleading, expostulant wailing,
That hopeless, monotonous moan, that crooning and droning for
    Peter.
Some say the witch in her wrath transmogrified all those good
    people;
That, wakened from slumber that day by the calling and bawling
    for Peter,
She out of her cave in a trice, and, waving the foot of a rabbit
(Crossed with the caul of a coon and smeared with the blood of a
    chicken),

She changed all those folk into birds and shrieked with demoniac
    venom:
"Fly away over the land, moaning your Peter forever,
Croaking of Peter, the boy who did n't believe there were hoodoos,
Crooning of Peter, the fool who scouted at stories of witches,
Crying of Peter for aye, forever outcalling for Peter!"

This is the story they tell; so in good sooth saith the legend;
As I have told it to you, so tell the folk and the legend.
That it is true I believe, for on the breezes this morning
Come the shrill voices of birds calling and calling for Peter;
Out of the maple and beech glitter the eyes of the wailers,
Peeping and peering for him who formerly lived in these places—
Peter, the heretic lad, lazy and careless and dreaming,
Sorely afflicted with books and with pubescent paresis,
Hating the things of the farm, care of the barn and the garden,
Always neglecting his chores—given to books and to reading,
Which, as all people allow, turn the young person to mischief,
Harden his heart against toil, wean his affections from tillage.

This is the legend of yore told in the state of Kentucky
When in the springtime the birds call from the beeches and maples,
Call from the petulant thorn, call from the acrid persimmon;
When from the woods by the creek and from the pastures and
    meadows,
When from the spring house and lane and from the mint-bed and
    orchard,
When from the redbud and gum and from the redolent lilac,
When from the dirt roads and pikes cometh that calling for Peter;
Cometh the dolorous cry, cometh that weird iteration
Of "Peter" and "Peter" for aye, of "Peter" and "Peter" forever!
This is the legend of old, told in the tumtitty metre
Which the great poets prefer, being less labor than rhyming
(My first attempt at the same, my *last* attempt, too, I reckon!);
Nor have I further to say, for the sad story is ended.

SISTER'S CAKE

I 'd not complain of Sister Jane, for she was good and kind,
Combining with rare comeliness distinctive gifts of mind;
Nay, I 'll admit it were most fit that, worn by social cares,
She 'd crave a change from parlor life to that below the stairs,
And that, eschewing needlework and music, she should take
Herself to the substantial art of manufacturing cake.

At breakfast, then, it would befall that Sister Jane would say:
"Mother, if you have got the things, I 'll make some cake to-day!"
Poor mother 'd cast a timid glance at father, like as not—
For father hinted sister's cooking cost a frightful lot—
But neither *she* nor *he* presumed to signify dissent,
Accepting it for gospel truth that what she wanted went!

No matter what the rest of 'em might chance to have in hand,
The whole machinery of the house came to a sudden stand;
The pots were hustled off the stove, the fire built up anew,
With every damper set just so to heat the oven through;
The kitchen-table was relieved of everything, to make
That ample space which Jane required when she compounded cake.

And, oh! the bustling here and there, the flying to and fro;
The click of forks that whipped the eggs to lather white as snow—
And what a wealth of sugar melted swiftly out of sight—
And butter? Mother said such waste would ruin father, quite!
But Sister Jane preserved a mien no pleading could confound
As she utilized the raisins and the citron by the pound.

Oh, hours of chaos, tumult, heat, vexatious din, and whirl!
Of deep humiliation for the sullen hired-girl;
Of grief for mother, hating to see things wasted so,
And of fortune for that little boy who pined to taste that dough!
It looked so sweet and yellow—sure, to taste it were no sin—
But, oh! how sister scolded if he stuck his finger in!

The chances were as ten to one, before the job was through,
That sister 'd think of something else she 'd great deal rather do!

So, then, she 'd softly steal away, as Arabs in the night,
Leaving the girl and ma to finish up as best they might;
These tactics (artful Sister Jane) enabled her to take
Or shift the credit or the blame of that too-treacherous cake!

And yet, unhappy is the man who has no Sister Jane—
For he who has no sister seems to me to live in vain.
I never had a sister—maybe that is why to-day
I 'm wizened and dyspeptic, instead of blithe and gay;
A boy who 's only forty should be full of romp and mirth,
But *I* (because I 'm sisterless) am the oldest man on earth!

Had I a little sister—oh, how happy I should be!
I 'd never let her cast her eyes on any chap but me;
I 'd love her and I 'd cherish her for better and for worse—
I 'd buy her gowns and bonnets, and sing her praise in verse;
And—yes, what 's more and vastly more—I tell you what I 'd do;
I 'd let her make her wondrous cake, and I would eat it, too!

I have a high opinion of the sisters, as you see—
Another fellow's sister is so very dear to me!
I love to work anear her when she 's making over frocks,
When she patches little trousers or darns prosaic socks;
But I draw the line at one thing—yes, I don my hat and take
A three hours' walk when she is moved to try her hand at cake!

ABU MIDJAN

"*When Father Time swings round his scythe,*
Intomb me 'neath the bounteous vine,
So that its juices, red and blithe,
May cheer these thirsty bones of mine.

"*Elsewise with tears and bated breath*
Should I survey the life to be.
But oh! How should I hail the death
That brings that vinous grace to me!"

So sung the dauntless Saracen,
    Whereat the Prophet-Chief ordains
That, curst of Allah, loathed of men,
    The faithless one shall die in chains.

But one vile Christian slave that lay
    A prisoner near that prisoner saith:
"God willing, I will plant some day
    A vine where liest thou in death."

Lo, over Abu Midjan's grave
    With purpling fruit a vine-tree grows;
Where rots the martyred Christian slave
    Allah, and only Allah, knows!

———

ED

ED was a man that played for keeps, 'nd when he tuk the notion,
You cudn't stop him any more 'n a dam 'ud stop the ocean;
For when he tackled to a thing 'nd sot his mind plum to it,
You bet yer boots he done that thing though it broke the bank to
    do it!
So all us boys uz knowed him best allowed he wuz n't jokin'
When on a Sunday he remarked uz how he 'd gin up smokin'.

Now this remark, that Ed let fall, fell, ez I say, on Sunday—
Which is the reason we wuz shocked to see him sail in Monday
A-puffin' at a snipe that sizzled like a Chinese cracker
An' smelt fur all the world like rags instead uv like terbacker;
Recoverin' from our first surprise, us fellows fell to pokin'
A heap uv fun at "folks uz said how they had gin up smokin'."

But Ed—sez he: "I found my work cud not be done without it—
Jes' try the scheme yourselves, my friends, ef any uv you doubt it!
It 's hard, I know, upon one's health, but there 's a certain beauty
In makin' sackerfices to the stern demands uv duty!
So, wholly in a sperrit uv denial 'nd concession,
I mortify the flesh 'nd smoke for the sake uv my perfession!"

JENNIE

SOME men affect a liking
    For the prim in face and mind,
And some prefer the striking
    And the loud in womankind;
Wee Madge is wooed of many,
    And buxom Kate, as well,
And Jennie—charming Jennie—
    Ah, Jennie doesn't tell!

What eyes so bright as Daisy's,
    And who as Maud so fair?
Who does not sing the praises
    Of Lucy's golden hair?
There 's Sophie—she is witty,
    A very sprite is Nell,
And Susie's, oh, so pretty—
    But Jennie doesn't tell!

And now for my confession:
    Of all the virtues rare,
I argue that discretion
    Doth most beseem the fair.
And though I hear the many
    Extol each other belle,
I—I pronounce for Jennie,
    For Jennie doesn't tell!

————

CONTENTMENT

HAPPY the man that, when his day is done,
    Lies down to sleep with nothing of regret—
The battle he has fought may not be won—
    The fame he sought be just as fleeting yet;

Folding at last his hands upon his breast,
  Happy is he, if hoary and forespent,
He sinks into the last, eternal rest,
  Breathing these only words: "I am content."

But happier he, that, while his blood is warm,
  Sees hopes and friendships dead about him lie—
Bares his brave breast to envy's bitter storm,
  Nor shuns the poison barbs of calumny;
And 'mid it all, stands sturdy and elate,
  Girt only in the armor God hath meant
For him who 'neath the buffetings of fate
  Can say to God and man: "I am content."

"GUESS"

THERE is a certain Yankee phrase
  I always have revered,
Yet, somehow, in these modern days,
  It's almost disappeared;
It was the usage years ago,
  But nowadays it's got
To be regarded coarse and low
  To answer: "I guess not!"

The height of fashion called the pink
  Affects a British craze—
Prefers "I fancy" or "I think"
  To that time-honored phrase;
But here's a Yankee, if you please,
  That brands the fashion rot,
And to all heresies like these
  He answers, "I—guess not!"—

When Chaucer, Wycliff, and the rest
  Express their meaning thus,
I guess, if not the very best,
  It's good enough for us!

Why! shall the idioms of our speech
    Be banished and forgot
For this vain trash which moderns teach?
    Well, no, sir; I guess not!

There's meaning in that homely phrase
    No other words express—
No substitute therefor conveys
    Such unobtrusive stress.
True Anglo-Saxon speech, it goes
    Directly to the spot,
And he who hears it always knows
    The worth of "I—guess—not!"

NEW-YEAR'S EVE

Good old days—dear old days
    When my heart beat high and bold—
When the things of earth seemed full of life,
    And the future a haze of gold!
Oh, merry was I that winter night,
    And gleeful our little one's din,
And tender the grace of my darling's face
    As we watched the new year in.
But a voice—a spectre's, that mocked at love—
    Came out of the yonder hall;
"Tick-tock, tick-tock!" 't was the solemn clock
    That ruefully croaked to all.
Yet what knew we of the griefs to be
    In the year we longed to greet?
Love—love was the theme of the sweet, sweet **dream**
    I fancied might never fleet!
But the spectre stood in that yonder gloom,
    And these were the words it spake,
"Tick-tock, tick-tock"—and they seemed to mock
    A heart about to break.

'T is new-year's eve, and again I watch
  In the old familiar place,
And I 'm thinking again of that old time when
  I looked on a dear one's face.
Never a little one hugs my knee
  And I hear no gleeful shout—
I am sitting alone by the old hearthstone,
  Watching the old year out.
But I welcome the voice in yonder gloom
  That solemnly calls to me:
"Tick-tock, tick-tock!" —for so the clock
  Tells of a life to be;
"Tick-tock, tick-tock!" —'t is so the clock
  Tells of eternity.

THE BROKEN RING

To the willows of the brookside
  The mill wheel sings to-day—
    Sings and weeps,
    As the brooklet creeps
  Wondering on its way;
And here is the ring *she* gave me
  With love's sweet promise then—
    It hath burst apart
    Like the trusting heart
That may never be soothed again!

Oh, I would be a minstrel
  To wander far and wide,
Weaving in song the merciless wrong
  Done by a perjured bride!
Or I would be a soldier,
  To seek in the bloody fray
What gifts of fate can compensate
  For the pangs I suffer to-day!
Yet may this aching bosom,
  By bitter sorrow crushed,

Be still and cold
In the churchyard mould
Ere *thy* sweet voice be hushed;
So sing, sing on forever,
O wheel of the brookside mill,
For you mind me again
Of the old time when
I felt love's gracious thrill.

THE BALLAD OF THE TAYLOR PUP

Now lithe and listen, gentles all,
Now lithe ye all and hark
Unto a ballad I shall sing
About Buena Park.

Of all the wonders happening there
The strangest hap befell
Upon a famous Aprile morn,
As I you now shall tell.

It is about the Taylor pup
And of his mistress eke
And of the prankish time they had
That I am fain to speak.

FITTE THE FIRST

The pup was of as noble mien
As e'er you gazed upon;
They called his mother Lady
And his father was a Don.

And both his mother and his sire
Were of the race Bernard—
The family famed in histories
And hymned of every bard.

His form was of exuberant mould,
  Long, slim, and loose of joints;
There never yet was pointer-dog
  So full as he of points.

His hair was like to yellow fleece,
  His eyes were black and kind,
And like a nodding, gilded plume
  His tail stuck up behind.

His bark was very, very fierce,
  And fierce his appetite,
Yet was it only things to eat
  That he was prone to bite.

But in that one particular
  He was so passing true
That never did he quit a meal
  Until he had got through.

Potatoes, biscuits, mush, or hash,
  Joint, chop, or chicken limb—
So long as it was edible,
  'T was all the same to him!

And frequently when Hunger's pangs
  Assailed that callow pup,
He masticated boots and gloves
  Or chewed a door-mat up.

So was he much beholden of
  The folk that him did keep;
They loved him when he was awake
  And better still asleep.

FITTE THE SECOND

Now once his master, lingering o'er
  His breakfast coffee-cup,
Observed unto his doting spouse:
  "You ought to wash the pup!"

"That shall I do this very day,"
    His doting spouse replied;
"You will not know the pretty thing
    When he is washed and dried.

"But tell me, dear, before you go
    Unto your daily work,
Shall I use Ivory soap on him,
    Or Colgate, Pears' or Kirk?"

"Odzooks, it matters not a whit—
    They all are good to use!
Take Pearline, if it pleases you—
    Sapolio, if you choose!

"Take any soap, but take the pup
    And also water take,
And mix the three discreetly up
    Till they a lather make.

"Then mixing these constituent parts,
    Let Nature take her way,"
With which advice that sapient sir
    Had nothing more to say.

Then fared he to his daily toil
    All in the Board of Trade,
While Mistress Taylor for that bath
    Due preparation made.

FITTE THE THIRD

She whistled gayly to the pup
    And called him by his name,
And presently the guileless thing
    All unsuspecting came.

But when she shut the bath-room door,
    And caught him as catch-can,
And hove him in that odious tub,
    His sorrows then began.

How did that callow, yellow thing
   Regret that Aprile morn—
Alas! how bitterly he rued
   The day that he was born!

Twice and again, but all in vain,
   He lifted up his wail;
His voice was all the pup could lift,
   For thereby hangs this tale.

'T was by that tail she held him down,
   And presently she spread
The creamy lather on his back,
   His stomach, and his head.

His ears hung down in sorry wise,
   His eyes were, oh! so sad—
He looked as though he just had lost
   The only friend he had.

And higher yet the water rose,
   The lather still increased,
And sadder still the countenance
   Of that poor martyred beast!

Yet all the time his mistress spoke
   Such artful words of cheer
As "Oh, how nice!" and "Oh, how clean!"
   And "There's a patient dear!"

At last the trial had an end,
   At last the pup was free;
She threw aside the bath-room door—
   "Now get you gone!" quoth she.

FITTE THE FOURTH

Then from that tub and from that room
   He gat with vast ado;
At every hop he gave a shake,
   And—how the water flew!

He paddled down the winding stairs
  And to the parlor hied,
Dispensing pools of foamy suds
  And slop on every side.

Upon the carpet then he rolled
  And brushed against the wall,
And, horror! whisked his lathery sides
  On overcoat and shawl.

Attracted by the dreadful din,
  His mistress came below—
Who, who can speak her wonderment—
  Who, who can paint her woe!

Great smears of soap were here and there—
  Her startled vision met
With blobs of lather everywhere,
  And everything was wet!

Then Mrs. Taylor gave a shriek
  Like one about to die:
"Get out—get out, and don't you dare
  Come in till you are dry!"

With that she opened wide the door
  And waved the critter through;
Out in the circumambient air
  With grateful yelps he flew.

FITTE THE FIFTH

He whisked into the dusty street
  And to the Waller lot,
Where bonnie Annie Evans played
  With charming Sissy Knott.

And with those pretty little dears
  He mixed himself all up—
Oh, fie upon such boisterous play—
  Fie, fie, you naughty pup!

Woe, woe on Annie's India mull,
    And Sissy's blue percale!
One got that pup's belathered flanks,
    And one his soapy tail!

Forth to the rescue of those maids
    Rushed gallant Willie Clow;
His panties they were white and clean—
    Where are those panties now?

Where is the nicely laundered shirt
    That Kendall Evans wore,
And Robbie James's tricot coat
    All buttoned up before?

The leaven, which, as we are told,
    Leavens a monstrous lump,
Hath far less reaching qualities
    Than a wet pup on the jump.

This way and that he swung and swayed,
    He gambolled far and near,
And everywhere he thrust himself
    He left a soapy smear.

FITTE THE SIXTH

That noon a dozen little dears
    Were spanked and put to bed
With naught to stay their appetite
    But cheerless crusts of bread.

That noon a dozen hired girls
    Washed out each gown and shirt
Which that exuberant Taylor pup
    Had frescoed o'er with dirt.

That whole day long the Aprile sun
    Smiled sweetly from above
On clotheslines flaunting to the breeze
    The emblems mothers love.

That whole day long the Taylor pup
  This way and that did hie
Upon his mad, erratic course,
  Intent on getting dry.

That night when Mr. Taylor came
  His vesper meal to eat,
He uttered things my pious pen
  Would liefer not repeat.

Yet still that noble Taylor pup
  Survives to romp and bark
And stumble over folks and things
  In fair Buena Park.

Good sooth, I wot he should be called
  Buena's favorite son
Who 's sired of such a noble sire
  And dammed by every one!

AFTER READING TROLLOPE'S HISTORY OF FLORENCE

My books are on their shelves again
And clouds lie low with mist and rain.
Afar the Arno murmurs low
The tale of fields of melting snow.
List to the bells of times agone
The while I wait me for the dawn.

Beneath great Giotto's Campanile
The gray ghosts throng; their whispers steal
From poets' bosoms long since dust;
They ask me now to go. I trust
Their fleeter footsteps where again
They come at night and live as men.

The rain falls on Ghiberti's gates;
The big drops hang on purple dates;

And yet beneath the ilex-shades—
Dear trysting-place for boys and maids—
There comes a form from days of old,
With Beatrice's hair of gold.

The breath of lands or lilied streams
Floats through the fabric of my dreams;
And yonder from the hills of song,
Where psalmists brood and prophets throng.
The lone, majestic Dante leads
His love across the blooming meads.

Along the almond walks I tread
And greet the figures of the dead.
Mirandula walks here with him
Who lived with gods and seraphim;
Yet where Colonna's fair feet go
There passes Michael Angelo.

In Rome or Florence, still with her
Stands lone and grand her worshipper.
In Leonardo's brain there move
Christ and the children of His love;
And Raphael is touching now,
For the last time, an angel's brow.

Angelico is praying yet
Where lives no pang of man's regret,
And, mixing tears and prayers within
His palette's wealth, absolved from sin,
He dips his brush in hues divine;
San Marco's angel faces shine.

Within Lorenzo's garden green,
Where olives hide their boughs between,
The lovers, as they read betimes
Their love within Petrarca's lines,
Stand near the marbles found at Rome,
Lost shades that search in vain for home.

They pace the paths along the stream,
Dark Vallombrosa in their dream.
They sing, amidst the rain-drenched pines,
Of Tuscan gold that ruddier shines
Behind a saint's auroral face
That shows e'en yet the master's trace.

But lo, within the walls of gray,
Ere yet there falls a glint of day,
And far without, from hill to vale,
Where honey-hearted nightingale
Or meads of pale anemones
Make sweet the coming morning breeze—

I hear a voice, of prophet tone,
A voice of doom, like his alone
That once in Gadara was heard;
The old walls trembled—lo, the bird
Has ceased to sing, and yonder waits
Lorenzo at his palace gates.

Some Romola in passing by
Turns toward the ruler, and his sigh
Wanders amidst the myrtle bowers
Or o'er the city's mantled towers,
For she is Florence! "Wilt thou hear
San Marco's prophet? Doom is near."

"Her liberties," he cries, "restore!
This much for Florence—yea, and more
To men and God!" The days are gone;
And in an hour of perfect dawn
I stand beneath the cypress trees
That shiver still with words like these.

"THE OLD HOMESTEAD"

JEST as atween the awk'ard lines a hand we love has penn'd
   Appears a meanin' hid from other eyes,
So, in your simple, homespun art, old honest Yankee friend,
   A power o' tearful, sweet seggestion lies.
We see it all—the pictur' that our mem'ries hold so dear—
   The homestead in New England far away,
An' the vision is so nat'ral-like we almost seem to hear
   The voices that were heshed but yesterday.

Ah, who 'd ha' thought the music of that distant childhood time
   Would sleep through all the changeful, bitter years
To waken into melodies like Chris'mas bells a-chime
   An' to claim the ready tribute of our tears!
Why, the robins in the maples an' the blackbirds round the pond,
   The crickets an' the locusts in the leaves,
The brook that chased the trout adown the hillside just beyond,
   An' the swallers in their nests beneath the eaves—
They all come troopin' back with you, dear Uncle Josh, to-day,
   An' they seem to sing with all the joyous zest
Of the days when we were Yankee boys an' Yankee girls at play,
   With nary thought of "livin' way out West"!

God bless ye, Denman Thomps'n, for the good y' do our hearts
   With this music an' these memories o' youth—
God bless ye for the faculty that tops all human arts,
   The good ol' Yankee faculty of Truth!

THE CONVALESCENT GRIPSTER

THE gods let slip that fiendish grip
   Upon me last week Sunday—
No fiercer storm than racked my form
   E'er swept the Bay of Fundy;

But now, good-by
To drugs, say I—
    Good-by to gnawing sorrow;
I am up to-day,
And, whoop, hooray!
    I 'm going out to-morrow!

What aches and pain in bones and brain
    I had I need not mention;
It seemed to me such pangs must be
    Old Satan's own invention;
Albeit I
Was sure I 'd die,
    The doctor reassured me—
And, true enough,
With his vile stuff,
    He ultimately cured me.

As there I lay in bed all day,
    How fair outside looked to me!
A smile so mild old Nature smiled
    It seemed to warm clean through me.
In chastened mood
The scene I viewed,
    Inventing, sadly solus,
Fantastic rhymes
Between the times
    I had to take a bolus.

Of quinine slugs and other drugs
    I guess I took a million—
Such drugs as serve to set each nerve
    To dancing a cotillon;
The doctors say
The only way
    To rout the grip instanter
Is to pour in
All kinds of sin—
    Similibus curantur!

'T was hard; and yet I 'll soon forget
   Those ills and cures distressing;
One's future lies 'neath gorgeous skies
   When one is convalescing!
  So now, good-by
  To drugs say I—
   Good-by, thou phantom Sorrow!
  I am up to-day,
  And, whoop, hooray!
   I 'm going out to-morrow.

THE SLEEPING CHILD

My baby slept—how calm his rest,
   As o'er his handsome face a smile
   Like that of angel flitted, while
He lay so still upon my breast!

My baby slept—his baby head
   Lay all unkiss'd 'neath pall and shroud:
   I did not weep or cry aloud—
I only wished I, too, were dead!

My baby sleeps—a tiny mound,
   All covered by the little flowers,
   Woos me in all my waking hours,
Down in the quiet burying-ground.

And when I sleep I seem to be
   With baby in another land—
   I take his little baby hand—
He smiles and sings sweet songs to me.

Sleep on, O baby, while I keep
   My vigils till this day be passed!
   Then shall I, too, lie down at last,
And with my baby darling sleep.

THE TWO COFFINS

In yonder old cathedral
　Two lovely coffins lie;
In one, the head of the state lies dead,
　And a singer sleeps hard by.

Once had that King great power
　And proudly ruled the land—
His crown e'en now is on his brow
　And his sword is in his hand.

How sweetly sleeps the singer
　With calmly folded eyes,
And on the breast of the bard at rest
　The harp that he sounded lies.

The castle walls are falling
　And war distracts the land,
But the sword leaps not from that mildewed spot
　There in that dead king's hand.

But with every grace of nature
　There seems to float along—
To cheer again the hearts of men—
　The singer's deathless song.

CLARE MARKET

In the market of Clare, so cheery the glare
Of the shops and the booths of the tradespeople there;
That I take a delight on a Saturday night
In walking that way and in viewing the sight.
For it 's here that one sees all the objects that please—
New patterns in silk and old patterns in cheese,

For the girls pretty toys, rude alarums for boys,
And baubles galore while discretion enjoys—
But here I forbear, for I really despair
Of naming the wealth of the market of Clare.

A rich man comes down from the elegant town
And looks at it all with an ominous frown;
He seems to despise the grandiloquent cries
Of the vender proclaiming his puddings and pies;
And sniffing he goes through the lanes that disclose
Much cause for disgust to his sensitive nose;
And free of the crowd, he admits he is proud
That elsewhere in London this thing 's not allowed
He has seen nothing there but filth everywhere,
And he 's glad to get out of the market of Clare.

But the child that has come from the gloom of the slum
Is charmed by the magic of dazzle and hum;
He feasts his big eyes on the cakes and the pies,
And they seem to grow green and protrude with surprise
At the goodies they vend and the toys without end—
And it 's oh! if he had but a penny to spend!
But alas, he must gaze in a hopeless amaze
At treasures that glitter and torches that blaze—
What sense of despair in this world can compare
With that of the waif in the market of Clare?

So, on Saturday night, when my custom invites
A stroll in old London for curious sights,
I am likely to stray by a devious way
Where goodies are spread in a motley array,
The things which some eyes would appear to despise
Impress me as pathos in homely disguise,
And my battered waif-friend shall have pennies to spen'
So long as I 've got 'em (or chums that will lend);
And the urchin shall share in my joy and declare
That there 's beauty and good in the market of Clare

A DREAM OF SPRINGTIME

I 'M weary of this weather and I hanker for the ways
Which people read of in the psalms and preachers paraphrase—
The grassy fields, the leafy woods, the banks where I can lie
And listen to the music of the brook that flutters by,
Or, by the pond out yonder, hear the redwing blackbird's call
Where he makes believe he has a nest, but has n't one at all;
And by my side should be a friend—a trusty, genial friend,
With plenteous store of tales galore and natural leaf to lend;
Oh, how I pine and hanker for the gracious boon of spring—
For *then* I 'm going a-fishing with John Lyle King!

How like to pigmies will appear creation, as we float
Upon the bosom of the tide in a three-by-thirteen boat—
Forgotten all vexations and all vanities shall be,
As we cast our cares to windward and our anchor to the lee;
Anon the minnow-bucket will emit batrachian sobs,
And the devil's darning-needles shall come wooing of our bobs;
The sun shall kiss our noses and the breezes toss our hair
(This latter metaphoric—we 've no fimbriæ to spare!);
And I—transported by the bliss—shan't do a plaguey thing
But cut the bait and string the fish for John Lyle King!

Or, if I angle, it will be for bullheads and the like,
While he shall fish for gamey bass, for pickerel, and for pike;
I really do not care a rap for all the fish that swim—
But it 's worth the wealth of Indies just to be along with him
In grassy fields, in leafy woods, beside the water-brooks,
And hear him tell of things he 's seen or read of in his books—
To hear the sweet philosophy that trickles in and out
The while he is discoursing of the things we talk about;
A fountain-head refreshing—a clear, perennial spring
Is the genial conversation of John Lyle King!

Should varying winds or shifting tides redound to our despite—
In other words, should we return all bootless home at night,
I 'd back him up in anything he had a mind to say
Of mighty bass he 'd left behind or lost upon the way;

I 'd nod assent to every yarn involving piscine game—
I 'd cross my heart and make my affidavit to the same;
For what is friendship but a scheme to help a fellow out—
And what a paltry fish or two to make such bones about!
Nay, Sentiment a mantle of sweet charity would fling
O'er perjuries committed for John Lyle King.

At night, when as the camp-fire cast a ruddy, genial flame,
He 'd bring his tuneful fiddle out and play upon the same;
No diabolic engine this—no instrument of sin—
No relative at all to that lewd toy, the violin!
But a godly hoosier fiddle—a quaint archaic thing
Full of all the proper melodies our grandmas used to sing;
With "Bonnie Doon," and "Nellie Gray," and "Sitting on the Stile,"
"The Heart Bowed Down," the "White Cockade," and "Charm-
    ing Annie Lisle"
Our hearts would echo and the sombre empyrean ring
Beneath the wizard sorcery of John Lyle King.

The subsequent proceedings should interest me no more—
Wrapped in a woolen blanket should I calmly dream and snore;
The finny game that swims by day is my supreme delight—
And *not* the scaly game that flies in darkness of the night!
Let those who are so minded pursue this latter game
But not repine if they should lose a boodle in the same;
For an example to you all one paragon should serve—
He towers a very monument to valor and to nerve;
No bob-tail flush, no nine-spot high, no measly pair can wring
A groan of desperation from John Lyle King!

A truce to badinage—I hope far distant is the day
When from these scenes terrestrial our friend shall pass away!
We like to hear his cheery voice uplifted in the land,
To see his calm, benignant face, to grasp his honest hand;
We like him for his learning, his sincerity, his truth,
His gallantry to woman and his kindliness to youth,
For the lenience of his nature, for the vigor of his mind,
For the fulness of that charity he bears to all mankind—
That 's why we folks who know him best so reverently cling
(And that is why I pen these lines) to John Lyle King.

And now adieu, a fond adieu to thee, O muse of rhyme—
I do remand thee to the shades until that happier time
When fields are green, and posies gay are budding everywhere,
And there's a smell of clover bloom upon the vernal air;
When by the pond out yonder the redwing blackbird calls,
And distant hills are wed to Spring in veils of water-falls;
When from his aqueous element the famished pickerel springs
Two hundred feet into the air for butterflies and things—
Then come again, O gracious muse, and teach me how to sing
The glory of a fishing cruise with John Lyle King!

HOW SALTY WIN OUT

USED to think that luck wuz luck and nuthin' else but luck—
It made no diff'rence how or when or where or why it struck;
But sev'ral years ago I changt my mind, an' now proclaim
That luck's a kind uv science—same as any other game;
It happened out in Denver in the spring uv '80 when
Salty teched a humpback an' win out ten.

Salty wuz a printer in the good ol' Tribune days,
An', natural-like, he fell into the good ol' Tribune ways;
So, every Sunday evenin' he would sit into the game
Which in this crowd uv thoroughbreds I think I need not name;
An' there he'd sit until he rose, an', when he rose, he wore
Invariably less wealth about his person than before.

But once there came a powerful change; one sollum Sunday night
Occurred the tidal wave that put ol' Salty out o' sight.
He win on deuce an' ace an' Jack—he win on king an' queen—
Clif Bell allowed the like uv how he win wuz never seen.
An' how he done it wuz revealed to all us fellers when
He said he teched a humpback to win out ten.

There must be somethin' in it, for he never win afore,
An' when he told the crowd about the humpback, how they
    swore!

For every sport allows it is a losin' game to luck
Agin the science uv a man who 's teched a hump f'r luck;
And there is no denyin' luck wuz nowhere in it when
Salty teched a humpback an' win out ten.

I 've had queer dreams an' seen queer things, an' allus tried to
    do
The thing that luck apparently intended f'r me to;
Cats, funerils, cripples, beggers have I treated with regard,
An' charity subscriptions have hit me powerful hard;
But what 's the use uv talkin'? I say, an' say again:
You 've got to tech a humpback to win out ten!

So, though I used to think that luck wuz lucky, I 'll allow
That luck, for luck, agin a hump ain't nowhere in it now!
An' though I can't explain the whys an' wherefores, I maintain
There must be somethin' in it when the tip 's so straight an' plain;
For I wuz there an' seen it, an' got full with Salty when
Salty teched a humpback an' win out ten!

BOCCACCIO

LOVE AFFAIRS OF A BIBLIOMANIAC

ONE day upon a topmost shelf
    I found a precious prize indeed,
Which father used to read himself,
    But did not want us boys to read;
A brown old book of certain age
    (As type and binding seemed to show),
While on the spotted title-page
    Appeared the name "Boccaccio."

I 'd never heard that name before,
    But in due season it became
To him who fondly brooded o'er
    Those pages a belovèd name!

Adown the centuries I walked
  Mid pastoral scenes and royal show;
With seigneurs and their dames I talked—
  The crony of Boccaccio!

Those courtly knights and sprightly maids,
  Who really seemed disposed to shine
In gallantries and escapades,
  Anon became great friends of mine.
Yet was there sentiment with fun,
  And oftentimes my tears would flow
At some quaint tale of valor done.
  As told by my Boccaccio.

In boyish dreams I saw again
  Bucolic belles and dames of court,
The princely youths and monkish men
  Arrayed for sacrifice or sport.
Again I heard the nightingale
  Sing as she sang those years ago
In his embowered Italian vale
  To my revered Boccaccio.

And still I love that brown old book
  I found upon the topmost shelf—
I love it so I let none look
  Upon the treasure but myself!
And yet I have a strapping boy
  Who (I have every cause to know)
Would to its full extent enjoy
  The friendship of Boccaccio!

But boys are, oh! so different now
  From what they were when I was one!
I fear my boy would not know how
  To take that old raconteur's fun!
In your companionship, O friend,
  I think it wise alone to go
Plucking the gracious fruits that bend
  Where'er you lead, Boccaccio.

So rest you there upon the shelf,
   Clad in your garb of faded brown;
Perhaps, sometime, my boy himself
   Shall find you out and take you down.
Then may he feel the joy once more
   That thrilled me, filled me years ago
When reverently I brooded o'er
   The glories of Boccaccio!

MARCUS VARRO

MARCUS VARRO went up and down
   The places where old books were sold;
He ransacked all the shops in town
   For pictures new and pictures old.
He gave the folk of earth no peace;
   Snooping around by day and night,
He plied the trade in Rome and Greece
   Of an insatiate Grangerite.

"Pictures!" was evermore his cry—
   "Pictures of old or recent date,"
And pictures only would he buy
   Wherewith to "extra-illustrate."
Full many a tome of ancient type
   And many a manuscript he took,
For nary purpose but to swipe
   Their pictures for some other book.

While Marcus Varro plied his fad
   There was not in the shops of Greece
A book or pamphlet to be had
   That was not minus frontispiece.
Nor did he hesitate to ply
   His baleful practices at home;
It was not possible to buy
   A perfect book in all of Rome!

What must the other folks have done—
　Who, glancing o'er the books they bought,
Came soon and suddenly upon
　The vandalism Varro wrough.
How must their cheeks have flamed with red—
　How did their hearts with choler beat!
We can imagine what they said—
　We can imagine, not repeat!

Where are the books that Varro made—
　The pride of dilettante Rome—
With divers portraitures inlaid
　Swiped from so many another tome?
The worms devoured them long ago—
　O wretched worms! ye should have fed
Not on the books "extended" so,
　But on old Varro's flesh instead!

Alas, that Marcus Varro lives
　And is a potent factor yet!
Alas, that still his practice gives
　Good men occasion for regret!
To yonder bookstall, pri'thee, go
　And by the "missing" prints and plates
And frontispieces you shall know
　He lives, and "extra-illustrates"!

MY GARDEN

My garden aboundeth in pleasant nooks
　And fragrance is over it all;
For sweet is the smell of my old, old books
　In their places against the wall.

Here is a folio that's grim with age
　And yellow and green with mould;
There's the breath of the sea on every page
　And the hint of a stanch ship's hold.

And here is a treasure from France la belle
   Exhaleth a faint perfume
Of wedded lily and asphodel
   In a garden of song abloom.

And this wee little book of Puritan mien
   And rude, conspicuous print
Hath the Yankee flavor of wintergreen,
   Or, may be, of peppermint.

In Walton the brooks a-babbling tell
   Where the cheery daisy grows,
And where in meadow or woodland dwell
   The buttercup and the rose.

But best beloved of books, I ween,
   Are those which one perceives
Are hallowed by ashes dropped between
   The yellow, well-thumbed leaves.

For it's here a laugh and it's there a tear,
   Till the treasured book is read;
And the ashes betwixt the pages here
   Tell us of one long dead.

But the gracious presence reappears
   As we read the book again,
And the fragrance of precious, distant years
   Filleth the hearts of men.

Come, pluck with me in my garden nooks
   The posies that bloom for all;
Oh, sweet is the smell of my old, old books
   In their places against the wall!

ONE DAY I GOT A MISSIVE

ONE day I got a missive
　　Writ in a dainty hand,
Which made my manly bosom
　　With vanity expand.
'T was from a "young admirer"
　　Who asked me would I mind
Sending her "favorite poem"
　　"In autograph, and signed."

She craved the boon so sweetly
　　That I had been a churl
Had I repulsed the homage
　　Of this gentle, timid girl;
With bright illuminations
　　I decked the manuscript,
And in my choicest paints and inks
　　My brush and pen I dipt.

Indeed it had been tedious
　　But that a flattered smile
Played on my rugged features
　　And eased my toil the while.
I was assured my poem
　　Would fill her with delight—
I fancied she was pretty—
　　I knew that she was bright!

And for a spell thereafter
　　That unknown damsel's face
With its worshipful expression
　　Pursued me every place;
Meseemed to hear her whisper:
　　"O, thank you, gifted sir,
For the overwhelming honor
　　You so graciously confer!"

But a catalogue from Benjamin's
   Disproves what things meseemed—
Dispels with savage certainty
   The flattering dreams I dreamed;
For that poor "favorite poem,"
   Done and signed in autograph,
Is listed in "Cheap Items"
   At a dollar-and-a-half.

POEMS OF CHILDHOOD

WITH TRUMPET AND DRUM

WITH big tin trumpet and little red drum,
Marching like soldiers, the children come!
   It's this way and that way they circle and file—
      My! but that music of theirs is fine!
   This way and that way, and after a while
      They march straight into this heart of mine!
A sturdy old heart, but it has to succumb
To the blare of that trumpet and beat of that drum!

Come on, little people, from cot and from hall—
This heart it hath welcome and room for you all!
   It will sing you its songs and warm you with love,
      As your dear little arms with my arms intertwine;
   It will rock you away to the dreamland above—
      Oh, a jolly old heart is this old heart of mine,
And jollier still is it bound to become
When you blow that big trumpet and beat that red drum!

So come; though I see not *his* dear little face
And hear not *his* voice in this jubilant place,
   I know he were happy to bid me enshrine
      His memory deep in my heart with your play—
   Ah me! but a love that is sweeter than mine
      Holdeth my boy in its keeping to-day!
And my heart it is lonely—so, little folk, come,
March in and make merry with trumpet and drum!

214

THE SUGAR-PLUM TREE

HAVE you ever heard of the Sugar-Plum Tree?
   'T is a marvel of great renown!
It blooms on the shore of the Lollipop sea
   In the garden of Shut-Eye Town;
The fruit that it bears is so wondrously sweet
   (As those who have tasted it say)
That good little children have only to eat
   Of that fruit to be happy next day.

When you 've got to the tree, you would have a hard time
   To capture the fruit which I sing;
The tree is so tall that no person could climb
   To the boughs where the sugar-plums swing!
But up in that tree sits a chocolate cat,
   And a gingerbread dog prowls below—
And this is the way you contrive to get at
   Those sugar-plums tempting you so:

You say but the word to that gingerbread dog
   And he barks with such terrible zest
That the chocolate cat is at once all agog,
   As her swelling proportions attest.
And the chocolate cat goes cavorting around
   From this leafy limb unto that,
And the sugar-plums tumble, of course, to the ground—
   Hurrah for that chocolate cat!

There are marshmallows, gumdrops, and peppermint canes,
   With stripings of scarlet or gold,
And you carry away of the treasure that rains
   As much as your apron can hold!
So come, little child, cuddle closer to me
   In your dainty white nightcap and gown,
And I 'll rock you away to that Sugar-Plum Tree
   In the garden of Shut-Eye Town.

KRINKEN

KRINKEN was a little child,—
It was summer when he smiled.
Oft the hoary sea and grim
Stretched its white arms out to him,
Calling, "Sun-child, come to me;
Let me warm my heart with thee!"
But the child heard not the sea.

Krinken on the beach one day
Saw a maiden Nis at play;
Fair, and very fair, was she,
Just a little child was he.
"Krinken," said the maiden Nis,
"Let me have a little kiss,—
Just a kiss, and go with me
To the summer-lands that be
Down within the silver sea."

Krinken was a little child,
By the maiden Nis beguiled;
Down into the calling sea
With the maiden Nis went he.

But the sea calls out no more;
It is winter on the shore,—
Winter where that little child
Made sweet summer when he smiled:
Though 't is summer on the sea
Where with maiden Nis went he,—
Summer, summer evermore,—
It is winter on the shore,
Winter, winter evermore.

Of the summer on the deep
Come sweet visions in my sleep;
His fair face lifts from the sea,
His dear voice calls out to me,—
These my dreams of summer be.

Krinken was a little child,
By the maiden Nis beguiled;
Oft the hoary sea and grim
Reached its longing arms to him,

Crying, "Sun-child, come to me;
Let me warm my heart with thee!"
But the sea calls out no more;
It is winter on the shore,—
Winter, cold and dark and wild;
Krinken was a little child,—
It was summer when he smiled;
Down he went into the sea,
And the winter bides with me.
Just a little child was he.

THE NAUGHTY DOLL

My dolly is a dreadful care,—
  Her name is Miss Amandy;
I dress her up and curl her hair,
  And feed her taffy candy.
Yet heedless of the pleading voice
  Of her devoted mother,
She will not wed her mother's choice,
  But says she 'll wed another.

I 'd have her wed the china vase,—
  There is no Dresden rarer;
You might go searching every place
  And never find a fairer.
He is a gentle, pinkish youth,—
  Of that there 's no denying;
Yet when I speak of him, forsooth,
  Amandy falls to crying!

She loves the drum—that 's very plain—
  And scorns the vase so clever;

And weeping, vows she will remain
  A spinster doll forever!
The protestations of the drum
  I am convinced are hollow;
When once distressing times should come,
  How soon would ruin follow!

Yet all in vain the Dresden boy
  From yonder mantel woos her;
A mania for that vulgar toy,
  The noisy drum, imbues her!
In vain I wheel her to and fro,
  And reason with her mildly,—
Her waxen tears in torrents flow,
  Her sawdust heart beats wildly.

I 'm sure that when I 'm big and tall,
  And wear long trailing dresses,
I sha' n't encourage beaux at all
  Till mamma acquiesces;
Our choice will be a suitor then
  As pretty as this vase is,—
Oh, how we 'll hate the noisy men
  With whiskers on their faces!

————

NIGHTFALL IN DORDRECHT

THE mill goes toiling slowly around
  With steady and solemn creak,
And my little one hears in the kindly sound
  The voice of the old mill speak.
While round and round those big white wings
  Grimly and ghostlike creep,
My little one hears that the old mill sings:
  "Sleep, little tulip, sleep!"

The sails are reefed and the nets are drawn,
  And, over his pot of beer,

The fisher, against the morrow's dawn,
  Lustily maketh cheer;
He mocks at the winds that caper along
  From the far-off clamorous deep,—
But we—we love their lullaby song
  Of "Sleep, little tulip, sleep!"

Old dog Fritz in slumber sound
  Groans of the stony mart—
To-morrow how proudly he'll trot you round,
  Hitched to our new milk-cart!
And you shall help me blanket the kine
  And fold the gentle sheep
And set the herring a-soak in brine—
  But now, little tulip, sleep!

A Dream-One comes to button the eyes
  That wearily droop and blink,
While the old mill buffets the frowning skies
  And scolds at the stars that wink;
Over your face the misty wings
  Of that beautiful Dream-One sweep,
And rocking your cradle she softly sings:
  "Sleep, little tulip, sleep!"

INTRY–MINTRY

WILLIE and Bess, Georgie and May—
Once, as these children were hard at play,
An old man, hoary and tottering, came
And watched them playing their pretty game.
  He seemed to wonder, while standing there,
    What the meaning thereof could be—
  Aha, but the old man yearned to share
    Of the little children's innocent glee
As they circled around with laugh and shout
And told their rime at counting out:
  "Intry-mintry, cutrey-corn,

Apple-seed and apple-thorn;
Wire, brier, limber, lock,
Twelve geese in a flock;
Some flew east, some flew west,
Some flew over the cuckoo's nest!'

Willie and Bess, Georgie and May—
Ah, the mirth of that summer-day!
'T was Father Time who had come to share
The innocent joy of those children there;
   He learned betimes the game they played
      And into their sport with them went he—
   How *could* the children have been afraid,
      Since little they recked whom he might be?
They laughed to hear old Father Time
Mumbling that curious nonsense rime
      Of "Intry-mintry, cutrey-corn,
      Apple-seed and apple-thorn;
      Wire, brier, limber, lock,
      Twelve geese in a flock;
      Some flew east, some flew west,
      Some flew over the cuckoo's nest!"

Willie and Bess, Georgie and May,
And joy of summer—where are they?
The grim old man still standeth near
Crooning the song of a far-off year;
   And into the winter I come alone,
      Cheered by that mournful requiem,
   Soothed by the dolorous monotone
      That shall count me off as it counted them—
The solemn voice of old Father Time
Chanting the homely nursery rime
      He learned of the children a summer morn
      When, with "apple-seed and apple-thorn,"
      Life was full of the dulcet cheer
      That bringeth the grace of heaven anear—
      The sound of the little ones hard at play—
      Willie and Bess, Georgie and May.

PITTYPAT AND TIPPYTOE

ALL day long they come and go—
Pittypat and Tippytoe;
    Footprints up and down the hall,
        Playthings scattered on the floor,
    Finger-marks along the wall,
        Telltale smudges on the door—
By these presents you shall know
Pittypat and Tippytoe.

How they riot at their play!
And a dozen times a day
    In they troop, demanding bread—
        Only buttered bread will do,
    And that butter must be spread
        Inches thick with sugar too!
And I never can say "No,
Pittypat and Tippytoe!"

Sometimes there are griefs to soothe,
Sometimes ruffled brows to smooth;
    For (I much regret to say)
        Tippytoe and Pittypat
    Sometimes interrupt their play
        With an internecine spat;
Fie, for shame! to quarrel so—
Pittypat and Tippytoe!

Oh the thousand worrying things
Every day recurrent brings!
    Hands to scrub and hair to brush,
        Search for playthings gone amiss,
    Many a wee complaint to hush,
        Many a little bump to kiss;
Life seems one vain, fleeting show
To Pittypat and Tippytoe!

And when day is at an end,
There are little duds to mend:
  Little frocks are strangely torn,
    Little shoes great holes reveal,
  Little hose, but one day worn,
    Rudely yawn at toe and heel!
Who but *you* could work such woe,
Pittypat and Tippytoe?

But when comes this thought to me:
"Some there are that childless be,"
  Stealing to their little beds,
    With a love I cannot speak,
  Tenderly I stroke their heads—
    Fondly kiss each velvet cheek.
God help those who do not know
A Pittypat or Tippytoe!

On the floor and down the hall,
Rudely smutched upon the wall,
  There are proofs in every kind
    Of the havoc they have wrought,
  And upon my heart you'd find
    Just such trade-marks, if you sought;
Oh, how glad I am 't is so,
Pittypat and Tippytoe!

———

BALOW, MY BONNIE

Hush, bonnie, dinna greit;
Moder will rocke her sweete,—
    Balow, my boy!
When that his toile ben done,
Daddie will come anone,—
Hush thee, my lyttel one;
    Balow, my boy!

Gin thou dost sleepe, perchaunce
Fayries will come to daunce,—
    Balow, my boy!
Oft hath thy moder seene
Moonlight and mirkland queene
Daunce on thy slumbering een,—
    Balow, my boy!

Then droned a bomblebee
Saftly this songe to thee:
    "Balow, my boy!"
And a wee heather bell,
Pluckt from a fayry dell,
Chimed thee this rune hersell:
    "Balow, my boy!"

Soe, bonnie, dinna greit;
Moder doth rocke her sweete,—
    Balow, my boy!
Give mee thy lyttel hand,
Moder will hold it and
Lead thee to balow land,—
    Balow, my boy!

THE HAWTHORNE CHILDREN

THE Hawthorne children—seven in all—
    Are famous friends of mine,
And with what pleasure I recall
How, years ago, one gloomy fall,
    I took a tedious railway line
And journeyed by slow stages down
Unto that sleepy seaport town
    (Albeit one worth seeing),
  Where Hildegarde, John, Henry, Fred,

And Beatrix and Gwendolen
And she that was the baby then—
 These famous seven, as aforesaid,
  Lived, moved, and had their being.

The Hawthorne children gave me such
 A welcome by the sea,
That the eight of us were soon in touch,
And though their mother marvelled much,
 Happy as larks were we!
Egad I was a boy again
With Henry, John, and Gwendolen!
 And, oh! the funny capers
 I cut with Hildegarde and Fred!
The pranks we heedless children played,
The deafening, awful noise we made—
 'T would shock my family, if they read
  About it in the papers!

The Hawthorne children all were smart;
 The girls, as I recall,
Had comprehended every art
Appealing to the head and heart,
 The boys were gifted, all;
'T was Hildegarde who showed me how
To hitch the horse and milk a cow
 And cook the best of suppers;
 With Beatrix upon the sands
I sprinted daily, and was beat,
While Henry stumped me to the feat
 Of walking round upon my hands
  Instead of on my "uppers."

The Hawthorne children liked me best
 Of evenings, after tea;
For then, by general request,
I spun them yarns about the west—
 And *all* involving Me!

I represented how I 'd slain
The bison on the gore-smeared plain,
 And divers tales of wonder
I told of how I 'd fought and bled
In Injun scrimmages galore,
Till Mrs. Hawthorne quoth, "No more!"
 And packed her darlings off to bed
  To dream of blood and thunder!

They must have changed a deal since then:
 The misses tall and fair
And those three lusty, handsome men,
Would they be girls and boys again
 Were I to happen there,
Down in that spot beside the sea
Where we made such tumultuous glee
 In dull autumnal weather?
  Ah me! the years go swiftly by,
And yet how fondly I recall
The week when we were children all—
 Dear Hawthorne children, you and I—
 Just eight of us, together!

LITTLE BLUE PIGEON

(JAPANESE LULLABY)

SLEEP, little pigeon, and fold your wings—
 Little blue pigeon with velvet eyes;
Sleep to the singing of mother-bird swinging—
 Swinging the nest where her little one lies.

Away out yonder I see a star—
 Silvery star with a tinkling song;
To the soft dew falling I hear it calling—
 Calling and tinkling the night along.

In through the window a moonbeam comes—
  Little gold moonbeam with misty wings;
All silently creeping, it asks: "Is he sleeping—
  Sleeping and dreaming while mother sings?"

Up from the sea there floats the sob
  Of the waves that are breaking upon the shore,
As though they were groaning in anguish, and moaning—
  Bemoaning the ship that shall come no more.

But sleep, little pigeon, and fold your wings—
  Little blue pigeon with mournful eyes;
Am I not singing?—see, I am swinging—
  Swinging the nest where my darling lies.

THE LYTTEL BOY

SOME time there ben a lyttel boy
  That wolde not renne and play,
And helpless like that little tyke
  Ben allwais in the way.
"Goe, make you merrie with the rest,"
  His weary moder cried;
But with a frown he catcht her gown
  And hong untill her side.

That boy did love his moder well,
  Which spake him faire, I ween;
He loved to stand and hold her hand
  And ken her with his een;
His cosset bleated in the croft,
  His toys unheeded lay,—
He wolde not goe, but, tarrying soe,
  Ben allwais in the way.

Godde loveth children and doth gird
  His throne with soche as these,

And he doth smile in plaisaunce while
  They cluster at his knees;
And some time, when he looked on earth
  And watched the bairns at play,
He kenned with joy a lyttel boy
  Ben allwais in the way.

And then a moder felt her heart
  How that it ben to-torne,
She kissed eche day till she ben gray
  The shoon he use to worn;
No bairn let hold untill her gown
  Nor played upon the floore,—
Godde's was the joy; a lyttel boy
  Ben in the way no more!

TEENY–WEENY

EVERY evening, after tea,
Teeny-Weeny comes to me,
And, astride my willing knee,
  Plies his lash and rides away;
Though that palfrey, all too spare,
Finds his burden hard to bear,
Teeny-Weeny doesn't care;
  He commands, and I obey!

First it 's trot, and gallop then;
Now it 's back to trot again;
Teeny-Weeny likes it when
  He is riding fierce and fast.
Then his dark eyes brighter grow
And his cheeks are all aglow:
"More!" he cries, and never "Whoa!"
  Till the horse breaks down at last.

Oh, the strange and lovely sights
Teeny-Weeny sees of nights,

As he makes those famous flights
  On that wondrous horse of his!
Oftentimes before he knows,
Wearylike his eyelids close,
And, still smiling, off he goes
  Where the land of By-low is.

There he sees the folk of fay
Hard at ring-a-rosie play,
And he hears those fairies say:
  "Come, let 's chase him to and fro!"
But, with a defiant shout,
Teeny puts that host to rout;
Of this tale I make no doubt,
  Every night he tells it so.

So I feel a tender pride
In my boy who dares to ride
That fierce horse of his astride,
  Off into those misty lands;
And as on my breast he lies,
Dreaming in that wondrous wise,
I caress his folded eyes,
  Pat his little dimpled hands.

On a time he went away,
Just a little while to stay,
And I 'm not ashamed to say
  I was very lonely then;
Life without him was so sad,
You can fancy I was glad
And made merry when I had
  Teeny-Weeny back again!

So of evenings, after tea,
When he toddles up to me
And goes tugging at my knee,
  You should hear his palfrey neigh!

You should see him prance and shy,
When, with an exulting cry,
Teeny-Weeny, vaulting high,
    Plies his lash and rides away!

NELLIE

His listening soul hears no echo of battle,
    No pæan of triumph nor welcome of fame;
But down through the years comes a little one's prattle,
    And softly he murmurs her idolized name.
And it seems as if now at his heart she were clinging
    As she clung in those dear, distant years to his knee;
He sees her fair face, and he hears her sweet singing—
    And Nellie is coming from over the sea.

While each patriot's hope stays the fulness of sorrow,
    While our eyes are bedimmed and our voices are low,
He dreams of the daughter who comes with the morrow
    Like an angel come back from the dear long ago.
Ah, what to him now is a nation's emotion,
    And what for our love or our grief careth he?
A swift-speeding ship is a-sail on the ocean,
    And Nellie is coming from over the sea!

O daughter—my daughter! when Death stands before me
    And beckons me off to that far misty shore,
Let me see your loved form bending tenderly o'er me,
    And feel your dear kiss on my lips as of yore.
In the grace of your love all my anguish abating,
    I'll bear myself bravely and proudly as he,
And know the sweet peace that hallowed his waiting
    When Nellie was coming from over the sea.

NORSE LULLABY

The sky is dark and the hills are white
    As the storm-king speeds from the north to-night;
And this is the song the storm-king sings,
As over the world his cloak he flings:
    "Sleep, sleep, little one, sleep";
He rustles his wings and gruffly sings:
    "Sleep, little one, sleep."

On yonder mountain-side a vine
Clings at the foot of a mother pine;
The tree bends over the trembling thing,
And only the vine can hear her sing:
    "Sleep, sleep, little one, sleep—
What shall you fear when I am here?
    Sleep, little one, sleep."

The king may sing in his bitter flight,
The tree may croon to the vine to-night,
But the little snowflake at my breast
Liketh the song *I* sing the best—
    Sleep, sleep, little one, sleep;
Weary thou art, a-next my heart
    Sleep, little one, sleep.

GRANDMA'S PRAYER

I pray that, risen from the dead,
    I may in glory stand—
A crown, perhaps, upon my head,
    But a needle in my hand.

I 've never learned to sing or play,
    So let no harp be mine;
From birth unto my dying day,
    Plain sewing 's been my line.

Therefore, accustomed to the end
  To plying useful stitches,
I 'll be content if asked to mend
  The little angels' breeches.

SOME TIME

LAST night, my darling, as you slept,
  I thought I heard you sigh,
And to your little crib I crept,
  And watched a space thereby;
Then, bending down, I kissed your brow—
  For, oh! I love you so—
You are too young to know it now,
  But some time you shall know.

Some time, when, in a darkened place
  Where others come to weep,
Your eyes shall see a weary face
  Calm in eternal sleep;
The speechless lips, the wrinkled brow,
  The patient smile may show—
You are too young to know it now,
  But some time you shall know.

Look backward, then, into the years,
  And see me here to-night—
See, O my darling! how my tears
  Are falling as I write;
And feel once more upon your brow
  The kiss of long ago—
You are too young to know it now,
  But some time you shall know.

THE FIRE-HANGBIRD'S NEST

As I am sitting in the sun upon the porch to-day,
I look with wonder at the elm that stands across the way;
I say and mean "with wonder," for now it seems to me
That elm is not as tall as years ago it used to be!
The old fire-hangbird 's built her nest therein for many springs-
High up amid the sportive winds the curious cradle swings,
But not so high as when a little boy I did my best
To scale that elm and carry off the old fire-hangbird's nest!

The Hubbard boys had tried in vain to reach the homely prize
That dangled from that upper outer twig in taunting wise,
And once, when Deacon Turner's boy had almost grasped the
    limb,
He fell! and had to have a doctor operate on him!
Philetus Baker broke his leg and Orrin Root his arm—
But what of that? The danger gave the sport a special charm!
The Bixby and the Cutler boys, the Newtons and the rest
Ran every risk to carry off the old fire-hangbird's nest!

I can remember that I used to knee my trousers through,
That mother used to wonder how my legs got black and blue,
And how she used to talk to me and make stern threats when
    she
Discovered that my hobby was the nest in yonder tree;
How, as she patched my trousers or greased my purple legs,
She told me 't would be wicked to destroy a hangbird's eggs,
And then she 'd call on father and on gran'pa to attest
That they, as boys, had never robbed an old fire-hangbird's nest!

Yet all those years I coveted the trophy flaunting there,
While, as it were in mockery of my abject despair,
The old fire-hangbird confidently used to come and go
As if she were indifferent to the bandit horde below!
And sometimes clinging to her nest we thought we heard her chide
The callow brood whose cries betrayed the fear that reigned in-
    side:
"Hush, little dears! all profitless shall be their wicked quest—
I knew my business when I built the old fire-hangbird's nest!"

For many, very many years that mother-bird has come
To rear her pretty little brood within that cosey home.
She is the selfsame bird of old—I 'm certain it is she—
Although the chances are that she has quite forgotten me.
Just as of old that prudent, crafty bird of compound name
(And in parenthesis I 'll say her nest is still the same);
Just as of old the passion, too, that fires the youthful breast
To climb unto and comprehend the old fire-hangbird's nest!

I like to see my old-time friend swing in that ancient tree,
And, if the elm 's as tall and sturdy as it *used* to be,
I 'm sure that many a year that nest shall in the breezes blow,
For boys are n't what they used to be a forty years ago!
The elm looks shorter than it did when brother Rufe and I
Beheld with envious hearts that trophy flaunted from on high;
He writes that in the city where he 's living 'way out West
His little boys have never seen an old fire-hangbird's nest!

Poor little chaps! how lonesomelike their city life must be—
I wish they 'd come and live awhile in this old house with me!
They 'd have the honest friends and healthful sports I used to know
When brother Rufe and I were boys a forty years ago.
So, when they grew from romping lads to busy, useful men,
They could recall with proper pride their country life again;
And of those recollections of their youth I 'm sure the best
Would be of how they sought in vain the old fire-hangbird's nest!

BUTTERCUP, POPPY, FORGET-ME-NOT

BUTTERCUP, Poppy, Forget-me-not—
These three bloomed in a garden spot;
And once, all merry with song and play,
A little one heard three voices say:
    "Shine and shadow, summer and spring,
      O thou child with the tangled hair
    And laughing eyes! we three shall bring
      Each an offering passing fair."
The little one did not understand,
But they bent and kissed the dimpled hand.

Buttercup gambolled all day long,
Sharing the little one's mirth and song;
Then, stealing along on misty gleams,
Poppy came bearing the sweetest dreams.
    Playing and dreaming—and that was all
        Till once a sleeper would not awake:
    Kissing the little face under the pall,
        We thought of the words the third flower spake;
And we found betimes in a hallowed spot
The solace and peace of Forget-me-not.

Buttercup shareth the joy of day,
Glinting with gold the hours of play;
Bringeth the Poppy sweet repose,
When the hands would fold and the eyes would close;
    And after it all—the play and the sleep
        Of a little life—what cometh then?
    To the hearts that ache and the eyes that weep
        A new flower bringeth God's peace again.
Each one serveth its tender lot—
Buttercup, Poppy, Forget-me-not.

WYNKEN, BLYNKEN, AND NOD

(DUTCH LULLABY)

WYNKEN, Blynken, and Nod one night
    Sailed off in a wooden shoe—
Sailed on a river of crystal light,
    Into a sea of dew.
"Where are you going, and what do you wish?"
    The old moon asked the three.
"We have come to fish for the herring fish
    That live in this beautiful sea;
    Nets of silver and gold have we!"
            Said Wynken,
            Blynken,
            And Nod.

The old moon laughed and sang a song,
 As they rocked in the wooden shoe,
And the wind that sped them all night long
 Ruffled the waves of dew.
The little stars were the herring fish
 That lived in that beautiful sea—
"Now cast your nets wherever you wish—
 Never afeard are we";
So cried the stars to the fishermen three:
   Wynken,
   Blynken,
   And Nod.

All night long their nets they threw
 To the stars in the twinkling foam—
Then down from the skies came the wooden shoe,
 Bringing the fishermen home;
'T was all so pretty a sail it seemed
 As if it could not be,
And some folks thought 't was a dream they 'd dreamed
 Of sailing that beautiful sea—
But I shall name you the fishermen three:
   Wynken,
   Blynken,
   And Nod.

Wynken and Blynken are two little eyes,
 And Nod is a little head,
And the wooden shoe that sailed the skies
 Is a wee one's trundle-bed.
So shut your eyes while mother sings
 Of wonderful sights that be,
And you shall see the beautiful things
 As you rock in the misty sea,
Where the old shoe rocked the fishermen three:
   Wynken,
   Blynken,
   And Nod.

GOLD AND LOVE FOR DEARIE

(CORNISH LULLABY)

OUT on the mountain over the town,
  All night long, all night long,
The trolls go up and the trolls go down,
  Bearing their packs and singing a song;
And this is the song the hill-folk croon,
As they trudge in the light of the misty moon—
This is ever their dolorous tune:
    "Gold, gold! ever more gold—
      Bright red gold for dearie!"

Deep in the hill a father delves
  All night long, all night long;
None but the peering, furtive elves
  Sees his toil and hears his song;
Merrily ever the cavern rings
As merrily ever his pick he swings,
And merrily ever this song he sings:
    "Gold, gold! ever more gold—
      Bright red gold for dearie!"

Mother is rocking thy lowly bed
  All night long, all night long,
Happy to smooth thy curly head,
  To hold thy hand and to sing *her* song:
'T is not of the hill-folk dwarfed and old,
Nor the song of thy father, stanch and bold,
And the burthen it beareth is not of gold:
    But it 's "Love, love! nothing but love—
      Mother's love for dearie!"

THE PEACE OF CHRISTMAS–TIME

DEAREST, how hard it is to say
    That all is for the best,
Since, sometimes, in a grievous way
    God's will is manifest.

See with what hearty, noisy glee
    Our little ones to-night
Dance round and round our Christmas tree
    With pretty toys bedight.

Dearest, one voice they may not hear,
    One face they may not see—
Ah, what of all this Christmas cheer
    Cometh to you and me?

Cometh before our misty eyes
    That other little face,
And we clasp, in tender, reverent wise,
    That love in the old embrace.

Dearest, the Christ-child walks to-night,
    Bringing his peace to men,
And he bringeth to you and to me the light
    Of the old, old years again.

Bringeth the peace of long ago,
    When a wee one clasped your knee
And lisped of the morrow—dear one, you know—
    And here come back is he!

Dearest, 't is sometimes hard to say
    That all is for the best,
For, often, in a grievous way
    God's will is manifest.

But in the grace of this holy night
  That bringeth us back our child,
Let us see that the ways of God are right,
  And so be reconciled.

TO A LITTLE BROOK

You 're not so big as you were then,
  O little brook!—
I mean those hazy summers when
We boys roamed, full of awe, beside
Your noisy, foaming, tumbling tide,
And wondered if it could be true
That there were bigger brooks than you,
  O mighty brook, O peerless brook!

All up and down this reedy place
  Where lives the brook,
We angled for the furtive dace;
The redwing-blackbird did his best
To make us think he 'd built his nest
Hard by the stream, when, like as not,
He 'd hung it in a secret spot
  Far from the brook, the telltale brook!

And often, when the noontime heat
  Parboiled the brook,
We 'd draw our boots and swing our feet
Upon the waves that, in their play,
Would tag us last and scoot away;
And mother never seemed to know
What burnt our legs and chapped them so—
  But father guessed it was the brook!

And Fido—how he loved to swim
  The cooling brook,
Whenever we 'd throw sticks for him;
And how we boys *did* wish that we

Could only swim as good as he—
Why, Daniel Webster never was
Recipient of such great applause
    As Fido, battling with the brook!

But once—O most unhappy day
    For you, my brook!—
Came Cousin Sam along that way;
And, having lived a spell out West,
Where creeks are n't counted much at best,
He neither waded, swam, nor leapt,
But, with superb indifference, *stept*
    Across that brook—our mighty brook!

Why do you scamper on your way,
    You little brook,
When I come back to you to-day?
Is it because you flee the grass
That lunges at you as you pass,
As if, in playful mood, it would
Tickle the truant if it could,
    You chuckling brook—you saucy brook?

Or is it you no longer know—
    You fickle brook—
The honest friend of long ago?
The years that kept us twain apart
Have changed my face, but not my heart—
Many and sore those years, and yet
I fancied you could not forget
    That happy time, my playmate brook!

Oh, sing again in artless glee,
    My little brook,
The song you used to sing for me—
The song that's lingered in my ears
So soothingly these many years;
My grief shall be forgotten when
I hear your tranquil voice again
    And that sweet song, dear little brook!

CROODLIN' DOO

Ho, pretty bee, did you see my croodlin' doo?
   Ho, little lamb, is she jinkin' on the lea?
   Ho, bonnie fairy, bring my dearie back to me—
Got a lump o' sugar an' a posie for you,
Only bring me back my wee, wee croodlin' doo!

Why! here you are, my little croodlin' doo!
   Looked in er cradle, but did n't find you there—
   Looked f'r my wee, wee croodlin' doo ever'where;
Be'n kind lonesome all er day withouten you—
Where you be'n, my teeny, wee, wee croodlin' doo?

Now you go balow, my little croodlin' doo;
   Now you go rockaby ever so far,—
   Rockaby, rockaby up to the star
That 's winkin' an' blinkin' an' singin' to you,
As you go balow, my wee, wee croodlin' doo!

LITTLE MISTRESS SANS-MERCI

LITTLE Mistress Sans-Merci
Fareth world-wide, fancy free:
   Trotteth cooing to and fro,
     And her cooing is command—
   Never ruled there yet, I trow,
     Mightier despot in the land.
And my heart it lieth where
Mistress Sans-Merci doth fare.

Little Mistress Sans-Merci—
She hath made a slave of me!
   "Go," she biddeth, and I go—
     "Come," and I am fain to come

Never mercy doth she show,
　　Be she wroth or frolicsome,
Yet am I content to be
Slave to Mistress Sans-Merci!

Little Mistress Sans-Merci
Hath become so dear to me
　　That I count as passing sweet
　　　　All the pain her moods impart,
　　And I bless the little feet
　　　　That go trampling on my heart:
Ah, how lonely life would be
But for little Sans-Merci!

Little Mistress Sans-Merci,
Cuddle close this night to me,
　　And the heart, which all day long
　　　　Ruthless thou hast trod upon,
　　Shall outpour a soothing song
　　　　For its best belovèd one—
All its tenderness for thee,
Little Mistress Sans-Merci!

LONG AGO

I ONCE knew all the birds that came
　　And nested in our orchard trees,
For every flower I had a name—
　　My friends were woodchucks, toads, and bees;
I knew where thrived in yonder glen
　　What plants would soothe a stone-bruised toe—
Oh, I was very learned then,
　　But that was very long ago.

I knew the spot upon the hill
　　Where checkerberries could be found,
I knew the rushes near the mill
　　Where pickerel lay that weighed a pound!

I knew the wood—the very tree
  Where lived the poaching, saucy crow,
And all the woods and crows knew me—
  But that was very long ago.

And pining for the joys of youth,
  I tread the old familiar spot
Only to learn this solemn truth:
  I have forgotten, am forgot.
Yet here 's this youngster at my knee
  Knows all the things I used to know;
To think I once was wise as he!—
  But that was very long ago.

I know it 's folly to complain
  Of whatsoe'er the fates decree,
Yet, were not wishes all in vain,
  I tell you what my wish should be:
I 'd wish to be a boy again,
  Back with the friends I used to know.
For I was, oh, so happy then—
  But that was very long ago!

———

IN THE FIRELIGHT

THE fire upon the hearth is low,
    And there is stillness everywhere,
    And, like wing'd spirits, here and there
The firelight shadows fluttering go.
And as the shadows round me creep,
    A childish treble breaks the gloom,
    And softly from a further room
Comes: "Now I lay me down to sleep."

And, somehow, with that little pray'r
    And that sweet treble in my ears,
    My thought goes back to distant years,
And lingers with a dear one there;

And as I hear my child's amen,
    My mother's faith comes back to me—
    Crouched at her side I seem to be,
And mother holds my hands again.

Oh, for an hour in that dear place—
    Oh, for the peace of that dear time—
    Oh, for that childish trust sublime—
Oh, for a glimpse of mother's face!
Yet, as the shadows round me creep,
    I do not seem to be alone—
    Sweet magic of that treble tone
And "Now I lay me down to sleep!"

COBBLER AND STORK

COBBLER

Stork, I am justly wroth,
    For thou hast wronged me sore;
The ash roof-tree that shelters thee
    Shall shelter thee no more!

STORK

Full fifty years I 've dwelt
    Upon this honest tree,
And long ago (as people know!)
    I brought thy father thee.
What hail hath chilled thy heart,
    That thou shouldst bid me go?
Speak out, I pray—then I 'll away,
    Since thou commandest so.

COBBLER

Thou tellest of the time
    When, wheeling from the west,
This hut thou sought'st and one thou brought'st
    Unto a mother's breast.

I was the wretched child
    Was fetched that dismal morn—
'T were better die than be (as I)
    To life of misery born!
And hadst thou borne me on
    Still farther up the town,
A king I 'd be of high degree,
    And wear a golden crown!
For yonder lives the prince
    Was brought that selfsame day:
How happy he, while—look at me!
    I toil my life away!
And see my little boy—
    To what estate he 's born!
Why, when I die no hoard leave I
    But poverty and scorn.
And *thou* hast done it all—
    I might have been a king
And ruled in state, but for thy hate,
    Thou base, perfidious thing!

STORK

Since, cobbler, thou dost speak
    Of one thou lovest well,
Hear of that king what grievous thing
    This very morn befell.
Whilst round thy homely bench
    Thy well-belovèd played,
In yonder hall beneath a pall
    A little one was laid;
Thy well-belovèd's face
    Was rosy with delight,
But 'neath that pall in yonder hall
    The little face is white;
Whilst by a merry voice
    Thy soul is filled with cheer,
Another weeps for one that sleeps
    All mute and cold anear;
One father hath his hope,
    And one is childless now;

He wears a crown and rules a town—
　Only a cobbler *thou!*
Wouldst thou exchange thy lot
　At price of such a woe?
I'll nest no more above thy door,
　But, as thou bidst me, go.

COBBLER

Nay, stork! thou shalt remain—
　I mean not what I said;
Good neighbors we must always be,
　So make thy home o'erhead.
I would not change my bench
　For any monarch's throne,
Nor sacrifice at any price
　My darling and my own!
Stork! on my roof-tree bide,
　That, seeing thee anear,
I'll thankful be God sent by thee
　Me and my darling here!

———

"LOLLYBY, LOLLY, LOLLYBY"

LAST night, whiles that the curfew bell ben ringing,
I heard a moder to her dearie singing
　　　"Lollyby, lolly, lollyby";
And presently that chylde did cease hys weeping,
And on his moder's breast did fall a-sleeping
　　　To "lolly, lolly, lollyby."

Faire ben the chylde unto his moder clinging,
But fairer yet the moder's gentle singing—
　　　"Lollyby, lolly, lollyby";
And angels came and kisst the dearie smiling
In dreems while him hys moder ben beguiling
　　　With "lolly, lolly, lollyby."

Then to my harte saies I: "Oh, that thy beating
Colde be assuaged by some sweete voice repeating
    'Lollyby, lolly, lollyby';
That like this lyttel chylde I, too, ben sleeping
With plaisaunt phantasies about me creeping,
    To 'lolly, lolly, lollyby'!"

Some time—mayhap when curfew bells are ringing—
A weary harte shall heare straunge voices singing
    "Lollyby, lolly, lollyby";
Some time, mayhap, with Chryst's love round me streaming.
I shall be lulled into eternal dreeming,
    With "lolly, lolly, lollyby."

A VALENTINE

Your gran'ma, in her youth, was quite
    As blithe a little maid as you.
And, though her hair is snowy white,
    Her eyes still have their maiden blue,
And on her cheeks, as fair as thine,
    Methinks a girlish blush would glow
If she recalled the valentine
    She got, ah! many years ago.

A valorous youth loved gran'ma then,
    And wooed her in that auld lang syne;
And first he told his secret when
    He sent the maid that valentine.
No perfumed page nor sheet of gold
    Was that first hint of love he sent,
But with the secret gran'pa told—
    "I love you"—gran'ma was content.

Go, ask your gran'ma, if you will,
    If—though her head be bowed and gray—
If—though her feeble pulse be chill—
    True love abideth not for aye;

By that quaint portrait on the wall,
  That smiles upon her from above,
Methinks your gran'ma can recall
  The sweet divinity of love.

Dear Elsie, here's no page of gold—
  No sheet embossed with cunning art—
But here's a solemn pledge of old:
  "I love you, love, with all my heart."
And if in what I send you here
  You read not all of love expressed,
Go—go to gran'ma, Elsie dear,
  And she will tell you all the rest!

———

AT THE DOOR

I THOUGHT myself, indeed, secure,
  So fast the door, so firm the lock;
But, lo! he toddling comes to lure
  My parent ear with timorous knock.

My heart were stone could it withstand
  The sweetness of my baby's plea,—
That timorous, baby knocking and
  "Please let me in,—it's only me."

I threw aside the unfinished book,
  Regardless of its tempting charms,
And, opening wide the door, I took
  My laughing darling in my arms.

Who knows but in Eternity,
  I, like a truant child, shall wait
The glories of a life to be,
  Beyond the Heavenly Father's gate?

And will that Heavenly Father heed
  The truant's supplicating cry,
As at the outer door I plead,
  " 'T is J O Father! only I "?

HI–SPY

STRANGE that the city thoroughfare,
  Noisy and bustling all the day,
Should with the night renounce its care
  And lend itself to children's play!

Oh, girls are girls, and boys are boys,
  And have been so since Abel's birth,
And shall be so till dolls and toys
  Are with the children swept from earth.

The self-same sport that crowns the day
  Of many a Syrian shepherd's son,
Beguiles the little lads at play
  By night in stately Babylon.

I hear their voices in the street,
  Yet 't is so different now from then!
Come, brother! from your winding-sheet,
  And let us two be boys again!

LITTLE BOY BLUE

THE little toy dog is covered with dust,
  But sturdy and stanch he stands;
And the little toy soldier is red with rust,
  And his musket moulds in his hands.
Time was when the little toy dog was new,
  And the soldier was passing fair;
And that was the time when our Little Boy Blue
  Kissed them and put them there.

"Now, don't you go till I come," he said,
  "And don't you make any noise!"
So, toddling off to his trundle-bed,
  He dreamt of the pretty toys;
And, as he was dreaming, an angel song
  Awakened our Little Boy Blue—
Oh! the years are many, the years are long,
  But the little toy friends are true!

Ay, faithful to Little Boy Blue they stand,
  Each in the same old place—
Awaiting the touch of a little hand,
  The smile of a little face;
And they wonder, as waiting the long years through
  In the dust of that little chair,
What has become of our Little Boy Blue,
  Since he kissed them and put them there.

———

FATHER'S LETTER

I 'M going to write a letter to our oldest boy who went
Out West last spring to practise law and run for president;
I 'll tell him all the gossip I guess he 'd like to hear,
For he has n't seen the home-folks for going on a year!
Most generally it 's Marthy does the writing, but as she
Is suffering with a felon, why, the job devolves on me—
So, when the supper things are done and put away to-night,
I 'll draw my boots and shed my coat and settle down to write.

I 'll tell him crops are looking up, with prospects big for corn,
That, fooling with the barnyard gate, the off-ox hurt his horn;
That the Templar lodge is doing well—Tim Bennett joined last
    week
When the prohibition candidate for Congress came to speak;
That the old gray woodchuck 's living still down in the pasture-lot,
A-wondering what 's become of little William, like as not!
Oh, yes, there 's lots of pleasant things and no bad news to tell,
Except that old Bill Graves was sick, but now he 's up and well.

Cy Cooper says—(but I 'll not pass my word that it is so,
For Cy he is some punkins on spinning yarns, you know)—
He says that, since the freshet, the pickerel are so thick
In Baker's pond you can wade in and kill 'em with a stick!
The Hubbard girls are teaching school, and Widow Cutler's Bill
Has taken Eli Baxter's place in Luther Eastman's mill;
Old Deacon Skinner's dog licked Deacon Howard's dog last week,
And now there are two lambkins in one flock that will not speak.

The yellow rooster froze his feet, a-wadin' through the snow
And now he leans ag'in' the fence when he starts in to crow;
The chestnut colt that was so skittish when *he* went away—
I 've broke him to the sulky and I drive him every day!
We 've got pink window curtains for the front spare-room up-
stairs,
And Lizzie's made new covers for the parlor lounge and chairs;
We 've roofed the barn and braced the elm that has the hangbird's
nest—
Oh, there 's been lots of changes since our William went out West!

Old Uncle Enos Packard is getting mighty gay—
He gave Miss Susan Birchard a peach the other day!
His late lamented Sarah hain't been buried quite a year,
So his purring 'round Miss Susan causes criticism here.
At the last donation party, the minister opined
That, if he 'd half suspicioned what was coming, he 'd resigned;
For, though they brought him slippers like he was a centipede,
His pantry was depleted by the consequential feed!

These are the things I 'll write him—our boy that 's in the West;
And I 'll tell him how we miss him—his mother and the rest;
Why, we never have an apple-pie that mother does n't say:
"*He* liked it so—I wish that he could have a piece to-day!"
I 'll tell him we are prospering, and hope he is the same—
That we hope he 'll have no trouble getting on to wealth and
fame;
And just before I write "good-by from father and the rest,"
I 'll say that "mother sends her love." and that will please him
best.

For when *I* went away from home, the weekly news I heard
Was nothing to the tenderness I found in that one word—
The sacred name of mother—why, even now as then,
The thought brings back the saintly face, the gracious love again
And in my bosom seems to come a peace that is divine,
As if an angel spirit communed awhile with mine;
And one man's heart is strengthened by the message from above,
And earth seems nearer heaven when "mother sends her love."

JEWISH LULLABY

My harp is on the willow-tree,
Else would I sing, O love, to thee
   A song of long-ago—
Perchance the song that Miriam sung
Ere yet Judea's heart was wrung
   By centuries of woe.

I ate my crust in tears to-day,
As scourged I went upon my way—
   And yet my darling smiled;
Ay, beating at my breast, he laughed—
My anguish curdled not the draught—
   'T was sweet with love, my child!

The shadow of the centuries lies
Deep in thy dark and mournful eyes—
   But, hush! and close them now;
And in the dreams that thou shalt dream
The light of other days shall seem
   To glorify thy brow!

Our harp is on the willow-tree—
I have no song to sing to thee,
   As shadows round us roll;
But, hush and sleep, and thou shalt hear
Jehovah's voice that speaks to cheer
   Judea's fainting soul!

OUR WHIPPINGS

COME, Harvey, let us sit awhile and talk about the times
Before you went to selling clothes and I to peddling rhymes—
The days when we were little boys, as naughty little boys
As ever worried home-folks with their everlasting noise!
Egad! and, were we so disposed, I 'll venture we could show
The scars of wallopings we got some forty years ago;
What wallopings I mean I think I need not specify—
Mother's whippings did n't hurt, but father's! oh, my!

The way that we played hookey those many years ago—
We 'd rather give 'most anything than have our children know!
The thousand naughty things we did, the thousand fibs we told—
Why, thinking of them makes my Presbyterian blood run cold!
How often Deacon Sabine Morse remarked if we were his
He 'd tan our "pesky little hides until the blisters riz!"
It 's many a hearty thrashing to that Deacon Morse we owe—
Mother's whippings did n't count—father's did, though!

We used to sneak off swimmin' in those careless, boyish days,
And come back home of evenings with our necks and backs ablaze;
How mother used to wonder why our clothes were full of sand,
But father, having been a boy, appeared to understand.
And, after tea, he 'd beckon us to join him in the shed
Where he'd proceed to tinge our backs a deeper, darker red;
Say what we will of mother's, there is none will controvert
The proposition that our father's lickings always hurt!

For mother was by nature so forgiving and so mild
That she inclined to spare the rod although she spoiled the child;
And when at last in self-defence she had to whip us, she
Appeared to feel those whippings a great deal more than we!
But how we bellowed and took on, as if we 'd like to die—
Poor mother really thought she hurt, and that 's what made *her* cry!
Then how we youngsters snickered as out the door we slid,
For mother's whippings never hurt, though father's always did.

In after years poor father simmered down to five feet four,
But in our youth he seemed to us in height eight feet or more!
Oh, how we shivered when he quoth in cold, suggestive tone:
"I 'll see you in the woodshed after supper all alone!"
Oh, how the legs and arms and dust and trouser buttons flew—
What florid vocalisms marked that vesper interview!
Yes, after all this lapse of years, I feelingly assert,
With all respect to mother, it was father's whippings hurt.

The little boy experiencing that tinglin' neath his vest
Is often loath to realize that all is for the best;
Yet, when the boy gets older, he pictures with delight
The buffetings of childhood—as we do here to-night.
The years, the gracious years, have smoothed and beautified the
    ways
That to our little feet seemed all too rugged in the days
Before you went to selling clothes and I to peddling rhymes—
So, Harvey, let us sit awhile and think upon those times.

THE ARMENIAN MOTHER

I WAS a mother, and I weep;
    The night is come—the day is sped—
The night of woe profound, for, oh,
    My little golden son is dead!

The pretty rose that bloomed anon
    Upon my mother breast, they stole;
They let the dove I nursed with love
    Fly far away—so sped my soul!

That falcon Death swooped down upon
    My sweet-voiced turtle as he sung;
'T is hushed and dark where soared the lark,
    And so, and so my heart was wrung!

Before my eyes, they sent the hail
  Upon my green pomegranate-tree—
Upon the bough where only now
  A rosy apple bent to me.

They shook my beauteous almond-tree,
  Beating its glorious bloom to death—
They strewed it round upon the ground,
  And mocked its fragrant dying breath.

I was a mother, and I weep;
  I seek the rose where nestleth none—
No more is heard the singing bird—
  I have no little golden son!

So fall the shadows over me,
  The blighted garden, lonely nest.
Reach down in love, O God above!
  And fold my darling to thy breast.

HEIGHO, MY DEARIE

(ORKNEY LULLABY)

A MOONBEAM floateth from the skies,
    Whispering: "Heigho, my dearie;
I would spin a web before your eyes—
A beautiful web of silver light
Wherein is many a wondrous sight
Of a radiant garden leagues away,
Where the softly tinkling lilies sway
And the snow-white lambkins are at play—
    Heigho, my dearie!"

A brownie stealeth from the vine,
    Singing: "Heigho, my dearie;
And will you hear this song of mine—

A song of the land of murk and mist
Where bideth the bud the dew hath kist?
Then let the moonbeam's web of light
Be spun before thee silvery white,
And I shall sing the livelong night—
    Heigho, my dearie!"

The night wind speedeth from the sea,
    Murmuring: "Heigho, my dearie;
I bring a mariner's prayer for thee;
So let the moonbeam veil thine eyes,
And the brownie sing thee lullabies—
But I shall rock thee to and fro,
Kissing the brow *he* loveth so.
And the prayer shall guard thy bed, I trow—
    Heigho, my dearie!"

TO A USURPER

AHA! a traitor in the camp,
    A rebel strangely bold,—
A lisping, laughing, toddling scamp,
    Not more than four years old!

To think that I, who 've ruled alone
    So proudly in the past,
Should be ejected from my throne
    By my own son at last!

He trots his treason to and fro,
    As only babies can,
And says he 'll be his mamma's beau
    When he 's a "gweat, big man"!

You stingy boy! you 've always had
    A share in mamma's heart.
Would you begrudge your poor old dad
    The tiniest little part?

That mamma, I regret to see,
  Inclines to take your part,—
As if a dual monarchy
  Should rule her gentle heart!

But when the years of youth have sped,
  The bearded man, I trow,
Will quite forget he ever said
  He 'd be his mamma's beau.

Renounce your treason, little son,
  Leave mamma's heart to me;
For there will come another one
  To claim your loyalty.

And when that other comes to you,
  God grant her love may shine,
Through all your life, as fair and true
  As mamma's does through mine!

THE BELL–FLOWER TREE

WHEN brother Bill and I were boys,
  How often in the summer we
Would seek the shade your branches made,
  O fair and gracious bell-flower tree!
Amid the clover bloom we sat
  And looked upon the Holyoke range,
While Fido lay a space away,
  Thinking our silence very strange.

The woodchuck in the pasture-lot,
  Beside his furtive hole elate,
Heard, off beyond the pickerel pond,
  The redwing-blackbird chide her mate.
The bumblebee went bustling round,
  Pursuing labors never done—
With drone and sting, the greedy thing
  Begrudged the sweets we lay upon!

Our eyes looked always at the hills—
  The Holyoke hills that seemed to stand
Between us boys and pictured joys
  Of conquest in a further land!
Ah, how we coveted the time
  When we should leave this prosy place
And work our wills beyond those hills,
  And meet creation face to face!

You must have heard our childish talk—
  Perhaps our prattle gave you pain;
For then, old friend, you seemed to bend
  Your kindly arms about us twain.
It might have been the wind that sighed,
  And yet I thought I heard you say:
"Seek not the ills beyond those hills—
  Oh, stay with me, my children, stay!"

See, I've come back; the boy you knew
  Is wiser, older, sadder grown;
I come once more, just as of yore—
  I come, but see! I come alone!
The memory of a brother's love,
  Of blighted hopes, I bring with me,
And here I lay my heart to-day—
  A weary heart, O bell-flower tree!

So let me nestle in your shade
  As though I were a boy again,
And pray extend your arms, old friend,
  And love me as you used to then.
Sing softly as you used to sing,
  And maybe I shall seem to be
A little boy and feel the joy
  Of thy repose, O bell-flower tree!

FAIRY AND CHILD

OH, listen, little Dear-My-Soul,
  To the fairy voices calling,
For the moon is high in the misty sky
  And the honey dew is falling;
To the midnight feast in the clover bloom
  The bluebells are a-ringing,
And it 's "Come away to the land of fay"
  That the katydid is singing.

Oh, slumber, little Dear-My-Soul,
  And hand in hand we 'll wander—
Hand in hand to the beautiful land
  Of Balow, away off yonder;
Or we 'll sail along in a lily leaf
  Into the white moon's halo—
Over a stream of mist and dream
  Into the land of Balow.

Or, you shall have two beautiful wings—
  Two gossamer wings and airy,
And all the while shall the old moon smile
  And think you a little fairy;
And you shall dance in the velvet sky,
  And the silvery stars shall twinkle
And dream sweet dreams as over their beams
  Your footfalls softly tinkle.

THE GRANDSIRE

I LOVED him so; his voice had grown
  Into my heart, and now to hear
The pretty song he had sung so long
  Die on the lips to me so dear!

He a child with golden curls,
      And I with head as white as snow—
I knelt down there and made this pray'r:
      "God, let me be the first to go!"

How often I recall it now:
      My darling tossing on his bed,
I sitting there in mute despair,
      Smoothing the curls that crowned his head.
They did not speak to me of death—
      A feeling *here* had told me so;
What could I say or do but pray
      That I might be the first to go?

Yet, thinking of him standing there
      Out yonder as the years go by,
Waiting for me to come, I see
      'T was better he should wait, not I.
For when I walk the vale of death,
      Above the wail of Jordan's flow
Shall rise a song that shall make me strong—
      The call of the child that was first to go.

HUSHABY, SWEET MY OWN

(LULLABY: BY THE SEA)

FAIR is the castle upon the hill—
            Hushaby, sweet my own!
The night is fair, and the waves are still,
And the wind is singing to you and to me
In this lowly home beside the sea—
            Hushaby, sweet my own!

On yonder hill is store of wealth—
            Hushaby, sweet my own!
And revellers drink to a little one's health;

But you and I bide night and day
For the other love that has sailed away—
        Hushaby, sweet my own!

See not, dear eyes, the forms that creep
        Ghostlike, O my own!
Out of the mists of the murmuring deep;
Oh, see them not and make no cry
Till the angels of death have passed us by—
        Hushaby, sweet my own!

Ah, little they reck of you and me—
        Hushaby, sweet my own!
In our lonely home beside the sea;
They seek the castle up on the hill,
And there they will do their ghostly will—
        Hushaby, O my own!

Here by the sea a mother croons
        "Hushaby, sweet my own!"
In yonder castle a mother swoons
While the angels go down to the misty deep,
Bearing a little one fast asleep—
        Hushaby, sweet my own!

CHILD AND MOTHER

O MOTHER-MY-LOVE, if you 'll give me your **hand**,
    And go where I ask you to wander,
I will lead you away to a beautiful land—
    The Dreamland that 's waiting out yonder.
We 'll walk in a sweet-posie garden out there
    Where moonlight and starlight are streaming
And the flowers and the birds are filling the air
    With the fragrance and music of dreaming.

There 'll be no little tired-out boy to undress,
   No questions or cares to perplex you;
There 'll be no little bruises or bumps to caress,
   Nor patching of stockings to vex you.
For I 'll rock you away on a silver-dew stream,
   And sing you asleep when you 're weary,
And no one shall know of our beautiful dream
   But you and your own little dearie.

And when I am tired I 'll nestle my head
   In the bosom that 's soothed me so often,
And the wide-awake stars shall sing in my stead
   A song which our dreaming shall soften.
So, Mother-My-Love, let me take your dear hand,
   And away through the starlight we 'll wander—
Away through the mist to the beautiful land—
   The Dreamland that 's waiting out yonder!

MEDIÆVAL EVENTIDE SONG

Come hither, lyttel childe, and lie upon my breast to-night,
For yonder fares an angell yclad in raimaunt white,
And yonder sings ye angell as onely angells may,
And his songe ben of a garden that bloometh farre awaye.

To them that have no lyttel childe Godde sometimes sendeth down
A lyttel childe that ben a lyttel angell of his owne;
And if so bee they love that childe, he willeth it to staye,
But elsewise, in his mercie, he taketh it awaye.

And sometimes, though they love it, Godde yearneth for ye childe,
And sendeth angells singing, whereby it ben beguiled;
They fold their arms about ye lamb that croodleth at his play,
And beare him to ye garden that bloometh farre awaye.

I wolde not lose ye lyttel lamb that Godde hath sent to me;
If I colde sing that angell songe, how joysome I sholde be!
For, with mine arms about him, and my musick in his eare,
What angell songe of paradize soever sholde I feare?

Soe come, my lyttel childe, and lie upon my breast to-night,
For yonder fares an angell yclad in raimaunt white,
And yonder sings that angell, as onely angells may,
And his songe ben of a garden that bloometh farre awaye.

ARMENIAN LULLABY

IF thou wilt shut thy drowsy eyes,
    My mulberry one, my golden sun!
The rose shall sing thee lullabies,
    My pretty cosset lambkin!
And thou shalt swing in an almond-tree,
With a flood of moonbeams rocking thee—
A silver boat in a golden sea,
    My velvet love, my nestling dove,
        My own pomegranate blossom!

The stork shall guard thee passing well
    All night, my sweet! my dimple-feet!
And bring thee myrrh and asphodel,
    My gentle rain-of-springtime!
And for thy slumbrous play shall twine
The diamond stars with an emerald vine
To trail in the waves of ruby wine,
    My myrtle bloom, my heart's perfume,
        My little chirping sparrow!

And when the morn wakes up to see
    My apple bright, my soul's delight!
The partridge shall come calling thee,
    My jar of milk-and-honey!

Yes, thou shalt know what mystery lies
In the amethyst deep of the curtained skies,
If thou wilt fold thy onyx eyes,
   You wakeful one, you naughty son,
     You cooing little turtle!

CHRISTMAS TREASURES

I count my treasures o'er with care,—
   The little toy my darling knew,
   A little sock of faded hue,
A little lock of golden hair.

Long years ago this holy time,
   My little one—my all to me—
   Sat robed in white upon my knee,
And heard the merry Christmas chime.

"Tell me, my little golden-head,
   If Santa Claus should come to-night,
   What shall he bring my baby bright,—
What treasure for my boy?" I said.

And then he named this little toy,
   While in his round and mournful eyes
   There came a look of sweet surprise,
That spake his quiet, trustful joy.

And as he lisped his evening prayer
   He asked the boon with childish grace;
   Then, toddling to the chimney-place,
He hung this little stocking there.

That night, while lengthening shadows crept,
   I saw the white-winged angels come
   With singing to our lowly home
And kiss my darling as he slept.

They must have heard his little prayer,
　For in the morn, with rapturous face,
　He toddled to the chimney-place,
And found this little treasure there.

They came again one Christmas-tide,—
　That angel host, so fair and white;
　And, singing all that glorious night,
They lured my darling from my side.

A little sock, a little toy,
　A little lock of golden hair,
　The Christmas music on the air,
A watching for my baby boy!

But if again that angel train
　And golden-head come back for me,
　To bear me to Eternity,
My watching will not be in vain.

OH, LITTLE CHILD

(SICILIAN LULLABY)

Hush, little one, and fold your hands—
　The sun hath set, the moon is high;
The sea is singing to the sands,
　　And wakeful posies are beguiled
　By many a fairy lullaby—
　　Hush, little child—my little child!

Dream, little one, and in your dreams
　Float upward from this lowly place—
Float out on mellow, misty streams
　　To lands where bideth Mary mild,
　And let her kiss thy little face,
　　You little child—my little child!

Sleep, little one, and take thy rest—
  With angels bending over thee,
Sleep sweetly on that Father's breast
    Whom our dear Christ hath reconciled—
  But stay not there—come back to me,
    Oh, little child—*my* little child!

————

GANDERFEATHER'S GIFT

I WAS just a little thing
  When a fairy came and kissed me;
Floating in upon the light
Of a haunted summer night,
Lo, the fairies came to sing
Pretty slumber songs and bring
  Certain boons that else had missed me.
From a dream I turned to see
What those strangers brought for me,
  When that fairy up and kissed me—
  Here, upon this cheek, he kissed me!

Simmerdew was there, but she
  Did not like me altogether;
Daisybright and Turtledove,
Pilfercurds and Honeylove,
Thistleblow and Amberglee
On that gleaming, ghostly sea
  Floated from the misty heather,
And around my trundle-bed
Frisked, and looked, and whispering said—
  Solemnlike and all together:
  "*You* shall kiss him, Ganderfeather!"

Ganderfeather kissed me then—
  Ganderfeather, quaint and merry!
No attenuate sprite was he,
—But as buxom as could be;—

Kissed me twice, and once again,
And the others shouted when
  On my cheek uprose a berry
Somewhat like a mole, mayhap,
But the kiss-mark of that chap
  Ganderfeather, passing merry—
Humorsome, but kindly, very!

I was just a tiny thing
  When the prankish Ganderfeather
Brought this curious gift to me
With his fairy kisses three;
Yet with honest pride I sing
That same gift he chose to bring
  Out of yonder haunted heather.
Other charms and friendships fly—
Constant friends this mole and I,
  Who have been so long together.
  Thank you, little Ganderfeather!

BAMBINO

(CORSICAN LULLABY)

BAMBINO in his cradle slept;
  And by his side his grandam grim
Bent down and smiled upon the child,
  And sung this lullaby to him,—
    This "ninna and anninia":

"When thou art older, thou shalt mind
  To traverse countries far and wide,
And thou shalt go where roses blow
  And balmy waters singing glide—
    So ninna and anninia!

"And thou shalt wear, trimmed up in points,
  A famous jacket edged in red,
And, more than that, a peakèd hat,
  All decked in gold, upon thy head—
    Ah! ninna and anninia!

"Then shalt thou carry gun and knife,
  Nor shall the soldiers bully thee;
Perchance, beset by wrong or debt,
  A mighty bandit thou shalt be—
    So ninna and anninia!

'No woman yet of our proud race
  Lived to her fourteenth year unwed;
The brazen churl that eyed a girl
  Bought her the ring or paid his head—
    So ninna and anninia!

"But once came spies (I know the thieves!)
  And brought disaster to our race;
God heard us when our fifteen men
  Were hanged within the market-place—
    But ninna and anninia!

'Good men they were, my babe, and true,—
  Right worthy fellows all, and strong;
Live thou and be for them and me
  Avenger of that deadly wrong—
    So ninna and anninia!"

LITTLE HOMER'S SLATE

AFTER dear old grandma died,
  Hunting through an oaken chest
In the attic, we espied
  What repaid our childish quest;
'T was a homely little slate,
Seemingly of ancient date.

On its quaint and battered face
  Was the picture of a cart,
Drawn with all that awkward grace
  Which betokens childish art;
But what meant this legend, pray:
"Homer drew this yesterday"?

Mother recollected then
  What the years were fain to hide—
She was but a baby when
  Little Homer lived and died;
Forty years, so mother said,
Little Homer had been dead.

This one secret through those years
  Grandma kept from all apart,
Hallowed by her lonely tears
  And the breaking of her heart;
While each year that sped away
Seemed to her but yesterday.

So the homely little slate
  Grandma's baby's fingers pressed,
To a memory consecrate,
  Lieth in the oaken chest,
Where, unwilling we should know,
Grandma put it, years ago.

THE ROCK-A-BY LADY

The Rock-a-By Lady from Hushaby street
  Comes stealing; comes creeping;
The poppies they hang from her head to her feet,
And each hath a dream that is tiny and fleet—
She bringeth her poppies to you, my sweet,
  When she findeth you sleeping!

There is one little dream of a beautiful drum—
    "Rub-a-dub!" it goeth;
There is one little dream of a big sugar-plum,
And lo! thick and fast the other dreams come
Of popguns that bang, and tin tops that hum,
    And a trumpet that bloweth!

And dollies peep out of those wee little dreams
    With laughter and singing;
And boats go a-floating on silvery streams,
And the stars peek-a-boo with their own misty gleams,
And up, up, and up, where the Mother Moon beams,
    The fairies go winging!

Would you dream all these dreams that are tiny and fleet?
    They 'll come to you sleeping;
So shut the two eyes that are weary, my sweet,
For the Rock-a-By Lady from Hushaby street,
With poppies that hang from her head to her feet,
    Comes stealing; comes creeping.

"BOOH!"

On afternoons, when baby boy has had a splendid nap,
And sits, like any monarch on his throne, in nurse's lap,
In some such wise my handkerchief I hold before my face,
And cautiously and quietly I move about the place;
Then, with a cry, I suddenly expose my face to view,
And you should hear him laugh and crow when I say "Booh!"

Sometimes the rascal tries to make believe that he is scared,
And really, when I first began, he stared, and stared, and stared;
And then his under lip came out and farther out it came,
Till mamma and the nurse agreed it was a "cruel shame"—
But now what does that same wee, toddling, lisping baby do
But laugh and kick his little heels when I say "Booh!"

He laughs and kicks his little heels in rapturous glee, and then
In shrill, despotic treble bids me "do it all aden!"
And I—of course I do it; for, as his progenitor,
It is such pretty, pleasant play as this that I am for!
And it is, oh, such fun! and I am sure that we shall rue
The time when we are both too old to play the game of "Booh!"

GARDEN AND CRADLE

WHEN our babe he goeth walking in his garden,
 Around his tinkling feet the sunbeams play;
  The posies they are good to him,
  And bow them as they should to him,
 As fareth he upon his kingly way;
  And birdlings of the wood to him
 Make music, gentle music, all the day,
  When our babe he goeth walking in his garden.

When our babe he goeth swinging in his cradle,
 Then the night it looketh ever sweetly down;
  The little stars are kind to him,
  The moon she hath a mind to him
 And layeth on his head a golden crown;
  And singeth then the wind to him
 A song, the gentle song of Bethle'm-town,
When our babe he goeth swinging in his cradle.

THE NIGHT WIND

HAVE you ever heard the wind go "Yooooo"?
 'T is a pitiful sound to hear!
It seems to chill you through and through
 With a strange and speechless fear.
'T is the voice of the night that broods outside
 When folk should be asleep,
And many and many 's the time I 've cried

To the darkness brooding far and wide
  Over the land and the deep:
"Whom do you want, O lonely night,
  That you wail the long hours through?"
And the night would say in its ghostly way:
    "Yoooooooo!
    Yoooooooo!
    Yoooooooo!"

My mother told me long ago
  (When I was a little tad)
That when the night went wailing so,
  Somebody had been bad;
And then, when I was snug in bed,
  Whither I had been sent,
With the blankets pulled up round my head,
I'd think of what my mother'd said,
  And wonder what boy she meant!
And "Who's been bad to-day?" I'd ask
  Of the wind that hoarsely blew,
And the voice would say in its meaningful way:
    "Yoooooooo!
    Yoooooooo!
    Yoooooooo!"

That this was true I must allow—
  You'll not believe it, though!
Yes, though I'm quite a model now,
  I was not always so.
And if you doubt what things I say,
  Suppose you make the test;
Suppose, when you've been bad some day
And up to bed are sent away
  From mother and the rest—
Suppose you ask, "Who has been bad?"
  And then you'll hear what's true;
For the wind will moan in its ruefullest tone:
    "Yoooooooo!
    Yoooooooo!
    Yoooooooo!"

KISSING TIME

'Tis when the lark goes soaring
　And the bee is at the bud,
When lightly dancing zephyrs
　Sing over field and flood;
When all sweet things in nature
　Seem joyfully achime—
'T is then I wake my darling,
　For it is kissing time!

Go, pretty lark, a-soaring,
　And suck your sweets, O bee;
Sing, O ye winds of summer,
　Your songs to mine and me;
For with your song and rapture
　Cometh the moment when
It 's half-past kissing time
　And time to kiss again!

So—so the days go fleeting .
　Like golden fancies free,
And every day that cometh
　Is full of sweets for me;
And sweetest are those moments
　My darling comes to climb
Into my lap to mind me
　That it is kissing time.

Sometimes, maybe, he wanders
　A heedless, aimless way—
Sometimes, maybe, he loiters
　In pretty, prattling play;
But presently bethinks him
　And hastens to me then,
For it 's half-past kissing time
　And time to kiss again!

JEST 'FORE CHRISTMAS

FATHER calls me William, sister calls me Will,
Mother calls me Willie, but the fellers call me Bill!
Mighty glad I ain't a girl—ruther be a boy,
Without them sashes, curls, an' things that's worn by Fauntleroy!
Love to chawnk green apples an' go swimmin' in the lake—
Hate to take the castor-ile they give for bellyache!
'Most all the time, the whole year round, there ain't no flies on me,
But jest 'fore Christmas I'm as good as I kin be!

Got a yeller dog named Sport, sick him on the cat;
First thing she knows she does n't know where she is at!
Got a clipper sled, an' when us kids goes out to slide,
'Long comes the grocery cart, an' we all hook a ride!
But sometimes when the grocery man is worrited an' cross,
He reaches at us with his whip, an' larrups up his hoss,
An' then I laff an' holler, "Oh, ye never teched *me!*"
But jest 'fore Christmas I'm as good as I kin be!

Gran'ma says she hopes that when I git to be a man,
I'll be a missionarer like her oldest brother, Dan,
As was et up by the cannibuls that lives in Ceylon's Isle,
Where every prospeck pleases, an' only man is vile!
But gran'ma she has never been to see a Wild West show,
Nor read the Life of Daniel Boone, or else I guess she'd know
That Buff'lo Bill an' cowboys is good enough for me!
Excep' jest 'fore Christmas, when I'm good as I kin be!

And then old Sport he hangs around, so solemnlike an' still,
His eyes they seem a-sayin': "What's the matter, little Bill?"
The old cat sneaks down off her perch an' wonders what's become
Of them two enemies of hern that used to make things hum!
But I am so perlite an' tend so earnestly to biz,
That mother says to father: "How improved our Willie is!"
But father, havin' been a boy hisself, suspicions me
When, jest 'fore Christmas, I'm as good as I kin be!

For Christmas, with its lots an' lots of candies, cakes, an' toys,
Was made, they say, for proper kids an' not for naughty boys;
So wash yer face an' bresh yer hair, an' mind yer p's and q's,
An' don't bust out yer pantaloons, and don't wear out yer shoes;
Say "Yessum" to the ladies, and "Yessur" to the men,
An' when they 's company, don't pass yer plate for pie again;
But, thinkin' of the things yer 'd like to see upon that tree,
Jest 'fore Christmas be as good as yer kin be!

BEARD AND BABY

I SAY, as one who never feared
    The wrath of a subscriber's bullet,
I pity him who has a beard
    But has no little girl to pull it!

When wife and I have finished tea,
    Our baby woos me with her prattle,
And, perching proudly on my knee,
    She gives my petted whiskers battle.

With both her hands she tugs away,
    While scolding at me kind o' spiteful;
You 'll not believe me when I say
    I find the torture quite delightful!

No other would presume, I ween,
    To trifle with this hirsute wonder,
Else would I rise in vengeful mien
    And rend his vandal frame asunder!

But when *her* baby fingers pull
    This glossy, sleek, and silky treasure,
My cup of happiness is full—
    I fairly glow with pride and pleasure!

And, sweeter still, through all the day
    I seem to hear her winsome prattle—
I seem to feel her hands at play,
    As though they gave me sportive battle.

Yes, heavenly music seems to steal
    Where thought of her forever lingers,
And round my heart I always feel
    The twining of her dimpled fingers!

THE DINKEY-BIRD

Iɴ an ocean, 'way out yonder
    (As all sapient people know),
Is the land of Wonder-Wander,
    Whither children love to go;
It 's their playing, romping, swinging,
    That give great joy to me
While the Dinkey-Bird goes singing
    In the amfalula tree!

There the gum-drops grow like cherries,
    And taffy's thick as peas—
Caramels you pick like berries
    When, and where, and how you please;
Big red sugar-plums are clinging
    To the cliffs beside that sea
Where the Dinkey-Bird is singing
    In the amfalula tree.

So when children shout and scamper
    And make merry all the day,
When there 's naught to put a damper
    To the ardor of their play;
When I hear their laughter ringing,
    Then I 'm sure as sure can be
That the Dinkey-Bird is singing
    In the amfalula tree.

For the Dinkey-Bird's bravuras
　And staccatos are so sweet—
His roulades, appoggiaturas,
　And robustos so complete,
That the youth of every nation—
　Be they near or far away—
Have especial delectation
　In that gladsome roundelay.

Their eyes grow bright and brighter,
　Their lungs begin to crow,
Their hearts get light and lighter,
　And their cheeks are all aglow;
For an echo cometh bringing
　The news to all and me,
That the Dinkey-Bird is singing
　In the amfalula tree.

I 'm sure you like to go there
　To see your feathered friend—
And so many goodies grow there
　You would like to comprehend!
Speed, little dreams, your winging
　To that land across the sea,
Where the Dinkey-Bird is singing
　In the amfalula tree!

THE DRUM

I 'M a beautiful red, red drum,
　And I train with the soldier boys;
As up the street we come,
　Wonderful is our noise!
There 's Tom, and Jim, and Phil,
　And Dick, and Nat, and Fred,
While Widow Cutler's Bill
　And I march on ahead,

With a r-r-rat-tat-tat
    And a tum-titty-um-tum-tum—
Oh, there's bushels of fun in that
    For boys with a little red drum!

The Injuns came last night
    While the soldiers were abed,
And they gobbled a Chinese kite
    And off to the woods they fled!
The woods are the cherry-trees
    Down in the orchard lot,
And the soldiers are marching to seize
    The booty the Injuns got.
With tum-titty-um-tum-tum,
    And r-r-rat-tat-tat,
When soldiers marching come
    Injuns had better scat!

Step up there, little Fred,
    And, Charley, have a mind!
Jim is as far ahead
    As you two are behind!
Ready with gun and sword
    Your valorous work to do—
Yonder the Injun horde
    Are lying in wait for you.
And their hearts go pitapat
    When they hear the soldiers come
With a r-r-rat-tat-tat
    And a tum-titty-um-tum-tum!

Course it's all in play!
    The skulking Injun crew
That hustled the kite away
    Are little white boys, like you!
But "honest" or "just in fun,"
    It is all the same to me;
And, when the battle is won,
    Home once again march we

With a r-r-rat-tat-tat
  And tum-titty-um-tum-tum;
And there's glory enough in that
  For the boys with their little red drum!

THE DEAD BABE

LAST night, as my dear babe lay dead,
In agony I knelt and said:
      "O God! what have I done,
Or in what wise offended Thee,
That thou shouldst take awa‒ from me
      My little son?

"Upon the thousand useless lives,
Upon the guilt that vaunting thrives,
      Thy wrath were better spent!
Why shouldst Thou take my little son—
Why shouldst Thou vent Thy wrath upon
      This innocent?"

Last night, as my dear babe lay dead,
Before mine eyes the vision spread
      Of things that *might* have been:
Licentious riot, cruel strife,
Forgotten prayers, a wasted life
      Dark-red with sin!

Then, with sweet music in the air,
I saw another vision there:
      A Shepherd in whose keep
A little lamb—my little child!
Of worldly wisdom undefiled,
      Lay fast asleep!

Last night, as my dear babe lay dead,
In those two messages I read

A wisdom manifest;
And though my arms be childless now,
I am content—to Him I bow
Who knoweth best.

THE HAPPY HOUSEHOLD

It's when the birds go piping and the daylight slowly breaks,
That, clamoring for his dinner, our precious baby wakes;
Then it's sleep no more for baby, and it's sleep no more for me,
For, when he wants his dinner, why it's dinner it must be!
And of that lacteal fluid he partakes with great ado,
      While gran'ma laughs,
      And gran'pa laughs,
      And wife, she laughs,
      And I—well, *I* laugh, *too!*

You'd think, to see us carrying on about that little tad,
That, like as not, that baby was the first we'd ever had;
But, sakes alive! he is n't, yet we people make a fuss
As if the only baby in the world had come to *us!*
And, morning, noon, and night-time, whatever he may do,
      Gran'ma, she laughs,
      Gran'pa, he laughs,
      Wife, she laughs,
      And *I*, of course, laugh, *too!*

But once—a likely spell ago—when that poor little chick
From teething or from some such ill of infancy fell sick,
You would n't know us people as the same that went about
A-feelin' good all over, just to hear him crow and shout;
And, though the doctor poohed our fears and said he'd pull him
   through,
      Old gran'ma cried,
      And gran'pa cried,
      And wife, she cried,
      And I—yes, *I* cried, *too!*

It makes us all feel good to have a baby on the place,
With his everlastin' crowing and his dimpling, dumpling face;
The patter of his pinky feet makes music everywhere,
And when he shakes those fists of his, good-by to every care!
No matter *what* our trouble is, when *he* begins to *coo*,
   Old gran'ma laughs,
   And gran'pa laughs,
   Wife, she laughs,
   And I—you bet, *I* laugh, *too!*

SO, SO, ROCK–A–BY SO!

So, so, rock-a-by so!
Off to the garden where dreamikins grow;
And here is a kiss on your winkyblink eyes,
 And here is a kiss on your dimpledown cheek,
And here is a kiss for the treasure that lies
In the beautiful garden 'way up in the skies
 Which you seek.
Now mind these three kisses wherever you go—
So, so, rock-a-by so!

There 's one little fumfay who lives there, I know,
For he dances all night where the dreamikins grow·
I send him this kiss on your droopydrop eyes,
 I send him this kiss on your rosyred cheek.
And here is a kiss for the dream that shall rise
When the fumfay shall dance in those far-away skies
 Which you seek.
Be sure that you pay those three kisses you owe—
So, so, rock-a-by so!

And, by-low, as you rock-a-by go,
Don't forget mother who loveth you so!
And here is her kiss on your weepydeep eyes,
 And here is her kiss on your peachypink cheek,

And here is her kiss for the dreamland that lies
Like a babe on the breast of those far-away skies
  Which you seek—
The blinkywink garden where dreamikins grow—
So, so, rock-a-by so!

THE SONG OF LUDDY-DUD

A SUNBEAM comes a-creeping
  Into my dear one's nest,
And sings to our babe a-sleeping
  The song that I love the best:
    "'T is little Luddy-Dud in the morning—
  'T is little Luddy-Dud at night;
      And all day long
      'T is the same sweet song
Of that waddling, toddling, coddling little mite, Luddy-Dud."

The bird to the tossing clover,
  The bee to the swaying bud,
Keep singing that sweet song over
  Of wee little Luddy-Dud.
    " 'T is little Luddy-Dud in the morning—
  'T is little Luddy-Dud at night;
      And all day long
      'T is the same dear song
Of that growing, crowing, knowing little sprite, Luddy-Dud."

Luddy-Dud's cradle is swinging
  Where softly the night winds blow,
And Luddy-Dud's mother is singing
  A song that is sweet and low;
    " 'T is little Luddy-Dud in the morning—
  'T is little Luddy-Dud at night;
      And all day long
      'T is the same sweet song
Of my nearest and my dearest heart's delight, Luddy-Dud!"

THE DUEL

THE gingham dog and the calico cat
Side by side on the table sat;
'T was half-past twelve, and (what do you think!)
Nor one nor t' other had slept a wink!
 The old Dutch clock and the Chinese plate
 Appeared to know as sure as fate
There was going to be a terrible spat.
  (I was n't there; I simply state
  What was told to me by the Chinese plate!)

The gingham dog went "Bow-wow-wow!"
And the calico cat replied "Mee-ow!"
The air was littered, an hour or so,
With bits of gingham and calico,
 While the old Dutch clock in the chimney-place
 Up with its hands before its face,
For it always dreaded a family row!
  (Now mind: I 'm only telling you
  What the old Dutch clock declares is true!)

The Chinese plate looked very blue,
And wailed, "Oh, dear! what shall we do!"
But the gingham dog and the calico cat
Wallowed this way and tumbled that,
 Employing every tooth and claw
 In the awfullest way you ever saw—
And, oh! how the gingham and calico flew!
  (Don't fancy I exaggerate—
  I got my news from the Chinese plate!)

Next morning, where the two had sat
They found no trace of dog or cat;
And some folks think unto this day
That burglars stole that pair away!
 But the truth about the cat and pup

Is this: they ate each other up!
Now what do you really think of that!
(*The old Dutch clock it told me so,*
And that is how I came to know.)

GOOD-CHILDREN STREET

THERE's a dear little home in Good-Children street—
  My heart turneth fondly to-day
Where tinkle of tongues and patter of feet
  Make sweetest of music at play;
Where the sunshine of love illumines each face
And warms every heart in that old-fashioned place.

For dear little children go romping about
  With dollies and tin tops and drums,
And, my! how they frolic and scamper and shout
  Till bedtime too speedily comes!
Oh, days they are golden and days they are fleet
With little folk living in Good-Children street.

See, here comes an army with guns painted red,
  And swords, caps, and plumes of all sorts;
The captain rides gayly and proudly ahead
  On a stick-horse that prances and snorts!
Oh, legions of soldiers you 're certain to meet—
Nice make-believe soldiers—in Good-Children street.

And yonder Odette wheels her dolly about—
  Poor dolly! I 'm sure she is ill,
For one of her blue china eyes has dropped out
  And her voice is asthmatic'ly shrill.
Then, too, I observe she is minus her feet,
Which causes much sorrow in Good-Children street.

'T is so the dear children go romping about
  With dollies and banners and drums,

And I venture to say they are sadly put out
  When an end to their jubilee comes:
Oh, days they are golden and days they are fleet
With little folk living in Good-Children street!

But when falleth night over river and town,
  Those little folk vanish from sight,
And an angel all white from the sky cometh down
  And guardeth the babes through the night,
And singeth her lullabies tender and swee.
To the dear little people in Good-Children street.

Though elsewhere the world be o'erburdened with care,
  Though poverty fall to my lot,
Though toil and vexation be always my share,
  What care I—they trouble me not!
This thought maketh life ever joyous and sweet:
There's a dear little home in Good-Children street.

———

THE DELECTABLE BALLAD OF THE WALLER LOT

Up yonder in Buena Park
  There is a famous spot,
In legend and in history
  Yclept the Waller Lot.

There children play in daytime
  And lovers stroll by dark,
For 't is the goodliest trysting-place
  In all Buena Park.

Once on a time that beauteous maid,
  Sweet little Sissy Knott,
Took out her pretty doll to walk
  Within the Waller Lot.

While thus she fared, from Ravenswood
   Came Injuns o'er the plain,
And seized upon that beauteous maid
   And rent her doll in twain.

Oh, 't was a piteous thing to hear
   Her lamentations wild;
She tore her golden curls and cried:
   "My child! My child! My child!"

Alas, what cared those Injun chiefs
   How bitterly wailed she?
They never had been mothers,
   And they could not hope to be!

"Have done with tears," they rudely quoth,
   And then they bound her hands;
For they proposed to take her off
   To distant border lands.

But, joy! from Mr. Eddy's barn
   Doth Willie Clow behold
The sight that makes his hair rise up
   And all his blood run cold.

He put his fingers in his mouth
   And whistled long and clear,
And presently a goodly horde
   Of cowboys did appear.

Cried Willie Clow: "My comrades bold,
   Haste to the Waller Lot,
And rescue from that Injun band
   Our charming Sissy Knott!

"Spare neither Injun buck nor squaw,
   But smite them hide and hair!
Spare neither sex nor age nor size,
   And no condition spare!"

Then sped that cowboy band away,
 Full of revengeful wrath,
And Kendall Evans rode ahead
 Upon a hickory lath.

And next came gallant Dady Field
 And Willie's brother Kent,
The Eddy boys and Robbie James,
 On murderous purpose bent.

For they were much beholden to
 That maid—in sooth, the lot
Were very, very much in love
 With charming Sissy Knott.

What wonder? She was beauty's queen,
 And good beyond compare;
Moreover, it was known she was
 Her wealthy father's heir!

Now when the Injuns saw that band
 They trembled with affright,
And yet they thought the cheapest thing
 To do was stay and fight.

So sturdily they stood their ground,
 Nor would their prisoner yield,
Despite the wrath of Willie Clow
 And gallant Dady Field.

Oh, never fiercer battle raged
 Upon the Waller Lot,
And never blood more freely flowed
 Than flowed for Sissy Knott!

An Injun chief of monstrous size
 Got Kendall Evans down,
And Robbie James was soon o'erthrown
 By one of great renown.

And Dady Field was sorely done,
  And Willie Clow was hurt,
And all that gallant cowboy band
  Lay wallowing in the dirt.

But still they strove with might and main
  Till all the Waller Lot
Was strewn with hair and gouts of gore—
  All, all for Sissy Knott!

Then cried the maiden in despair:
  "Alas, I sadly fear
The battle and my hopes are lost,
  Unless some help appear!"

Lo, as she spoke, she saw afar
  The rescuer looming up—
The pride of all Buena Park,
  Clow's famous yellow pup!

"Now, sick 'em, Don," the maiden cried,
  "Now, sick 'em, Don!" cried she;
Obedient Don at once complied—
  As ordered, so did he.

He sicked 'em all so passing well
  That, overcome by fright,
The Indian horde gave up the fray
  And safety sought in flight.

They ran and ran and ran and ran
  O'er valley, plain, and hill;
And if they are not walking now,
  Why, then, they're running still.

The cowboys rose up from the dust
  With faces black and blue;
"Remember, beauteous maid," said they,
  "We"ve bled and died for you!

"And though we suffer grievously,
   We gladly hail the lot
That brings us toils and pains and wounds
   For charming Sissy Knott!"

But Sissy Knott still wailed and wept,
   And still her fate reviled;
For who could patch her dolly up—
   Who, who could mend her child?

Then out her doting mother came,
   And soothed her daughter then;
"Grieve not, my darling, I will sew
   Your dolly up again!"

Joy soon succeeded unto grief,
   And tears were soon dried up,
And dignities were heaped upon
   Clow's noble yellow pup.

Him all that goodly company
   Did as deliverer hail—
They tied a ribbon round his neck,
   Another round his tail.

And every anniversary day
   Upon the Waller Lot
They celebrate the victory won
   For charming Sissy Knott.

And I, the poet of these folk,
   Am ordered to compile
This truly famous history
   In good old ballad style.

Which having done as to have earned
   The sweet rewards of fame,
In what same style I did begin
   I now shall end the same.

So let us sing: Long live the King,
  Long live the Queen and Jack,
Long live the ten-spot and the ace,
  And also all the pack.

THE STORK

Last night the Stork came stalking,
  And, Stork, beneath your wing
Lay, lapped in dreamless slumber,
  The tiniest little thing!
From Babyland, out yonder
  Beside a silver sea,
You brought a priceless treasure
  As gift to mine and me!

Last night my dear one listened—
  And, wife, you knew the cry—
The dear old Stork has sought our home
  A many times gone by!
And in your gentle bosom
  I found the pretty thing
That from the realm out yonder
  Our friend the Stork did bring.

Last night a babe awakened,
  And, babe, how strange and new
Must seem the home and people
  The Stork has brought you to;
And yet methinks you like them—
  You neither stare nor weep,
But closer to my dear one
  You cuddle, and you sleep!

Last night my heart grew fonder—
  O happy heart of mine,
Sing of the inspirations
  That round my pathway shine!

And sing your sweetest love-song
To this dear nestling wee
The Stork from 'Way-Out-Yonder
Hath brought to mine and me!

THE BOTTLE-TREE

A BOTTLE-TREE bloometh in Winkyway land—
    Heigh-ho for a bottle, I say!
A snug little berth in that ship I demand
    That rocketh the Bottle-Tree babies away
    Where the Bottle-Tree bloometh by night and by day
And reacheth its fruit to each wee, dimpled hand;
        You take of that fruit as much as you list,
        For colic 's a nuisance that doesn't exist!
So cuddle me close, and cuddle me fast,
    And cuddle me snug in my cradle away,
For I hunger and thirst for that precious repast—
    Heigho-ho for a bottle, I say!

The Bottle-Tree bloometh by night and by day!
    Heigh-ho for Winkyway land!
And Bottle-Tree fruit (as I 've heard people say)
    Makes bellies of Bottle-Tree babies expand—
    And that is a trick I would fain understand!
Heigh-ho for a bottle to-day!
        And heigh-ho for a bottle to-night—
        A bottle of milk that is creamy and white!
So cuddle me close, and cuddle me fast,
    And cuddle me snug in my cradle away,
For I hunger and thirst for that precious repast—
    Heigh-ho for a bottle, I say!

GOOGLY–GOO

Of mornings, bright and early,
  When the lark is on the wing
And the robin in the maple
  Hops from her nest to sing,
From yonder cheery chamber
  Cometh a mellow coo—
'T is the sweet, persuasive treble
  Of my little Googly-Goo!

The sunbeams hear his music,
  And they seek his little bed,
And they dance their prettiest dances
  Round his golden curly head:
Schottisches, galops, minuets,
  Gavottes and waltzes, too,
Dance they unto the music
  Of my googling Googly-Goo.

My heart—my heart it leapeth
  To hear that treble tone;
What music like *thy* music,
  My darling and mine own!
And patiently—yes, cheerfully
  I toil the long day through—
My labor seemeth lightened
  By the song of Googly-Goo!

I may not see his antics,
  Nor kiss his dimpled cheek:
I may not smooth the tresses
  The sunbeams love to seek;
It mattereth not—the echo
  Of his sweet, persuasive coo
Recurreth to remind me
  Of my little Googly-Goo.

And when I come at evening,
  I stand without the door
And patiently I listen
  For that dear sound once more;
And oftentimes I wonder,
  "Oh, God! what should I do
If any ill should happen
  To my little Googly-Goo!"

Then in affright I call him—
  I hear his gleeful shouts!
Begone, ye dread forebodings—
  Begone, ye killing doubts!
For, with my arms about him,
  My heart warms through and through
With the oogling and the googling
  Of my little Googly-Goo!

THE BENCH-LEGGED FYCE

SPEAKIN' of dorgs, my bench-legged fyce
Hed most o' the virtues, an' nary a vice.
Some folks called him Sooner, a name that arose
From his predisposition to chronic repose;
But, rouse his ambition, he couldn't be beat—
Yer bet yer he got thar on all his four feet!

Mos' dorgs hez some forte—like huntin' an' such,
But the sports o' the field didn't bother *him* much;
Wuz just a plain dorg, an' contented to be
On peaceable terms with the neighbors an' me;
Used to fiddle an' squirm, and grunt "Oh, how nice,
When I tickled the back of that bench-legged fyce!

He wuz long in the bar'l, like a fyce oughter be;
His color wuz yaller as ever you see;
His tail, curlin' upward, wuz long, loose, an' slim—

When he didn't wag *it*, why, the tail it wagged *him!*
His legs wuz so crooked, my bench-legged pup
Wuz as tall settin' down as he wuz standin' up!

He 'd lie by the stove of a night an' regret
The various vittles an' things he had et;
When a stranger, most likely a tramp, come along,
He 'd lift up his voice in significant song—
You wondered, by gum! how there ever wuz space
In that bosom o' his'n to hold so much bass!

Of daytimes he 'd sneak to the road an' lie down,
An' tackle the country dorgs comin' to town;
By common consent he wuz boss in St. Jo,
For what he took hold of he never let go!
An' a dude that come courtin' our girl left a slice
Of his white flannel suit with our bench-legged fyce!

He wuz good to us kids—when we pulled at his fur
Or twisted his tail he would never demur;
He seemed to enjoy all our play an' our chaff,
For his tongue 'u'd hang out an' he 'd laff an' he'd laff;
An' once, when the Hobart boy fell through the ice,
He wuz drug clean ashore by that bench-legged fyce!

We all hev our choice, an' you, like the rest,
Allow that the dorg which you 've got is the best;
I wouldn't give much for the boy 'at grows up
With no friendship subsistin' 'tween him an' a pup!
When a fellow gits old—I tell you it 's nice
To think of his youth and his bench-legged fyce!

To think of the springtime 'way back in St. Jo—
Of the peach-trees abloom an' the daises ablow;
To think of the play in the medder an' grove,
When little legs wrassled an' little han's strove;
To think of the loyalty, valor, an' truth
Of the friendships that hallow the season of youth!

LITTLE MISS BRAG

LITTLE Miss Brag has much to say
To the rich little lady from over the way,
And the rich little lady puts out a lip
As she looks at her own white, dainty slip,
And wishes that *she* could wear a gown
As pretty as gingham of faded brown!
For little Miss Brag she lays much stress
On the privileges of a gingham dress—
    "Aha,
    Oho!"

The rich little lady from over the way
Has beautiful dolls in vast array;
Yet she envies the raggedy home-made doll
She hears our little Miss Brag extol.
For the raggedy doll can fear no hurt
From wet, or heat, or tumble, or dirt!
Her nose is inked, and her mouth is, too,
And one eye's black and the other's blue—
    "Aha,
    Oho!"

The rich little lady goes out to ride
With footmen standing up outside,
Yet wishes that, sometimes, after dark
Her father would trundle *her* in the park;—
That, sometimes, *her* mother would sing the things
Little Miss Brag says *her* mother sings
When through the attic window streams
The moonlight full of golden dreams—
    "Aha,
    Oho!"

Yes, little Miss Brag has much to say
To the rich little lady from over the way;
And yet who knows but from her heart
Often the bitter sighs upstart—

Uprise to lose their burn and sting
In the grace of the tongue that loves to sing
Praise of the treasures all its own!
So I 've come to love that treble tone—
    "Aha,
    Oho!"

THE HUMMING TOP

THE top it hummeth a sweet, sweet song
  To my dear little boy at play—
Merrily singeth all day long,
  As it spinneth and spinneth away.
        And my dear little boy
        He laugheth with joy
When he heareth the monotone
        Of that busy thing
        That loveth to sing
The song that is all its own.

Hold fast the string and wind it tight,
  That the song be loud and clear;
Now hurl the top with all your might
  Upon the banquette here;
        And straight from the string
        The joyous thing
Boundeth and spinneth along,
        And it whirrs and it chirrs
        And it birrs and it purrs
Ever its pretty song.

Will ever my dear little boy grow old,
  As some have grown before?
Will ever his heart feel faint and cold,
  When he heareth the songs of yore?
        Will ever this toy
        Of my dear little boy,

When the years have worn away,
　　Sing sad and low
　　Of the long ago,
As it singeth to me to-day?

LADY BUTTON-EYES

WHEN the busy day is done,
And my weary little one
Rocketh gently to and fro;
When the night winds softly blow,
And the crickets in the glen
Chirp and chirp and chirp again;
When upon the haunted green
Fairies dance around their queen—
Then from yonder misty skies
Cometh Lady Button-Eyes.

Through the murk and mist and gloam
To our quiet, cozy home,
Where to singing, sweet and low,
Rocks a cradle to and fro;
Where the clock's dull monotone
Telleth of the day that 's done;
Where the moonbeams hover o'er
Playthings sleeping on the floor—
Where my weary wee one lies
Cometh Lady Button-Eyes.

Cometh like a fleeting ghost
From some distant eerie coast;
Never footfall can you hear
As that spirit fareth near—
Never whisper, never word
From that shadow-queen is heard.

In ethereal raiment dight,
From the realm of fay and sprite
In the depth of yonder skies
Cometh Lady Button-Eyes.

Layeth she her hands upon
My dear weary little one,
And those white hands overspread
Like a veil the curly head,
Seem to fondle and caress
Every little silken tress;
Then she smooths the eyelids down
Over those two eyes of brown—
In such soothing, tender wise
Cometh Lady Button-Eyes.

Dearest, feel upon your brow
That caressing magic now;
For the crickets in the glen
Chirp and chirp and chirp again,
While upon the haunted green
Fairies dance around their queen,
And the moonbeams hover o'er
Playthings sleeping on the floor—
Hush, my sweet! from yonder skies
Cometh Lady Button-Eyes!

THE RIDE TO BUMPVILLE

PLAY that my knee was a calico mare
    Saddled and bridled for Bumpville;
Leap to the back of this steed, if you dare,
    And gallop away to Bumpville!
I hope you 'll be sure to sit fast in your seat,
For this calico mare is prodigiously fleet,
And many adventures you 're likely to meet
    As you journey along to Bumpville.

This calico mare both gallops and trots
    While whisking you off to Bumpville;
She paces, she shies, and she stumbles, in spots,
    In the tortuous road to Bumpville;
And sometimes this strangely mercurial steed
Will suddenly stop and refuse to proceed,
Which, all will admit, is vexatious indeed,
    When one is en route to Bumpville!

She's scared of the cars when the engine goes "Toot!"
    Down by the crossing at Bumpville;
You'd better look out for that treacherous brute
    Bearing you off to Bumpville!
With a snort she rears up on her hindermost heels,
And executes jigs and Virginia reels—
Words fail to explain how embarrassed one feels
    Dancing so wildly to Bumpville!

It's bumpytybump and it's jiggytyjog,
    Journeying on to Bumpville;
It's over the hilltop and down through the bog
    You ride on your way to Bumpville;
It's rattletybang over boulder and stump,
There are rivers to ford, there are fences to jump,
And the corduroy road it goes bumpytybump,
    Mile after mile to Bumpville!

Perhaps you'll observe it's no easy thing
    Making the journey to Bumpville,
So I think, on the whole, it were prudent to bring
    An end to this ride to Bumpville;
For, though she has uttered no protest or plaint,
The calico mare must be blowing and faint—
What's more to the point, I'm blowed if I ain't!
    So play we have got to Bumpville!

THE BROOK

I LOOKED in the brook and saw a face—
    Heigh-ho, but a child was I!
There were rushes and willows in that place,
    And they clutched at the brook as the brook ran by;
And the brook it ran its own sweet way,
As a child doth run in heedless play,
And as it ran I heard it say:
        "Hasten with me
        To the roistering sea
That is wroth with the flame of the morning sky!"

I look in the brook and see a face—
    Heigh-ho, but the years go by!
The rushes are dead in the old-time place,
    And the willows I knew when a child was I.
And the brook it seemeth to me to say,
As ever it stealeth on its way—
Solemnly now, and not in play:
        "Oh, come with me
        To the slumbrous sea
That is gray with the peace of the evening sky!"

Heigh-ho, but the years go by—
I would to God that a child were I!

PICNIC-TIME

IT 's June ag'in, an' in my soul I feel the fillin' joy
That 's sure to come this time o' year to every little boy;
For, every June, the Sunday-schools at picnics may be seen,
Where "fields beyont the swellin' floods stand dressed in livin'
    green";
Where little girls are skeered to death with spiders, bugs, and ants,
An' little boys get grass-stains on their go-to-meetin' pants.
It 's June ag'in, an' with it all what happiness is mine—
There 's goin' to be a picnic, an' I 'm goin' to jine!

One year I jined the Baptists, an' goodness! how it rained!
(But granpa says that that 's the way "baptizo" is explained.)
And once I jined the 'Piscopils an' had a heap o' fun—
But the boss of all the picnics was the Presbyteriun!
They had so many puddin's, sallids, sandwidges, an' pies,
That a feller wisht his stummick was as hungry as his eyes!
Oh, yes, the eatin' Presbyteriuns give yer is so fine
That when *they* have a picnic, you bet *I* 'm goin' to jine!

But at this time the Methodists have special claims on me,
For they 're goin' to give a picnic on the 21st, D. V,;
Why should a liberal Universalist like me object
To share the joys of fellowship with every friendly sect?
However het'rodox their articles of faith elsewise may be,
Their doctrine of fried chick'n is a savin' grace to me!
So on the 21st of June, the weather bein' fine,
They 're goin' to give a picnic, and I 'm goin' to jine!

―――――

SHUFFLE–SHOON AND AMBER–LOCKS

Shuffle-shoon and Amber-Locks
Sit together, building blocks;
   Shuffle-Shoon is old and gray,
    Amber-Locks a little child,
   But together at their play
    Age and Youth are reconciled,
And with sympathetic glee
Build their castles fair to see.

"When I grow to be a man"
(So the wee one's prattle ran),
   "I shall build a castle so—
    With a gateway broad and grand;
   Here a pretty vine shall grow,
    There a soldier guard shall stand;
And the tower shall be so high,
Folks will wonder, by and by!"

Shuffle-Shoon quoth: "Yes, I know;
Thus I builded long ago!
   Here a gate and there a wall,
     Here a window, there a door;
   Here a steeple wondrous tall
     Riseth ever more and more!
But the years have levelled low
What I builded long ago!"

So they gossip at their play,
Heedless of the fleeting day;
   One speaks of the Long Ago
     Where his dead hopes buried lie;
   One with chubby cheeks aglow
     Prattleth of the By and By;
Side by side, they build their blocks—
Shuffle-Shoon and Amber-Locks.

THE SHUT-EYE TRAIN

COME, my little one, with me!
There are wondrous sights to see
  As the evening shadows fall;
  In your pretty cap and gown,
     Don't detain
     The Shut-Eye train—
  "Ting-a-ling!" the bell it goeth,
  "Toot-toot!" the whistle bloweth,
And we hear the warning call:
"All aboard for Shut-Eye Town!"

Over hill and over plain
Soon will speed the Shut-Eye train!
  Through the blue where bloom the stars
  And the Mother Moon looks down
     We'll away
     To land of Fay—

Oh, the sights that we shall see there!
Come, my little one, with me there—
'T is a goodly train of cars—
All aboard for Shut-Eye Town!

Swifter than a wild bird's flight,
Through the realms of fleecy light
We shall speed and speed away!
Let the Night in envy frown—
What care we
How wroth she be!
To the Balow-land above us,
To the Balow-folk who love us,
Let us hasten while we may—
All aboard for Shut-Eye Town!

Shut-Eye Town is passing fair—
Golden dreams await us there:
We shall dream those dreams, my dear,
Till the Mother Moon goes down—
See unfold
Delights untold!
And in those mysterious places
We shall see beloved faces
And beloved voices hear
In the grace of Shut-Eye Town.

Heavy are your eyes, my sweet,
Weary are your little feet—
Nestle closer up to me
In your pretty cap and gown;
Don't detain
The Shut-Eye train!
"Ting-a-ling!" the bell it goeth,
"Toot-toot!" the whistle bloweth—
Oh, the sights that we shall see!
All aboard for Shut-Eye Town!

LITTLE–OH–DEAR

SEE, what a wonderful garden is here,
Planted and trimmed for my Little-Oh-Dear!
Posies so gaudy and grass of such brown—
Search ye the country and hunt ye the town
And never ye 'll meet with a garden so queer
As this one I 've made for my Little-Oh-Dear!

Marigolds white and buttercups blue,
Lilies all dabbled with honey and dew,
The cactus that trails over trellis and wall,
Roses and pansies and violets—all
Make proper obeisance and reverent cheer
When into her garden steps Little-Oh-Dear.

And up at the top of that lavender-tree
A silver-bird singeth as only can she;
For, ever and only, she singeth the song
"I love you—I love you!" the happy day long;—
Then the echo—the echo that smiteth me here!
"I love you, I love you," my Little-Oh-Dear!

The garden may wither, the silver-bird fly—
But what careth my little precious, or I?
From her pathway of flowers that in springtime upstart
She walketh the tenderer way in my heart;
And, oh, it is always the summer-time *here*
With that song of "I love you," my Little-Oh-Dear!

THE FLY–AWAY HORSE

OH, a wonderful horse is the Fly-Away Horse—
  Perhaps you have seen him before;
Perhaps, while you slept, his shadow has swept
  Through the moonlight that floats on the floor.

For it 's only at night, when the stars twinkle bright,
   That the Fly-Away Horse, with a neigh
And a pull at his rein and a toss of his mane,
   Is up on his heels and away!
         The Moon in the sky,
         As he gallopeth by,
    Cries: "Oh! what a marvellous sight!"
        And the Stars in dismay
        Hide their faces away
   In the lap of old Grandmother Night.

It is yonder, out yonder, the Fly-Away Horse
   Speedeth ever and ever away—
Over meadows and lanes, over mountains and plains,
   Over streamlets that sing at their play;
And over the sea like a ghost sweepeth he,
   While the ships they go sailing below,
And he speedeth so fast that the men at the mast
   Adjudge him some portent of woe.
       "What ho there!" they cry,
       As he flourishes by
   With a whisk of his beautiful tail;
       And the fish in the sea
       Are as scared as can be,
   From the nautilus up to the whale!

And the Fly-Away Horse seeks those far-away lands
   You little folk dream of at night—
Where candy-trees grow, and honey-brooks flow,
   And corn-fields with popcorn are white;
And the beasts in the wood are ever so good
   To children who visit them there—
What glory astride of a lion to ride,
   Or to wrestle around with a bear!
       The monkeys, they say:
       "Come on, let us play,"
   And they frisk in the cocoanut-trees:
       While the parrots, that cling
       To the peanut-vines, sing
   Or converse with comparative ease!

Off! scamper to bed—you shall ride him to-night!
  For, as soon as you 've fallen asleep,
With a jubilant neigh he shall bear you away
  Over forest and hillside and deep!
But tell us, my dear, all you see and you hear
  In those beautiful lands over there,
Where the Fly-Away Horse wings his far-away course
  With the wee one consigned to his care.
       Then grandma will cry
       In amazement: "Oh, my!"
   And she 'll think it could never be so;
       And only we two
       Shall know it is true—
   You and I, little precious! shall know!

SWING HIGH AND SWING LOW

     Swing high and swing low
     While the breezes they blow—
It 's off for a sailor thy father would go;
And it 's here in the harbor, in sight of the sea,
He hath left his wee babe with my song and with me:
    "Swing high and swing low
    While the breezes they blow!"

     Swing high and swing low
     While the breezes they blow—
It 's oh for the waiting as weary days go!
And it 's oh for the heartache that smiteth me when
I sing my song over and over again:
    "Swing high and swing low
    While the breezes they blow!"

     "Swing high and swing low"—
     The sea singeth so,
And it waileth anon in its ebb and its flow;

And a sleeper sleeps on to that song of the sea
Nor recketh he ever of mine or of me!
> *"Swing high and swing low*
> *While the breezes they blow—*
> *'T was off for a sailor thy father would go!"*

WHEN I WAS A BOY

Up in the attic where I slept
     When I was a boy, a little boy,
In through the lattice the moonlight crept,
Bringing a tide of dreams that swept
Over the low, red trundle-bed,
Bathing the tangled curly head,
While moonbeams played at hide-and-seek
With the dimples on the sun-browned cheek—
     When I was a boy, a little boy!

And, oh! the dreams—the dreams I dreamed!
     When I was a boy, a little boy!
For the grace that through the lattice streamed
Over my folded eyelids seemed
To have the gift of prophecy,
And to bring me glimpses of times to be
When manhood's clarion seemed to call—
Ah! *that* was the sweetest dream of all,
     When I was a boy, a little boy!

I'd like to sleep where I used to sleep
     When I was a boy, a little boy!
For in at the lattice the moon would peep,
Bringing her tide of dreams to sweep
The crosses and griefs of the years away
From the heart that is weary and faint to-day;
And those dreams should give me back again
A peace I have never known since then—
     When I was a boy, a little boy!

AT PLAY

PLAY that you are mother dear,
　And play that papa is your beau;
Play that we sit in the corner here,
　Just as we used to, long ago.
Playing so, we lovers two
　Are just as happy as we can be,
And I 'll say "I love you" to you,
　And you say "I love you" to me!
"I love you" we both shall say,
All in earnest and all in play.

Or, play that you are that other one
　That some time came, and went away;
And play that the light of years agone
　Stole into my heart again to-day!
Playing that you are the one I knew
　In the days that never again may be,
I 'll say "I love you" to you,
　And you say "I love you" to me!
"I love you!" my heart shall say
To the ghost of the past come back to-day!

Or, play that you sought this nestling-place
　For your own sweet self, with that dual guise
Of your pretty mother in your face
　And the look of that other in your eyes!
So the dear old loves shall live anew
　As I hold my darling on my knee,
And I 'll say "I love you" to you,
　And you say "I love you" to me!
Oh, many a strange, true thing we say
And do when we pretend to play,

A VALENTINE

Go, Cupid, and my sweetheart tell
I love her well.
Yes, though she tramples on my heart
And rends that bleeding thing apart;
And though she rolls a scornful eye
On doting me when I go by;
And though she scouts at everything
As tribute unto her I bring—
Apple, banana, caramel,—
Haste, Cupid, to my love and tell,
In spite of all, I love her well!

And further say I have a sled
Cushioned in blue and painted red!
The groceryman has promised I
Can "hitch" whenever he goes by—
Go, tell her that, and, furthermore,
Apprise my sweetheart that a score
Of other little girls impiore
The boon of riding on that sled
Painted and hitched, as aforesaid;—
And tell her, Cupid, only she
Shall ride upon that sled with me!
Tell her this all, and further tell
        I love her well.

————

LITTLE ALL-ALONEY

Little all-aloney's feet
    Pitter-patter in the hall,
And his mother runs to meet
And to kiss her toddling sweet,
    Ere perchance he fall.

He is, oh, so weak and small!
  Yet what danger shall he fear
  When his mother hovereth near,
And he hears her cheering call:
    "All-Aloney"?

Little All-Aloney's face
  It is all aglow with glee,
As around that romping-place
At a terrifying pace
  Lungeth, plungeth he!
And that hero seems to be
  All unconscious of our cheers—
  Only one dear voice he hears
Calling reassuringly:
    "All-Aloney!"

Though his legs bend with their load,
  Though his feet they seem so small
That you cannot help forebode
Some disastrous episode
  In that noisy hall,
Neither threatening bump nor fall
  Little All-Aloney fears,
  But with sweet bravado steers
Whither comes that cheery call:
    "All-Aloney!"

Ah, that in the years to come,
  When he shares of Sorrow's store,—
When his feet are chill and numb,
When his cross is burdensome,
  And his heart is sore:
Would that he could hear once more
  The gentle voice he used to hear—
  Divine with mother love and cheer—
Calling from yonder spirit shore:
    "All, all alone!"

SEEIN' THINGS

I AIN'T afeard uv snakes, or toads, or bugs, or worms, or mice,
An' things 'at girls are skeered uv I think are awful nice!
I 'm pretty brave, I guess; an' yet I hate to go to bed,
For, when I 'm tucked up warm an' snug an' when my prayers
  are said,
Mother tells me "Happy dreams!" and takes away the light,
An' leaves me lyin' all alone an' seein' things at night!

Sometimes they 're in the corner, sometimes they 're by the door,
Sometimes they 're all a-standin' in the middle uv the floor;
Sometimes they are a-sittin' down, sometimes they 're walkin'
  round
So softly an' so creepylike they never make a sound!
Sometimes they are as black as ink, an' other times they 're white—
But the color ain't no difference when you see things at night!

Once, when I licked a feller 'at had just moved on our street,
An' father sent me up to bed without a bite to eat,
I woke up in the dark an' saw things standin' in a row,
A-lookin' at me cross-eyed an' p'intin' at me—so!
Oh, my! I wuz so skeered that time I never slep' a mite—
It 's almost alluz when I 'm bad I see things at night!

Lucky thing I ain't a girl, or I 'd be skeered to death!
Bein' I 'm a boy, I duck my head an' hold my breath;
An' I am, oh! *so* sorry I 'm a naughty boy, an' then
I promise to be better an' I say my prayers again!
Gran'ma tells me that 's the only way to make it right
When a feller has been wicked an' sees things at night!

An' so, when other naughty boys would coax me into sin,
I try to skwush the Tempter's voice 'at urges me within;
An' when they 's pie for supper, or cakes 'at 's big an' nice,
I want to—but I do not pass my plate f'r them things twice!
No, ruther let Starvation wipe me slowly out o' sight
Than I should keep a-livin' on an' seein' things at night!

THE CUNNIN' LITTLE THING

WHEN baby wakes of mornings,
    Then it 's wake, ye people all!
        For another day
        Of song and play
    Has come at our darling's call!
And, till she gets her dinner,
    She makes the welkin ring,
And she *won't* keep still till she 's had her fill—
    The cunnin' little thing!

When baby goes a-walking,
    Oh, how her paddies fly!
        For that 's the way
        The babies say
    To other folk "by-by";
The trees bend down to kiss her,
    And the birds in rapture sing,
As there she stands and waves her hands—
    The cunnin' little thing!

When baby goes a-rocking
    In her bed at close of day,
        At hide-and-seek
        On her dainty cheek
    The dreams and the dimples play;
Then it 's sleep in the tender kisses
    The guardian angels bring
From the Far Above to my sweetest love—
    You cunnin' little thing!

THE DOLL'S WOOING

THE little French doll was a dear little doll
    Tricked out in the sweetest of dresses;
        Her eyes were of hue
        A most delicate blue

And dark as the night were her tresses;
Her dear little mouth was fluted and red,
And this little French doll was so very well bred
That whenever accosted her little mouth said:
"Mamma! mamma!"

The stockinet doll, with one arm and one leg,
 Had once been a handsome young fellow,
  But now he appeared
  Rather frowzy and bleared
 In his torn regimentals of yellow;
Yet his heart gave a curious thump as he lay
In the little toy cart near the window one day
And heard the sweet voice of that French dolly say:
 "Mamma! mamma!"

He listened so long and he listened so hard
 That anon he grew ever so tender,
  For it 's everywhere known
  That the feminine tone
 Gets away with all masculine gender!
He up and he wooed her with soldierly zest
But all she 'd reply to the love he professed
Were *these* plaintive words (which perhaps you have guessed):
 "Mamma! mamma!"

Her mother—a sweet little lady of five—
 Vouchsafed her parental protection,
  And although stockinet
  Was n't blue-blooded, yet
 She really could make no objection!
So soldier and dolly were wedded one day,
And a moment ago, as I journeyed that way,
I 'm sure that I heard a wee baby voice say:
 "Mamma! mamma!"

INSCRIPTION FOR MY LITTLE SON'S SILVER PLATE

WHEN thou dost eat from off this plate,
I charge thee be thou temperate;
Unto thine elders at the board
Do thou sweet reverence accord;
And, though to dignity inclined,
Unto the serving-folk be kind;
Be ever mindful of the poor,
Nor turn them hungry from the door;
And unto God, for health and food
And all that in thy life is good,
Give thou thy heart in gratitude.

FISHERMAN JIM'S KIDS

FISHERMAN JIM lived on the hill
  With his bonnie wife an' his little boys;
'T wuz "Blow, ye winds, as blow ye will—
  Naught we reck of your cold and noise!"
    For happy and warm were he an' his,
And he dandled his kids upon his knee
To the song of the sea.

Fisherman Jim would sail all day,
  But, when come night, upon the sands
His little kids ran from their play,
  Callin' to him an' wavin' their hands;
    Though the wind was fresh and the sea was high,
He 'd hear 'em—you bet—above the roar
Of the waves on the shore!

Once Fisherman Jim sailed into the bay
  As the sun went down in a cloudy sky,
And never a kid saw he at play,

And he listened in vain for the welcoming cry.
In his little house he learned it all,
And he clinched his hands and he bowed his head—
"The fever!" they said.

'T wuz a pitiful time for Fisherman Jim,
With them darlin's a-dyin' afore his eyes,
A-stretchin' their wee hands out to him
An' a-breakin' his heart with the old-time cries
He had heerd so often upon the sands;
For they thought they wuz helpin' his boat ashore—
Till they spoke no more.

But Fisherman Jim lived on and on,
Castin' his nets an' sailin' the sea;
As a man will live when his heart is gone,
Fisherman Jim lived hopelessly,
Till once in those years they come an' said:
"Old Fisherman Jim is powerful sick—
Go to him, quick!"

Then Fisherman Jim says he to me:
"It's a long, long cruise—you understand—
But over beyont the ragin' sea
I kin see my boys on the shinin' sand
Waitin' to help this ol' hulk ashore,
Just as they used to—ah, mate, you know!—
In the long ago."

No, sir! he wuz n't afeard to die;
For all night long he seemed to see
His little boys of the days gone by,
An' to hear sweet voices forgot by me!
An' just as the mornin' sun come up—
"They're holdin' me by the hands!" he cried,
An' so he died.

"FIDDLE–DEE–DEE"

THERE once was a bird that lived up in a tree,
And all he could whistle was "Fiddle-dee-dee"—
A very provoking, unmusical song
For one to be whistling the summer day long!
Yet always contented and busy was he
With that vocal recurrence of "Fiddle-dee-dee."

Hard by lived a brave little soldier of four,
That weird iteration repented him sore;
"I prithee, Dear-Mother-Mine! fetch me my gun,
For, by our St. Didy! the deed must be done
That shall presently rid all creation and me
Of that ominous bird and his 'Fiddle-dee-dee'!"

Then out came Dear-Mother-Mine, bringing her son
His awfully truculent little red gun;
The stock was of pine and the barrel of tin,
The "bang" it came out where the bullet went in—
The right kind of weapon I think you 'll agree
For slaying all fowl that go "Fiddle-dee-dee"!

The brave little soldier quoth never a word,
But he up and he drew a straight bead on that bird;
And, while that vain creature provokingly sang,
The gun it went off with a terrible bang!
Then loud laughed the youth—"By my Bottle," cried he
"I have put a quietus on 'Fiddle-dee-dee'!"

Out came then Dear-Mother-Mine, saying: "My son,
Right well have you wrought with your little red gun!
Hereafter no evil at all need I fear,
With such a brave soldier as You-My-Love here!"
She kissed the dear boy.
                    [The bird in the tree
Continued to whistle his "Fiddle-dee-dee"!]

OVER THE HILLS AND FAR AWAY

OVER the hills and far away,
A little boy steals from his morning play
And under the blossoming apple-tree
He lies and he dreams of the things to be:
Of battles fought and of victories won,
Of wrongs o'erthrown and of great deeds done—
Of the valor that he shall prove some day,
Over the hills and far away—
     Over the hills, and far away!

Over the hills and far away
It 's, oh, for the toil the livelong day!
But it mattereth not to the soul aflame
With a love for riches and power and fame!
On, O man! while the sun is high—
On to the certain joys that lie
Yonder where blazeth the noon of day,
Over the hills and far away—
     Over the hills, and far away!

Over the hills and far away,
An old man lingers at close of day;
Now that his journey is almost done,
His battles fought and his victories won—
The old-time honesty and truth,
The trustfulness and the friends of youth,
Home and mother—where are they?
Over the hills and far away—
     Over the years, and far away!

CRADLE SONG

THE twinkling stars, that stud the skies
    Throughout the quiet night,
Are only precious little eyes
    Of babies fair and bright;

For, when the babies are asleep,
  An angel comes and takes
Their little eyes to guard and keep
  Until the morning breaks.
So, in the sky and on the earth,
  Those little eyes divine,
With quiet love and twinkling mirth,
  Through all the darkness shine.
The golden and majestic moon
  Beholds these baby eyes,
And, mother-like, she loves to croon
  Her softest lullabies,
  Her gentlest hushabies.

The tiny flow'rs the baby knew
  Throughout the noisy day,
Now ope their blossoms to the dew
  And, smiling, seem to say:
"We know you, stars, serene and small,
  Up yonder in the skies—
You are no little stars at all—
  You're only baby eyes!"
The lambkins scamper to and fro
  And chase the night away,
For they are full of joy to know
  The stars behold their play.
The wind goes dancing, free and light,
  O'er tree and hilltop high.
And murmurs all the happy night
  The sweetest lullaby,
  The gentlest hushaby.

So let thy little eyelids close
  Like flow'rs at set of sun.
And tranquil be thy soul's repose,
  My precious weary one!
The still and melancholy night
  Is envious of thine eyes,
And longs to see their glorious light
  In yonder azure skies.

The daisies wonder all the while
   Why all is dark above,
And clamor for the radiant smile
   Of little orbs they love;
And, lo! an angel hovers near
   To bear thine eyes on high.
So sleep, my babe, if thou would'st hear
   The music of the sky—
   Sweet nature's hushaby.

THE ROSE AND THE ICEBERG

I HASTEN from the land of snows,
   Where sunbeams dance and quiver,
Unto the dwelling of a rose,
   Hard by a southern river.
An iceberg loves the blooming thing,
   But she will pay no heeding
Unto the splendid polar king,
   Nor to his piteous pleading.

Abashed that she is hostile to
   His amorous pursuing,
The iceberg wills that I should go
   To do his kingly wooing.
He bids me lure her from her tree,
   And from her balmy places;
And bear her swiftly back with me.
   Unto his fond embraces.

So, swiftly o'er the mountains high,
   And through the forests gloomy,
Unto the distant vale I fly
   To win this blossom to me.
To-morrow evening shall I ride—
   More merrisome and faster—
For I shall bear the blooming bride
   Back to my knightly master.

A HUSHABY

BA-BA, baby sheep,
 Chill and sombre grows the night—
 Only stars from heaven's height
 Shed on us their golden light—
Ba-ba, go to sleep—
Go to sleep, baby sheep!

Ba-ba, baby sheep—
 Never mind the goblin's growl—
 Never heed the hoodoo's howl—
 Let the hippogriffin prowl—
Ba-ba, mother 'll keep
Watch over baby sheep!

Ba-ba, baby sheep—
 Up above, serene and far,
 Beams a tiny golden star
 Listening to the ba-ba
I am singing to the sheep,
As they rock the lambs to sleep.

———

SONG OF THE CLOUDS

FAR, far beyond yon Eastern steeps
 There is an humble little cot,
 And in that homely, lonely spot
A mother prays and weeps.
Be calm, dear one, the Father hears
 Thy softest plaint and faintest sigh,
 And He hath bless'd thy pray'rful cry
And sanctified thy tears.

And He hath sent us clouds to bear
 Thy mother's tears, in form of rain,
 Unto the distant desert plain,

To cool the desert air.
The fainting youth will feel our breath
  Upon his bronzed and fevered face,
  And have new strength to leave that place—
That arid haunt of death.

The mother heart need not despair—
  To-morrow eve the son shall rest
  Upon that mother's joyful breast,
For God hath heard her pray'r.
So, gentle stars, stay not our flight—
  A mother's tears, in form of rain,
  We bear unto that distant plain
Where faints a son to-night.

THE PRINCESS MING

THERE was a prince by the name of Tsing
  Who lived in the Chinese town of Lung
And fell in love with the Princess Ming
  Who lived in the neighboring town of Jung;
      'Twas a terrible thing
      For Tsing and Ming,
As you 'll allow, when you 've heard me sing.

Now it happened so that the town of Lung,
  Where lived the prince who longed to woo,
Went out to war with the town of Jung
  With junks and swords and matchlocks, too—
      'Twas a terrible thing
      For Tsing and Ming,
As you 'll allow, when you 've heard me sing.

Miss Ming's papa was eating rice
  On yestermorn at half-past eight,
And had carved a pie composed of mice,
  When the soldiers knocked at his palace gate;

They were led by Tsing,
And they called for Ming,
Which all will allow was a terrible thing!

Miss Ming's papa girt on his sword—
"For this," quoth he, "I 'll have his gore!"
In vain the Princess Ming implored—
In vain she swooned on the palace floor—
The Princess Ming
Who was wooed of Tsing
Could not prevail with the gruff old King!

The old King opened the palace gate
And in marched Tsing with his soldiers grim,
And the King smote Tsing on his princely pate—
Stating this stern rebuke to him:
"It 's a fatal thing
For you, Mr. Tsing,
To come a-courting the Princess Ming!"

The prince most keenly felt this slight,
But still more keenly the cut on his head;
So, suddenly turning cold and white,
He fell to the earth and lay there dead.
Which act of the King
To the handsome Tsing
Was a brutal shock to the Princess Ming.

No sooner did the young prince die
Than Princess Ming from the palace flew,
And jumped straight into the River Ji,
With the dreadful purpose of dying, too!
'Twas a natural thing
For the Princess Ming
To do for love of the handsome Tsing!

And when she leaped in the River Ji,
And gasped and choked till her face was blue,
A crocodile fish came paddling by
And greedily bit Miss Ming in two—

The horrid old thing
Devoured Miss Ming,
Who had hoped to die for the love of Tsing.

When the King observed her life adjourned,
By the crocodile's biting the girl in twain,
Up to the ether his toes he turned,
With a ghastly rent in his jugular vein;
So the poor old King,
And Tsing, and Ming
Were dead and gone—what a terrible thing!

And as for the crocodile fish that had
Devoured Miss Ming in this off-hand way,
He caught the dyspepsy so dreadful bad
That he, too, died that very day!
So, now, with the King,
And Tsing, and Ming,
And the crocodile dead, what more can I sing?

AN ELFIN SUMMONS

From the flow'rs and from the trees
Come, O tiny midnight elves,
And, to music of the breeze,
Merrily disport yourselves.
Harnessing the glow-worm's wing,
Drive the glow-worm for your steed,
Or with crickets dance and sing
On the velvet, perfumed mead.
Forth from pretty blue-bells creep
To coquette with starlight gleam—
See, the lambkins are asleep
And the daisies sleeping dream.
Hasten to engage yourselves
In your frolics, midnight elves!

See, a toad with jewelled eyes
 Comes and croaks his homely song
To the spider as she plies
 Her deft spinning all night long;
See the bat with rustling wings
 Darting nervously above—
Hear the cricket as she sings
 To her little violet love.
All the goblins are asleep
 And no flimflam hovers near,
So from out the posies creep
 With your Elfin ladies dear;
Merrily disport yourselves,
Frisky little midnight elves!

A BROOK SONG

I 'M hastening from the distant hills
 With swift and noisy flowing,
Nursed by a thousand tiny rills,
 I 'm ever onward going.
The willows cannot stay my course,
 With all their pliant wooing.
I sing and sing till I am hoarse,
 My prattling way pursuing.
I kiss the pebbles as I pass,
 And hear them say they love me;
I make obeisance to the grass
 That kindly bends above me.
So onward through the meads and dells
 I hasten, never knowing
The secret motive that impels,
 Or whither I am going.

A little child comes often here
 To watch my quaint commotion,
As I go tumbling, swift and clear,
 Down to the distant ocean;

And as he plays upon my brink,
  So thoughtless like and merry,
And full of noisy song, I think
  The child is like me, very.
Through all the years of youthful play,
  With ne'er a thought of sorrow,
We, prattling, speed upon our way,
  Unmindful of the morrow;
Aye, through these sunny meads and dells
  We gambol, never trowing
The solemn motive that impels,
  Or whither we are going.

And men come here to say to me:
  "Like you, with weird commotion,
O little singing brooklet, we
  Are hastening to an ocean;
Down to a vast and misty deep,
  With fleeting tears and laughter,
We go, nor rest until we sleep
  In that profound Hereafter.
What tides may bear our souls along—
  What monsters rise appalling—
What distant shores may hear our song
  And answer to our calling?
Ah, who can say! through meads and dells
  We wander, never knowing.
The awful motive that impels,
  Or whither we are going!"

THE DISMAL DOLE OF THE DOODLEDOO

A BINGO bird once nestled her nest
  On the lissom bough of an I O yew,
Hard by a burrow that was possess'd
  Of a drear and dismal doodledoo.

Eftsoons this doodledoo descried
  The blithe and beautiful bingo bird,
He vowed he 'd woo her to be his bride
  With many a sleek and winsome word.
"Oh, doo! oh, doo!" sang the doodledoo
To the bingo bird in the yarrish yew.

Now a churlish chit was the bingo bird,
  Though her plumes were plumes of cardinal hue,
And she smithered a smirk whenever she heard
  The tedious yawp of the doodledoo;
For she loved, alas! a subtile snaix,
  Which had a sting at the end of his tail
And lived in a tarn of sedge and brakes
  On the murky brink of a gruesome swail.
"Oh, doo! oh, doo!" moaned the doodledoo,
As dimmer and danker each day he grew.

Now, when this doodledoo beheld
  The snaix go wooing the bingo bird,
With envious rancor his bosom swelled—
  His soul with bitter remorse was stirred.
And a flubdub said to the doodledoo,
  "The subtile snaix isn't toting square—
I tell no tales—but if I were you,
  I 'd stop his courting the bingo fair!
Aye, marry, come up, I 'd fain imbrue,
If I were only a doodledoo!"

These burning words which the flubdub said
  Inflamed the reptile's tortured soul
Till the bristles rose on his livid head,
  And his slimy tongue began for to roll;
His skin turned red and his fangs turned black
  And his eyes exuded a pool of tears,
And the scales stood up on his bony back,
  And fire oozed out of his nose and ears!
Oh, he was a terrible sight to view—
This fierce and vengeful doodledoo!

The very next morn, as the bingo bird
  Was nursing her baby bingoes three,
She gave a start, for she plainly heard
  An ominous sound at the foot of the tree!
Her keen eye lit on the gruesome brakes,
  From whence proceeded the hullaballoo—
And, lo and behold! 'twas the subtile snaix,
  Busy at work with the doodledoo.
Boo-hoo! boo-hoo! how the feathers flew,
When the snaix imbrued with the doodledoo!

They fought and scratched, and they bit and bled,
  Dispensing gore and their vitals, too,
And never pausing till both were dead—
  The subtile snaix and the doodledoo!
And the bingo bird—she didn't mind,
  But giving her shoulders a careless shrug,
She went the way of her female kind,
  And straightway wedded the straddlebug!
And there was nobody left to rue
The doom of the snaix and the doodledoo—
Unless, mayhap, 'twas the I O yew.

THE VIOLET'S LOVE STORY

HERE died a robin in the spring,
  And, when he fluttered down to me,
I tried to bind his broken wing,
  And soothe his dying agony.

I loved the wounded little bird—
  And, though my heart was full to break,
I loved in silence—ne'er a word
  Of that dear, hopeless love I spake.

I saw his old companions bring
  Their funeral tributes to his dell;
But, when they went, I stayed to sing
  The love I had not dared to tell.

So, while the little robin sleeps,
  The sorrowing violet bides above:
And still she sings, as still she weeps,
  A requiem to her buried love.

AN INVITATION TO SLEEP

LITTLE eyelids, cease your winking;
  Little orbs, forget to beam;
Little soul, to slumber sinking,
  Let the fairies rule your dream.
Breezes, through the lattice sweeping,
  Sing their lullabies the while—
And a star-ray, softly creeping
  To thy bedside, woos thy smile.
But no song nor ray entrancing
  Can allure thee from the spell
Of the tiny fairies dancing
  O'er the eyes they love so well.
See, we come in countless number—
  I, their queen, and all my court—
Haste, my precious one, to slumber
  Which invites our fairy sport.

COQUETRY

TIDDLE-DE-DUMPTY, tiddle-de-dee—
The spider courted the frisky flea;
Tiddle-de-dumpty, tiddle-de-doo—
The flea ran off with the bugaboo!
      "Oh, tiddle-de-dee!"
      Said the frisky flea—
      For what cared she
      For the miseree
      The spider knew,
      When, tiddle-de-doo,
The flea ran off with the bugaboo!

Rumpty-tumpty, pimplety-pan—
The flubdub courted a catamaran
But timplety-topplety, timpity-tare—
The flubdub wedded the big blue bear!
  The fun began
  With a pimplety-pan,
  When the catamaran
  Tore up a man
  And streaked the air
  With his gore and hair
Because the flubdub wedded the bear!

THE CRICKET'S SONG

When all around from out the ground
 The little flowers are peeping,
And from the hills the merry rills
 With vernal songs are leaping,
I sing my song the whole day long
 In woodland, hedge, and thicket—
And sing it, too, the whole night through,
 For I 'm a merry cricket.

The children hear my chirrup clear
 As, in the woodland straying,
They gather flow'rs through summer hours—
 And then I hear them saying:
"Sing, sing away the livelong day,
 Glad songster of the thicket—
With your shrill mirth you gladden earth,
 You merry little cricket!"

When summer goes, and Christmas snows
 Are from the north returning,
I quit my lair and hasten where
 The old yule-log is burning.

And where at night the ruddy light
  Of that old log is flinging
A genial joy o'er girl and boy,
  There I resume my singing.

And, when they hear my chirrup clear,
  The children stop their playing—
With eager feet they haste to greet
  My welcome music, saying:
"The little thing has come to sing
  Of woodland, hedge, and thicket—
Of summer day and lambs at play—
  Oh, how we love the cricket!"

———

THE FATE OF THE FLIMFLAM

A FLIMFLAM flopped from a fillamaloo,
  Where the pollywog pinkled so pale,
And the pipkin piped a petulant "pooh"
  To the garrulous gawp of the gale.
"Oh, woe to the swap of the sweeping swipe
  That booms on the bobbling bay!"
Snickered the snark to the snoozing snipe
  That lurked where the lamprey lay.

The gluglug glinked in the glimmering gloam,
  Where the buzbuz bumbled his bee—
When the flimflam flitted, all flecked with foam,
  From the sozzling and succulent sea.
"Oh, swither the swipe, with its sweltering sweep!"
  She swore as she swayed in a swoon,
And a doleful dank dumped over the deep,
  To the lay of the limpid loon!

CONTENTMENT

ONCE on a time an old red hen
　　Went strutting 'round with pompous clucks,
For she had little babies ten,
　　A part of which were tiny ducks.
" 'T is very rare that hens," said she,
　　"Have baby ducks as well as chicks—
But I possess, as you can see,
　　Of chickens four and ducklings six!"

A season later, this old hen
　　Appeared, still cackling of her luck,
For, though she boasted babies ten,
　　Not one among them was a duck!
" 'T is well," she murmured, brooding o'er
　　The little chicks of fleecy down—
"My babies now will stay ashore,
　　And, consequently, cannot drown!"

The following spring the old red hen
　　Clucked just as proudly as of yore—
But lo! her babes were ducklings ten,
　　Instead of chickens, as before!
" 'T is better," said the old red hen,
　　As she surveyed her waddling brood;
"A little water now and then
　　Will surely do my darlings good!"

But oh! alas, how very sad!
　　When gentle spring rolled round again
The eggs eventuated bad,
　　And childless was the old red hen!
Yet patiently she bore her woe,
　　And still she wore a cheerful air,
And said: " 'T is best these things are so,
　　For babies are a dreadful care!"

I half suspect that many men,
  And many, many women, too,
Could learn a lesson from the hen
  With foliage of vermilion hue;
She ne'er presumed to take offence
  At any fate that might befall,
But meekly bowed to Providence—
  She was contented—that was all!

A FAIRY LULLABY

THERE are two stars in yonder steeps
That watch the baby while he sleeps.
  But while the baby is awake
    And singing gayly all day long,
  The little stars their slumbers take
    Lulled by the music of his song.
So sleep, dear tired baby, sleep
While little stars their vigils keep.

Beside his loving mother-sheep
A little lambkin is asleep;
  What does he know of midnight gloom—
    He sleeps, and in his quiet dreams
  He thinks he plucks the clover bloom
    And drinks at cooling, purling streams.
And those same stars the baby knows
Sing softly to the lamb's repose.

Sleep, little lamb; sleep, little child—
The stars are dim—the night is wild;
  But o'er the cot and o'er the lea
    A sleepless eye forever beams—
  A shepherd watches over thee
    In all thy little baby dreams;
The shepherd loves his tiny sheep—
Sleep, precious little lambkin, sleep!

BALLAD OF THE JELLY–CAKE

A LITTLE boy whose name was Tim
   Once ate some jelly-cake for tea—
Which cake did not agree with him,
   As by the sequel you shall see.
"My darling child," his mother said,
   "Pray do not eat that jelly-cake,
For, after you have gone to bed,
   I fear 't will make your stomach ache!"
But foolish little Tim demurred
Unto his mother's warning word.

That night, while all the household slept,
   Tim felt an awful pain, and then
From out the dark a nightmare leapt
   And stood upon his abdomen!
"I cannot breathe!" the infant cried—
   "Oh, Mrs. Nightmare, pity take!"
"There is no mercy," she replied,
   "For boys who feast on jelly-cake!"
And so, despite the moans of Tim,
The cruel nightmare went for him.

At first, she 'd tickle Timmy's toes
   Or roughly smite his baby cheek—
And now she 'd rudely tweak his nose
   And other petty vengeance wreak;
And then, with hobnails in her shoes
   And her two horrid eyes aflame,
The mare proceeded to amuse
   Herself by prancing o'er his frame—
First to his throbbing brow, and then
Back to his little feet again.

At last, fantastic, wild, and weird,
   And clad in garments ghastly grim,
A scowling hoodoo band appeared
   And joined in worrying little Tim.

Each member of this hoodoo horde
　Surrounded Tim with fierce ado
And with long, cruel gimlets bored
　His aching system through and through,
And while they labored all night long
The nightmare neighed a dismal song.

Next morning, looking pale and wild,
　Poor little Tim emerged from bed—
"Good gracious! what can ail the child!"
　His agitated mother said.
"We live to learn," responded he,
　"And I have lived to learn to take
Plain bread and butter for my tea,
　And never, never, jelly-cake!
For when my hulk with pastry teems,
I must *expect* unpleasant dreams!"

MORNING SONG

The eastern sky is streaked with red,
　The weary night is done,
And from his distant ocean bed
　Rolls up the morning sun.
The dew, like tiny silver beads
　Bespread o'er velvet green,
Is scattered on the wakeful meads
　By angel hands unseen.
"Good-morrow, robin in the trees!"
　The star-eyed daisy cries;
"Good-morrow," sings the morning breeze
　Unto the ruddy skies;
"Good-morrow, every living thing!"
　Kind Nature seems to say,
And all her works devoutly sing
　A hymn to birth of day,
　　So, haste, without delay,
Haste, fairy friends, on silver wing,
　And to your homes away!

TO A SLEEPING BABY'S EYES

AND thou, twin orbs of love and joy!
 Unveil thy glories with the morn—
 Dear eyes, another day is born—
Awake, O little sleeping boy!
Bright are the summer morning skies,
 But in this quiet little room
 There broods a chill, oppressive gloom—
All for the brightness of thine eyes.
Without those radiant orbs of thine
 How dark this little world would be—
 This sweet home-world that worships thee—
So let their wondrous glories shine
On those who love their warmth and joy—
Awake, O sleeping little boy.

DREAM, DREAM, DREAM!

DREAM, dream, dream
Of meadow, wood, and stream;
 Of bird and bee,
 Of flower and tree,
All under the noonday gleam;
 Of the song and play
 Of mirthful day—
Dream, dream, dream!

Dream, dream, dream
Of glamour, glint, and gleam;
 Of the hushaby things
 The night wind sings
To the moon and the stars abeam;
 Of whimsical sights
 In the land o' sprites
Dream, dream, dream!

A LULLABY

THE stars are twinkling in the skies,
   The earth is lost in slumbers deep;
So hush, my sweet, and close thine eyes,
   And let me lull thy soul to sleep.
Compose thy dimpled hands to rest,
   And like a little birdling lie
Secure within thy cosey nest
Upon my loving mother breast
   And slumber to my lullaby,
   So hushaby—O hushaby.

The moon is singing to a star
   The little song I sing to you;
The father sun has strayed afar,
   As baby's sire is straying too.
And so the loving mother moon
   Sings to the little star on high;
And as she sings, her gentle tune
Is borne to me, and thus I croon
   For thee, my sweet, that lullaby
   Of hushaby—O hushaby.

There is a little one asleep
   That does not hear his mother's song;
But angel watchers—as I weep—
   Surround his grave the night-tide long.
And as I sing, my sweet, to you,
   Oh, would the lullaby I sing—
The same sweet lullaby he knew
While slumb'ring on this bosom too—
   Were borne to him on angel's wing!
   So hushaby—O hushaby.

THE DEATH OF ROBIN HOOD

"Give me my bow," said Robin Hood,
　"An arrow give to me;
And where 't is shot mark thou that spot,
　For there my grave shall be."

Then Little John did make no sign,
　And not a word he spake;
But he smiled, altho' with mickle woe
　His heart was like to break.

He raised his master in his arms,
　And set him on his knee;
And Robin's eyes beheld the skies,
　The shaws, the greenwood tree.

The brook was babbling as of old,
　The birds sang full and clear,
And the wild-flowers gay like a carpet lay
　In the path of the timid deer.

"O Little John," said Robin Hood,
　"Meseemeth now to be
Standing with you so stanch and true
　Under the greenwood tree.

"And all around I hear the sound
　Of Sherwood long ago,
And my merry men come back again,—
　You know, sweet friend, you know!

"Now mark this arrow; where it falls,
　When I am dead dig deep,
And bury me there in the greenwood where
　I would forever sleep."

He twanged his bow. Upon its course
  The clothyard arrow sped,
And when it fell in yonder dell,
  Brave Robin Hood was dead.

The sheriff sleeps in a marble vault,
  The king in a shroud of gold;
And upon the air with a chanted pray'r
  Mingles the mock of mould.

But the deer draw to the shady pool,
  The birds sing blithe and free,
And the wild-flow'rs bloom o'er a hidden tomb
  Under the greenwood tree.

———

MOTHER AND CHILD

ONE night a tiny dewdrop fell
  Into the bosom of a rose,—
"Dear little one, I love thee well,
  Be ever here thy sweet repose!"

Seeing the rose with love bedight,
  The envious sky frowned dark, and then
Sent forth a messenger of light
  And caught the dewdrop up again.

"Oh, give me back my heavenly child,—
  My love!" the rose in anguish cried;
Alas! the sky triumphant smiled,
  And so the flower, heart-broken, died.

ASHES ON THE SLIDE

WHEN Jim and Bill and I were boys a many years ago,
How gayly did we use to hail the coming of the snow!
Our sleds, fresh painted red and with their runners round and
     bright,
Seemed to respond right briskly to our clamor of delight
As we dragged them up the slippery road that climbed the rugged
     hill
Where perched the old frame meetin'-house, so solemn-like and still.

Ah, coasting in those days—those good old days—was fun indeed!
Sleds at that time I'd have you know were paragons of speed!
And if the hill got bare in spots, as hills will do, why then
We'd haul on ice and snow to patch those bald spots up again;
But, oh! with what sad certainty our spirits would subside
When Deacon Frisbee sprinkled ashes where we used to slide!

The deacon he would roll his eyes and gnash his toothless gums,
And clear his skinny throat, and twirl his saintly, bony thumbs,
And tell you: "When I wuz a boy, they taught me to eschew
The godless, ribald vanities which modern youth pursue!
The pathway that leads down to hell is slippery, straight, and
     wide;
And Satan lurks for prey where little boys are wont to slide!"

Now, he who ever in his life has been a little boy
Will not reprove me when he hears the language I employ
To stigmatize as wickedness the deacon's zealous spite
In interfering with the play wherein we found delight;
And so I say, with confidence, not unalloyed of pride:
"Gol durn the man who sprinkles ashes where the youngsters slide!"

But Deacon Frisbee long ago went to his lasting rest,
His money well invested in farm mortgages out West;
Bill, Jim, and I, no longer boys, have learned through years of strife
That the troubles of the little boy pursue the man through life;
That here and there along the course wherein we hoped to glide
Some envious hand has sprinkled ashes just to spoil our slide!

And that malicious, envious hand is not the deacon's now.
Grim, ruthless Fate, that evil sprite none other is than thou!
Riches and honors, peace and care come at thy beck and go;
The soul, elate with joy to-day, to-morrow writhes in woe;
And till a man has turned his face unto the wall and died,
He must expect to get his share of ashes on his slide!

CHRISTMAS EVE

OH, hush thee, little Dear-my-Soul,
    The evening shades are falling,—
Hush thee, my dear, dost thou not hear
    The voice of the Master calling?

Deep lies the snow upon the earth,
    But all the sky is ringing
With joyous song, and all night long
    The stars shall dance, with singing.

Oh, hush thee, little Dear-my-Soul,
    And close thine eyes in dreaming,
And angels fair shall lead thee where
    The singing stars are beaming.

A shepherd calls his little lambs,
    And he longeth to caress them;
He bids them rest upon his breast,
    That his tender love may bless them.

So, hush thee, little Dear-my-Soul,
    Whilst evening shades are falling,
And above the song of the heavenly throng
    Thou shalt hear the Master calling.

TELLING THE BEES

Out of the house where the slumberer lay
Grandfather came one summer day,
And under the pleasant orchard trees
He spake this wise to the murmuring bees:
  "The clover-bloom that kissed her feet
    And the posie-bed where she used to play
  Have honey store, but none so sweet
    As ere our little one went away.
O bees, sing soft, and, bees, sing low;
For she is gone who loved you so."

A wonder fell on the listening bees
Under those pleasant orchard trees,
And in their toil that summer day
Ever their murmuring seemed to say:
  "Child, O child, the grass is cool,
    And the posies are waking to hear the song
  Of the bird that swings by the shaded pool,
    Waiting for one that tarrieth long."
'T was so they called to the little one then,
As if to call her back again.

O gentle bees, I have come to say
That grandfather fell asleep to-day,
And we know by the smile on grandfather's face
He has found his dear one's biding-place.
  So, bees, sing soft, and, bees, sing low,
    As over the honey-fields you sweep,—
  To the trees abloom and the flowers ablow
    Sing of grandfather fast asleep;
And ever beneath these orchard trees
Find cheer and shelter, gentle bees.

TWO VALENTINES

I—TO MISTRESS BARBARA

THERE were three cavaliers, all handsome and true,
On Valentine's day came a maiden to woo,
And quoth to your mother: "Good-morrow, my dear,
We came with some songs for your daughter to hear!"

Your mother replied: "I 'll be pleased to convey
To my daughter what things you may sing or may say!"

Then the first cavalier sung: "My pretty red rose,
I 'll love you and court you some day, I suppose!"
And the next cavalier sung, with make-believe tears:
"I 've loved you! I 've loved you these many long years!"

But the third cavalier (with the brown, bushy head
And the pretty blue jacket and necktie of red)
He drew himself up with a resolute air,
And he warbled: "O maiden, surpassingly fair!
I 've loved you long years, and I love you to-day,
And, if you will let me, I 'll love you for aye!"

I (the third cavalier) sang this ditty to you,
In my necktie of red and my jacket of blue;
I 'm sure you 'll prefer the song that was mine
And smile your approval on your valentine.

II—TO A BABY BOY

WHO I am I shall not say,
But I send you this bouquet
With this query, baby mine:
"Will you be my valentine?"

See these roses blushing blue,
Very like your eyes of hue;
While these violets are the red
Of your cheeks.   It can be said
Ne'er before was babe like you.

And I think it is quite true
No one e 'er before to-day
Sent so wondrous a bouquet
As these posies aforesaid—
Roses blue and violets red!

Sweet, repay me sweets for sweets—
'T is your lover who entreats!
Smile upon me, baby mine—
Be my little valentine!

THE LIMITATIONS OF YOUTH

I 'D like to be a cowboy an' ride a firey hoss
   Way out into the big an' boundless West;
I 'd kill the bears an' catamounts an' wolves I come across,
   An' I 'd pluck the bal' head eagle from his nest!
         With my pistols at my side,
         I would roam the prarers wide,
   An' to scalp the savage Injun in his wigwam would I ride—
         If I darst; but I darse n't!

I 'd like to go to Afriky an' hunt the lions there,
  An' the biggest ollyfunts you ever saw!
I would track the fierce gorilla to his equatorial lair,
  An' beard the cannybull that eats folks raw!
      I 'd chase the pizen snakes
      An' the 'pottimus that makes
His nest down at the bottom of unfathomable lakes—
      If I darst; but I darse n't!

I would I were a pirut to sail the ocean blue,
  With a big black flag aflyin' overhead;
I would scour the billowy main with my gallant pirut crew
  An' dye the sea a gouty, gory red!
      With my cutlass in my hand
      On the quarterdeck I 'd stand
And to deeds of heroism I 'd incite my pirut band—
      If I darst; but I darse n't!

And, if I darst, I 'd lick my pa for the times that he 's licked me!
  I 'd lick my brother an' my teacher, too!
I 'd lick the fellers that call round on sister after tea,
  An' I 'd keep on lickin' folks till I got through!
      You bet! I 'd run away
      From my lessons to my play,
An' I 'd shoo the hens, an' tease the cat, an' kiss the girls all
  day—
      If I darst; but I darse n't!

A PITEOUS PLAINT

I CANNOT eat my porridge,
  I weary of my play;
No longer can I sleep at night,
  No longer romp by day!
Though forty pounds was once my weight,
  I 'm shy of thirty now;
I pine, I wither and I fade
  Through ,ove of Martha Clow.

As she rolled by this morning
  I heard the nurse girl say:
"She weighs just twenty-seven pounds
  And she 's one year old to-day."
I threw a kiss that nestled
  In the curls upon her brow,
But she never turned to thank me—
  That bouncing Martha Clow!

She ought to know I love her,
  For I 've told her that I do;
And I 've brought her nuts and apples,
  And sometimes candy, too!
I 'd drag her in my little cart
  If her mother would allow
That delicate attention
  To her daughter, Martha Clow.

O Martha! pretty Martha!
  Will you always be so cold?
Will you always be as cruel
  As you are at one-year-old?

Must your two-year-old admirer
　Pine as hopelessly as now
For a fond reciprocation
　Of his love for Martha Clow?

You smile on Bernard Rogers
　And on little Harry Knott;
You play with them at peek-a-boo
　All in the Waller Lot!
Wildly I gnash my new-cut teeth
　And beat my throbbing brow,
When I behold the coquetry
　Of heartless Martha Clow!

I cannot eat my porridge,
　Nor for my play care I;
Upon the floor and porch and lawn
　My toys neglected lie;
But on the air of Halsted Street
　I breathe this solemn vow:
"Though *she* be *false, I* will be true
　To pretty Martha Clow!"

———

THE TWO LITTLE SKEEZUCKS

THERE were two little skeezucks who lived in the isle
　Of Boo in a southern sea;
They clambered and rollicked in heathenish style
　In the boughs of their cocoanut tree.
They didn't fret much about clothing and such
　And they recked not a whit of the ills
　　　That sometimes accrue
　　　From having to do
With tailor and laundry bills.

The two little skeezucks once heard of a Fair
  Far off from their native isle,
And they asked of King Fan if they mightn't go there
  To take in the sights for awhile.
      Now old King Fan
        Was a good-natured man
(As good-natured monarchs go),
And howbeit he swore that all Fairs were a bore,
He hadn't the heart to say "No."

So the two little skeezucks sailed off to the Fair
  In a great big gum canoe,
And I fancy they had a good time there,
  For they tarried a year or two.
And old King Fan at last began
  To reckon they 'd come to grief,
      When glory! one day
      They sailed into the bay
To the tune of "Hail to the Chief!"

The two little skeezucks fell down on the sand,
  Embracing his majesty's toes,
Till his majesty graciously bade them stand
  And salute him nose to nose.
      And then quoth he:
      "Divulge unto me
What happenings have hapt to you:
And how did they dare to indulge in a Fair
  So far from the island of Boo?"

The two little skeezucks assured their king
  That what he surmised was true;
That the Fair would have been a different thing
  Had it only been held in Boo!

"The folk over there in no wise compare
With the folk of the southern seas;
  Why, they comb out their heads
  And they sleep in beds
Instead of in caverns and trees!"

The two little skeezucks went on to say
 That children (so far as they knew)
Had a much harder time in that land far away
 Than here in the island of Boo!
  They have to wear clo'es
  Which (as every one knows)
 Are irksome to primitive laddies,
While, with forks and with spoons, they 're denied the sweet
  boons
 That accrue from free use of one's paddies!

"And now that you 're speaking of things to eat,"
 Interrupted the monarch of Boo,
"We beg to inquire if you happened to meet
 With a nice missionary or two?"
"No, that we did not; in that curious spot
Where were gathered the fruits of the earth,
  Of that special kind
  Which Your Nibs has in mind
There appeared a deplorable dearth!"

Then loud laughed that monarch in heathenish mirth
 And loud laughed his courtiers, too,
And they cried: "There is elsewhere no land upon earth
 So good as our island of Boo!"
  And the skeezucks, tho' glad
  Of the journey they 'd had,
 Climbed up in their cocoanut trees,
Where they still may be seen with no shirts to keep clean
Or trousers that bag at the knees.

THE BOW–LEG BOY

WHO should come up the road one day
But the doctor-man in his two-wheel shay!
And he whoaed his horse and he cried "Ahoy!
I have brought you folks a bow-leg boy!
　　Such a cute little boy!
　　　　Such a funny little boy!
　　　　　　Such a dear little bow-leg boy!"

He took out his box and he opened it wide,
And there was the bow-leg boy inside!
And when they saw that cunning little mite,
They cried in a chorus expressive of delight:
　　"What a cute little boy!
　　　　What a funny little boy!
　　　　　　What a dear little bow-leg boy!"

Observing a strict geometrical law,
They cut out his panties with a circular saw;
Which gave such a stress to his oval stride
That the people he met invariably cried:
　　"What a cute little boy!
　　　　What a funny little boy!
　　　　　　What a dear little bow-leg boy!"

They gave him a wheel and away he went
Speeding along to his heart's content;
And he sits so straight and he pedals so strong
That the folks all say as he bowls along:
　　"What a cute little boy!
　　　　What a funny little boy!
　　　　　　What a dear little bow-leg boy!"

With his eyes aflame and his cheeks aglow,
He laughs "aha" and he laughs "oho";
And the world is filled and thrilled with the joy
Of that jolly little human, the bow-leg boy—
  The cute little boy!
   The funny little boy!
    The dear little bow-leg boy!

If ever the doctor-man comes *my* way
With his wonderful box in his two-wheel shay,
I 'll ask for the treasure I 'd fain possess—
Now, honest Injun! can't you guess?
  Why, a cute little boy—
   A funny little boy—
    A dear little bow-leg boy!

ECHOES FROM THE SABINE FARM

By Eugene and Roswell Martin Field

TO M. L. GRAY

(DEDICATION)

Come, dear old friend, and with us twain
  To calm Digentian groves repair;
The turtle coos his sweet refrain
  And posies are a-blooming there;
And there the romping Sabine girls
Bind myrtle in their lustrous curls.

I know a certain ilex-tree
  Whence leaps a fountain cool and clear.
Its voices summon you and me;
  Come, let us haste to share its cheer!
Methinks the rapturous song it sings
Should woo our thoughts from mortal things.

But, good old friend, I charge thee well,
  Watch thou my brother all the while,
Lest some fair Lydia cast her spell
  Round him unschooled in female guile.
Those damsels have no charms for me;
Guard thou that brother,—I 'll guard thee!

And, lo, sweet friend! behold this cup,
  Round which the garlands intertwine;
With Massic it is foaming up,
  And we would drink to thee and thine.
And of the draught thou shalt partake,
Who lov'st us for our father's sake

Hark you! from yonder Sabine farm
  Echo the songs of long ago,
With power to soothe and grace to charm
  What ills humanity may know;
With that sweet music in the air,
'T is Love and Summer everywhere.

So, though no grief consumes our lot
  (Since all our lives have been discreet),
Come, in this consecrated spot,
  Let's see if pagan cheer be sweet.
Now, then, the songs; but, first, more wine.
The gods be with you, friends of mine!

AN INVITATION TO MÆCENAS

DEAR, noble friend! a virgin cask
  Of wine solicits your attention;
And roses fair, to deck your hair,
  And things too numerous to mention.
So tear yourself awhile away
  From urban turmoil, pride, and splendor,
And deign to share what humble fare
  And sumptuous fellowship I tender.
The sweet content retirement brings
Smoothes out the ruffled front of kings.

The evil planets have combined
  To make the weather hot and hotter;
By parboiled streams the shepherd dreams
  Vainly of ice-cream soda-water.
And meanwhile you, defying heat,
  With patriotic ardor ponder
On what old Rome essays at home,
  And what her heathen do out yonder.
Mæcenas, no such vain alarm
Disturbs the quiet of this farm!

God in His providence obscures
　　The goal beyond this vale of sorrow,
And smiles at men in pity when
　　They seek to penetrate the morrow.
With faith that all is for the best,
　　Let's bear what burdens are presented,
That we shall say, let come what may,
　　"We die, as we have lived, contented!
Ours is to-day; God's is the rest,—
He doth ordain who knoweth best."

Dame Fortune plays me many a prank.
　　When she is kind, oh, how I go it!
But if again she 's harsh,—why, then
　　I am a very proper poet!
When favoring gales bring in my ships,
　　I hie to Rome and live in clover;
Elsewise I steer my skiff out here,
　　And anchor till the storm blows over.
Compulsory virtue is the charm
Of life upon the Sabine farm!

CHLORIS PROPERLY REBUKED

Chloris, my friend, I pray you your misconduct to forswear;
The wife of poor old Ibycus should have more *savoir faire.*
A woman at your time of life, and drawing near death's door,
Should not play with the girly girls, and think she 's *en rapport.*

What 's good enough for Pholoe you cannot well essay;
Your daughter very properly courts the *jeunesse dorée,*—
A Thyiad, who, when timbrel beats, cannot her joy restrain,
But plays the kid, and laughs and giggles *à l'Américaine.*

'T is more becoming, madame, in a creature old and poor,
To sit and spin than to engage in an *affaire d'amour.*
The lutes, the roses, and the wine drained deep are not for you;
Remember what the poet says: *Ce monde est plein de fous!*

TO THE FOUNTAIN OF BANDUSIA

O FOUNTAIN of Bandusia!
  Whence crystal waters flow,
With garlands gay and wine I 'll pay
  The sacrifice I owe;
A sportive kid with budding horns
  I have, whose crimson blood
Anon shall dye and sanctify
  Thy cool and babbling flood.

O fountain of Bandusia!
  The Dog-star's hateful spell
No evil brings into the springs
  That from thy bosom well;
Here oxen, wearied by the plough,
  The roving cattle here
Hasten in quest of certain rest,
  And quaff thy gracious cheer.

O fountain of Bandusia!
  Ennobled shalt thou be,
For I shall sing the joys that spring
  Beneath yon ilex-tree.
Yes, fountain of Bandusia,
  Posterity shall know
The cooling brooks that from thy nooks
  Singing and dancing go.

TO THE FOUNTAIN OF BANDUSIA

O FOUNTAIN of Bandusia! more glittering than glass,
And worthy of th pleasant wine and toasts that freely pass;
More worthy of the flowers with which thou modestly art hid
To-morrow willing hands shall sacrifice to thee a kid.

In vain the glory of the brow where proudly swell above
The growing horns, significant of battle and of love;
For in thy honor he shall die,—the offspring of the herd,—
And with his crimson life-blood thy cold waters shall be stirred.

The Dog-star's cruel season, with its fierce and blazing heat,
Has never sent its scorching rays into thy glad retreat;
The oxen, wearied with the plough, the herd which wanders near,
Have found a grateful respite and delicious coolness here.

When of the graceful ilex on the hollow rocks I sing,
Thou shalt become illustrious, O sweet Bandusian spring!
Among the noble fountains which have been enshrined in fame,
Thy dancing, babbling waters shall in song our homage claim.

THE PREFERENCE DECLARED

Boy, I detest the Persian pomp;
   I hate those linden-bark devices;
And as for roses, holy Moses!
   They can't be got at living prices!
Myrtle is good enough for us,—
   For *you*, as bearer of my flagon;
For *me*, supine beneath this vine,
   Doing my best to get a jag on!

A TARDY APOLOGY

I

Mæcenas, you will be my death,—though friendly you profess
   yourself,—
If to me in a strain like this so often you address yourself:
"Come, Holly, why this laziness? Why indolently shock you us?
Why with Lethean cups fall into desuetude innocuous?"

A god, Mæcenas! yea, a god hath proved the very curse of me!
If my iambics are not done, pray, do not think the worse of me;
Anacreon for young Bathyllus burned without apology,
And wept his simple measures on a sample of conchology.

Now, you yourself, Mæcenas, are enjoying this beatitude;
If by no brighter beauty Ilium fell, you 've cause for gratitude.
A certain Phryne keeps me on the rack with lovers numerous;
This is the artful hussy's neat conception of the humorous!

A TARDY APOLOGY

II

You ask me, friend,
Why I don't send
The long since due-and-paid-for numbers;
Why, songless, I
As drunken lie
Abandoned to Lethean slumbers.

Long time ago
(As well you know)
I started in upon that carmen;
My work was vain,—
But why complain?
When gods forbid, how helpless are men!

Some ages back,
The sage Anack
Courted a frisky Samian body,
Singing her praise
In metered phrase
As flowing as his bowls of toddy.

Till I was hoarse
Might I discourse
Upon the cruelties of Venus;
'T were waste of time
As well of rhyme,
For you 've been there yourself, Mæcenas!

Perfect your bliss
If some fair miss
Love you yourself and *not* your minæ;
I, fortune's sport,
All vainly court
The beauteous, polyandrous Phryne!

TO THE SHIP OF STATE

O SHIP of state,
Shall new winds bear you back upon the sea?
What are you doing?　Seek the harbor's lee
Ere 't is too late!

Do you bemoan
Your side was stripped of oarage in the blast?
Swift Africus has weakened, too, your mast;
The sailyards groan.

Of cables bare,
Your keel can scarce endure the lordly wave.
Your sails are rent; you have no gods to save,
Or answer pray'r.

Though Pontic pine,
The noble daughter of a far-famed wood,
You boast your lineage and title good,—
A useless line!

The sailor there
In painted sterns no reassurance finds;
Unless you owe derision to the winds,
Beware—beware!

My grief erewhile,
But now my care—my longing! shun the seas
That flow between the gleaming Cyclades,
Each shining isle.

QUITTING AGAIN

THE hero of
Affairs of love
By far too numerous to be mentioned,
And scarred as I 'm,
It seemeth time
That I were mustered out and pensioned.

So on this wall
My lute and all
I hang, and dedicate to Venus;
And I implore
But one thing more
Ere all is at an end between us.

O goddess fair
Who reignest where
The weather 's seldom bleak and snowy,
This boon I urge:
In anger scourge
My old cantankerous sweetheart, Chloe!

SAILOR AND SHADE

SAILOR

You, who have compassed land and sea,
Now all unburied lie;
All vain your store of human lore,
For you were doomed to die.
The sire of Pelops likewise fell,—
Jove's honored mortal guest;
So king and sage of every age
At last lie down to rest.
Plutonian shades enfold the ghost
Of that majestic one

Who taught as truth that he, forsooth,
　　Had once been Pentheus' son;
Believe who may, he 's passed away,
　　And what he did is done.
A last night comes alike to all;
　　One path we all must tread,
Through sore disease or stormy seas
　　Or fields with corpses red.
Whate'er our deeds, that pathway leads
　　To regions of the dead.

SHADE

The fickle twin Illyrian gales
　　O'erwhelmed me on the wave;.
But you that live, I pray you give
　　My bleaching bones a grave!
Oh, then when cruel tempests rage
　　You all unharmed shall be;
Jove's mighty hand shall guard by land
　　And Neptune's on the sea.
Perchance you fear to do what may
　　Bring evil to your race?
Oh, rather fear that like me here
　　You 'll lack a burial place.
So, though you be in proper haste,
　　Bide long enough, I pray,
To give me, friend, what boon shall send
　　My soul upon its way!

LET US HAVE PEACE

In maudlin spite let Thracians fight
　　Above their bowls of liquor;
But such as we, when on a spree,
　　Should never brawl and bicker!

These angry words and clashing swords
  Are quite *de trop*, I 'm thinking;
Brace up, my boys, and hush your noise,
  And drown your wrath in drinking.

Aha, 't is fine,—this mellow wine
  With which our host would dope us!
Now let us hear what pretty dear
  Entangles him of Opus.

I see you blush,—nay, comrades, hush!
  Come, friend, though they despise you,
Tell me the name of that fair dame,—
  Perchance I may advise you.

O wretched youth! and is it truth
  You love that fickle lady?
I, doting dunce, courted her once;
  Since when, she 's reckoned shady!

TO QUINTUS DELLIUS

BE tranquil, Dellius, I pray;
For though you pine your life away
  With dull complaining breath,
Or speed with song and wine each day,
  Still, still your doom is death.

Where the white poplar and the pine
In glorious arching shade combine,
  And the brook singing goes,
Bid them bring store of nard and wine
  And garlands of the rose.

Let 's live while chance and youth obtain;
Soon shall you quit this fair domain
  Kissed by the Tiber's gold,
And all your earthly pride and gain
  Some heedless heir shall hold.

One ghostly boat shall some time bear
From scenes of mirthfulness or care
   Each fated human soul,—
Shall waft and leave its burden where
   The waves of Lethe roll.

So come, I prithee, Dellius mine;
Let's sing our songs and drink our wine
   In that sequestered nook
Where the white poplar and the pine
   Stand listening to the brook.

POKING FUN AT XANTHIAS

OF your love for your handmaid you need feel no shame.
   Don't apologize, Xanthias, pray;
Remember, Achilles the proud felt a flame
   For Brissy, his slave, as they say.
Old Telamon's son, fiery Ajax, was moved
   By the captive Tecmessa's ripe charms;
And Atrides, suspending the feast, it behooved
   To gather a girl to his arms.

Now, how do you know that this yellow-haired maid
   (This Phyllis you fain would enjoy)
Hasn't parents whose wealth would cast you in the shade,—
   Who would ornament you, Xan, my boy?
Very likely the poor chick sheds copious tears,
   And is bitterly thinking the while
Of the royal good times of her earlier years,
   When her folks regulated the style!

It won't do at all, my dear boy, to believe
   That she of whose charms you are proud
Is beautiful only as means to deceive,—
   Merely one of the horrible crowd.

So constant a sweetheart, so loving a wife,
  So averse to all notions of greed
Was surely not born of a mother whose life
  Is a chapter you'd better not read.

As an unbiased party I feel it my place
  (For I don't like to do things by halves)
To compliment Phyllis,—her arms and her face
  And (excuse me) her delicate calves.
Tut, tut! don't get angry, my boy, or suspect
  You have any occasion to fear
A man whose deportment is always correct,
  And is now in his forty-first year!

―――――

TO ARISTIUS FUSCUS

Fuscus, whoso to good inclines,
  And is a faultless liver,
Nor Moorish spear now bow need fear,
  Nor poison-arrowed quiver.

Ay, though through desert wastes he roam,
  Or scale the rugged mountains,
Or rest beside the murmuring tide
  Of weird Hydaspan fountains!

Lo, on a time, I gayly paced
  The Sabine confines shady,
And sung in glee of Lalage,
  My own and dearest lady;

And as I sung, a monster wolf
  Slunk through the thicket from me;
But for that song, as I strolled along,
  He would have overcome me!

Set me amid those poison mists
　　Which no fair gale dispelleth,
Or in the plains where silence reigns,
　　And no thing human dwelleth,—

Still shall I love my Lalage,
　　Still sing her tender graces;
And while I sing, my theme shall bring
　　Heaven to those desert places!

TO ALBIUS TIBULLUS

I

Not to lament that rival flame
　　Wherewith the heartless Glycera scorns you,
Nor waste your time in maudlin rhyme,
　　How many a modern instance warns you!

Fair-browed Lycoris pines away
　　Because her Cyrus loves another;
The ruthless churl informs the girl
　　He loves her only as a brother!

For he, in turn, courts Pholoe,—
　　A maid unscotched of love's fierce virus;
Why, goats will mate with wolves they hate
　　Ere Pholoe will mate with Cyrus!

Ah, weak and hapless human hearts,
　　By cruel Mother Venus fated
To spend this life in hopeless strife,
　　Because incongruously mated!

Such torture, Albius, is my lot;
　　For, though a better mistress wooed me,
My Myrtale has captured me,
　　And with her cruelties subdued me!

TO ALBIUS TIBULLUS

II

Grieve not, my Albius, if thoughts of Glycera may haunt you,
  Nor chant your mournful elegies because she faithless proves;
  If now a younger man than you this cruel charmer loves,
Let not the kindly favors of the past rise up to taunt you.

Lycoris of the little brow for Cyrus feels a passion,
  And Cyrus, on the other hand, toward Pholoe inclines;
  But ere this crafty Cyrus can accomplish his designs
She-goats will wed Apulian wolves in deference to fashion.

Such is the will, the cruel will, of love-inciting Venus,
  Who takes delight in wanton sport and ill-considered jokes,
  And brings ridiculous misfits beneath her brazen yokes,—
A very infelicitous proceeding, just between us.

As for myself, young Myrtale, slave-born and lacking graces,
  And wilder than the Adrian tides which form Calabrian bays,
  Entangled me in pleasing chains and compromising ways,
When—just my luck—a better girl was courting my embraces.

TO MÆCENAS

Mæcenas, thou of royalty's descent,
Both my protector and dear ornament,
Among humanity's conditions are
Those who take pleasure in the flying car,
Whirling Olympian dust, as on they roll,
And shunning with the glowing wheel the goal;
While the ennobling palm, the prize of worth,
Exalts them to the gods, the lords of earth.

Here one is happy if the fickle crowd
His name the threefold honor has allowed;
And there another, if into his stores
Comes what is swept from Libyan threshing-floors.

He who delights to till his father's lands,
And grasps the delving-hoe with willing hands,
Can never to Attalic offers hark,
Or cut the Myrtoan Sea with Cyprian bark.
The merchant, timorous of Afric's breeze,
When fiercely struggling with Icarian seas
Praises the restful quiet of his home,
Nor wishes from the peaceful fields to roam;
Ah, speedily his shattered ships he mends,—
To poverty his lesson ne'er extends.

One there may be who never scorns to fill
His cups with mellow draughts from Massic's hill,
Nor from the busy day an hour to wean,
Now stretched at length beneath the arbute green,
Now at the softly whispering spring, to dream
Of the fair nymphs who haunt the sacred stream.
For camp and trump and clarion some have zest,—
The cruel wars the mothers so detest.
'Neath the cold sky the hunter spends his life,
Unmindful of his home and tender wife,
Whether the doe is seen by faithful hounds
Or Marsian boar through the fine meshes bounds.

But as for me, the ivy-wreaths, the prize
Of learned brows, exalt me to the skies;
The shady grove, the nymphs and satyrs there,
Draw me away from people everywhere;
If it may be, Euterpe's flute inspires,
Or Polyhymnia strikes the Lesbian lyres;
And if you place me where no bard debars,
With head exalted I shall strike the stars!

TO HIS BOOK

You vain, self-conscious little book,
Companion of my happy days,
  How eagerly you seem to look
For wider fields to spread your lays;
    My desk and locks cannot contain you,
    Nor blush of modesty restrain you.

  Well, then, begone, fool that thou art!
But do not come to me and cry,
  When critics strike you to the heart:
"Oh, wretched little book am I!"
    You know I tried to educate you
    To shun the fate that must await you.

  In youth you may encounter friends
(Pray this prediction be not wrong),
  But wait until old age descends
And thumbs have smeared your gentlest song:
    Then will the moths connive to eat you
    And rural libraries secrete you.

  However, should a friend some word
Of my obscure career request,
  Tell him how deeply I was stirred
To spread my wings beyond the nest;
    Take from my years, which are before you,
    To boom my merits, I implore you.

  Tell him that I am short and fat,
Quick in my temper, soon appeased,
  With locks of gray,—but what of that?
Loving the sun, with nature pleased.
    I'm more than four and forty, hark you,
    But ready for a night off, mark you!

FAME *vs.* RICHES

THE Greeks had genius,—'t was a gift
　The Muse vouchsafed in glorious measure;
The boon of Fame they made their aim
　And prized above all worldly treasure.

But *we*,—how do we train *our* youth?
　Not in the arts that are immortal,
But in the greed for gains that speed
　From him who stands at Death's dark portal.

Ah, when this slavish love of gold
　Once binds the soul in greasy fetters,
How prostrate lies,—how droops and dies
　The great, the noble cause of letters!

THE LYRIC MUSE

I LOVE the lyric muse!
For when mankind ran wild in grooves
　Came holy Orpheus with his songs
And turned men's hearts from bestial loves,
　From brutal force and savage wrongs;
Amphion, too, and on his lyre
　Made such sweet music all the day
That rocks, instinct with warm desire,
　Pursued him in his glorious way.

I love the lyric muse!
Hers was the wisdom that of yore
　Taught man the rights of fellow man,
Taught him to worship God the more,
　And to revere love's holy ban.
Hers was the hand that jotted down
　The laws correcting divers wrongs;
And so came honor and renown
　To bards and to their noble songs.

I love the lyric muse!
Old Homer sung unto the lyre;
  Tyrtæus, too, in ancient days;
Still warmed by their immortal fire,
  How doth our patriot spirit blaze!
The oracle, when questioned, sings;
  So our first steps in life are taught.
In verse we soothe the pride of kings,
  In verse the drama has been wrought.

I love the lyric muse!
Be not ashamed, O noble friend,
  In honest gratitude to pay
Thy homage to the gods that spend
  This boon to charm all ill away.
With solemn tenderness revere
  This voiceful glory as a shrine
Wherein the quickened heart may hear
  The counsels of a voice divine!

A COUNTERBLAST AGAINST GARLIC

MAY the man who has cruelly murdered his sire—
  A crime to be punished with death—
Be condemned to eat garlic till he shall expire
  Of his own foul and venomous breath!
What stomachs these rustics must have who can eat
  This dish that Canidia made,
Which imparts to my colon a torturous heat,
  And a poisonous look, I 'm afraid!

They say that ere Jason attempted to yoke
  The fire-breathing bulls to the plough
He smeared his whole body with garlic,—a joke
  Which I fully appreciate now.
When Medea gave Glauce her beautiful dress,
  In which garlic was scattered about,
It was cruel and rather low-down, I confess,
  But it settled the point beyond doubt.

On thirsty Apulia ne'er has the sun
  Inflicted such terrible heat;
As for Hercules' robe, although poisoned, 't was fun
  When compared with this garlic we eat!
Mæcenas, if ever on garbage like this
  You express a desire to be fed,
May Mrs. Mæcenas object to your kiss,
  And lie at the foot of the bed!

AN EXCUSE FOR LALAGE

To bear the yoke not yet your love's submissive neck is bent,
To share a husband's toil, or grasp his amorous intent;
Over the fields, in cooling streams, the heifer longs to go,
Now with the calves disporting where the pussy-willows grow.

Give up your thirst for unripe grapes, and, trust me, you shall learn
How quickly in the autumn time to purple they will turn.
Soon she will follow you, for age steals swiftly on the maid;
And all the precious years that you have lost she will have paid.

Soon she will seek a lord, beloved as Pholoe, the coy,
Or Chloris, or young Gyges, that deceitful, girlish boy,
Whom, if you placed among the girls, and loosed his flowing locks,
The wondering guests could not decide which one decorum shocks.

AN APPEAL TO LYCE

Lyce, the gods have heard my prayers, as gods will hear the dutiful,
And brought old age upon you, though you still affect the beautiful.
You sport among the boys, and drink and chatter on quite aim-
    lessly;
And in your cups with quavering voice you torment Cupid shame-
    lessly.

For blooming Chia, Cupid has a feeling more than brotherly;
He knows a handsaw from a hawk whenever winds are southerly.
He pats her pretty cheeks, but looks on you as a monstrosity;
Your wrinkles and your yellow teeth excite his animosity.

For jewels bright and purple Coan robes you are not dressable;
Unhappily for you, the public records are accessible.
Where is your charm, and where your bloom and gait so firm
    and sensible,
That drew my love from Cinara,—a lapse most indefensible?

To my poor Cinara in youth Death came with great celerity
Egad, that never can be said of you with any verity!
The old crow that you are, the teasing boys will jeer, compelling
    you
To roost at home. Reflect, all this is straight that I am telling
    you.

————

A ROMAN WINTER-PIECE

I

> See, Thaliarch mine, how, white with snow,
>   Soracte mocks the sullen sky;
> How, groaning loud, the woods are bowed,
>   And chained with frost the rivers lie.
>
> Pile, pile the logs upon the hearth;
>   We 'll melt away the envious cold:
> And, better yet, sweet friend, we 'll wet
>   Our whistles with some four-year-old.
>
> Commit all else unto the gods,
>   Who, when it pleaseth them, shall bring
> To fretful deeps and wooded steeps
>   The mild, persuasive grace of Spring.
>
> Let not To-morrow, but To-day,
>   Your ever active thoughts engage;

Frisk, dance, and sing, and have your fling,
   Unharmed, unawed of crabbed Age.

Let 's steal content from Winter's wrath,
   And glory in the artful theft,
That years from now folks shall allow
   'T was cold indeed when we got left.

So where the whisperings and the mirth
   Of girls invite a sportive chap,
Let 's fare awhile,—aha, you smile;
   You guess my meaning,—*verbum sap.*

A ROMAN WINTER-PIECE

II

Now stands Soracte white with snow, now bend the laboring trees,
And with the sharpness of the frost the stagnant rivers freeze.
Pile up the billets on the hearth, to warmer cheer incline,
And draw, my Thaliarchus, from the Sabine jar the wine.

The rest leave to the gods, who still the fiercely warring wind,
And to the morrow's store of good or evil give no mind.
Whatever day your fortune grants, that day mark up for gain;
And in your youthful bloom do not the sweet amours disdain.

Now on the Campus and the squares, when evening shades descend,
Soft whisperings again are heard, and loving voices blend;
And now the low delightful laugh betrays the lurking maid,
While from her slowly yielding arms the forfeiture is paid.

TO DIANA

O VIRGIN, tri-formed goddess fair,
   The guardian of the groves and hills,
Who hears the girls in their despair
   Cry out in childbirth's cruel ills,
      And saves them from the Stygian flow!

Let the pine-tree my cottage near
  Be sacred to thee evermore,
That I may give to it each year
  With joy the life-blood of the boar,
    Now thinking of the sidelong blow.

TO HIS LUTE

IF ever in the sylvan shade
A song immortal we have made,
Come now, O lute, I prithee come,
Inspire a song of Latium!

A Lesbian first thy glories proved;
In arms and in repose he loved
To sweep thy dulcet strings, and raise
His voice in Love's and Liber's praise.
The Muses, too, and him who clings
To Mother Venus' apron-strings,
And Lycus beautiful, he sung
In those old days when you were young.

O shell, that art the ornament
Of Phœbus, bringing sweet content
To Jove, and soothing troubles all,—
Come and requite me, when I call!

TO LEUCONÖE

I

WHAT end the gods may have ordained for me,
  And what for thee,
    Seek not to learn, Leuconöe; we may not know
Chaldean tables cannot bring us rest
  'T is for the best
    To bear in patience what may come, or weal or woe.

If for more winters our poor lot is cast,
Or this the last,
    Which on the crumbling rocks has dashed Etruscan seas,
Strain clear the wine; this life is short, at best.
Take hope with zest,
    And, trusting not To-morrow, snatch To-day for ease!

TO LEUCONÖE

II

SEEK not, Leuconöe, to know how long you're going to live yet,
What boons the gods will yet withhold, or what they're going to
    give yet;
For Jupiter will have his way, despite how much we worry,—
Some will hang on for many a day, and some die in a hurry.
The wisest thing for you to do is to embark this diem
Upon a merry escapade with some such bard as I am.
And while we sport I'll reel you off such odes as shall surprise ye;
To-morrow, when the headache comes,—well, then I'll satirize ye!

TO LIGURINUS

I

THOUGH mighty in Love's favor still,
    Though cruel yet, my boy,
When the unwelcome dawn shall chill
    Your pride and youthful joy,
The hair which round your shoulder grows
    Is rudely cut away,
Your color, redder than the rose,
    Is changed by youth's decay,—

Then, Ligurinus, in the glass
    Another you will spy.
And as the shaggy face, alas!
    You see, your grief will cry:

"Why in my youth could I not learn
    The wisdom men enjoy?
Or why to men cannot return
    The smooth cheeks of the boy?"

TO LIGURINUS

II

O CRUEL fair,
    Whose flowing hair
The envy and the pride of all is,
    As onward roll
    The years, that poll
Will get as bald as a billiard ball is;
Then shall your skin, now pink and dimply,
Be tanned to parchment, sear and pimply!

    When you behold
    Yourself grown old,
These words shall speak your spirits moody;
    "Unhappy one!
    What heaps of fun
I've missed by being goody-goody!
Oh, that I might have felt the hunger
Of loveless age when I was younger!"

THE HAPPY ISLES

OH, come with me to the Happy Isles
    In the golden haze off yonder,
Where the song of the sun-kissed breeze beguiles
    And the ocean loves to wander.

Fragrant the vines that mantle those hills,
    Proudly the fig rejoices,
Merrily dance the virgin rills,
    Blending their myriad voices.

Our herds shall suffer no evil there,
  But peacefully feed and rest them;
Never thereto shall prowling bear
  Or serpent come to molest them.

Neither shall Eurus, wanton bold,
  Nor feverish drought distress us,
But he that compasseth heat and cold
  Shall temper them both to bless us.

There no vandal foot has trod,
  And the pirate hordes that wander
Shall never profane the sacred sod
  Of those beautiful isles out yonder.

Never a spell shall blight our vines,
  Nor Sirius blaze above us,
But you and I shall drink our wines
  And sing to the loved that love us.

So come with me where Fortune smiles
  And the gods invite devotion,—
Oh, come with me to the Happy Isles
  In the haze of that far-off ocean!

CONSISTENCY

SHOULD painter attach to a fair human head
  The thick, turgid neck of a stallion,
Or depict a spruce lass with the tail of a bass,
  I am sure you would guy the rapscallion.

Believe me, dear Pisos, that just such a freak
  Is the crude and preposterous poem
Which merely abounds in a torrent of sounds,
  With no depth of reason below 'em.

'T is all very well to give license to art,—
  The wisdom of license defend I;
But the line should be drawn at the fripperish spawn
  Of a mere *cacoethes scribendi.*

It is too much the fashion to strain at effects,—
  Yes, that 's what 's the matter with Hannah!
Our popular taste, by the tyros debased,
  Paints each barnyard a grove of Diana!

Should a patron require you to paint a marine,
  Would you work in some trees with their barks on?
When his strict orders are for a Japanese jar,
  Would you give him a pitcher like Clarkson?

Now, this is my moral: Compose what you may,
  And Fame will be ever far distant
Unless you combine with a simple design
  A treatment in toto consistent.

TO POSTUMUS

O POSTUMUS, my Postumus, the years are gliding past,
And piety will never check the wrinkles coming fast,
The ravages of time old age's swift advance has made,
And death, which unimpeded comes to bear us to the shade.

Old friend, although the tearless Pluto you may strive to please,
And seek each year with thrice one hundred bullocks to appease,
Who keeps the thrice-huge Geryon and Tityus his slaves,
Imprisoned fast forevermore with cold and sombre waves,

Yet must that flood so terrible be sailed by mortals all;
Whether perchance we may be kings and live in royal hall,
Or lowly peasants struggling long with poverty and dearth,
Still must we cross who live upon the favors of the earth.

And all in vain from bloody war and contest we are free,
And from the waves that hoarsely break upon the Adrian Sea;
For our frail bodies all in vain our helpless terror grows
In gloomy autumn seasons, when the baneful south wind blows.

Alas! the black Cocytus, wandering to the world below,
That languid river to behold we of this earth must go;
To see the grim Danaides, that miserable race,
And Sisyphus of Æolus, condemned to endless chase.

Behind you must you leave your home and land and wife so dear,
And of the trees, except the hated cypresses, you rear,
And which around the funeral piles as signs of mourning grow,
Not one will follow you, their short-lived master, there below.

Your worthier heir the precious Cæcuban shall drink galore,
Now with a hundred keys preserved and guarded in your store,
And stain the pavements, pouring out in waste the nectar proud,
Better than that with which the pontiffs' feasts have been endowed.

————

TO MISTRESS PYRRHA

I

WHAT perfumed, posie-dizened sirrah,
        With smiles for diet,
Clasps you, O fair but faithless Pyrrha,
        On the quiet?
For whom do you bind up your tresses,
        As spun-gold yellow,—
Meshes that go with your caresses,
        To snare a fellow?

How will he rail at fate capricious,
        And curse you duly,
Yet now he deems your wiles delicious,—
        You perfect, truly!

Pyrrha, your love 's a treacherous ocean;
     He 'll soon fall in there!
Then shall I gloat on his commotion,
     For *I* have been there!

TO MISTRESS PYRRHA

II

WHAT dainty boy with sweet perfumes bedewed
Has lavished kisses, Pyrrha, in the cave?
For whom amid the roses, many-hued,
Do you bind back your tresses' yellow wave?

How oft will he deplore your fickle whim,
And wonder at the storm and roughening deeps,
Who now enjoys you, all in all to him,
And dreams of you, whose only thoughts he keeps.

Wretched are they to whom you seem so fair;—
That I escaped the storms, the gods be praised!
My dripping garments, offered with a prayer,
Stand as a tablet to the sea-god raised.

TO MELPOMENE

LOFTY and enduring is the monument I 've reared:
     Come, tempests, with your bitterness assailing;
And thou, corrosive blasts of time, by all things mortal feared,
     Thy buffets and thy rage are unavailing!

I shall not altogether die: by far my greater part
     Shall mock man's common fate in realms infernal;
My works shall live as tributes to my genius and my art,—
     My works shall be my monument eternal!

While this great Roman empire stands and gods protect our fanes,
     Mankind with grateful hearts shall tell the story
How one most lowly born upon the parched Apulian plains
     First raised the native lyric muse to glory.

Assume, revered Melpomene, the proud estate I 've won,
   And, with thine own dear hand the meed supplying,
Bind thou about the forehead of thy celebrated son
   The Delphic laurel-wreath of fame undying!

TO PHYLLIS

I

Come, Phyllis, I 've a cask of wine
   That fairly reeks with precious juices,
And in your tresses you shall twine
   The loveliest flowers this vale produces.

My cottage wears a gracious smile;
   The altar, decked in floral glory,
Yearns for the lamb which bleats the while
   As though it pined for honors gory.

Hither our neighbors nimbly fare,
   The boys agog, the maidens snickering;
And savory smells possess the air,
   As skyward kitchen flames are flickering.

You ask what means this grand display,
   This festive throng and goodly diet?
Well, since you're bound to have your way,
   I don't mind telling, on the quiet.

'T is April 13, as you know,
   A day and month devote to Venus,
Whereon was born, some years ago,
   My very worthy friend, Mæcenas.

Nay, pay no heed to Telephus;
   Your friends agree he does n't love you.
The way he flirts convinces us
   He really is not worthy of you.

Aurora's son, unhappy lad!
  You know the fate that overtook him?
And Pegasus a rider had,—
  I say he *had*, before he shook him!

Hoc docet (as you must agree)
  'T is meet that Phyllis should discover
A wisdom in preferring me,
  And mittening every other lover.

So come, O Phyllis, last and best
  Of loves with which this heart 's been smitten,
Come, sing my jealous fears to rest,
  And let your songs be those *I 've* written.

TO PHYLLIS

II

Sweet Phyllis, I have here a jar of old and precious wine,
The years which mark its coming from the Alban hills are nine
And in the garden parsley, too, for wreathing garlands fair,
And ivy in profusion to bind up your shining hair.

Now smiles the house with silver; the altar, laurel-bound,
Longs with the sacrificial blood of lambs to drip around;
The company is hurrying, boys and maidens with the rest;
The flames are flickering as they whirl the dark smoke on their crest.

Yet you must know the joys to which you have been summoned here
To keep the Ides of April, to the sea-born Venus dear,—
Ah, festal day more sacred than my own fair day of birth,
Since from its dawn my loved Mæcenas counts his years of earth.

A rich and wanton girl has caught, as suited to her mind,
The Telephus whom you desire,—a youth not of your kind.
She holds him bound with pleasing chains, the fetters of her
    charms,—
Remember how scorched Phaëthon ambitious hopes alarms.

The winged Pegasus the rash Bellerophon has chafed,
To you a grave example for reflection has vouchsafed,—
Always to follow what is meet, and never try to catch
That which is not allowed to you, an inappropriate match.

Come now, sweet Phyllis, of my loves the last, and hence the best
(For nevermore shall other girls inflame this manly breast);
Learn loving measures to rehearse as we may stroll along,
And dismal cares shall fly away and vanish at your song.

———

TO CHLOE

I

Why do you shun me, Chloe, like the fawn,
    That, fearful of the breezes and the wood,
Has sought her timorous mother since the dawn,
    And on the pathless mountain tops has stood?

Her trembling heart a thousand fears invites,
    Her sinking knees with nameless terrors shake,—
Whether the rustling leaf of spring affrights,
    Or the green lizards stir the slumbering brake.

I do not follow with a tigerish thought,
    Or with the fierce Gætulian lion's quest;
So, quickly leave your mother, as you ought,
    Full ripe to nestle on a husband's breast.

———

TO CHLOE

II

Chloe, you shun me like a hind
    That, seeking vainly for her mother,
Hears danger in each breath of wind,
    And wildly darts this way and t' other;

Whether the breezes sway the wood
　　Or lizards scuttle through the brambles,
She starts, and off, as though pursued,
　　The foolish, frightened creature scrambles.

But, Chloe, you 're no infant thing
　　That should esteem a man an ogre;
Let go your mother's apron-string,
　　And pin your faith upon a toga!

III

A PARAPHRASE

How happens it, my cruel miss,
　　You 're always giving me the mitten?
You seem to have forgotten this:
　　That you no longer are a kitten!

A woman that has reached the years
　　Of that which people call discretion
Should put aside all childish fears
　　And see in courtship no transgression.

A mother's solace may be sweet,
　　But Hymen's tenderness is sweeter;
And though all virile love be meet,
　　You 'll find the poet's love is metre.

IV

A PARAPHRASE, CIRCA 1715

SINCE Chloe is so monstrous fair,
With such an eye and such an air,
What wonder that the world complains
When she each am'rous suit disdains?

Close to her mother's side she clings,
And mocks the death her folly brings
To gentle swains that feel the smarts
Her eyes inflict upon their hearts.

Whilst thus the years of youth go by,
Shall Colin languish, Strephon die?
Nay, cruel nymph! come, choose a mate,
And choose him ere it be too late!

V

A PARAPHRASE, BY DR. I. W.

WHY, Mistress Chloe, do you bother
    With prattlings and with vain ado
Your worthy and industrious mother,
    Eschewing them that come to woo?

Oh, that the awful truth might quicken
    This stern conviction to your breast:
You are no longer now a chicken
    Too young to quit the parent nest.

So put aside your froward carriage,
    And fix your thoughts, whilst yet there's time,
Upon the righteousness of marriage
    With some such godly man as I 'm.

VI

A PARAPHRASE, BY CHAUCER

SYN that you, Chloe, to your moder sticken,
Maketh all ye yonge bacheloures full sicken;
Like as a lyttel deere you ben y-hiding
Whenas come lovers with theyre pityse chiding.
Sothly it ben faire to give up your moder
For to beare swete company with some oder;
Your moder ben well enow so farre shee goeth,
But that ben not farre enow, God knoweth;
Wherefore it ben sayed that foolysh ladyes
That marrye not shall leade an aype in Hadys;
But all that do with gode men wed full quicklye
When that they be on dead go to ye seints full sickerly.

TO MÆCENAS

THAN you, O valued friend of mine,
  A better patron *non est!*
Come, quaff my home-made Sabine wine,—
  You 'll find it poor but honest.

I put it up that famous day
  You patronized the ballet,
And the public cheered you such a way
  As shook your native valley.

Cæcuban and the Calean brand
  May elsewhere claim attention;
But *I* have none of these on hand,—
  For reasons I 'll not mention.

ENVOY

So, come! though favors I bestow
  Cannot be called extensive,
Who better than my friend should know
  That they 're at least expensive?

————

TO BARINE

IF for your oath broken, or word lightly spoken,
A plague comes, Barine, to grieve you;
If on tooth or on finger a black mark shall linger
Your beauty to mar, I 'll believe you.

But no sooner, the fact is, you bind, as your tact is,
Your head with the vows of untruth,
Than you shine out more charming, and, what 's more
    alarming,
You come forth beloved of our youth.

It is advantageous, but no less outrageous,
Your poor mother's ashes to cheat;
While the gods of creation and each constellation
You seem to regard as your meat.

Now Venus, I own it, is pleased to condone it;
The good-natured nymphs merely smile;
And Cupid is merry,—'t is humorous, very,—
And sharpens his arrows the while.

Our boys you are making the slaves for your taking,
A new band is joined to the old;
While the horrified matrons your juvenile patrons
In vain would bring back to the fold.

The thrifty old fellows your loveliness mellows
Confess to a dread of your house;
But a more pressing duty, in view of your beauty,
Is the young wife's concern for her spouse.

THE RECONCILIATION

I

HE

WHEN you were mine, in auld lang syne,
    And when none else your charms might ogle,
I 'll not deny, fair nymph, that I
    Was happier than a heathen mogul.

SHE

Before *she* came, that rival flame
    (Had ever mater saucier filia?),
In those good times, bepraised in rhymes,
    I was more famed than Mother Ilia.

HE

Chloe of Thrace! With what a grace
  Does she at song or harp employ her!
I'd gladly die, if only I
  Could live forever to enjoy her!

SHE

Mẏ Sybaris so noble is
  That, by the gods, I love him madly!
That I might save him from the grave,
  I'd give my life, and give it gladly!

HE

What if *ma belle* from favor fell,
  And I made up my mind to shake her;
Would Lydia then come back again,
  And to her quondam love betake her?

SHE

My other beau should surely go,
  And you alone should find me gracious;
For no one slings such odes and things
  As does the lauriger Horatiu !

THE RECONCILIATION

II

HORACE

While favored by thy smiles no other youth in amorous teasing
  Around thy snowy neck his folding arms was wont to fling;
As long as I remained your love, acceptable and pleasing,
  I lived a life of happiness beyond the Persian king.

LYDIA

While Lydia ranked Chloe in your unreserved opinion,
  And for no other cherished thou a brighter, livelier flame,
I, Lydia, distinguished throughout the whole dominion,
  Surpassed the Roman Ilia in eminence of fame.

HORACE

'T is now the Thracian Chloe whose accomplishments inthrall
   me,—
So sweet in modulations, such a mistress of the lyre.
In truth the fates, however terrible, could not appall me;
   If they would spare her, sweet my soul, I gladly would expire.

LYDIA

And now the son of Ornytus, young Calais, inflames me
   With mutual, restless passion and an all-consuming fire;
And if the fates, however dread, would spare the youth who claims
   me,
   Not only once would I face death, but gladly twice expire.

HORACE

What if our early love returns to prove we were mistaken
   And bind with brazen yoke the twain, to part, ah! nevermore?
What if the charming Chloe of the golden locks be shaken
   And slighted Lydia again glide through the open door?

LYDIA

Though he is fairer than the star that shines so far above you,
   Thou lighter than a cork, more stormy than the Adrian Sea,
Still should I long to live with you, to live for you and love
   you,
   And cheerfully see death's approach if thou wert near to me.

THE ROASTING OF LYDIA

No more your needed rest at night
   By ribald youth is troubled;
No more your windows, fastened tight,
   Yield to their knocks redoubled.

No longer you may hear them cry,
  "Why art thou, Lydia, lying
In heavy sleep till morn is nigh,
  While I, your love, am dying?"

Grown old and faded, you bewail
  The rake's insulting sally,
While round your home the Thracian gale
  Storms through the lonely alley.

What furious thoughts will fill your breast,
  What passions, fierce and tinglish
(Cannot be properly expressed
  In calm, reposeful English/.

Learn this, and hold your carping tongue:
  Youth will be found rejoicing
In ivy green and myrtle young,
  The praise of fresh life voicing;

And not content to dedicate,
  With much protesting shiver,
The sapless leaves to winter's mate,
  Hebrus, the cold dark river.

TO GLYCERA

The cruel mother of the Loves,
  And other Powers offended,
Have stirred my heart, where newly roves
  The passion that was ended.

'T is Glycera, to boldness prone,
  Whose radiant beauty fires me;
While fairer than the Parian stone
  Her dazzling face inspires me.

And on from Cyprus Venus speeds,
  Forbidding—ah! the pity—
The Scythian lays, the Parthian meeds,
  And such irrelevant ditty.

Here, boys, bring turf and vervain too;
  Have bowls of wine adjacent;
And ere our sacrifice is through
  She may be more complaisant.

TO LYDIA

I

WHEN, Lydia, you (once fond and true,
  But now grown cold and supercilious)
Praise Telly's charms of neck and arms—
  Well, by the dog! it makes me bilious!

Then with despite my cheeks wax white,
  My doddering brain gets weak and giddy,
My eyes o'erflow with tears which show
  That passion melts my vitals, Liddy!

Deny, false jade, your escapade,
  And, lo! your wounded shoulders show it!
No manly spark left such a mark—
  Leastwise he surely was no poet!

With savage buss did Telephus
  Abrade your lips, so plump and mellow;
As you would save what Venus gave,
  I charge you shun that awkward fellow!

And now I say thrice happy they
  That call on Hymen to requite 'em;
For, though love cools, the wedded fools
  Must cleave till death doth disunite 'em.

TO LYDIA

II

WHEN praising Telephus you sing
　His rosy neck and waxen arms,
Forgetful of the pangs that wring
　This heart for my neglected charms,

Soft down my cheek the tear-drop flows,
　My color comes and goes the while,
And my rebellious liver glows,
　And fiercely swells with laboring bile.

Perchance yon silly, passionate youth,
　Distempered by the fumes of wine,
Has marred your shoulder with his tooth,
　Or scarred those rosy lips of thine.

Be warned; he cannot faithful prove,
　Who, with the cruel kiss you prize,
Has hurt the little mouth I love,
　Where Venus's own nectar lies.

Whom golden links unbroken bind,
　Thrice happy—more than thrice are they;
And constant, both in heart and mind,
　In love await the final day.

TO QUINTIUS HIRPINUS

To Scythian and Cantabrian plots,
　Pay them no heed, O Quintius!
　　So long as we
　　From care are free,
Vexations cannot cinch us.

Unwrinkled youth and grace, forsooth,
　Speed hand in hand together;
　　The songs we sing
　　In time of spring
　Are hushed in wintry weather.

Why, even flow'rs change with the hours,
　And the moon has divers phases·
　　And shall the mind
　　Be racked to find
　A clew to Fortune's mazes?

Nay; 'neath this tree let you and me
　Woo Bacchus to caress us;
　　We 're old, 't is true,
　　But still we two
　Are thoroughbreds, God bless us!

While the wine gets cool in yonder pool,
　Let's spruce up nice and tidy;
　　Who knows, old boy,
　　But we may decoy
　The fair but furtive Lyde?

She can execute on her ivory lute
　Sonatas full of passion,
　　And she bangs her hair
　　(Which is passing fair)
　In the good old Spartan fashion.

WINE, WOMEN, AND SONG

O Varus mine,
Plant thou the vine
Within this kindly soil of Tibur;
　Nor temporal woes,
　Nor spiritual, knows
The man who 's a discreet imbiber.

For who doth croak
Of being broke,
Or who of warfare, after drinking?
With bowl atween us,
Of smiling Venus
And Bacchus shall we sing, I 'm thinking.

Of symptoms fell
Which brawls impel,
Historic data give us warning;
The wretch who fights
When full, of nights,
Is bound to have a head next morning.
I do not scorn
A friendly horn,
But noisy toots, I can't abide 'em!
Your howling bat
Is stale and flat
To one who knows, because he 's tried 'em!

The secrets of
The life I love
(Companionship with girls and toddy)
I would not drag
With drunken brag
Into the ken of everybody;
But in the shade
Let some coy maid
With smilax wreathe my flagon's nozzle,
Then all day long,
With mirth and song,
Shall I enjoy a quiet sozzle!

AN ODE TO FORTUNE

O Lady Fortune! 't is to thee I call,
Dwelling at Antium, thou hast power to crown
The veriest clod with riches and renown,

And change a triumph to a funeral.
The tillers of the soil and they that vex the seas,
Confessing thee supreme, on bended knees
    Invoke thee, all.

Of Dacian tribes, of roving Scythian bands,
Of cities, nations, lawless tyrants red
With guiltless blood, art thou the haunting dread;
    Within thy path no human valor stands,
And, arbiter of empires, at thy frown
The sceptre, once supreme, slips surely down
    From kingly hands.

Necessity precedes thee in thy way;
Hope fawns on thee, and Honor, too, is seen
Dancing attendance with obsequious mien;
    But with what coward and abject dismay
The faithless crowd and treacherous wantons fly
When once their jars of luscious wine run dry,—
    Such ingrates they!

Fortune, I call on thee to bless
Our king,—our Cæsar girt for foreign wars!
Help him to heal these fratricidal scars
    That speak degenerate shame and wickedness;
And forge anew our impious spears and swords,
Wherewith we may against barbarian hordes
    Our Past redress!

―――――――

TO A JAR OF WINE

O GRACIOUS jar,—my friend, my twin,
    Born at the time when I was born,—
Whether tomfoolery you inspire
Or animate with love's desire,
    Or flame the soul with bitter scorn,

Or lull to sleep, O jar of mine!
  Come from your place this festal day;
  Corvinus hither wends his way,
And there 's demand for wine!

Corvinus is the sort of man
  Who dotes on tedious argument.
An advocate, his ponderous pate
  Is full of Blackstone and of Kent;
Yet not insensible is he,
O genial Massic flood! to thee.
Why, even Cato used to take
  A modest, surreptitious nip
At meal-times for his stomach's sake,
  Or to forefend la grippe.

How dost thou melt the stoniest hearts,
  And bare the cruel knave's design;
How through thy fascinating arts
  We discount Hope, O gracious wine!
And passing rich the poor man feels
As through his veins thy affluence steals.

Now, prithee, make us frisk and sing,
  And plot full many a naughty plot
With damsels fair—nor shall we care
  Whether school keeps or not!
And whilst thy charms hold out to burn
  We shall not deign to go to bed,
  But we shall paint creation red;
So, fill, sweet wine, this friend of mine,—
  My lawyer friend, as aforesaid.

TO POMPEIUS VARUS

Pompey, what fortune gives you back
  To the friends and the gods who love you?
Once more you stand in your native land,
  With your native sky above you.

Ah, side by side, in years agone,
  We 've faced tempestuous weather,
    And often quaffed
    The genial draught
From the same canteen together.

When honor at Philippi fell
  A prey to brutal passion,
I regret to say that my feet ran away
  In swift Iambic fashion.
You were no poet; soldier born,
  You stayed, nor did you wince then.
    Mercury came
    To my help, which same
Has frequently saved me since then.

But now you 're back, let 's celebrate
  In the good old way and classic;
Come, let us lard our skins with nard,
  And bedew our souls with Massic!
With fillets of green parsley leaves
  Our foreheads shall be done up;
    And with song shall we
    Protract our spree
Until the morrow's sun-up.

THE POET'S METAMORPHOSIS

Mæcenas, I propose to fly
  To realms beyond these human portals;
No common things shall be my wings,
  But such as sprout upon immortals.

Of lowly birth, once shed of earth,
  Your Horace, precious (so you 've told him),
Shall soar away; no tomb of clay
  Nor Stygian prison-house shall hold him.

Upon my skin feathers begin
  To warn the songster of his fleeting;
But never mind, I leave behind
  Songs all the world shall keep repeating.

Lo! Boston girls, with corkscrew curls,
  And husky westerns, wild and woolly,
And southern climes shall vaunt my rhymes,
  And all profess to know me fully.

Methinks the West shall know me best,
  And therefore hold my memory dearer;
For by that lake a bard shall make
  My subtle, hidden meanings clearer.

So cherished, I shall never die;
  Pray, therefore, spare your dolesome praises,
Your elegies, and plaintive cries,
  For I shall fertilize no daisies!

TO VENUS

VENUS, dear Cnidian-Paphian queen!
  Desert that Cyprus way off yonder,
And fare you hence, where with incense
  My Glycera would have you fonder;
And to your joy bring hence your boy,
  The Graces with unbelted laughter,
The Nymphs, and Youth,—then, then, in sooth,
  Should Mercury come tagging after.

IN THE SPRINGTIME

I

'T IS spring! The boats bound to the sea;
  The breezes, loitering kindly over
The fields, again bring herds and men
  The grateful cheer of honeyed clover.

Now Venus hither leads her train;
  The Nymphs and Graces join in orgies;
The moon is bright, and by her light
  Old Vulcan kindles up his forges.

Bind myrtle now about your brow,
  And weave fair flowers in maiden tresses;
Appease god Pan, who, kind to man,
  Our fleeting life with affluence blesses;

But let the changing seasons mind us,
  That Death's the certain doom of mortals,—
Grim Death, who waits at humble gates,
  And likewise stalks though kingly portals.

Soon, Sestius, shall Plutonian shades
  Enfold you with their hideous seemings;
Then love and mirth and joys of earth
  Shall fade away like fevered dreamings.

IN THE SPRINGTIME

II

THE western breeze is springing up, the ships are in the bay,
And spring has brought a happy change as winter melts away.
No more in stall or fire the herd or ploughman finds delight;
No longer with the biting frosts the open fields are white.

Our Lady of Cythera now prepares to lead the dance,
While from above the kindly moon gives an approving glance;
The Nymphs and comely Graces join with Venus and the choir,
And Vulcan's glowing fancy lightly turns to thoughts of fire.

Now it is time with myrtle green to crown the shining pate,
And with the early blossoms of the spring to decorate;
To sacrifice to Faunus, on whose favor we rely,
A sprightly lamb, mayhap a kid, as he may specify.

Impartially the feet of Death at huts and castles strike;
The influenza carries off the rich and poor alike.
O Sestius, though blessed you are beyond the common run,
Life is too short to cherish e'en a distant hope begun.

The Shades and Pluto's mansion follow hard upon the grip.
Once there you cannot throw the dice, nor taste the wine you sip;
Nor look on blooming Lycidas, whose beauty you commend,
To whom the girls will presently their courtesies extend.

TO A BULLY

You, blatant coward that you are,
　Upon the helpless vent your spite.
Suppose you ply your trade on me;
Come, monkey with this bard, and see
　How I 'll repay your bark with bite!

Ay, snarl just once at me, you brute!
　And I shall hound you far and wide,
As fiercely as through drifted snow
The shepherd dog pursues what foe
　Skulks on the Spartan mountain-side.

The chip is on my shoulder—see?
　But touch it and I 'll raise your fur;
I 'm full of business, so beware!
For, though I 'm loaded up for bear,
　I 'm quite as like to kill a cur!

TO MOTHER VENUS

O MOTHER VENUS, quit, I pray,
    Your violent assailing!
The arts, forsooth, that fired my youth
    At last are unavailing;
My blood runs cold, I 'm getting old,
    And all my powers are failing.

Speed thou upon thy white swan's wings,
    And elsewhere deign to mellow
With thy soft arts the anguished hearts
    Of swains that writhe and bellow;
And right away seek out, I pray,
    Young Paullus,—he 's your fellow!

You 'll find young Paullus passing fair,
    Modest, refined, and tony;
Go, now, incite the favored wight!
    With Venus for a crony
He 'll outshine all at feast and ball
    And conversazione!

Then shall that godlike nose of thine
    With perfumes be requited,
And then shall prance in Salian dance
    The girls and boys delighted,
And while the lute blends with the flute
    Shall tender loves be plighted.

But as for me, as you can see,
    I 'm getting old and spiteful.
I have no mind to female kind,
    That once I deemed delightful;
No more brim up the festive cup
    That sent me home at night full.

Why do I falter in my speech,
    O cruel Ligurine?

Why do I chase from place to place
In weather wet and shiny?
Why down my nose forever flows
The tear that 's cold and briny?

TO LYDIA

TELL me, Lydia, tell me why,
By the gods that dwell above,
Sybaris makes haste to die
Through your cruel, fatal love.

Now he hates the sunny plain;
Once he loved its dust and heat.
Now no more he leads the train
Of his peers on coursers fleet.

Now he dreads the Tiber's touch,
And avoids the wrestling-rings,—
He who formerly was such
An expert with quoits and things.

Come, now, Mistress Lydia, say
Why your Sybaris lies hid,
Why he shuns the martial play,
As we 're told Achilles did.

TO NEOBULE

A SORRY life, forsooth, these wretched girls are undergoing,
Restrained from draughts of pleasant wine, from loving favors
showing,
For fear an uncle's tongue a reprimand will be bestowing!

Sweet Cytherea's winged boy deprives you of your spinning,
And Hebrus, Neobule, his sad havoc is beginning,
Just as Minerva thriftily gets ready for an inning.

Who could resist this gallant youth, as Tiber's waves he breasted,
Or when the palm of riding from Bellerophon he wrested,
Or when with fists and feet the sluggers easily he bested?

He shot the fleeting stags with regularity surprising;
The way he intercepted boars was quite beyond surmising,—
No wonder that your thoughts this youth has been monopolizing!

So I repeat that with these maids fate is unkindly dealing,
Who never can in love's affair give license to their feeling,
Or share those sweet emotions when a gentle jag is stealing.

AT THE BALL GAME

WHAT gods or heroes, whose brave deeds none can dispute,
Will you record, O Clio, on the harp and flute?
What lofty names shall sportive Echo grant a place
On Pindus' crown or Helicon's cool, shadowy space?

Sing not, my Orpheus, sweeping oft the tuneful strings,
Of gliding streams and nimble winds and such poor things;
But lend your measures to a theme of noble thought,
And crown with laurel these great heroes, as you ought.

Now steps Ryanus forth at call of furious Mars,
And from his oaken staff the sphere speeds to the stars;
And now he gains the tertiary goal, and turns,
While whiskered balls play round the timid staff of Burns.

Lo! from the tribunes on the bleachers comes a shout,
Beseeching bold Ansonius to line 'em out;
And as Apollo's flying chariot cleaves the sky,
So stanch Ansonius lifts the frightened ball on high.

Like roar of ocean beating on the Cretan cliff,
The strong Komiske gives the panting sphere a biff;
And from the tribunes rise loud murmurs everywhere,
When twice and thrice Mikellius beats the mocking air.

And as Achilles' fleet the Trojan waters sweeps,
So horror sways the throng,—Pfefferius sleeps!
And stalwart Konnor, though by Mercury inspired,
The Equus Carolus defies, and is retired.

So waxes fierce the strife between these godlike men;
And as the hero's fame grows by Virgilian pen,
So let Clarksonius Maximus be raised to heights
As far above the moon as moon o'er lesser lights.

But as for me, the ivy leaf is my reward,
If you a place among the lyric bards accord;
With crest exalted, and O "People," with delight,
I'll proudly strike the stars, and so be out of sight.

EPILOGUE

THE day is done; and, lo! the shades
  Melt 'neath Diana's mellow grace.
Hark, how those deep, designing maids
  Feign terror in this sylvan place!
Come, friends, it's time that we should go;
We're honest married folk, you know.

Was not the wine delicious cool
  Whose sweetness Pyrrha's smile enhanced?
And by that clear Bandusian pool
  How gayly Chloe sung and danced!
And Lydia Dic,—aha, methinks
You'll not forget the saucy minx!

But, oh, the echoes of those songs
  That soothed our cares and lulled our hearts!
Not to that age nor this belongs
  The glory of what heaven-born arts
Speak with the old distinctive charm
From yonder humble Sabine farm!

The day is done. Now off to bed,
  Lest by some rural ruse surprised,
And by those artful girls misled,
  You two be sadly compromised.
You go; perhaps *I* 'd better stay
To shoo the giddy things away!

But sometime we shall meet again
  Beside Digentia, cool and clear,—
You and we twain, old friend; and then
  We 'll have our fill of pagan cheer.
Then, could old Horace join us three,
How proud and happy he would be!

Or if we part to meet no more
  This side the misty Stygian Sea,
Be sure of this: on yonder shore
  Sweet cheer awaiteth such as we;
A Sabine pagan's heaven, O friend,—
The fellowship that knows no end!

LYDIA DICK

WHEN I was a boy at college,
Filling up with classic knowledge,
  Frequently I wondered why
Old Professor Demas Bentley
Used to praise so eloquently
  "Opera Horatii."

Toiling on a season longer
Till my reasoning powers got stronger,
  As my observation grew,
I became convinced that mellow,
Massic-loving poet fellow,
  Horace, knew a thing or two.

Yes, we sophomores figured duly
That, if we appraised him truly,
    Horace must have been a brick;
And no wonder that with ranting
Rhymes he went a-gallivanting
    Round with sprightly Lydia Dick!

For that pink of female gender
Tall and shapely was, and slender,
    Plump of neck and bust and arms;
While the raiment that invested
Her so jealously suggested
    Certain more potential charms.

Those dark eyes of hers that fired him,
Those sweet accents that inspired him,
    And her crown of glorious hair,—
These things baffle my description:
I should have a fit conniption
    If I tried; so I forbear.

Maybe Lydia had her betters;
Anyway, this man of letters
    Took that charmer as his pick.
Glad—yes, glad I am to know it!
I, a *fin de siecle* poet,
    Sympathize with Lydia Dick!

Often in my arbor shady
I fall thinking of that lady,
    And the pranks she used to play;
And I 'm cheered,—for all we sages
Joy when from those distant ages
    Lydia dances down our way.

Otherwise some folks might wonder,
With good reason, why in thunder
    Learned professors, dry and prim,
Find such solace in the giddy
Pranks that Horace played with Liddy
    Or that Liddy played on him.

Still this world of ours rejoices
In those ancient singing voices,
     And our hearts beat high and quick,
To the cadence of old Tiber
Murmuring praise of roistering Liber
     And of charming Lydia Dick.

Still Digentia, downward flowing,
Prattleth to the roses blowing
     By the dark, deserted grot.
Still Soracte, looming lonely,
Watcheth for the coming only
     Of a ghost that cometh not.

IN PRAISE OF CONTENTMENT

I HATE the common, vulgar herd!
     Away they scamper when I "booh" em!
But pretty girls and nice young men
Observe a proper silence when
     I choose to sing my lyrics to 'em.

The kings of earth, whose fleeting pow'r
     Excites our homage and our wonder,
Are precious small beside old Jove,
The father of us all, who drove
     The giants out of sight, by thunder!

This man loves farming, that man law,
     While this one follows pathways martial—
What boots it whither mortals turn?
Grim fate from her mysterious urn
     Doles out the lots with hand impartial.

Nor sumptuous feasts nor studied sports
     Delight the heart by care tormented;

The mightiest monarch knoweth not
The peace that to the lowly cot
   Sleep bringeth to the swain contented.

On him untouched of discontent
   Care sits as lightly as a feather;
He does n't growl about the crops,
Or worry when the market drops,
   Or fret about the changeful weather.

Not so with him who, rich in fact,
   Still seeks his fortune to redouble;
Though dig he deep or build he high,
Those scourges twain shall lurk anigh—
   Relentless Care, relentless Trouble!

If neither palaces nor robes
   Nor unguents nor expensive toddy
Insure Contentment's soothing bliss,
Why should I build an edifice
   Where Envy comes to fret a body?

Nay, I 'd not share your sumptuous cheer,
   But rather sup my rustic pottage,
While that sweet boon the gods bestow—
The peace your mansions cannot know—
   Blesseth my lowly Sabine cottage.

VARIOUS TRANSLATIONS

UHLAND'S WHITE STAG

Into the woods three huntsmen came,
Seeking the white stag for their game.

They laid them under a green fir-tree
And slept, and dreamed strange things to see.

(FIRST HUNTSMAN)

I dreamt I was beating the leafy brush,
When out popped the noble stag—hush, hush!

(SECOND HUNTSMAN)

As ahead of the clamorous pack he sprang,
I pelted him hard in the hide—piff, bang!

(THIRD HUNTSMAN)

And as that stag lay dead I blew
On my horn a lusty tir-ril-la-loo!

So speak the three as there they lay
When lo! the white stag sped that way,

Frisked his heels at those huntsmen three,
Then leagues o'er hill and dale was he—
Hush, hush! Piff, bang! Tir-ril-la-loo!

A PARAPHRASE OF HEINE

(LYRIC INTERMEZZO)

THERE fell a star from realms above—
　A glittering, glorious star to see!
Methought it was the star of love,
　So sweetly it illumined me.

And from the apple branches fell
　Blossoms and leaves that time in June;
The wanton breezes wooed them well
　With soft caress and amorous tune.

The white swan proudly sailed along
　And vied her beauty with her note—
The river, jealous of her song,
　Threw up its arms to clasp her throat.

But now—oh, now the dream is past—
　The blossoms and the leaves are dead,
The swan's sweet song is hushed at last,
　And not a star burns overhead.

OLD SPANISH SONG

I 'M thinking of the wooing
　That won my maiden heart
When he—he came pursuing
　A love unused to art.
Into the drowsy river
　The moon transported flung
Her soul that seemed to quiver
　With the songs my lover sung.
And the stars in rapture twinkled
　On the slumbrous world below—
You see that, old and wrinkled,
　I 'm not forgetful—no!

He still should be repeating
  The vows he uttered then—
Alas! the years, though fleeting,
  Are truer yet than men!
The summer moonlight glistens
  In the favorite trysting spot
Where the river ever listens
  For a song it heareth not.
And I, whose head is sprinkled
  With time's benumbing snow,
I languish, old and wrinkled,
  But not forgetful—no!

What though he elsewhere turneth
  To beauty strangely bold?
Still in my bosom burneth
  The tender fire of old;
And the words of love he told me
  And the songs he sung me then
Come crowding to uphold me,
  And I live my youth again!
For when love's feet have tinkled
  On the pathway women go,
Though one be old and wrinkled,
  She 's not forgetful—no!

———

UHLAND'S "CHAPEL"

YONDER stands the hillside chapel
  'Mid the evergreens and rocks,
All day long it hears the song
  Of the shepherd to his flocks.

Then the chapel bell goes tolling—
  Knelling for a soul that 's sped;
Silent and sad the shepherd lad
  Hears the requiem for the dead.

Shepherd, singers of the valley,
  Voiceless now, speed on before;
Soon shall knell that chapel bell
  For the songs you 'll sing no more.

———

A HEINE LOVE SONG

THE image of the moon at night
  All trembling in the ocean lies,
But she, with calm and steadfast light,
  Moves proudly through the radiant skies.

How like the tranquil moon thou art—
  Thou fairest flower of womankind!
And, look, within my fluttering heart
  Thy image trembling is enshrined!

———

BÉRANGER'S "TO MY OLD COAT."

STILL serve me in my age, I pray,
  As in my youth, O faithful one;
For years I 've brushed thee every day—
  Could Socrates have better done?
What though the fates would wreak on thee
  The fulness of their evil art?
Use thou philosophy, like me—
  And we, old friend, shall never part!

I think—I *often* think of it—
  The day we twain first faced the crowd;
My roistering friends impeached your fit,
  But you and I were very proud!
Those jovial friends no more make free
  With us (no longer new and smart),
But rather welcome you and me
  As loving friends that should not part.

The patch?   Oh, yes—one happy night—
   "Lisette," says I, "it 's time to go"—
She clutched this sleeve to stay my flight,
   Shrieking: "What! leave so early? No!"
To mend the ghastly rent she 'd made,
   Three days she toiled, dear patient heart!
And I—right willingly I stayed—
   Lisette decreed we should not part!

No incense ever yet profaned
   This honest, shiny warp of thine,
Nor hath a courtier's eye disdained
   Thy faded hue and quaint design;
Let servile flattery be the price
   Of ribbons in the royal mart—
A roadside posie shall suffice
   For us two friends that must not part!

Fear not the recklessness of yore
   Shall reoccur to vex thee now;
Alas, I am a youth no more—
   I 'm old and sere, and so art thou!
So bide with me unto the last
   And with thy warmth caress this heart
That pleads, by memories of the Past,
   That two such friends should never part!

———

A SPRING POEM FROM BION

               ONE asketh:
      "Tell me, Myrson, tell me true:
      What 's the season pleaseth you?
      Is it summer suits you best,
      When from harvest toil we rest?
         Is it autumn with its glory
            Of all surfeited desires?

Is it winter, when with story
    And with song we hug our fires?
Or is spring most fair to you—
Come, good Myrson, tell me true!"

    Another answereth:
"What the gods in wisdom send
We should question not, my friend;
Yet, since you entreat of me,
I will answer reverently:
    Me the summertime displeases,
      For its sun is scorching hot;
    Autumn brings such dire diseases
      That perforce I like it not;
As for biting winter, oh!
How I hate its ice and snow!

"But, thrice welcome, kindly spring,
With the myriad gifts you bring!
Not too hot nor yet too cold,
Graciously your charms unfold—
    Oh, your days are like the dreaming
      Of those nights which love beseems,
    And your nights have all the seeming
      Of those days of golden dreams!
Heaven smiles down on earth, and then
Earth smiles up to heaven again!"

MOTHER AND SPHINX

(EGYPTIAN FOLK-SONG)

GRIM is the face that looks into the night
    Over the stretch of sands;
A sullen rock in a sea of white—
A ghostly shadow in ghostly light,
    Peering and moaning it stands.
"Oh, is it the king that rides this way—

Oh, is it the king that rides so free?
I have looked for the king this many a day,
But the years that mock me will not say
    Why tarrieth he!"

'T is not your king that shall ride to-night,
    But a child that is fast asleep;
And the horse he shall ride is the Dream-horse white—
Aha, he shall speed through the ghostly light
    Where the ghostly shadows creep!
"My eyes are dull and my face is sere,
    Yet unto the word he gave I cling,
For he was a Pharaoh that set me here—
And, lo! I have waited this many a year
    For him—my king!"

Oh, past thy face my darling shall ride
    Swift as the burning winds that bear
The sand clouds over the desert wide—
Swift to the verdure and palms beside
    The wells off there!
"And is it the mighty king I shall see
    Come riding into the night?
Oh, is it the king come back to me—
Proudly and fiercely rideth he,
    With centuries dight!"

I know no king but my dark-eyed dear
    That shall ride the Dream-Horse white;
But see! he wakes at my bosom here,
While the Dream-Horse frettingly lingers near
    To speed with my babe to-night!
And out of the desert darkness peers
    A ghostly, ghastly, shadowy thing
Like a spirit come out of the mouldering years,
And ever that waiting spectre hears
    The coming king!

HYMN

(FROM THE GERMAN OF MARTIN LUTHER)

O HEART of mine! lift up thine eyes
And see who in yon manger lies!
Of perfect form, of face divine—
It is the Christ-child, heart of mine!

O dearest, holiest Christ-child, spread
Within this heart of mine thy bed;
Then shall my breast forever be
A chamber consecrate to thee!

Beat high to-day, O heart of mine,
And tell, O lips, what joys are thine;
For with your help shall I prolong
Old Bethlehem's sweetest cradle-song.

Glory to God, whom this dear Child
Hath by His coming reconciled,
And whose redeeming love again
Brings peace on earth, good will to men!

TWO IDYLS FROM BION THE SMYRNEAN

I

ONCE a fowler, young and artless,
    To the quiet greenwood came;
Full of skill was he and heartless
    In pursuit of feathered game.
And betimes he chanced to see
Eros perching in a tree.

"What strange bird is that, I wonder?"
  Thought the youth, and spread his snare;
Eros, chuckling at the blunder,
  Gayly scampered here and there.
Do his best, the simple clod
Could not snare the agile god!

Blubbering, to his aged master
  Went the fowler in dismay,
And confided his disaster
  With that curious bird that day;
"Master, hast thou ever heard
Of so ill-disposed a bird?"

"Heard of him? Aha, most truly!"
  Quoth the master with a smile;
"And thou, too, shalt know him duly—
  Thou art young, but bide awhile,
And old Eros will not fly
From thy presence by and by!

"For when thou art somewhat older
  That same Eros thou didst see,
More familiar grown and bolder,
  Shall become acquaint with thee;
And when Eros comes thy way
Mark my word, he comes to stay!"

II

Once came Venus to me, bringing
  Eros where my cattle fed—
"Teach this little boy your singing,
  Gentle herdsman," Venus said.
I was young—I did not know
  Whom it was that Venus led—
That was many years ago!

In a lusty voice but mellow—
  Callow pedant! I began

To instruct the little fellow
    In the mysteries known to man;
Sung the noble cithern's praise,
    And the flute of dear old Pan,
And the lyre that Hermes plays.

But he paid no heed unto me—
    Nay, that graceless little boy
Coolly plotted to undo me—
    With his songs of tender joy;
And my pedantry o'erthrown,
    Eager was I to employ
His sweet ritual for mine own!

Ah, these years of ours are fleeting!
    Yet I have not vainly wrought,
Since to-day I am repeating
    What dear lessons Eros taught;
Love, and always love, and then—
    Counting all things else for naught—
Love and always love again!

A RHINE-LAND DRINKING SONG

IF our own life is the life of a flower
    (And that's what some sages are thinking),
We should moisten the bud with a health-giving flood
        And 't will bloom all the sweeter—
        Yes, life 's the completer
    For drinking,
            and drinking,
                    and drinking.

If it be that our life is a journey
    (As many wise folk are opining),
We should sprinkle the way with the rain while we may;

Though dusty and dreary,
'T is made cool and cheery
With wining,
and wining,
and wining.

If this life that we live be a dreaming
(As pessimist people are thinking),
To induce pleasant dreams there is nothing, meseems,
Like this sweet prescription,
That baffles description—
This drinking,
and drinking,
and drinking.

HUGO'S "POOL IN THE FOREST"

How calm, how beauteous and how cool—
How like a sister to the skies,
Appears the broad, transparent pool
That in this quiet forest lies.
The sunshine ripples on its face,
And from the world around, above,
It hath caught down the nameless grace
Of such reflections as we love.

But deep below its surface crawl
The reptile horrors of the night—
The dragons, lizards, serpents—all
The hideous brood that hate the light;
Through poison fern and slimy weed
And under ragged, jagged stones
They scuttle, or, in ghoulish greed,
They lap a dead man's bleaching bones.

And as, O pool, thou dost cajole
With seemings that beguile us well,
So doeth many a human soul
That teemeth with the lusts of hell.

HUGO'S "CHILD AT PLAY"

A CHILD was singing at his play—
  I heard the song, and paused to hear;
His mother moaning, groaning lay,
  And, lo! a spectre stood anear!

The child shook sunlight from his hair,
  And carolled gayly all day long—
Ay, with that spectre gloating there,
  The innocent made mirth and song!

How like to harvest fruit wert thou,
  O sorrow, in that dismal room—
God ladeth not the tender bough
  Save with the joy of bud and bloom!

LOVE SONG—HEINE

MANY a beauteous flower doth spring
  From the tears that flood my eyes,
And the nightingale doth sing
  In the burthen of my sighs.

If, O child, thou lovest me,
  Take these flowerets fair and frail,
And my soul shall waft to thee
  Love songs of the nightingale.

TO CINNA

CINNA, the great Venusian, told
  In songs that will not die
How in Augustan days of old
  Your love did glorify

His life, and all his being seemed
   Thrilled by that rare incense
Till, grudging him the dreams he dreamed,
   The gods did call you hence.

Cinna, I 've looked into your eyes,
   And held your hands in mine,
And seen your cheeks in sweet surprise
   Blush red as Massic wine;
Now let the songs in Cinna's praise
   Be chanted once again,
For, oh! alone I walk the ways
   We walked together then!

Perhaps upon some star to-night,
   So far away in space
I cannot see that beacon light
   Nor feel its soothing grace—
Perhaps from that far-distant sphere
   Her quickened vision seeks
For this poor heart of mine that here
   To its lost Cinna speaks.

Then search this heart, beloved eyes,
   And find it still as true
As when in all my boyhood skies
   My guiding stars were you!
Cinna, you know the mystery
   That is denied to men—
Mine is the lot to feel that we
   Shall elsewhere love again!

DER MANN IM KELLER

How cool and fair this cellar where
   My throne a dusky cask is;
To do no thing but just to sing
   And drown the time my task is.

The cooper he 's
Resolved to please,
And, answering to my winking,
He fills me up
Cup after cup
For drinking, drinking, drinking.

Begrudge me not
This cosey spot
In which I am reclining—
Why, who would burst
With envious thirst,
When he can live by wining?
A roseate hue seems to imbue
The world on which I 'm blinking;
My fellow-men—I love them when
I 'm drinking, drinking, drinking.

And yet I think, the more I drink,
It 's more and more I pine for—
Oh, such as I (forever dry)
God made this land of Rhine for
And there is bliss
In knowing this,
As to the floor I 'm sinking:
I 've wronged no man
And never can
While drinking, drinking, drinking.

"TROT, MY GOOD STEED, TROT!"

WHERE my true love abideth
I make my way to-night;
Lo! waiting, she
Espieth me,
And calleth in delight:

"I see his steed anear
Come trotting with my dear,—
Oh, idle not, good steed, but trot,
Trot thou my lover here!"

Aloose I cast the bridle,
And ply the whip and spur,
And gayly I
Speed this reply,
While faring on to her:
"Oh, true love, fear thou not!
I seek our trysting spot;
And double feed be yours, my steed,
If you more swiftly trot."

I vault from out the saddle,
And make my good steed fast;
Then to my breast
My love is pressed,—
At last, true heart, at last!
The garden drowsing lies,
The stars fold down their eyes,—
In this dear spot, my steed, neigh not,
Nor stamp in restless wise!

O passing sweet communion
Of young hearts, warm and true!
To thee belongs
The old, old songs
Love finds forever new.
We sing those songs, and then
Cometh the moment when
It 's "Good steed, trot from this dear spot,—
Trot, trot me home again!"

BION'S SONG OF EROS

EROS is the god of love;
He and I are hand-in-glove.
　All the gentle, gracious Muses
　　Follow Eros where he leads,
　And they bless the bard who chooses
　　To proclaim love's famous deeds;
Him they serve in rapturous glee,—
That is why they 're good to me.

Sometimes I have gone astray
From love's sunny, flowery way:
　How I floundered, how I stuttered!
　　And, deprived of ways and means,
　What egregious rot I uttered,—
　　Such as suits the magazines!
I was rescued only when
Eros called me back again.

Gods forefend that I should shun
That benignant Mother's son!
　Why, the poet who refuses
　　To emblazon love's delights
　Gets the mitten from the Muses,—
　　Then what balderdash he writes!
I love Love; which being so,
See how smooth my verses flow!

Gentle Eros, lead the way,—
I will follow while I may:
　Be thy path by hill or hollow,
　　I will follow fast and free;
　And when I 'm too old to follow,
　　I will sit and sing of thee,—
Potent still in intellect,
Sit, and sing, and retrospect.

FIDUCIT

THREE comrades on the German Rhine,
　Defying care and weather,
Together quaffed the mellow wine,
　And sung their songs together.
What recked they of the griefs of life,
　With wine and song to cheer them?
Though elsewhere trouble might be rife,
　It would not come anear them.

Anon one comrade passed away,
　And presently another,
And yet unto the tryst each day
　Repaired the lonely brother;
And still, as gayly as of old,
　That third one, hero-hearted,
Filled to the brim each cup of gold,
　And called to the departed,—

"O comrades mine! I see ye not,
　Nor hear your kindly greeting,
Yet in this old, familiar spot
　Be still our loving meeting!
Here have I filled each bouting-cup
　With juices red and cheery;
I pray ye drink the potion up,
　And as of old make merry!"

And once before his tear-dimmed eyes,
　All in the haunted gloaming,
He saw two ghostly figures rise,
　And quaff the beakers foaming;
He heard two spirit voices call,
　"Fiducit, jovial brother!"
And so forever from that hall
　Went they with one another.

THE LOST CUPID OF MOSCHUS

"Cupid!" Venus went a-crying;
    "Cupid, whither dost thou stray?
Tell me, people, hither hieing,
    Have you seen my runaway?
    Speak,—my kiss shall be your pay!
Yes, and sweets more gratifying,
    If you bring him back to-day.

"Cupid," Venus went a-calling,
    "Is a rosy little youth,
But his beauty is enthralling.
    He will speak you fair, in sooth,
    Wheedle you with glib untruth,—
Honey-like his words; but galling
    Are his deeds, and full of ruth!

"Cupid's hair is curling yellow,
    And he hath a saucy face;
With his chubby hands the fellow
    Shooteth into farthest space,
    Heedless of all time and place;
King and squire and punchinello
    He delighteth to abase!

"Nude and winged the prankish blade is,
    And he speedeth everywhere,
Vexing gentlemen and ladies,
    Callow youths and damsels fair
    Whom he catcheth unaware;—
Venturing even into Hades,
    He hath sown his torments there!

"For that bow, that bow and quiver,—
    Oh, they are a cruel twain!
Thinking of them makes me shiver.

Oft, with all his might and main,
Cupid sends those darts profane
Whizzing through my heart and liver,
Setting fire to every vein!

"And the torch he carries blazing,—
Truly 't is a tiny one;
Yet, that tiny torch upraising,
Cupid scarifies the sun!
Ah, good people, there is none
Knows what mischief most amazing
Cupid's evil torch hath done!

"Show no mercy when you find him!
Spite of every specious plea
And of all his whimpering, bind him!
Full of flatteries is he;
Armed with treachery, *cap-a-pie*,
He 'll play 'possum; never mind him,—
March him straightway back to me!

"Bow and arrows and sweet kisses
He will offer you, no doubt;
But beware those proffered blisses,—
They are venomous throughout!
Seize and bind him fast about;
Mind you,—most important this is:
Bind him, bring him, but—watch out!"

AN ECLOGUE FROM VIRGIL

[The exile Melibœus finds Tityrus in possession of his own farm, re-
stored to him by the Emperor Augustus, and a conversation ensues. The
poem is in praise of Augustus, peace, and pastoral life.]

MELIBŒUS

ƒITYRUS, all in the shade of the wide-spreading beech-tree reclining,
 Sweet is that music you've made on your pipe that is oaten and
  slender;
Exiles from home, you beguile our hearts from their hopeless re-
 pining,
 As you sing Amaryllis the while in pastorals tuneful and tender.

TITYRUS

A god—yes, a god, I declare—vouchsafes me these pleasant con-
 ditions,
 And often I gayly repair with a tender white lamb to his altar;
He gives me the leisure to play my greatly admired compositions,
 While my heifers go browsing all day, unhampered of bell and
  of halter.

MELIBŒUS

I do not begrudge you repose; I simply admit I 'm confounded
 To find you unscathed of the woes of pillage and tumult and
  battle.
To exile and hardship devote, and by merciless enemies hounded,
 I drag at this wretched old goat and coax on my famishing
  cattle.
Oh, often the omens presaged the horrors which now overwhelm
 me—
But, come, if not elsewise engaged, who *is* this good deity, tell me!

TITYRUS
(reminiscently)

The city—the city called Rome, with my head full of herding and
 tillage,
 I used to compare with my home, these pastures wherein you
  now wander;

But I didn't take long to find out that the city surpasses the village
  As the cypress surpasses the sprout that thrives in the thicket
    out yonder.

MELIBŒUS

Tell me, good gossip, I pray, what led you to visit the city?

TITYRUS

Liberty! which on a day regarded my lot with compassion;
My age and distresses, forsooth, compelled that proud mistress
  to pity,
  That had snubbed the attentions of youth in most reprehensible
    fashion.
Oh, happy, thrice happy, the day when the cold Galatea forsook me;
And equally happy, I say, the hour when that other girl took me!

MELIBŒUS
(slyly, as if addressing the damsel)

So now, Amaryllis, the truth of your ill-disguised grief I discover!
  You pined for a favorite youth with citified damsels hobnobbing;
And soon your surroundings partook of your grief for your rec-
  usant lover,—
  The pine-trees, the copse, and the brook, for Tityrus ever went
    sobbing.

TITYRUS

Melibœus, what else could I do? Fate doled me no morsel of
  pity;
  My toil was all vain the year through, no matter how earnest or
    clever,
Till, at last, came that god among men, that king from that won-
  derful city,
  And quoth: "Take your homesteads again; they are yours
    and your assigns' forever!"

MELIBŒUS

Happy, oh, happy old man! rich in what's better than money,—
  Rich in contentment, you can gather sweet peace by mere lis-
    tening;

Bees with soft murmurings go hither and thither for honey,
  Cattle all gratefully low in pastures where fountains are glistening—
Hark! in the shade of that rock the pruner with singing rejoices,—
  The dove in the elm and the flock of wood-pigeons hoarsely
    repining,
The plash of the sacred cascade,—ah, restful, indeed, are these
    voices,
  Tityrus, all in the shade of your wide-spreading beech-tree reclining!

TITYRUS

And he who insures this to me—oh, craven I were not to love
    him!
  Nay, rather the fish of the sea shall vacate the water they swim
    in,
The stag quit his bountiful grove to graze in the ether above
    him,
  While folk antipodean rove along with their children and women!

MELIBŒUS
(suddenly recalling his own misery)

But we who are exiled must go; and whither—ah, whither—God
    knoweth!
  Some into those regions of snow or of desert where Death reigneth only;
Some off to the country of Crete, where rapid Oaxes down floweth;
  And desperate others retreat to Britain, the bleak isle and lonely.
Dear land of my birth! shall I see the horde of invaders oppress
    thee?
  Shall the wealth that outspringeth from thee by the hand of the
    alien be squandered?
Dear cottage wherein I was born! shall another in conquest possess thee,
  Another demolish in scorn the fields and the groves where I 've
    wandered?
My flock! nevermore shall you graze on that furze-covered hillside above me;
  Gone, gone are the halcyon days when my reed piped defiance
    to sorrow!

Nevermore in the vine-covered grot shall I sing of the loved ones
    that love me,—
    Let yesterday's peace be forgot in dread of the stormy to-mor-
        row!

TITYRUS

But rest you this night with me here; my bed,—we will share it
    together,
    As soon as you 've tasted my cheer, my apples and chestnuts
        and cheeses;
The evening already is nigh,—the shadows creep over the heather,
    And the smoke is rocked up to the sky to the lullaby song of the
        breezes.

CATULLUS TO LESBIA

Come, my Lesbia, no repining;
    Let us love while yet we may!
Suns go on forever shining;
    But when we have had our day,
Sleep perpetual shall o'ertake us,
And no morrow's dawn awake us.

Come, in yonder nook reclining,
    Where the honeysuckle climbs,
Let us mock at Fate's designing,
    Let us kiss a thousand times!
And if they shall prove too few, dear,
When they 're kissed we 'll start anew, dear!

And should any chance to see us,
    Goodness! how they 'll agonize!
How they 'll wish that they could be us,
    Kissing in such liberal wise!
Never mind their envious whining;
Come, my Lesbia, no repining!

KÖRNER'S BATTLE PRAYER

FATHER, I cry to Thee!
Round me the billows of battle are pouring,
Round me the thunders of battle are roaring;
    Father on high, hear Thou my cry,—
    Father, oh, lead Thou me!

Father, oh, lead Thou me!
Lead me, o'er Death and its terrors victorious,—
See, I acknowledge Thy will as all-glorious;
    Point thou the way, lead where it may,—
    God, I acknowledge Thee!

God, I acknowledge Thee!
As when the dead leaves of autumn whirl round me
So, when the horrors of war would confound me,
    Laugh I at fear, knowing Thee near,—
    Father, oh, bless Thou me!

Father, oh, bless Thou me!
Living or dying, waking or sleeping,
Such as I am, I commit to Thy keeping:
    Frail though I be, Lord, bless Thou me!
    Father, I worship Thee!

Father, I worship Thee!
Not for the love of the riches that perish,
But for the freedom and justice we cherish,
    Stand we or fall, blessing Thee, all—
    God, I submit to Thee!

God, I submit to Thee!
Yea, though the terrors of Death pass before me,
Yea, with the darkness of Death stealing o'er me,
    Lord, unto Thee bend I the knee,—
    Father, I cry to Thee!

BÉRANGER'S "MA VOCATION"

MISERY is my lot,
  Poverty and pain;
Ill was I begot,
  Ill must I remain;
Yet the wretched days
  One sweet comfort bring,
When God whispering says,
  "Sing, O singer, sing!"

Chariots rumble by,
  Splashing me with mud;
Insolence see I
  Fawn to royal blood;
Solace have I then
  From each galling sting
In that voice again,—
  "Sing, O singer, sing!"

Cowardly at heart,
  I am forced to play
A degraded part
  For its paltry pay;
Freedom is a prize
  For no starving thing;
Yet that small voice cries,
  "Sing, O singer, sing!"

I *was* young, but now,
  When I'm old and gray,
Love—I know not how
  Or why—hath sped away;
Still, in winter days
  As in hours of spring,
Still a whisper says,
  "Sing, O singer, sing!"

Ah, too well I know
  Song's my only friend!
Patiently I'll go
  Singing to the end;
Comrades, to your wine!
  Let your glasses ring!
Lo, that voice divine
  Whispers, "Sing, oh, sing!"

———

HUGO'S "FLOWER TO BUTTERFLY"

SWEET, bide with me and let my love
  Be an enduring tether;
Oh, wanton not from spot to spot,
  But let us dwell together.

You've come each morn to sip the sweets
  With which you found me dripping,
Yet never knew it was not dew
  But tears that you were sipping.

You gambol over honey meads
  Where siren bees are humming;
But mine the fate to watch and wait
  For my beloved's coming.

The sunshine that delights you now
  Shall fade to darkness gloomy;
You should not fear if, biding here,
  You nestled closer to me.

So rest you, love, and be my love,
  That my enraptured blooming
May fill your sight with tender light,
  Your wings with sweet perfuming.

Or, if you will not bide with me
  Upon this quiet heather,
Oh, give me wing, thou beauteous thing,
  That we may soar together.

———

BÉRANGER'S "MY LAST SONG PERHAPS"

[JANUARY, 1814]

WHEN, to despoil my native France,
  With flaming torch and cruel sword
And boisterous drums her foeman comes,
  I curse him and his vandal horde !
Yet, what avail accrues to her,
  If we assume the garb of woe?
Let's merry be,—in laughter we
  May rescue somewhat from the foe !

Ah, many a brave man trembles now.
  I (coward!) show no sign of fear;
When Bacchus sends his blessing, friends,
  I drown my panic in his cheer.
Come, gather round my humble board,
  And let the sparkling wassail flow,—
Chuckling to think, the while you drink,
  "This much we rescue from the foe !"

My creditors beset me so
  And so environed my abode,
That I agreed, despite my need,
  To settle up the debts I owed;
When suddenly there came the news
  Of this invasion, as you know;
I'll pay no score; pray, lend me more,—
  I—*I* will keep it from the foe !

Now here's my mistress,—pretty dear!—
  Feigns terror at this martial noise,
And yet, methinks, the artful minx
  Would like to meet those soldier boys
I tell her that they're coarse and rude,
  Yet feel she don't believe 'em so,—
Well, never mind; so she be kind,
  That much I rescue from the foe !

If, brothers, hope shall have in store
  For us and ours no friendly glance,
Let's rather die than raise a cry
  Of welcome to the foes of France !
But, like the swan that dying sings,
  Let us, O Frenchmen, singing go,—
Then shall our cheer, when death is near,
  Be so much rescued from the foe !

UHLAND'S "THREE CAVALIERS"

THERE were three cavaliers that went over the Rhine,
And gayly they called to the hostess for wine.
"And where is thy daughter?   We would she were here,—
Go fetch us that maiden to gladden our cheer !"

"I 'll fetch thee thy goblets full foaming," she said,
"But in yon darkened chamber the maiden lies dead."
And lo! as they stood in the doorway, the white
Of a shroud and a dead shrunken face met their sight.

Then the first cavalier breathed a pitiful sigh,
And the throb of his heart seemed to melt in his eye,
And he cried, "Hadst thou lived, O my pretty white rose,
I ween I had loved thee and wed thee—who knows?"

The next cavalier drew aside a small space,
And stood to the wall with his hands to his face;
And this was the heart-cry that came with his tears:
"I loved her, I loved her these many long years !"

But the third cavalier kneeled him down in that place,
And, as it were holy, he kissed that dead face:
"I loved thee long years, and I love thee to-day,
And I'll love thee, dear maiden, forever and aye!"

HEINE'S "WIDOW OR DAUGHTER?"

SHALL I woo the one or other?
  Both attract me—more's the pity!
Pretty is the widowed mother,
  And the daughter, too, is pretty.

When I see that maiden shrinking,
  By the gods I swear I'll get 'er!
But anon I fall to thinking
  That the mother'll suit me better!

So, like any idiot ass
  Hungry for the fragrant fodder,
Placed between two bales of grass,
  Lo, I doubt, delay, and dodder!

BÉRANGER'S "BROKEN FIDDLE"

I

THERE, there, poor dog, my faithful friend,
  Pay you no heed unto my sorrow:
But feast to-day while yet you may,—
  Who knows but we shall starve to-morrow!

II

"Give us a tune," the foemen cried,
  In one of their profane caprices;
I bade them "No"—they frowned, and, lo!
  They dashed this innocent in pieces!

III

This fiddle was the village pride—
  The mirth of every fête enhancing;
Its wizard art set every heart
  As well as every foot to dancing.

IV

How well the bridegroom knew its voice,
  As from its strings its song went gushing!
Nor long delayed the promised maid
  Equipped for bridal, coy and blushing.

V

Why, it discoursed so merrily,
  It quickly banished all dejection;
And yet, when pressed, our priest confessed
  I played with pious circumspection.

VI

And though, in patriotic song,
  It was our guide, compatriot, teacher,
I never thought the foe had wrought
  His fury on the helpless creature!

VII

But there, poor dog, my faithful friend,
  Pay you no heed unto my sorrow;
I prithee take this paltry cake,—
  Who knows but we shall starve to-morrow!

VIII

Ah, who shall lead the Sunday choir
  As this old fiddle used to do it?
Can vintage come, with this voice dumb
  That used to bid a welcome to it?

IX

It soothed the weary hours of toil,
   It brought forgetfulness to debtors;
Time and again from wretched men
   It struck oppression's galling fetters.

X

No man could hear its voice, and hate;
   It stayed the teardrop at its portal;
With that dear thing I was a king
   As never yet was monarch mortal!

XI

Now has the foe—the vandal foe—
   Struck from my hands their pride and glory;
There let it lie!   In vengeance, I
   Shall wield another weapon, gory!

XII

And if, O countrymen, I fall,
   Beside our grave let this be spoken
"No foe of France shall ever dance
   Above the heart and fiddle, broken!"

XIII

So come, poor dog, my faithful friend,
   I prithee do not heed my sorrow,
But feast to-day while yet you may,
   For we are like to starve to-morrow.

SHARPS AND FLATS

THE OFFICIAL EXPLANATION

ONE night aside the fire at hum,
  Ez I wuz sittin' nappin',
Deown frum the lower hall there come
  The seound of some one rappin'.
The son uv old Nat Hawthorne he—
  Julian, I think his name wuz—
Uv course he feound a friend in me,
  Not knowin' what his game wuz.

An' ez we visited a spell,
  Our talk ranged wide an' wider,
An' if we struck dry subjects—well,
  We washed 'em deown with cider.
Neow, with that cider coursin' thru
  My system an' a-playin'
Upon my tongue, I hardly knew
  Just what I was a-sayin'.

I kin remember that I spun
  A hifalutin story
Abeout the Prince uv Wales, an' one
  Abeout old Queen Victory.
But, sakes alive! I never dreamed
  The cuss would get it printed—
(By that old gal I 'm much esteemed,
  Ez she hez often hinted.)

Oh, if I had that critter neow,
  You bet your boots I 'd l'arn him
In mighty lively fashion heow
  To walk the chalk, gol darn him!

Meanwhile between his folks an' mine
    The breach grows wide an' wider,
An', by the way, it 's my design
    To give up drinkin' cider.

November 1, 1886.

THE POET'S RETURN

A POET, crazed by Mammon, hung
    His harp upon the willows, and
Forgot the songs which he had sung,
    Sweeping that harp with master hand.
Long wailed the Muse with much ado,
    The votary which Mammon stole,
Till Mammon pitying her withdrew
    The spell that bound the poet's soul.

The poet then with master hand
    Took down the old familiar lyre
And sang unto a listening land
    His song aflame with heav'nly fire.
Sing on, O poet, while ye may,
    As sweetly as in years of old,
For thy sweet songs shall live for aye,
    A grander heritance than gold!

August 17, 1883.

A SHOSHONE LEGEND

THE brave Shoshones much revere
    Our presidential Arthur,
And they proclaim him, far and near
    The mighty pale-face father.

This reverence, 't is said, is due
   Unto a little caper,
Which, whether false or whether true,
   Hath ne'er before seen paper.

Down in the Yellowstone, one eve,
   Quoth Vest, the statesman-joker:
"Since time hangs heavy, I believe
   I 'll start a game of poker."
He called the bold Shoshones round
   And filled their pipes with Gravely,
And, seated on the dewy ground,
   They all chipped in right bravely.

And lo! the President did choose
   To lend approval hearty;
So, purchasing a stack of blues,
   He sat in with the party.
Out spake the brave Po-Dunk-a-Wee,
   Rending his purse asunder:
"Big Injun bet heap dollar he
   Beat pale-face all to thunder!"

Whereat the pale-face chief sublime
   Did manifest a wincing—
And yet allowed it was no time
   For presidential mincing.
So none dropped out, but all came in,
   Till groaned the pot with stuffing—
And, consequently, rose the din
   Of multifarious bluffing.

And when the show-down word was spoke—
   Alas, its dreadful uses!
The brave Po-Dunk-a-Wee went broke
   On sixes full on deuces;
"Two pair," the brave Tim-Tom-Kee moaned
   Amid regretful blushes,
While other rash Shoshones groaned
   O'er various bobtail flushes.

And then a miracle ensued
  Which blanched the copper faces—
Our Arthur, with rare fortitude,
  Showed down five awful aces.

August 22, 1883.

A ZEPHYR FROM ZULULAND

FROM Onathlamba in the west,
  Where rise the walls of Quangar,
And where the brave Bapedis rest,
  Is heard a joyous clangor:
From Unyanyembe's pagan towers—
  The Umtamtuna River—
Where dark Kabompo's noisome bowers
  Disturb the Kaffir's liver;
Where bloom the nutmeg and the rose
  And thrives the tapir greasy,
And where the Unzimkulu flows
  Into the fair Zambesi;
Where dwells the cruel assagai
  Among the fierce Potgeiters,
And Sekukunis live and die
  As Amaswazai fighters;
And from the huts of Mozambique
  Upon the northern shore,
Unto old Umoolosi peak,
  And fragrant Delagoa—
Around and round the tidings go,
  Inspiring vast thanksgiving
That all in spite of dastard foe
  Their monarch still is living.
Hail, monarch! Cetewayo, hail!—
  Great England's pagan hobby—
And bless thy fate that foes should **fail**
  To slay a nibs so nobby!

August 22, 1883.

THE FRENCH MUST GO

UNTO his valiant aide-de-camp
    Remarked the brave Bouet:
"To-morrow we will move along
    To battle, *s'il vous plaît.*
Hard by the walls of Hue, we
    Our pagan foe shall meet,
And then and there, *mon cher ami,*
    We 'll warm him *tout de suite.*"

Next morn, as brave Wun Lung with zest
    Partook his matin rice,
And stored away beneath his vest
    A pie composed of mice,
Into his presence rushed Gin Sing,
    And cried in sore dismay:
"Oh, save thyself, most potent king—
    The Flenchmen come this way!"

Wun Lung looked daggers, and replied:
    "If that 's the Flenchman's gamee,
We 'll meet him on the plain outside,
    And lick him allee samee.
Close up the laundries, whet your swords;
    And, with your spears in hand,
Call in the servile cooly hordes
    And let the junks be manned."

When this commotion brave Bouet
    Discovered from afar—
"I fear," he muttered in dismay,
    "I 've made *un grand faux pas.*
I do not understand," quoth he,
    "This hurrying to and fro;
But I suspect, from what I see
    And hear, *je suis de trop !*"

The hostile forces soon imbrued
  With murd'rous shock and blow,
And in the struggle that ensued
  The Frenchman had to go.
The fierce Wun Lung, amid the strife,
  Beheld brave Bouet near,
And took his horse-du-combat's life
  With battle-axe and spear.

And when his horse-du-combat fell
  All lifeless at his feet,
Brave Bouet, with a sickening yell,
  Commanded a retreat.
Wun Lung now lolls in his abode
  From morn till dewy eve,
And eats his rat-pie *a la mode*—
  And Bouet takes "French leave."

August 22, 1883

A BATTLE IN YELLOWSTONE PARK

THE sun had slipped down
  The blue slant of the west;
The pale, queenly moon
  Sat upon the night's crest,
With her face from the world
  Turned in shame half away,
As she fondly pursued
  Her loved king of the day.

The Yellowstone camp
  In the valley below,
With its tents like tombstones
  Set out in a row,
Was quaking with fear;
  For the word had been brought
That a train was en route
  With bold kidnappers fraught.

The President lay
  In his well-guarded tent;
The general hither
  And thither had sent
The men of his staff
  And the men of his troop;
The visiting statesmen
  Were crouched in a group.

On the soft summer breeze
  Came a sharp, startling sound.
For a moment all stood
  As in fear's fetters bound.
"What was that?" whispered Robert.
  Said Rufus: "Fly! Hide!
'T is the savage war-whoop
  Of the robber's red guide."

"Man the outposts! Look sharp!"
  The brave general said.
"Guard the President well."
  And with field-glass he read
The circling horizon,
  To south and to east,
Till his eye fell, at last,
  On the skulking red beast.

Every eye in the camp
  Strained, the pale night to pierce;
Every hand clutched a gun,
  As by fear rendered fierce;
Every heart pounded hard
  At the ribs of its cage
As forms were spied, veiled
  By a thicket of sage.

Flash! each gun laughed a flame
  Like a demon at sport.
Crash! the still night was rent
  By the awful report,

And the craggy old mountains
  Re-echoed "Ha, ha!"
Till the sounds seemed to blend
  In a giant guffaw.

Hours and hours the camp watched
  Till the bright threads of dawn
Wove a shining gold veil
  For the night to put on.
Then, there in the sage-brush,
  In bullet-torn coats,
Lay the earthly remains
  Of a pair of coyotes.

August 28, 1883.

HIS LORDSHIP, THE CHIEF JUSTICE

WHEREAS, it is alleged, to wit:
  There cometh from afar
A certain party in whose cause
  Herewith these presents are;
One Coleridge is said party's name,
  A lord of high degree,
Well known unto this court and fame—
  A judge, so called, is he.

As parties of the second part,
  We, the appellants, pray
That sundry courtesies be shown
  Said judge who comes this way;
And, furthermore, appellants crave
  Said judge be dined and fêted
As would become said judge and court
  Hereinbefore narrated;
And that said divers compliments
  Be also well intentioned,
As to delight said judge, so called,
  Above and afore mentioned.

August 29, 1883.

A HINT FOR 1884

THE sage of Greystone, so they say,
  Has two imported steeds;
The one is black, the other bay,
  And both of noble breeds.
Before he bought these chargers rare—
  Of stylish blood and tone—
He used to drive another pair,
  A humble gray and roan.

When Tilden hankers after style
  On boulevard or street,
A coachman reins the chargers,
  While he lolls on cushioned seat.
But when he 's out for holiday
  To scour the hedge and thicket,
Alone he drives the roan and gray—
  The good old-fashioned ticket.

August 31, 1883.

THE INDIAN AND THE TROUT

THE morning sun in splendor shone
On the mellow park of the Yellowstone.
The President at the break of day
Had packed his duds and moved away.
A brave Shoshone chief came out
With his willow pole to fish for trout.
It was half-past six when he cast his line,
And he kept on fishing till half-past nine;
And then he baited his hook anew
And patiently fished until half-past two—
The meanwhile swearing a powerful sight
For fishing all day with nary a bite.

And he swore and fished, and fished and swore
Till his Elgin watch tolled half-past four;
When a big, fat trout came swimming by
And winked at the chief with his cold, sad eye.

"And do you reckon, you pagan soul,
You can catch us trout with a willow pole?
The President taught us manners while
He fished for us in the latest style.
You 've no idea how proud we feel
To be jerked ashore with a Frankfort reel!"

The red man gathered his dinner-pail
And started home by the shortest trail,
And he told his faithful squaw he guess'd
They 'd better move still farther west,
Where presidents didn't come fooling about,
Turning the heads of the giddy trout.
September 5, 1883.

A PLAY ON WORDS

(TO BE READ ALOUD RAPIDLY)

Assert ten Barren love day made
    Dan woo'd her hart buy nigh tan day;
Butt wen knee begged she 'd marry hymn,
    The crewel bell may dancer neigh.
Lo atter fee tin vein he side
    Ant holder office offal pane—
A lasses mown touched knot terse sole—
    His grown was sever awl Lynn vane.

"Owe, beam my bride, my deer, rye prey,
    And here mice size beef ore rye dye;
Oak caste mean knot tin scorn neigh way—
    Yew are the apple love me nigh!"

She herd Dan new we truly spoke.
  Key was of noble berth, and bread
Tool lofty mean and hie renown,
  The air too grate testates, 't was head.

"Ewe wood due bettor, sir," she bald,
  "Took court sum mother girl, lie wean—
Ewer knot mice stile, lisle never share
  The thrown domestic azure quean!"
" 'T is dun, no farebutt Scilly won—
  Aisle waiste know father size on the!"
Oft tooth the nay bring porte tea flue
  And through himself into the see.

September 12, 1883.

HOW FLAHERTY KEPT THE BRIDGE

Out spake Horatius Flaherty,—a Fenian bold was he,—
"Lo, I will stand at thy right hand and turn the bridge with thee!
So ring the bell, O'Grady, and clear the railway track—
Muldoon will heed the summons well and keep the street-cars
    back."

Forthwith O'Grady rang the bell, and straightway from afar
There came a rush of humankind and over-loaded car.
"Back, back! a schooner cometh," the brave O'Grady cried;
"She cometh from Muskegon, packed down with horn and hide."

And "Back!" Muldoon demanded and Flaherty declaimed,
While many a man stopped short his course and muttered, "I 'll
    be blamed!"
And many a horse-car jolted, and many a driver swore,
As the tother gangway of the bridge swung off from either shore.
And bold Horatius Flaherty a storm of curses heard,
But pushing bravely at his key, he answered not a word;
And round and round he turned the bridge to let the schooner
    through,

And round and round and round again O'Grady turned it too;
Till now at last the way is clear, and with a sullen toot
'Twixt bridge and shore, ten rods or more, the tug and schooner
　　shoot.

"Now swing her round the tother way," the brave O'Grady cried.
" 'T is well!" Horatius Flaherty in thunder tones replied.
Muldoon waved high his club in air, his handkerchief waved
　　high,
To see the stanch Muskegon ship go sailing calmly by;
And as the rafters of the bridge swung round to either shore,
Vast was the noise of men and boys and street-cars passing o'er.
And Flaherty quoth proudly, as he mopped his sweaty brow,
"Well done for you, and here's a chew, O'Grady, for you now."
September 19, 1883.

———

THE THREE–CENT STAMP

Good-by, old stamp; it's nasty luck
　　That ends our friendship so.
When others failed, you gamely stuck,
　　But now you've got to go.
So here's a flood of honest tears,
　　And here's an honest sigh.
Good-by, old friend of many years—
　　Good-by, old stamp, good-by!

Your life has been a varied one,
　　With curious phases fraught—
Sometimes a check, sometimes a dun,
　　Your daily coming brought;
Smiles to a waiting lover's face,
　　Tears to a mother's eye,
Or joy or pain to every place—
　　Good-by, old stamp, good-by!

You bravely toiled, and better men
　Will vouch for what I say;
Although you have been licked, 't was when
　Your face turned t' other way.
'T was often in a box you got
　(As you will not deny)
For going through the mails, I wot—
　Good-by, old stamp, good-by!

Ah, in your last expiring breath
　The tale of years is heard—
The sound of voices hushed in death,
　A mother's dying word,
A maiden's answer, soft and sweet,
　A wife's regretful sigh,
The patter of a baby's feet—
　Good-by, old stamp, good-by!

What wonder, then, that at this time
　When you and I must part,
I should aspire to speak in rhyme
　The promptings of my heart?
Go, bide with all those mem'ries dear
　That live when others die;
You' ve nobly served your purpose here—
　Good-by, old stamp, good-by!
September 24, 1883.

———

BIG THURSDAY

In this week's history of the Fair,
　To-day will be the banner day.
The commonwealth will all be there
　To view the truly grand display.
The country folk from miles around
　Will gather in this monstrous hive,
And will in wondering groups be found
　Where pigs and cows and squashes thrive.

The rural bumpkin and his gal
  Will proudly note the Lima bean
And golden pumpkin from La Salle,
  The sweet potato from Moline,
The toothsome cheese from Kankakee,
  The turnip bred in Kickapoo;
And squashes fair and round we 'll see
  From Crete and Big Foot Prairie, too.

Or, fancying live stock, they will ponder
  On blooded cattle by the drove—
Sleek Berkshire bullocks from Golconda,
  And Durham swine from Downer's Grove;
On gentle Southdown mules from Pana,
  On Poland China sheep from Niles,
On calves from Buda and Urbana,
  And likewise cows in divers styles.

Unhappy, most unhappy being
  Who thinks to stay away from there—
Who misses all such sights worth seeing
  At and around our glorious Fair!
So don, O youth, your paper collar,
  And prink your best, O maiden gay,
A ticket costs but half a dollar—
  Go join the multitude to-day!

September 27, 1883.

THE MYSTERY OF PASADENE

Come, now, who is this Pasadene
That such a whirl of praises warrants?
    And is a rose
    Her only clo'es?
Oh, fie upon you, Billy Florence!

Ah, no; that's your poetic way
Of turning loose your rhythmic torrents.
    This Pasadene
    Is not your queen—
We know you know we know it, Florence!

So sing your song of women-folks;
We'll read without the least abhorrence,
    Because we know
    Through weal and woe
Your queen is Mrs. Billy Florence!

January 3, 1887.

A NIGHTMARE

(CAUSED BY FAILURE TO DIGEST A BLANKET-SHEET)

    Did I dream? Was 't a fancy
    Of weird necromancy
That mingled the living with shades of the dead
    Was 't a deep meditation,
    Or hallucination
Provoked by a paper I had but just read?

    Blanket-sheet editor
      Sat in his den,
    With his yardstick and tape-measure,
      Paste-pot and pen,
    When there came to the doorway
      And stood in a row

    The spirits of Shakspere,
      Of Addison, Poe,
    And a multitude more
      Of the same brainy school;
    And one in clown's raiment—
      A poor verbose fool.

"So you 're looking for places?"
    The editor said.
Each shade in his turn
    Gave a nod of the head.
"How much can you write
    In the course of a day?"
The spirits proceeded
    Their work to display.

One had written a sonnet
    Of usual length;
Another a paragraph
    Towering in strength;
Still another romanced
    In sensational strain—
Every thought a rare gem
    From a procreant brain.

Then forth from his bag
    The poor, motley clown brought
A haymow of words
    With a needle of thought;
And the editor measured
    Them all with his rule,
And dismissed every spirit
    Save that of the fool.

October 3, 1883.

———

BACHELOR HALL

It seems like a dream—that sweet wooing of old—
Like a legend of fairies on pages of gold—
Too soon the sweet story of loving was closed,
Too rudely awakened the soul that reposed;
I kissed the white lips that lay under the pall,
And crept back to you, lonely Bachelor Hall.

Mine eyes have grown dim and my hair has turned white,
But my heart beats as warmly and gayly to-night
As in days that are gone and years that are fled—
Though I fill up my flagon and drink to the dead;
For over my senses sweet memories fall,
And the dead is come back to old Bachelor Hall.

I see her fair face through a vapor of tears,
And her sweet voice comes back o'er the desert of years,
And I hear, oh, so gently, the promises she spoke,
And a soft, spirit hand soothes the heart that is broke;
So I fill up the flagon, and drink—that is all—
To the dead and the dying of Bachelor Hall.

October 5, 1883.

HUMAN NATURE

A BEGGAR-MAN crept to my side
   One bitter, wintry time;
"I want to buy a drink," he cried;
   "Please give me, sir, a dime."
If he had craved this boon forlorn
   To buy his family meat,
I had passed on in silent scorn,
   And left him in the street.

I tossed the money in his hand,
   And quoth: "As o'er your wine
Within the tippling-room you stand
   Drink thou to me and mine."
He let an earnest "Thank ye" drop—
   Then up the street he sped,
And rushed into a baker's shop,
   And bought a loaf of bread!

I know not why it was, and yet,
  So sudden was the blow,
I felt emotions of regret
  That he had duped me so.
Yet, had the hungry beggar said
  That he was sore in need
Of that necessity called "bread,"
  What man would pay him heed?

October 10, 1883.

A VERY WEARY ACTOR

Amber clouds on a cobalt sky,
The hour for work is drawing nigh!

An all-night journey, an aching head,
A longing to strike and go to bed!

Not a friend to greet or a friend to meet,
A lonely room on a noisy street.

A silent meal in a crowded room,
A silent smoke in a cloud of gloom.

A scene rehearsed, a stammering crew,
Letters received, and more work to do.

Business bothers, intrigues, and war;
The future a blank, the present a bore.

A cup of strong tea, a smoke, and I'd better
Screw up my courage, and seek the theatre.

Dress for an hour in a cell that is stifling,
And then play a part with a heart—but I'm trifling.

(Attributed to) Richard Mansfield.

October 25, 1883.

GETTYSBURG

You wore the blue and I the gray
  On this historic field;
And all throughout the dreadful fray
  We felt our muscles steeled
For deeds which men may never know,
Nor page of history ever show.

My father, sir, with soul to dare,
  Throughout the day and night,
Stood on old Little Round Top there,
  And watched the changeful fight,
And, with a hoarse, inspiring cry,
Held up the stars and bars on high.

At last the flag went down, and then—
  Ah, you can guess the rest—
I never saw his face again.
  My father's loyal breast
Is strewn with these sweet flow'rs, I wot,
That seem to love this sacred spot.

The smoke of battle 's cleared away,
  And all its hatreds, too;
And as I clasp your hand to-day,
  O man who wore the blue,
On yonder hill I seem to see
My father smiling down on me.

October 27, 1883.

HER FAIRY FEET

"Bring me a tiny mouse's skin,"
  The boisterous tanner cried;
"It must be as a rose-leaf thin
  And scarce three fingers wide."

He seized the fragile, tiny bit
  Within his brawny hand,
And cast it in the seething pit,
  And so the skin was tann'd.

Then came a cobbler to his side.
  With tools that cobblers use,
And deft they wrought that mouse's hide
  Into a pair of shoes.

"Tell me," I asked, "O cobbler, tell
  For whom these morceaux be?"
"A lover bade me build them well
  For his true love," quoth he.

"Where dwells this maid with fairy feet?"
  In wonderment I cried;
The old man shifted in his seat—
  "Chicago," he replied.

October 29, 1883.

THE REMORSEFUL CAKES

A LITTLE boy named Thomas ate
  Hot buckwheat cakes for tea—
A very rash proceeding, as
  We presently shall see.

He went to bed at eight o'clock,
  As all good children do,
But scarce had closed his little eyes,
  When he most restless grew.

He flopped on this side, then on that,
  Then keeled upon his head,
And covered all at once each spot
  Of his wee trundle-bed.

He wrapped one leg around his waist
  And t' other round his ear,
While mamma wondered what on earth
  Could ail her little dear.

But sound he slept, and as he slept
  He dreamt an awful dream
Of being spanked with hickory slabs
  Without the power to scream.

He dreamt a great big lion came
  And ripped and raved and roared—
While on his breast two furious bulls
  In mortal combat gored.

He dreamt he heard the flop of wings
  Within the chimney-flue—
And down there crawled, to gnaw his ears,
  An awful bugaboo!

When Thomas rose next morn, his face
  Was pallid as a sheet;
"I nevermore," he firmly said,
  "Will cakes for supper eat!"

November 6, 1883.

A PATRIOT'S TRIUMPH

GEORGE WILLIAM CURTIS met a lad
  As down the street he hied.
"Pray tell me, boy, if eke you can,
  Where Schurz doth now reside."
"In sooth I can, my gentle sir,"
  The honest lad replied;
"Proceed due north and soon you 'll come
  To where he doth abide."

"You speak some words I ken not of,"
  George William Curtis cried;
"Now tell in speech non-sectional
  Where doth my friend reside.
I know not north—Schurz knows no south;
  Such terms do ill betide.
The north is south—the south is north—
  The west the east, beside."

"Good sir, you jest," complained the youth,
  And hung his fuddled head.
"Nay, foolish boy, I speak the truth,"
  George William Curtis said;
"Lo, from the south the north wind blows
  And eke the rising tide,
That splashes on our eastern shores,
  Laves all the western side.

"The snows do fall on southern soil
  And on the prairies wide;
The cotton on the northern hills
  Is now the Yankee's pride.
There is no north—there is no south—
  These terms have long since died;
So tell in reconstructed speech
  Where now doth Schurz reside."

"Good master, turn ye to the west,
  And on the eastern side
Adown the northern path, due south,
  Two blocks he doth abide."
George William Curtis missed his way,
  But still it gave him joy
To know our land had gained that day
  A reconstructed boy.

November 7, 1883.

"YOURS FRATERNALLY"

An editor in Kankakee
  Once falling in a burning passion
With a vexatious rival, he
  Wrote him a letter in this fashion:
"You are an ass uncouth and rude,
  And will be one eternally."
Then, in an absent-minded mood,
  He signed it "Yours fraternally."

November 9, 1883.

SONG OF THE ALL-WOOL SHIRT

My father bought an undershirt
  Of bright and flaming red—
"All wool, I'm ready to assert,
  Fleece-dyed," the merchant said;
"Your size is thirty-eight, I think;
  A forty you should get,
Since all-wool goods are bound to shrink
  A trifle when they're wet."

That shirt two weeks my father wore—
  Two washings, that was all;
From forty down to thirty-four
  It shrank like leaf in fall.
I wore it then a day or two,
  But when 't was washed again
My wife said, "Now 't will only do
  For little brother Ben."

A fortnight Ben squeezed into it;
  At last he said it hurt.
We put it on our babe—the fit
  Was good as any shirt.

We ne'er will wash it more while yet
We see its flickering light,
For if again that shirt is wet
'T will vanish from our sight.

December 6, 1883.

OF BLESSED MEMORY

I OFTEN wonder mother loves to creep
Up to the garret where a cupboard stands,
And sit upon the musty floor and weep,
Holding a baby's dresses in her hands.

I often wonder grandma loves to sit
Alone where hangs a picture on the wall—
A handsome face across whose features flit
The phantoms of a love she would recall.

I wonder, too, that sister, pale and sad,
Waits at the gate, and, waiting, seems to hear
The footfalls of the brave, heroic lad
Who nevermore may woo her waiting there.

ENVOY

The little lips in voiceless death are sealed;
The haughty squire seeks now a lasting sleep;
The lover's bones bleach on a battle-field—
And broken-hearted women live to weep.

December 11, 1883.

A LEAP-YEAR EPISODE

CAN I forget that winter night
In eighteen eighty-four,
When Nellie, charming little sprite,
Came tapping at the door?

"Good evening, miss," I, blushing, said,
　　For in my heart I knew—
And, knowing, hung my pretty head—
　　That Nellie came to woo.

She clasped my big red hand, and fell
　　Adown upon her knees,
And cried: "You know I love you well,
　　So be my husband, please!"
And then she swore she 'd ever be
　　A tender wife and true.
Ah, what delight it was to me
　　That Nellie came to woo!

She 'd lace my shoes, and darn my hose,
　　And mend my shirts, she said;
And grease my comely Roman nose
　　Each night on going to bed;
She 'd build the fires, and fetch the coal,
　　And split the kindling, too.
Love's perjuries o'erwhelmed her soul
　　When Nellie came to woo.

And as I, blushing, gave no check
　　To her advances rash,
She twined her arms about my neck,
　　And toyed with my mustache;
And then she pleaded for a kiss,
　　While I—what could I do
But coyly yield me to that bliss
　　When Nellie came to woo?

I am engaged, and proudly wear
　　A gorgeous diamond ring,
And I shall wed my lover fair
　　Sometime in gentle spring.
I face my doom without a sigh;
　　And so, forsooth, would you,
If you but loved as fond as I,
　　And Nellie came to woo.

December 22, 1883.

THE DÉBUTANTE

HAVE you got the jellies made, mother?
　　Are the sandwiches *au fait?*
Are the salads wrought and the wine all bought
　　For the splurge on New Year's day?
You look serene as a regnant queen,
　　But there 'll be some hitch, I fear,
For I 'm to receive this year, mother—
　　I 'm to receive this year.

My dress is such a daisy, mother,
　　What wonder if I am vain?
'T is a white piqué, décolleté,
　　With a princesse skirt, en train.
That 's why I yearn and impatient burn
　　For the splurge that is, oh, so near,
For I 'm to receive this year, mother—
　　I 'm to receive this year.

Jack says he will come at ten, mother,
　　And tarry the rest of the day.
Why turn up your nose?　You don't suppose
　　He 'd dare to stay away?
Though Jack is proud and hates a crowd,
　　I 'm certain he will be here,
For I 'm to receive this year, mother—
　　I 'm to receive this year.

So call me at half-past eight, mother—
　　Don't let me sleep till nine.
I 've crimped my hair, and over the chair
　　I 've thrown my dresses fine;
At half-past eight—now don't be late—
　　Come early, O mother dear,
For I 'm to receive this year, mother—
　　I 'm to receive this year.

December 27, 1883.

THE MODERN MARTYR

"Only an editor's wife," they say,
As she rides along in her proud coupé;
But they all confess that her face is fair,
That her form is lovely beyond compare,
That her robes are rich and her jewels rare,
That her heart is warm and her gold is free;
Yet "only an editor's wife" is she!

Do they envy her laces and silks so grand,
Or the diamonds she wears on her white left hand,
Or the satin train that sweeps in her track,
Or the elegant three-ply sealskin sack
That gracefully covers her shapely back?
Or why do the people derisively cry
When "only an editor's wife" rides by?

Do they envy the palace where she abides,
Or the gilded coach in which she rides,
Or her yacht that sports with the lake's white foam,
Or the troop of servants that go and come
To do her will in her regal home?
Do they envy her gold when they descry
That it's "only an editor's wife" goes by?

They never think of the man who writes
Through the weary days and the darksome nights,
To earn the ducats with which to pay
For the laces fine and the jewels gay,
And the robes en train and décolleté,
And the other trappings that greet the eye
When "only an editor's wife" sails by.

Oh, could they go to his working-place,
And see his furrowed and pallid face,
And know the grind of his daily life,—

How he freely encounters all toil and strife
To humor the whims of his petted wife,—
Methinks they would raise their plaudits high
When "only an editor's wife" rode by.

January 10, 1884.

AN OHIO IDYL

O FATHERS all, reflect upon
    The touching story and the fate
Of hapless Mr. Pendleton,
    Who had a daughter and a gate.

Once said this Mr. Pendleton
    To dapper little John McLean:
"Here, now, get off that gate, my son,
    And don't come hanging round again!
You 're not their style, my daughters say;
    Your visits do not bring them joy.
Get off the gate and run away—
    Come, there 's a clever little boy!"

Then dapper little John McLean
    Sought out another quiet street,
Where lived a certain Mr. Payne,
    Who had a daughter young and sweet;
Engaging this enchanting miss
    In many a twilight tête-à-tête,
He whiled away long hours of bliss
    In swinging on the old man's gate.

Lo, some years after, Messrs. Payne
    And Pendleton were candidates;
Then did the dapper John McLean
    Recall the story of the gates.
He lent his vengeful nature to
    Manipulations darkly deft—
And Mr. Payne pulled glibly through,
    While Pendleton got badly left.

So, fathers all, reflect upon
  The touching story and the fate
Of hapless Mr. Pendleton,
  Who had a daughter and a gate.

January 15, 1884.

A SCHERZO

ONE night the charming Gerster said,
  "Now listen, colonel, to me:
I will not sing—I 'll quit instead—
  Unless I 'm paid what 's due me.
I 'm mad to think that you should think
  That I am such a greeny
To let you lavish all the chink
  On Mrs. Nicolini!"

Then Mapleson in guileful vein
  Protested he was busted;
And Gerster on the midnight train
  Incontinently dusted.
Back to her babe in York she hied,—
  This operatic charmer,—
And put all other roles aside
  For that of simple mamma.

But Mapleson, when she had fled,
  Forthwith began to worry;
The telegram he sent her said:
  "Come back, and please to hurry.
I 'll build a palace-car for you,
  And bear your tantrums meekly,
And pay your salary when it 's due—
  That is to say, tri-weekly."

So back to Mapleson went she
  As sweet as dripping honey,
And now is happy as can be
  Because she got her money.

When asked what caused the recent row
   They answer 't was the baby;
This fairy tale 's sufficient now
   To fool the public, maybe

January 29, 1884.

AN OHIO DITTY

MARY had a little lamb,
   Down in Ohio state,
And, ere it grew to be a ram,
   Most dismal was its fate.

Its fleece was long and white and full,
   And Mary loved to shear
Her lamb for the amount of wool
   It brought her twice a year.

But once, upon a summer's day,
   She learned, to her dejection,
Her wool investment didn't pay—
   And so she craved protection.

And then, with many a pleading word
   And copious flow of tears,
She flew to genial Mr. Hurd
   To set at rest her fears.

But Mr. Hurd in scorn did hold
   Poor Mary and her kid,
And when their tale of woe was told
   No kindly act he did.

In vain for help the maiden cried
   Upon her bended knees.
"No tariff, girl," the man replied;
   "Go, serve your lamb with peas!"

So Mary slew her little lamb—
    As might have been expected,
For little lambs are n't worth a d——
    When they are not protected

January 28, 1884.

A GOOD MAN'S SORROW

ABOU BEN HALSTEAD—may his tribe increase!—
Thinking one night to steal a sweet surcease
From office work, of which he 'd had a greed,
Called to his side his faithful Romeo Reed,
And quoth: "By Allah and his great horned spoon,
I will go home and sleep me until noon
If I can get a paragraph from you
To pull to-morrow's editorial through;
Now, mind you, one short paragraph will do!"

Good Romeo Reed inclined his reverend head—
"Ismillah robang!" ("Good enough!") he said;
And Halstead straightway hied himself to bed.

Abou Ben Halstead woke next day at nine,
And having quaffed, as is his wont, his wine,
Called for the paper, which he always read
Propped up by pillows in his regal bed.
He seized the sheet, and with an eager flout
He turned the mammoth paper inside out
To see what Romeo Reed had writ about.
Abou Ben Halstead's cheeks grew very red;
He frothed awhile, and stood upon his head;
His mournful eyes were all ablaze with fire,
His noble frame quaked with demoniac ire.
Lo! Romeo's paragraph filled up the page entire!

February 20, 1884.

LAMENT OF A NEGLECTED BOSS

WITH not a faithful lackey nigh,
  With all my vast resources spent,
I find myself enshrouded by
  The winter of my discontent.
Gone are the hours of tranquil bliss
  I fondly used to count mine own,
And I, at last, am come to this—
  The running of a telephone!

Before I took this paltry thing
  That keeps a-jingling all the day,
I was a most puissant king,
  And most despotic was my sway.
Proud was my lot and proud my mien;
  I sat upon a gilded throne
And bossed a radical machine
  Where now I boss a telephone!

Pause, O ye countrymen of mine,
  And drop a sympathetic tear,
And carve to me this touching line:
  "Oh, what a falling off is here!"
Dear Riddleberger and Mahone,
  Grant sweet surcease unto my woe
By wafting through my telephone
  A fond, occasional hello!

March 17, 1884.

ROMANCE OF A "CUSS-WORD"

BROAD expanse of shiny shirt-front,
  Cuffs and collar white to match,
Overcoat with silken facing—
  Just the rig to make a catch.

Pretty lady coming toward him;
  He prepares to make a mash;
Meets a stumbling horse on crossing—
  Mud flies o'er him with a splash!

Man who looked so sweet and gentle,
  Like a little suckling lamb,
Now becomes a raving lion;
  Girl goes by and hears him d—n.

Girl is shocked beyond expression—
  Thinks his language simply vile;
Yet believes that she can save him—
  Meets him next time with a smile.

Man apologizes bravely,
  Says his anger made him rash.
Girl replies it but convinced her
  He's a man of proper dash.

They are married in November;
  Wife is over all her scare;
Says she thought him soft and sickish
  Till the day she heard him swear.

March 20, 1884.

COLD CONSOLATION

I AM booming, brother, booming;
  As the tide of time rolls on
Thou wilt see me higher looming
  In thy pathway, dearest John.
But oh, brother, in thy sorrow
  Turn thou not thy face away;
Be for me, dear John, to-morrow,
  As for thee I am to-day.

I am booming, brother, booming;
  See the tempests toss my plume;
See the friends about me grooming,
  Grooming lovingly my boom.
Lose no time, nor stumble blindly
  Into error, Brother John;
To my boom, I tell thee kindly,
  Soon or late thou must catch on.

March 21, 1884.

MR. HOLMAN'S FAREWELL

THE little boom they said was vain
  Will strike them now as vainer,
Since you have got aboard the train
And started o'er the cactus plain,
  O frail and fickle Dana!

For when you reach the marble halls
  Of pagan Montezuma,
What ear will heed my piteous calls
Amid the havoc that appalls
  A boom without a boomer?

Perhaps some charm of that proud place
  Will swerve you from your duty—
Will tempt you to forget my face,
My artless ways and simple grace,
  My modest Hoosier beauty.

If so it be, my face will haunt
  Your soul where'er you linger;
Within your ears I 'll breathe a taunt,
Within your eyes I 'll ever flaunt
  My pale and bony finger.

Like amorous Dido am I left
  To torturesome reflection—
Deceived, cajoled, betrayed, bereft,
My trusting heart by anguish cleft—
  Though not without OBJECTION.

March 22, 1884.

THE APRIL FOOL

FAIR was her young and girlish face,
  Her lips were luscious red as wine;
Her willowy form betrayed a grace
  That seemed to me to be divine.
One evening at the trysting-place
  I asked this maiden to be mine.
Unhappy, thrice-unhappy youth
  Was I to court the crushing blow;
But why delay the awful truth—
  She April-fooled me years ago!

Filled with a ghastly, grim dismay
  As kneeling at her feet I heard
This fair but cruel angel say
  That last, unhappy, severing word,
I fluttered hopelessly away
  Like some forlorn and stricken bird.
For years I played the cynic's part,
  For years I nursed my secret woe;
And this reflection galled my heart—
  She April-fooled me years ago!

But she is forty now, and fat,
  And vanished all her graces are:
And many a lusty, brawling brat
  Pulls at her skirts and calls her "ma,"
And I have information that
  Her horrid husband tends a bar.

And when I see that fleeting years
  Have changed my quondam angel so,
I thank my stars, 'mid grateful tears,
  She April-fooled me years ago!

March 27, 1884.

THE OLD SEXTON

NIGH to a boom that was newly made
Leaned Charles A. Dana on his pick and spade:
He smiled sardonic and paused to wait
The funeral train through the open gate.
A savage editor man was he,
And his eyes were aflame with demoniac glee
As these words came from his lips so thin:
"I gather them in—I gather them in!

"I gather them in, and their final rest
Is here—down here in the earth's dark breast.
Hancock I buried four years ago
'Neath a mossy mound where the daisies blow;
Holman and Bayard and Field I boom,
Only to leave them where violets bloom;
For, heedless of what their grandeur has been,
I gathered them in—I gathered them in!

"I gather them in, and I never care
How the victims rage or the people swear;
Thurman, McDonald, and Flower, too,
Have gently flocked to my hullabaloo,
And now I am patiently waiting here
For the Grover Cleveland boom to appear;
And, blind to the chances it has to win,
I 'll gather it in—I 'll gather it in!"

July 5, 1884.

OGLESBY (1884)

WHEN treason boldly stalked the land
  And poisoned hearts of men
Till traitors rose on every hand,
  A patriot called us then;
We followed, comrade,—you and I,—
  Where death and wounds were thick,
And gloried in the battle-cry,
  "Hurrah for Uncle Dick!"

They say that we, who knew no fears
  Of death and carnage then,
Are summoned in these after years,
  To follow him again;
Not with the gun nor with the sword,
  But with the hoe and pick,
We come, a brave, determined horde—
  Hurrah for Uncle Dick!

His waving hair was black as night
  In that dear long ago;
But now with care and age 't is white
  As first December snow;
But round that old and whitened head
  Have honors, fast and thick,
A grand, majestic halo shed—
  Hurrah for Uncle Dick!

Once tall and stately was the form
  That now is stooped and bent;
Wait till he scents the coming storm
  And marks the base intent
Of foemen circling round about,
  And see how pow'rful quick
That grave old body straightens out—
  Hurrah for Uncle Dick!

And as we rallied in the fray
  With him long years ago,

So do we rally round, to-day,
　　The chief we reverence so.
Beware the foe, O patriots true,
　　Beware each traitorous trick.
We still are soldiers of the blue—
　　Hurrah for Uncle Dick!

July 10, 1884.

THE POLITICAL MAUD

BEN BUTLER, on a summer's day,
Stood in a convention making hay;
The hay was sweet and the hay was dry,
But it was n't as cocked as old Ben's eye;
For old Ben saw on a gelding gay
Judge Nomination ride that way.

When the judge saw Ben in the hay at work,
He stopped his horse with a sudden jerk,
And he rolled his eyes on the winsome face
And the buxom form and the air of grace
And the wealth of cheek and the mesh of hair
Of sweet Ben Butler a-working there.

"Oh," sighed the judge, "that the fate were mine
To wed with a creature so divine!
With Ben for a mate, my life would seem
Like a poet's song or an artist's dream;
But, when they heard of my marital pick,
How like a steer some folks would kick!"

So, fearful of what his folks might say,
Judge Nomination rode away,
And left Ben Butler standing there
With her wealth of cheek and her mesh of hair;
And of all sad words of tongue and pen
The saddest are these: "He would n't have Ben."

July 11, 1884.

A VIRGILIAN PICNIC

"Come, Chloe, beauteous maiden, come,
  And here, within the flowery shade,
Enjoy with me the tuneful hum
  Of bees that swarm throughout the glade.
Upon the velvet moss reclining,
  And with thy murmurings in mine ear,
What thought have I of love's repining?
  So come, sweet Chloe, rest thee here."

"Nay, Corydon; I fear, alack!
The ants would clamber up my back."

"Ah, Chloe, here amongst the flow'rs,
  While linnets coo in vines above,
How sweet to dream away the hours,
  Or weave fair sonnets to my love!
A zephyr, coming to delight me,
  Breathes in mine ear a soothing tone,
And tells me Chloe shall requite me,
  And so I smile as eke I prone."

"Rise, Corydon! I prithee rise!
You're proning on the custard-pies."
July 31, 1884.

AN ILLINOIS WAR-SONG

Come, let us quaff a stirrup-cup
  To Virtue undismayed.
Fill, comrades, fill your glasses up
  With sparkling Lemonade!

Here's death to Whiskey, Wine, and Beer,
  To Brandy, Gin, and Rum!
We have a million voters here—
  A million more will come.

We 'll pulverize the Liquor pow'r,
  With all its odious jobs,
Until the Demon Drink shall cow'r
  Beneath the sword of Hobbs!

The sale of cocktail, punch, and sling,
  We are resolved, must stop.
As substitute therefor we bring
  The fragrant Ginger-pop;

Or else, perchance, refreshing Mead,
  Or Soda-water cool:
But liquor is a fiend indeed
  We don't intend shall rule.

Oh, 't is a thief that steals our wits
  And all our manhood robs;
So we propose to give it fits
  With gallant Brother Hobbs!

So let us quaff a stirrup-cup
  Before we join the raid.
Fill, comrades, fill your glasses up
  With sparkling Lemonade!

August 6, 1884.

———

THOMAS A. HENDRICKS'S APPEAL

How infamous that men should raise
  The foul and bitter lie
That in the old secession days,
  When din of war was high,
I dealt in traitorous sneer and brag
  And did not dare to go
To battle for my country's flag
  Against the rebel foe!

Who was it for the Stripes and Stars
  Risked fortune, fame, and life?
Who bore away the purple scars
  Of many a bloody strife?
Who was it led the patriot band
  And held the flag on high?
Ay, tell me truly, if you can
  Who was it, if not I?

At Vicksburg, braving sword and shell,
  I gloried in the fray
Till finally I fainting fell
  With one leg shot away;
But on to Corinth's ghastly field
  I hastened to imbrue,
And did not hesitate to yield
  A paltry arm or two!

And when with Sherman to the sea
  Our gallant army cross'd,
The rebel bullets followed me—
  Another leg I lost;
But still I gladly drained the cup
  Of deep misfortune's harm,
And down at Gettysburg gave up
  Another leg and arm!

So, gallant boys who wore the blue
  Through all that dismal tide,
By all those bloody days we knew
  When battling side by side,
Choke off the hideous lying throats
  These slanders issue from—
And next November cast your vote
  For patriotic Tom!

August 8, 1884.

THE EXPLORER'S WOOING

Oh, come with me to the arctic seas
  Where the blizzards and icebergs grow,
And dally awhile with the polar breeze
  In the land of the Esquimau.
We will fish for seal and the great white bears
  In their caves on the frozen shores;
We will spread our nets in the frigid lairs
  Of the walrus that snorts and roars.

When the rest of creation swoons with heat
  All pleasant and chipper we 'll be;
'T would be hard to find a summer retreat
  As cool as the arctic sea.
We will ramble along in some snowy glade
  With never a sultry sigh,
Or loll at ease in the grateful shade
  Of an iceberg four miles high.

So come with me to the arctic pole—
  To the land of the walrus and bear,
Where the glaciers wave and the blizzards roll,
  And victuals are frequently rare.
You are plump and fat—with such a mate
  In my iceberg I would dwell,
In the pleasing hope I could baffle fate
  By eating you *au naturel*.

September 3, 1884.

THE AHKOOND OF SWAT

When the writer has written with all of his might
  Of Blaine and of Cleveland a column or more,
And the editor happens along in the night
  (As he generally does betwixt midnight and four)

And kills all the stuff that that writer has writ,
  And calls for more copy at once, on the spot—
There is none for the writer to turn on and hit
  But that distant old party, the Ahkoond of Swat.

Now the Ahkoond of Swat is a vague sort of man
  Who lives in a country far over the sea;
Pray tell me, good reader, if tell me you can,
  What 's the Ahkoond of Swat to you folks or to me?
Yet when one must be careful, conservative, too,
  Since the canvass is getting unpleasantly hot,
If we must abuse some—let us haste to imbrue
  With that foreign old bloomer, the Ahkoond of Swat!

Yet why should we poke this insipid old king,
  Who lives in the land of the tiger and cane,
Since the talk we might make on the dotard can't bring
  The sweet satisfaction of a Cleveland or Blaine?
A plague on these politics, statesmen, and all
  Who conspire to embarrass the editor's lot;
And a plague on the man, we implore, who will call
  On a fellow to write of the Ahkoond of Swat!

But vain is this fuming, this frenzy, this storm—
  The printers care naught for this protest or that;
A long, dreadful hollow appears in the "form"—
  And it 's copy they want, with a preference for "fat."
So here 's to our friend who 's so handy in need,
  Whose useful acquaintance too soon is forgot—
That distant old party and senile old seed,
  The loathsome and pestilent Ahkoond of Swat!
September 19, 1884.

A PLEA FOR THE CLASSICS

A Boston gentleman declares,
  By all the gods above, below,
That our degenerate sons and heirs
  Must let their Greek and Latin go!

Forbid, O Fate, we loud implore,
  A dispensation harsh as that;
What! wipe away the sweets of yore;
  The dear "Amo, amas, amat"?

The sweetest hour the student knows
  Is not when poring over French,
Or twisted in Teutonic throes,
  Upon a hard collegiate bench;
'T is when on roots and kais and gars
  He feeds his soul and feels it glow,
Or when his mind transcends the stars
  With "Zoa mou, sas agapo"!

So give our bright, ambitious boys
  An inkling of these pleasures, too—
A little smattering of the joys
  Their dead and buried fathers knew;
And let them sing—while glorying that
  Their sires so sang, long years ago—
The songs "Amo, amas, amat,"
  And "Zoa mou, sas agapo"!
September 23, 1884.

THE SECRET OF THE SPHINX

Upon the hot Egyptian sands,
  Beneath the lurid, blistering skies,
  With stolid face and fireless eyes
The Sphinx in sombre grandeur stands.
Within that doleful desert place,
  By desolation's doom oppress'd,
  No sweet emotion fills her breast—
No smile illumes the Sphinx's face.

They say that many years ago
  A Roman pretor left his home,
  Resolved to go from Rome to roam—

A Roman roamin' to and fro.
This pretor happened, so they say,
    To meet a humorist, whose name
    Was heralded on wings of fame
Through Boston leagues and leagues **away.**

They roamed together far and wide—
    The pretor and the Boston wit—
    Till finally one night they lit
In Egypt by the Sphinx's side.
"Now tell me, ere we go to bed
    Within our tents, some funny tale;
    With humorous anecdote regale
My jaded soul," the pretor said.

The Sphinx was then as fair a bit
    Of female flesh as you could find,
    And, womanlike, she had a mind
For stories that partook of wit.
She, therefore, smiling bent her ear
    To hear the Massachusetts joke
    The famous Boston humorist spoke
Unto the pretor, listening near.

What was the joke we do not know—
    The ancient hist'ries do not state,
    Nor legendary lore relate,
Nor hieroglyphic tablets show;
But since that Boston wit beguiled
    The Roman pretor with the joke
    Which centuries ago was spoke,
The hapless Sphinx has never smiled.

September 23, 1884.

FANCHON THE CRICKET

My grandsire, years and years ago,
   In round old English used to praise
   Sweet Maggie Mitchell's pretty ways
And her fair face that charmed him so.

Her tuneful voice and curly hair,
   Her coquetry and subtle art
   Ensnared my grandsire's willing heart
And ever reigned supremely there.

In time my father felt the force
   Of cunning Maggie Mitchell's smiles,
   And, dazzled by her thousand wiles,
He sang her glories too, of course.

Quite natural, then, it was that I—
   Of such a sire and grandsire, too—
   When this dear sprite first met my view
Should learn to rhapsodize and sigh.

And now my boy—of tender age—
   Indites a sonnet to the curl
   Of this most fascinating girl
That ever romped the mimic stage!

O prototype of girlhood truth,
   Of girlhood glee and girlhood prank,
   By what good fortune hast thou drank
The waters of eternal youth?

September 26, 1884.

NOVEMBER

THE wold is drear and the sedges sere,
　And gray is the autumn sky,
And sorrows roll through my riven soul
　As lonely I sit and sigh
　　"Good-by"
　To the goose-birds as they fly.

With his weird wishbone to the temperate zone
　Came the goose-bird in the spring;
And he built his nest in the glorious west,
　And sat on a snag to sing,
　　Sweet thing!
　Or flap his beautiful wing.

But the boom of the blast has come at last
　To the goose-bird on the lea,
And the succulent thing, with shivering wing,
　Flies down to a southern sea.
　　Ah me,
　That such separation should be!

But it's always so in this world of woe:
　The things that gladden our eye
Are the surest to go to the bugs, and so
　We can only wearily sigh
　　"Good-by"
　To the goose-birds as they fly.

November 5, 1884.

————

PARLEZ–VOUS FRANÇAIS?

THE old man sits inveiled by gloom,
　His bosom heaves with dire dismay;
For in that editorial room

There booms no presidential boom,
　　And folks no longer come that way
To whisper, "Parlez-vous Français?"

Gone is the time he hoped to be
　　A diplomat in Paris gay—
When, far across the briny sea,
The festive gamins, *très jolis,*
　　And fair *grisettes decolletées*
　　Should murmur, "Parlez-vous Français?"

So let the poor old Joseph rest
　　And let him pine his life away;
Nor vex that journalistic breath
Which by a hopeless grief 's distressed—
　　The hopeless grief he never may
　　Respond to "Parlez-vous Français?"
November 10, 1884.

"GEE SWEE ZAMERICANE"

WHY should I pine and languish so?
　　Why should I droop and sigh?
Why should my soul be bowed in woe,
　　As weary days go by?
Why should I drown in sorrow's sea,
　　When, through the surf of pain,
This sweet salvation comes to me:
　　"Gee swee Zamericane!"

I thought diplomacy my forte,
　　And yearned for deeds of state
Amid the solemn pomps of court
　　In monarchies effete;
And most I hankered to abide
　　Hard by the river Seine,
Where I could say, with swelling pride,
　　"Gee swee Zamericane!"

And this is why I made the flop
  Which Reid and Halstead made,
And this is why I took a drop
  On matters of free trade;
I ate my words of '76,
  And boomed the "rascal" Blaine,
And played a thousand Jingo tricks—
  "Gee swee Zamericane!"

The die is cast, the boom is o'er,
  And Blaine is beaten bad—
The which is why I 'm feeling sore,
  And, likewise, very mad;
For, after all this harrowing strife,
  I 'm likely to remain
What I have been through all my life—
  "Gee swee Zamericane!"

November 11, 1884.

———

CHRISTMAS

My little child comes to my knee
  And tugging pleads that he may climb
    Into my lap to hear me tell
    The Christmas tale he loves so well—
A tale my mother told to me,
  Beginning "Once upon a time."

It is a tale of skies that rang
  With angel rhapsodies sublime;
    Of that great host, serene and white,
    The shepherds saw one winter night;
And of the glorious stars that sang
  An anthem, once upon a time.

This story of the hallowed years
  Tells of the sacrifice sublime
    Of One who prayed alone and wept
    While his awearied followers slept—
And how his blood and Mary's tears
  Commingled, once upon a time.

And now my darling at my side
  And echoes of the distant clime
    Bring that sweet story back to me—
    Of Bethlehem and Calvary,
And of the gentle Christ that died
  For sinners, once upon a time.

The mighty deeds that men have told
  In ponderous tomes or fluent rhyme,
    Like misty shadows fade away;
    But this sweet story bides for aye,
And, like the stars that sang of old,
  We sing of "Once upon a time."
December 1, 1884.

CHICAGO WEATHER

To-day, fair Thisbe, winsome girl!
  Strays o'er the meads where daisies blow,
Or, ling'ring where the brooklets purl,
  Laves in the cool, refreshing flow.

To-morrow, Thisbe, with a host
  Of amorous suitors in her train,
Comes like a goddess forth to coast
  Or skate upon the frozen main.

To-day, sweet posies mark her track,
  While birds sing gayly in the trees;
To-morrow morn, her sealskin sack
  Defies the piping polar breeze.

So Doris is to-day enthused
  By Thisbe's soft, responsive sighs,
And on the morrow is confused
  By Thisbe's cold, repellent eyes.

December 6, 1884.

THE COLLECTOR'S DISCONTENT

A DIBDIN properly displayed,
  An Elzevir ensconced on high,
My hand upon an Aldus laid—
  I felt a tear fall from my eye.

The cause? And is there none who knows
  The pangs ambition idly wields?
Is there a man that to the throes
  Of covetousness never yields?

Perhaps some day some graven urn
  Or parchment old may bring to view
The name of him that did not yearn
  For the books that dear old Burton knew.
  I don't believe it, though—do you?

January 30, 1889.

A LEAP-YEAR LAMENT

THE golden year is nearly sped—
  This year of girlish wooing;
And lo, my hope of love is dead,
  And fate is past undoing!
When suitors came in gentle spring
  And proffered their caresses,
Like some coquettish, giddy thing,
  I spurned their fond addresses.

So Minnie, Maggie, Maud, and Belle,
　Miranda, Jane, and Jessie,
Maria, Nannie, Ruth, and Nell,
　And charming blue-eyed Bessie
Went wooing other kindlier men
　Too numerous to mention·
And I, by this hegira, then
　Was left without attention.

But in the sere of autumn came
　That sweetest maid of many,
With wit and beauty known to fame—
　The blithe and winsome Jennie;
And having wooed as women can,
　Protesting she adored me,
She wed her father's hired man;
　And that completely floored me!

O silly celibate, that spurned
　The leap-year wooing vernal,
How hast thy haughty scorning turned
　To self-reproach eternal!
I'd give my wealth, my life, my fame,
　If I could summon to me
In this bleak hour those nymphs that came
　In early spring to woo me!

December 17, 1884.

———

ILL REQUITED

Oh, hand me down my spectacles,
　Oh, hand them down to me,
That I may read and know, indeed,
　If our good Grover C.
Hath bid me stand at his right hand.
　Where I have longed to be

Oh, hand me down my microscope;
   These specs ill serveth me:
But I have hope the microscope
   Will give me pow'r to see
My noble name where lasting fame
   Intended it should be.

Alas! nor specs nor microscope
   Nor aught availeth me.
My name is missed from all the list
   Where it should surely be.
And if, ere long, affairs go wrong,
   The blame 's with Grover C.

March 5, 1885.

GRANT

His was the sword that from its scabbard leapt
   To cleave the way where freedom could be won,
And where it led a conquering army swept
   Till all was done.

Then that same valorous hand which swung the sword
   Back to its sheath returned the patriot blade,
And bore sweet peace where crushed rebellion's horde
   Stood all dismayed.

And now a spirit, speeding from above,
   Chills that great heart with his destroying breath,
And all a people's reverence and love
   Are mocked by death.

April 1, 1885.

FROM THE SAME CANTEEN

From hill and plain to the State of Maine
    The veterans toiled along,
And they rent the air with the tuneful blare
    Of trumpets and of song;
That their throats were dry there will none deny,
    But little they recked, I ween,
As they gathered round on the old camp-ground
    To drink from the same canteen.

The tales of old were again retold,
    And they sang of the war once more—
Till the word went round like a thunder sound,
    "Let us drink to the days of yore!"
A rapturous glee that was fair to see
    Enveloped the martial scene—
But there came a change that was pitiful strange
    When they drank from the old canteen.

The veteran throng sings now no song
    That is keyed in the grand old strain,
And the air is blue with the hullabaloo
    Of the soldiers who marched to Maine.
Not even beer is the proffered cheer,
    Nor a jug nor a flask is seen;
But it 's lemonade of a watery grade
    That they drink from the same canteen!

June 26, 1885.

LITTLE MISS DANDY

The other night as in my bed
    I lay profoundly sleeping,
An angel babe with hairless head
    Came through the darkness creeping;

And, waking at the dawn of day,
  Bliss percolated through me
When, smiling in her artless way,
  She murmured "papa" to me.

Strange, was it not? But stranger still
  What next claimed my attention—
The robes of wealth with tuck and frill
  Too numerous to mention.
Whence came these bibs with lace bedecked—
  These flannels all so handy?
And who could possibly suspect
  The coming of Miss Dandy?

Well, she shall live a thousand years,
  Unmindful of each morrow;
Her eyes shall know no plash of tears,
  Her heart no touch of sorrow;
And she shall dress in silk and lace
  And feed on taffy candy—
God bless her fuzzy little face,
  My little angel dandy!

August 11, 1885.

SPIRIT LAKE

UPON this beautiful expanse
  Of purple waves and spray
The wanton prairie zephyrs dance
  With sunbeams all the day.
And ships go sailing to and fro;
  The sea-gulls circle round;
Above the plash of ebb and flow
  The children's voices sound.

See how the playful pickerel speeds
  Upon his devious way
Among the lissome, clinging weeds,
  In hot pursuit of prey;

And here or there the greedy bass
  In their erratic flight
Like dark electric shadows pass
  Before our wondering sight.

Oh, what a wealth of life is here—
  What pike and carp abound!
Within these waters, cool and clear,
  What game may not be found!
You only have to bait your hook
  And cast it in the spray;
Down—fathoms down—it sinks; and look!
  You 've caught your finny prey.

O beauteous lake with pebbly shore
  And skies of azure hue,
With gulls and zephyrs skimming o'er
  Thy waves of restless blue,
To thee I dedicate this hymn
  In melancholic spite—
To thee, where bass and pickerel swim,
  But only bullheads bite.

TO DENMAN THOMPSON

THERE 's somethin' in your homely ways,
  Your simple speech, and honest face
That takes us back to other days
  And to a distant, cherished place.
We seem to see the dear old hills,
  The clover-patch, the pickerel pond,
And we can hear the mountain rills
  A-singin' in the haze beyond.

There is the lane wherein we played,
  An' there the hillside, rough an' gray,
O'er which we little Yankees strayed
  A-checkerberryin' ev'ry day;

The big red barn, the old stone wall,
  The pippin-tree, the fav'rite beach—
We seem to recognize 'em all
  In thy quaint face an' honest speech!

An' somehow when we see 'em rise
  Like spectres of those distant years,
We kinder weaken, and our eyes
  See dimly through a mist o' tears;
For there's no thing will touch the heart
  Like mem'ry's subtle wand, I trow,
An' there's no tear that will not start
  At thought of home an' long ago.

You make us boys an' girls again,
  An' like a tender, sweet surprise,
Come thoughts of those dear moments when
  Our greatest joy was mother's pies!
I'd ruther have your happy knack
  Than all the arts which critics praise—
The knack o' takin' old folks back
  To childhood homes and childhood days.

September 2, 1885.

"PURITAN"—"GENESTA"

A CENTURY or so ago,
  When we was young an' skittish,
We started out to let folks know
  That we could tan the British;
From Bunker Hill ter Southern sile,
  And on the ragin' water,
We warmed 'em in sich hearty style,
  They quickly begged fur quarter.

Waal, ever sence them early days
   When we was young an' skittish,
We Yanks hev been disposed to raise
   Ther devil with ther British;
Thar 's nary game they kin suggest
   But thet we Yankees larn 'em
That we are cuter than the best
   Of all their lords—goll darn 'em!

With our Kintucky colts we 've beat
   Their stables highfalutin;
Their sportin' men hev met defeat
   At cricket and at shootin';
Our pugilists, with skill an' ease,
   Hev stopped all furrin blowin';
Our oarsmen on the lakes an' seas
   Hev beat 'em all a-rowin'!

An' now, ter save that silver cup
   From England's proud "Genesta,"
The Yankee folks have kunjured up
   A skimmin' dish ter best 'er.
Thar ain't no ship thet swims the sea
   Or sails the briny ocean—
No matter what her flag may be—
   Kin beat a Yankee notion!

But what o' thet? It 's all in fun,
   And thar won't be no squealin';
Fur Yank an' Britisher is one
   In language, blud, an' feelin'!
An' though the times we've played 'em smart
   Are numbered by the dozens,
The Yankee feels, down in his heart,
   "God bless our British cousins!"

September 15, 1885.

THE SONG OF THE MUGWUMP

THE Mugwump sat on a hickory limb,
    "Too-hoo!"
In the autumn twilight, dank and dim,
    "Too-hoo!"
When, coming along, a Democrat heard
The doleful voice of the curious bird
Sadly moaning this wild, weird word,
    "Too-hoo!"

"Oh, why do you sit on that limb and cry
    'Too-hoo?'
Does it mean a lingering, last good-by—
    Adieu?
You 've been our guest a paltry year,
And now you are going to disappear
With a parting flip-flop, sad and sear—
    Boo-hoo!"

But the Mugwump scorned the Democrat's wail,
    "Too-hoo!"
And flirting its false, fantastic tail,
    "Too-hoo!"
It spread its wings and it soared away,
And left the Democrat in dismay,
With no pitch hot and the devil to pay—
    "Too-hoo!"

October 6, 1885.

SONG FOR THE DEPARTED

OH, what has become of the Mugwump-bird
    In this weather of wind and snow,
And does he roost as high as we heard
    He roosted a year ago?

A year ago and his plumes were red
  As the deepest of cardinal hues,
But in the year they 've changed, 't is said,
  To the bluest of bilious blues!

A year ago and this beautiful thing
  Warbled in careless glee;
But now the tune he is forced to sing
  Is pitched in a minor key.

It 's oh, we sigh, for the times gone by
  When the Mugwump lived to laugh—
When, coy and shy, he roosted high,
  And could n't be caught with chaff.

And it 's oh, we say, for the good old day
  Which never again may come—
When the Mugwump threaded his devious way
  And whistled his lumpty-tum!

November 5, 1885.

A SONG OF THE CHRISTMAS WIND

As on my roving way I go
  Beneath the starlight's gleaming,
Upon a bank of feathery snow
  I find a moonbeam dreaming;
I crouch beside the pretty miss
  And cautiously I give her
My gentlest, tend'rest little kiss,
  And frown to see her shiver.
      Oho! Oho!
      On bed of snow
Beneath the starlight's gleaming,
      I steal the bliss
      Of one sweet kiss
From that fair friend a-dreaming.

I scamper up the gloomy street
  With wild, hilarious shrieking,
And each rheumatic sign I meet
  I set forthwith to creaking;
The sooty chimneys wheeze and sigh
  In dismal apprehension,
And when the rich man passes by
  I pay him marked attention.
      Oho! Oho!
      With gusts of snow
I love to pelt and blind him;
      But I kiss the curls
      Of the beggar-girls
Who crouch in the dark behind him.

In summer-time a posy fair
  Bloomed on the distant heather,
And every day we prattled there
  And sang our songs together;
And thither, as we sang or told
  Of love's unchanging glory,
A maiden and her lover strolled,
  Repeating our sweet story.
      "Oho! Oho!"
      We murmur low—
The maid and I, together;
      For summer 's sped
      And love is dead
Upon the distant heather.

December 26, 1885.

AN OVERWORKED WORD

  We wake up and make up,
  We rake up, we fake up,
And use the word "up" when we can.

We drink up and think up,
We kink up and shrink up,
And do up a shirt or a man.

We slack up or back up,
We stack up and whack up,
And hold up a man or an ace;
We beer up and cheer up,
We steer up and clear up,
And work up ourselves or a case.

We walk up and talk up,
We stalk up and chalk up,
And everywhere "up" 's to be heard;
We wet up and set up,
But hanged if we let up
On "up," the much overworked word.

March 6, 1886.

A WESTERN BOY'S LAMENT

I wish 't I lived away down East, where codfish salt the sea,
And where the folks have pumpkin pie and apple-sass for tea.
Us boys who 's livin' here out West don't get more 'n half a show;
We don't have nothin' else to do but jest to sort of grow.

Oh, if I was a bird I 'd fly a million miles away
To where they feed their boys on pork and beans three times a
    day;
To where the place they call the Hub gives out its shiny spokes,
And where the folks—so father says—is mostly women-folks.

March 26, 1886.

HUMANITY

THE big-eyed baby, just across the way,
  Longs for the moon and reaches out to clasp it;
He lunges at the crescent cold and gray,
  And waxes wroth to find he cannot grasp it.

Be hushed, O babe, and give thy grief a rest;
  Better a thousand times for thee to ponder
Upon the lacteal wealth of mother's breast
  Than reach for that vain Milky Way up yonder.

Yet am I like this man of recent birth
  That lets a foolish disappointment fret it;
Scorning the sky, I 'm reaching for the earth,
  And grunt and groan because I do not get it.

April 12, 1886.

THE WHITE HOUSE BALLADS

KING GROVER CRAVES PIE

KING GROVER at his table round
Sate feasting once, and there was sound
  Of good things said and sly;
When presently King Grover spake:
"A murrain seize this futile cake—
  Come, Daniel, pass the pie!"

Then quoth Sir Daniel, flaming hot:
"Pie hath not been in Camelot
  Since Arthur was our King;
Soothly, I ween, 't were vain to make
Demand for pie where there is cake,
  For pie 's a ribald thing!"

"Despite King Arthur's rash decree,
Which ill beseemeth mine and me,"
　King Grover answered flat,
"I will have pie three times a day—
Let dotards cavil as they may—
　And pumpkin pie at that!"

Then, frowning a prodigious frown,
Sir Daniel pulled his visor down,
　And, with a mighty sigh,
Out strode he to the kitchen, where
He bade the varlet slaves prepare
　Three times each day a pie.

Thenceforth King Grover was content,
And all his reign in peace was spent;
　And when 't was questioned why
He waxed so hale, and why, the while,
The whole domain was free from guile,
　He simply answered, "Pie."

April 21, 1886

SISTER ROSE'S SUSPICIONS

"WHAT of these tidings, Grover dear,
That are reported far and near
　Upon suspicion's breath?
And is it true, as eke 't is said,
That you have made your mind to wed?"
　Quoth Rose Elizabeth.

With that his conscience smote him sore—
He cast his eyes upon the floor,
　But not a word he saith.
Then did she guess his secret flame;
In sooth she was a crafty dame,
　Was Rose Elizabeth.

She flaunted out into the hall
In grievous wrath and tears withal,
   Did Rose Elizabeth;
And when he saw her grewsome rage
That no entreaties could assuage,
   He fiercely muttered, " 'S death!"

April 24, 1886.

THE WEDDING-DAY

Oh, hand me down my spike-tail coat
   And reef my waistband in,
And tie this necktie round my throat
   And fix my bosom-pin;
I feel so weak and flustered like,
   I don't know what to say—
For I 'm to be wedded to-day, Dan'l,
   I 'm to be wedded to-day!

Put double sentries at the doors
   And pull the curtains down,
And tell the Democratic bores
   That I am out of town:
It 's funny folks hain't decency
   Enough to stay away
When I 'm to be wedded to-day, Dan'l,
   I 'm to be wedded to-day!

The bride, you say, is calm and cool
   In satin robes of white.
Well, I am stolid, as a rule,
   But now I 'm flustered quite;
Upon a surging sea of bliss
   My soul is borne away,
For I 'm to be wedded to-day, Dan'l,
   I 'm to be wedded to-day!

May 2, 1886.

THE TYING OF THE TIE

Now was Sir Grover passing wroth.
"A murrain seize the man," he quoth,
  "Who first invented ties!
Egad, they are a grievous bore,
And tying of them vexeth sore
  A person of my size!"

Lo, at his feet upon the floor
Were sprent the neckties by the score,
  And collars all a-wreck;
And good Sir Grover's cheeks were flame,
And good Sir Grover's arms were lame
  With wrestling at his neck.

But much it joyed him when he heard
Sir Daniel say: "I fain will gird
  Your necktie on for you,
As 't will not cause you constant fear
Of bobbing round beneath your ear
  Or setting you askew."

Sir Daniel grasped one paltry tie
And, with a calm, heroic eye
  And confidential air
(As who should say, "Odds bobs, I vow
There 's nothing like the knowing how"),
  He mounted on a chair.

And whilst Sir Grover raised his chin
(For much he did respect the pin)
  Sir Daniel tied the tie,
The which when good Sir Grover viewed—
Albeit it belike a dude—
  He heaved a grateful sigh.

May 3, 1886.

THE KISSING OF THE BRIDE

AND when at last, with priestly pray'r
And music mingling in the air,
  The nuptial knot was tied,
Sir Grover, flaming crimson red,
"Soothly, it is my mind," he said,
  "That I salute the bride!"

Whereat upon her virgin cheek,
So smooth, so plump, and comely eke,
  He did implant a smack
So lusty that the walls around
Gave such an echo to the sound
  As they had like to crack.

No modern salutation this,
No mincing, maudlin Mugwump kiss,
  To chill a bride's felicity;
Exploding on her blushing cheek,
Its virile clamor did bespeak
  Arcadian simplicity.

May 3, 1886.

THE CUTTING OF THE CAKE

SIR GROVER quoth: "Let each one here
Of soups and wine and sumptuous cheer
    Most heartily partake;
And whilst you are thus well employed,
I ween my consort will be joyed
    To cut the bridal cake!"

Then saith the bride, as courtesying low:
"There is no sweeter task, I trow,
    Than which is now my life,
To do thy will, my liege; so I
Would fain with thy request comply
    If I but had a knife."

Thereat of shining blades a score
Leaped from their knightly sheaths before
    You could have counted two;
As each brave knight right humbly prayed
The lady to accept his blade
    Wherewith her will to do.

But Lady Frances shook her head
And with sweet dignity she said:
    "None other's blade I 'll take
Save his who hath my rev'rence won—
My pole-star and my central sun—
    And his shall cut the cake!"

Then did Sir Grover bend him to
His trousers pockets, whence he drew
    A jack-knife, big and fat,
The which he gave into her hand,
Whereat the others murmured, and
    They marvelled much thereat.

But when the cake was cut, the rest
Made proper hurry to attest
    In knightly phrase emphatic
How that the cake was passing nice,
And how the blade that cleft each slice
    Was truly democratic.

May 4, 1886.

THE PASSING OF THE COMPLIMENT

Eftsoons the priest had made his say,
The courtly knights and ladies gay
    Did haste from every side,
With honeyed words and hackneyed phrase
And dainty smiles withal, to praise
    Sir Grover's blushing bride.

Out spake the courtly Sir Lamar:
"Of all fair brides, you, lady, are
    The fairest I have seen;
Not only of this castle grand,
But of all hearts throughout the land,
    Are you acknowledged queen!"

Whereat the Lady Frances bowed;
And rapturous murmurs in the crowd
    Did presently attest
That of the chestnuts uttered there
This chestnut was without compare—
    Foredating all the rest.

May 4, 1886.

THREE DAYS IN SPRINGTIME

I

On such a day as this old Notting Wood
    Made gentle answer from her secret glades
    Unto the tumult of the lusty blades
That owned no liege save merry Robin Hood.
    Deep in the haunts of velvet doe and buck
    Lolled gallant Will and pursy Friar Tuck,
Quaffing brown ale but last October brewed.
    Whilst of his flame the amorous Allen troll'd,
Upon the sward beyond, 'mid blithesome shouts
    That mocked each broken pate, the yeomen bold
Plied their stout quarter-staffs in bloody bouts.
Apart from all the rest, good Robin lay,
And sorely grieved that, lo, for many a day
The varlet sheriff had not rode that way.

II

On such a day as this the Nazarene
    Came from his lowly fisher home and stood
    Upon the shore of restless Galilee;

And as he viewed the ever-changing scene,
  He heard the breezes whisper to the sea
  How they had come that morning from a wood,
Where, in the warmth of springtime, all was green;
  How they had lingered there in furtive mood;
  How they had kissed a crucifixion tree
That angels guarded; and the listening One
  Bowed down His head in sweet humility.
"Father, Thy will," He cried, "not mine, be done."

Then sped the vernal breezes, fair and free,
To bear the tidings back to Calvary.
April 26, 1886.

SAG HARBOR

Three authors stood upon the beach
  And watched the fishing-smacks heave to;
As far as human eye could reach,
  Swept one expanse of saline blue.
First Hawthorne spoke: "While ebbs the tide,
  Suppose we three a-fishing go?"
" 'T is well," the white-haired Stoddard cried.
  "Amen," quoth Reverend E. P. Roe

" 'Neath yonder hedge, where burdocks blow
  And chirps the cricket to his mate,
Methinks the plethoric gentles grow;
  Come, let us dig a few for bait."
Thus big, strong Julian Hawthorne said;
  But with a smile that answered "No,"
The dear old Stoddard shook his head;
  And quoth to Reverend E. P. Roe:

"Although, assuredly, I am
  Unlearn'd in piscatorial lore,
I mind me that the modest clam
  Beats all your bait that grows ashore;

Still care I not, and you, friend Roe,
   Shall name the bait and fix the terms;
So now decide before we go—
   Shall it be clams or angleworms?"

" 'T is not for such a wretch as I
   To say what shall or shall not be,
For He who heeds the raven's cry
   Will care, in His good time, for me.
Whether upon the ocean tides
   Or by the water-brooks I go,
I 'll take the bait the Lord provides!"
   Remarked the Reverend E. P. Roe.

July 3, 1886.

THE 5TH OF JULY

The sun climbs up, but still the tyrant Sleep
   Holds fast our baby boy in his embrace;
   The slumb'rer sighs, anon athwart his face
Faint, half-suggested frowns like shadows creep.
One little hand lies listless on his breast,
   One little thumb sticks up with mute appeal,
   While motley burns and powder-marks reveal
The fruits of boyhood's patriotic zest.

Our baby's faithful poodle crouches near;
   He, too, is weary of the din and play
   That come with glorious Independence Day,
But which, thank God! come only once a year!
And Fido, too, has suffered in this cause,
   Which once a year right noisily obtains;
   For Fido's tail—or what thereof remains—
Is not so fair a sight as once it was.

July 7, 1886.

A POEM IN THREE CANTOS

I

FROM the land of logs and peaches
　　Came a callow jay-bird dressed
In homespun coat and breeches
　　And a gaudy velvet vest;
His eyes were red and wistful,
　　And he gawped a rural stare,
Yet, withal, he had a fistful
　　Of the stuff that speeds the mare.

II

9 to 4.

III

Confound the tarnal tallies
　　That mulct the callow jay!
Confound the sharp that dallies
　　With Detroit's wealth to-day!
Confound the fate that teaches
　　The jay to warble low!
But bless the land of peaches
　　Where the royal suckers grow!

July 9, 1886.

IN PRAISE OF TRUTH AND SIMPLICITY IN SONG

OH, for the honest, blithesome times
　　Of bosky Sherwood long ago,
When Allen trolled his amorous rhymes
　　And Robin twanged his crafty bow;
When Little John and Friar Tuck
　　Traversed the greenwood far and near,
Feasting on many a royal buck
　　Washed down with brown October beer!

Beside their purling sylvan rills,
　　What knew these yeomen bold and free
Of envious cares and grewsome ills
　　That now, sweet friend, vex you and me?
Theirs but to roam the leafy glade,
　　Beshrewing sheriffs, lords, and priests,
To loll supine beneath the shade,
　　Regaling monarchs with their feasts.

The murrain seize these ribald times
　　When there is such a lust for gold
That poets fashion all their rhymes,
　　Like varlet tradesfolk, to be sold!
Not so did Allen when he troll'd
　　His ballads in that merry glade;
Nay, in those courteous days of old
　　The minstrel spurned the tricks of trade!

So, joyous friend, when you and I
　　Sing to the world our chosen theme,
Let's do as do the birds that fly
　　Careless o'er woodland, wold, and stream:
Sing Nature's song, untouched of art—
　　Sing of the forest, brook, and plain;
And, hearing it, each human heart
　　Will vibrate with the sweet refrain.

August 16, 1886.

THE FOOL

A FOOL, when plagued by fleas by night,
　　Quoth: "Since these neighbors so despite me,
I think I will put out the light
　　And then they cannot see to bite me!"

November 26, 1886.

TO THE LADYE JULIA

ON HER X BIRTHDAY
Belle semper eadem

PUELLA PULCHRA

TIME, by Julia's face enchanted,
  Made with Love a bargain rare;
These the terms that Eros granted
  In the interest of his fair:
When old Chronos, in his yearly
  Round, must visit beauty's queen,
Love should turn the glass, while idly
  Time would bask beneath her een—
  Julia being then sweet 'steen.

UXOR PULCHRIOR

Cupid, cunning rogue, delighted
  At the chance to cheat his foe,
Bound the pact with kisses plighted—
  This was several years ago.
Of the scheme no doubt that you 'll u-
  Nite in saying: "Well we ween
'Gainst the charms of Ladye Julia
  Love 's but time in quarantine—
  Julia 'll always be sweet 'steen!"

MATRE PULCHERRIMA

Since, in all the white Decembers,
  For this day doth Chronos yearn;
Love sets the glass, then straight remembers
  Back the dial's hand to turn.
So old Tempus, edax rerum,
  May not mar the peerless sheen
Of her beauty.   Dixi verum.
  This is why I envy . . . —
  Julia 's always lovely 'steen!

                                    THE DOCTOR.

December 14, 1886

A BALLAD OF ANCIENT OATHS

THER ben a knyghte, Sir Hoten hight,
 That on a time did swere
In mighty store othes mickle sore,
 Which grieved his wiffe to here.

Soth, whenne she scofft, his wiffe did oft
 Swere as a ladye may;
"I' faith," "I' sooth," or "lawk," in truth,
 Ben alle that wiffe wold say.

Soe whenne her goodman waxed him wood
 She mervailed much to here
The hejeous sound of othes full round
 The which her lord did swere.

"Now pray thee, speke and tell me eke
 What thing hath vexed thee soe?"
The wiffe she cried; but hee replied
 By swereing moe and moe.

He sweren zounds which be Gog's wounds,
 By bright Marie and Gis,
By sweit Sanct Ann and holle Tan,
 And by Bryde's bell, ywis;

By holle grails, by 'slids and 'snails,
 By old Sanct Dunstan bauld,
The Virgin faire that Him did beare,
 By Him that Judas sauld;

By Arthure's sword, by Paynim horde,
 By holie modyr's teir,
By Cokis breath, by Zooks and 'sdeath,
 And by Sanct Swithen deir;

By divells alle, both greate and smalle,
  And all in hell there be,
By bread and salt, and by Gog's malt,
  And by the blody tree;

By Him that worn the crown of thorn,
  And by the sun and mone,
By deir Sanct Blane and Sanct Fillane,
  And three kings of Cologne;

By the gude Lord and His sweit word,
  By him that herryit hell,
By blessed Jude, by holie Rude,
  And eke by Gad himsel'!

He sweren soe (and mickle moe)
  It made man's flesch to creepen;
The air ben blue with his ado,
  And sore his wiffe ben wepen.

Giff you wold know why sweren soe
  The good man hight Sir Hoten,
He ben full wroth because, in soth,
  He leesed his coler boten.

March 1, 1887.

THE SUSCEPTIBLE WIDOW

I SHOW, by my distressful tones
  And by my doleful features,
How much I miss the Reverend Jones,
  That best of modern preachers.
When his Chicago work was done
  He paused not to consider
What grief the parting wrought upon
  One lorn and lonely widder.

I used to wend my way each night
   To revel in his teachings;
My burdened soul grew airy light
   Beneath his magic preachings.
I occupied a seat reserved
   For struggling young beginners,
And hung upon the blasts he served
   To unrepentant sinners.

Farewell to those delicious times
   For silent adoration!
My idol speeds to other climes
   To ply his sweet vocation.
Oh that he might forget her not
   Who boldly makes assertion
That from her lonely, widowed lot
   She hankers for conversion!

April 6, 1886.

PIKE'S PEAK

I STOOD upon the peak, amid the air;
   Below me lay the peopled, busy earth.
Life, life, and life again was everywhere,
   And everywhere were melody and mirth,
Save on that peak, and silence brooded there.

I vaunted then myself, and half aloud
   I gloried in the journey I had done:
Eschewing earth and earth's seductive crowd,
   I'd scaled this steep, despite the rocks and sun;
Of such a feat might any man be proud!

But, as I boasted thus, my burro brayed;
   I turned, and lo! a tear was in his eye,
And as I gazed, methought the burro sayed:
   "Prithee, who brought you up this mountain high—
Was it your legs or mine the journey made?"

Then moralled I: The sturdiest peak is Fame's!
  And there be many on its very height,
Who strut in pride and vaunt their empty claims,
  While those poor human asses who delight
To place them there have unremembered names!
April 6, 1887.

LONGINGS

I LONG for some intenser life,
Some wilder joy, some sterner strife!
A dull, slow stream whose waters pass
Through weary wastes of dry morass,
Through reptile-breeding levels low—
A sluggish ooze and not a flow—
Choked up with fat and slimy weeds
The current of my life proceeds.

Once more to meet the advancing sun
Earth puts her bridal glories on;
Once more beneath the summer moons
The whippoorwill her song attunes;
Once more the elements are rife
With countless forms of teeming life.
Life fills the air and fills the deeps;
Life from the quickened clod upleaps;

But all too feeble is the ray
That glances on our Northern day;
And man, beneath its faint impress,
Grows sordid, cold, and passionless.

I long to greet those ardent climes
Where the sun's burning heat sublimes
All forms of being, and imparts
Its fervor even to human hearts;
To see uptowering, grand and calm,
The king of trees, the lordly palm,

And, when night darkens through the skies,
Watch the strange constellations rise;
The floral pomps, the fruits of gold,
The fiery life I would behold;
The swart, warm beauties, luscious-lipped,
With hearts in passion's lava dipped;
Nature's excess and overgrowth—
The light and splendor of the South!

Or if it be my lot to bear
This pulseless life, this blank despair,
Waft me, ye winds, unto those isles
Round which the fair Pacific smiles;
Where, through the sun-bright atmosphere,
Their purple peaks the mountains rear;
Where earth is garmented in light,
And with unfading spring is bright
Then, if my life must be a dream,
Without a plan, without a scheme,
From purpose as from action free,
A dream of beauty it shall be.

(Attributed to) HORACE RUBLEE.

July 4, 1888.

FROM THE RUBAIYAT OF OMAR KHAYYAM

UNTO a withered palm-tree clinging,
A yusef-bird was wildly singing,
  And "yusef, yusef" was the word
That to my very soul went winging.

And came to me in my dejection
The keen and harrowing reflection:
  "Thou art indeed a yusef-bird;
I ate your kind the last election!"

August 3, 1889.

MEIN FAEDER BED

Ach, faeder bed! mein faeder bed!
Upon thy body softly spread,
What Cold von Winter shall I dread?

All through the night no touch of storm
Shall come to nip or chill my form—
Du bist so grosser goot und warm!

The winds that howl I need not fear,
But with that faeder bed to cheer,
I dream von Wiener wurst und beer!

Sometimes at night, in turning o'er,
I made that bed upon the floor.
Ach, then I shivered some, and swore!

But now I either turn mit skill
Or lie in bed sahr grosser still;
I make me not to swear or chill.

My Faderland is auf der sea,
Und when I sleep wo Yankees be
How vainly shall I pine for thee!

How, when I lay my weary head
Below ein cotton sheet and spread,
Shall I lament das faeder bed!

Yet still shall pleasing dreams combine
To waft me hence what joys are thine,
O faeder bed, beyond the Rhine!

December 14, 1889.

BETHLEHEM TOWN

THERE burns a star o'er Bethlehem town—
    See, O my eyes!
And gloriously it beameth down
Upon a virgin mother meek
And Him whom solemn Magi seek.
Burn on, O star! and be the light
To guide us all to Him this night!

The angels walk in Bethlehem town—
    Hush, O my heart!
The angels come and bring a crown
To Him, our Saviour and our King;
And sweetly all this night they sing.
Sing on in rapturous angel throng,
That we may learn that heavenly song!

Near Bethlehem town there blooms a tree—
    O heart, beat low!
And it shall stand on Calvary!
But from the shade thereof we turn
Unto the star that still shall burn
When Christ is dead and risen again
To mind us that He died for men.

There is a cry in Bethlehem town—
    Hark, O my soul!
'T is of the Babe that wears the crown.
It telleth us that man is free—
That He redeemeth all and me!
The night is sped—behold the morn!
Sing, O my soul; the Christ is born!

December 27, 1889.

IN HOLLAND

Our course lay up a smooth canal,
  Through tracts of velvet green,
And through the shade that windmills made
  And pasture-lands between.
The kine had canvas on their backs
  To temper autumn's spite,
And everywhere there was an air
  Of comfort and delight.

My wife, dear philosophic soul!
  Saw here whereof to prate:
"Vain fools are we across the sea
  To boast our nobler state!
Go North or South or East or West,
  Or whereso'er you please,
You shall not find what's here combined—
  Equality and ease.

"How tidy are these honest homes
  In every part and nook!
The men-folk wear a prosperous air,
  The women happy look.
Seeing the peace that smiles around,
  I would our land were such.
Think as you may, I'm free to say,
  I would we were the Dutch!"

Just then we overtook a boat,
  The Golden Tulip hight;
Big with the weight of motley freight,
  It was a goodly sight!
Mynheer van Blarcom sat on deck,
  With pipe in lordly pose,
And with his son of twenty-one
  He played at dominos.

Then quoth my wife: "How fair to see
  This sturdy, honest man
Beguile all pain and lust of gain
  With whatso joys he can!
Methinks his spouse is down below,
  Beading a kerchief gay;
A babe, mayhap, lolls in her lap
  In the good old milky way

"Where in the land from whence we came
  Is there content like this?
Where such disdain of sordid gain—
  Such sweet domestic bliss?
A homespun woman I, this land
  Delights me overmuch.
Think as you will and argue still,
  I like the honest Dutch."

And then my wife made end of speech;
  Her voice stuck in her throat:
For, swinging round the turn, we found
  What motor moved the boat.
Hitched up in towpath-harness there
  Was neither horse nor cow,
But the buxom frame of a Hollandish dame—
  Mynheer van Blarcom's frau!
January 27, 1890.

IN PRAISE OF PIE

I 'D like to weave a pretty rhyme
  To send my *Daily News*.
What shall I do? In vain I woo
  The too-exacting Muse;
In vain I coax the tyrant minx,
  And this the reason why:
She will not sing a plaguy thing,
  Because I 've eaten pie.

A pretty pass it is, indeed,
   That I have reached at last,
If I, in spite of appetite,
   Must fast, and fast, and fast!
The one dear boon I am denied
   Is that for which I sigh.
Take all the rest that men hold best,
   But leave, oh, leave me pie!

I hear that Whittier partakes
   Of pie three times a day;
And it is rife that with a knife
   He stows that pie away.
There 's Stoddard—he was raised on pie,
   And he is hale and fat.
And Stedman's cry is always "pie,"
   And hot mince-pie at that!

Of course I 'm not at all like those
   Great masters in their art,
Except that pie doth ever lie
   Most sweetly next my heart,
And that I fain would sing my songs
   Without surcease or tiring
If 'neath my vest and else could rest
   That viand all-inspiring!

What I object to is the harsh,
   Vicarious sacrifice
I 'm forced to make if I partake
   Of fair and proper pies;
The pangs I suffer are the pangs
   To other sinners due.
I 'd gladly bear my righteous share,
   But not the others', too.

How vain the gift of heavenly fire,
   How vain the laurel wreath,
If these crown not that godlike spot,
   A well-filled paunch beneath!

And what is glory but a sham
  To those who pine and sigh
For bliss denied, which (as implied)
  Is pie, and only pie!

Well, since it 's come to such a pass,
  I boldly draw the line;
Go thou, O Muse, which way you choose,
  While I meander mine.
Farewell, O fancies of the pen,
  That dazzled once mine eye;
My choice may kill, but still, oh. still,
  I choose and stand for pie!

April 8, 1890.

UNCLE EPH

My Uncle Ephraim was a man who did not live in vain,
And yet, why he succeeded so I never could explain.
By nature he was not endowed with wit to a degree,
But folks allowed there nowhere lived a better man than he.
He started poor, but soon got rich; he went to Congress then,
And held that post of honor long against much brainier men;
He never made a famous speech nor did a thing of note,
And yet the praise of Uncle Eph welled up from every throat.

I recollect I never heard him say a bitter word;
He never carried to and fro unpleasant things he heard;
He always doffed his hat and spoke to every one he knew;
He tipped to poor and rich alike a genial "howdy-do";
He kissed the babies, praised their looks, and said, "That child
    will grow
To be a Daniel Webster or our President, I know!"
His voice was so mellifluous, his smile so full of mirth,
That folks declared he was the best and smartest man on earth!

Now, father was a smarter man, and yet he never won
Such wealth and fame as Uncle Eph, "the deestrick's fav'rite son."

He had "convictions," and he was not loath to speak his mind;
He went his way and said his say as he might be inclined.
Yes, he was brainy; yet his life was hardly a success—
He was too honest and too smart for this vain world, I guess!
At any rate, I wondered he was unsuccessful when
My Uncle Eph, a duller man, was so revered of men!

When Uncle Eph was dying he called me to his bed,
And in a tone of confidence inviolate he said:
"Dear Willyum, ere I seek repose in yonder blissful sphere,
I fain would breathe a secret in your adolescent ear:
Strive not to hew your path through life—it really does n't pay;
Be sure the salve of flattery soaps all you do and say;
Herein the only royal road to fame and fortune lies:
Put not your trust in vinegar—molasses catches flies!"
October 11, 1890.

CHRISTMAS MORNING

THE angel host that sped last night,
　　Bearing the wondrous news afar,
Came in their ever-glorious flight
　　Unto a slumbering little star.

"Awake and sing, O star!" they cried.
　　"Awake and glorify the morn!
Herald the tidings far and wide—
　　He that shall lead His flock is born!"

The little star awoke and sung
　　As only stars in rapture may,
And presently where church bells hung
　　The joyous tidings found their way.

"Awake, O bells! 't is Christmas morn—
　　Awake and let thy music tell
To all mankind that now is born
　　What Shepherd loves His lambkins well!"

Then rang the bells as fled the night
  O'er dreaming land and drowsing deep,
And coming with the morning light,
  They called, my child, to you asleep.

Sweetly and tenderly they spoke,
  And lingering round your little bed,
Their music pleaded till you woke,
  And this is what their music said:

"Awake and sing! 't is Christmas morn,
  Whereon all earth salutes her King!
In Bethlehem is the Shepherd born.
  Awake, O little lamb, and sing!"

So, dear my child, kneel at my feet,
  And with those voices from above
Share thou this holy time with me,
  The universal hymn of love.

December 25, 1890.

HYMN: MIDNIGHT HOUR

MIDNIGHT hour! how sweet the calm
  Thy solemn cadences impart;
What solace as of healing balm
  Cometh with thee unto this heart!
Yet bring me not thy grace alone—
  Let others share thy dear delight;
Oh, let thy soothing monotone
  Be heard of all this holy night!

Anon shall angels walk the sky,
  The stars cry out in rapturous glee,
And radiant splendors glorify
  The waking earth and wondering sea;

Jehovah's reassuring word
  Shall be proclaimed abroad again,
And tidings everywhere be heard
  Of peace on earth, good will to men!

'T is of those glories of the morn,
  The sacrifice that makes man free,
And of the Babe in Bethlehem born
  That midnight's voices speak to me.
Speak on, O voices sweet and low,
  Soothing our griefs and doubts away—
That all mankind may hear and know
  What rapture cometh with the day!

December 25, 1890.

WHEN STEDMAN COMES TO TOWN

WE 'RE cleaning up the boulevards
  And divers thoroughfares;
Our lawns, our fences, and our yards
  Are bristling with repairs;
And soon Chicago 'll be abloom
  With splendor and renown;
For ain't we going to have a boom
  When Stedman comes to town?

And gosh! the things we 'll have to eat—
  The things we 'll have to drink!
O 'er hecatombs of corn-fed meat
  How shall the glasses clink!
Our culture, having started in,
  Will do the thing up brown.
'T will be a race 'twixt brass and tin
  When Stedman comes to town!

There 's Mr. Wayback Canvass Hamm,
    Old Crœsus' counterpart;
He don't know nor give a damn
    About poetic art;
And he has such amount of pelf
    As would weigh mountains down,
And he has sworn to spread himself
    When Stedman comes to town.

And Mrs. Hamm, a faded belle,
    And one no longer young,—
She speaks the native quite as well
    As any foreign tongue,—
At Mr. Hamm's reception she
    Will wear a gorgeous gown
That shows all else but modesty,
    When Stedman comes to town.

Now, Stedman knows a thing or two
    Besides poetic art;
Yes, truth to say, 'twixt me and you,
    Stedman is mighty smart;
And so I wonder will he smile
    Good-naturedly or frown
At our flamboyant Western style,
    When Stedman comes to town.

April 23, 1891.

THE STRAW HAT

THE sweet shade falls athwart her face,
    And leaves half shadow and half light—
Dimples and lips in open day,
    And dreamy brows and eyes in night.

So low the languid eyelids fall,
　　They rest their silk upon her cheek,
And give delicious laziness
　　To glances arch and cunning meek.

It cannot frown, the placid brow
　　Hidden in rare obscurity;
They cannot hate, the indolent eyes,
　　The sins they do not strive to see.

And in the sunshine of her cheeks
　　The wanton dimples are at play,
So frolic-earnest in their sport
　　They do not care to look away.

And, oh, if love, kiss-winged, should come
　　And light on such a rose as this,
Could brow or eye or dimples blame
　　Such lips for giving back a kiss?
June 24, 1891.

————

A WAR–SONG

Awake! arise, ye patriot brave,
　　Your duty to fulfill!
Rush in your righteous wrath to save
　　The land from threatened ill.
Foul treachery's vengeful shadows flit
　　Like demons everywhere;
And Baby Cleveland wants to sit
　　In grandpa's baby's chair.

Shall this spoiled darling vanquish that
　　Sweet Hoosier younkit?　Nay!
She'll never wear her grandpa's hat—
　　She isn't built that way.

Out—out upon the pampered chit!
　The patriot legions swear
That Baby Cleveland shall not sit
　In grandpa's baby's chair!

So come!　We'll lift our standard high—
　A tiny pair of pants!
This "In hoc signo" 'll petrify
　All Mugwump sycophants!
Stern common sense shall soon outwit
　Each sentimental snare;
And Baby Cleveland shall not sit
　In grandpa's baby's chair!

　June 24, 1892.

EXTINCT MONSTERS

Oh, had I lived in the good old days,
　When the Ichthyosaurus ramped around,
When the Elasmosaur swam the bays,
　And the Sivatherium pawed the ground,
Would I have spent my precious time
At weaving golden thoughts in rhyme?

When the Tinoceras snooped about,
　And the Pterodactyl flapped its wings,
When the Brontops with the warty snout
　Noseyed around for herbs and things,
Would I have bothered myself o'ermuch
About divine afflatus and such?

The Dinotherium flourished then;
　The Pterygotus lashed the seas;
The Rhamphorhynchus prospered when
　The Scaphognathus perched in trees;
And every creature, wild and tame,
Rejoiced in some rococo name.

Pause and ponder; who could write
   A triolet or roundelay
While a Megatherium yawped all night
   And a Hesperornis yamped all day,
While now and again the bray sonorous
Of Glyptodon Asper swelled the chorus?

If I 'd been almost anything
   But a poet, I might have got along:
Those extinct monsters of hoof and wing
   Were not conducive to lyric song;
So Nature reserved this tender bard
For the kindlier Age of Pork and Lard.

May 11, 1893.

MRS. REILLY'S PEACHES

WHETHER in Michigan they grew,
   Or by the far Pacific,
Or Jerseywards, I never knew
   Or cared; they were magnifique!
They set my hungry eyes aflame,
   My heart to beating quicker,
When trotted out by that good dame,
   A-drowned in spicy liquor!

Of divers sweets in many a land
   I have betimes partaken,
Yet now for those old joys I stand,
   My loyalty unshaken!
My palate, weary of the ways
   Of modern times, beseeches
The toothsome grace of halcyon days
   And Mrs. Reilly's peaches!

Studded with cloves and cinnamon,
   And duly spiced and pickled,
That viand was as choice an one
   As ever palate tickled!

And by those peaches on his plate
   No valorous soul was daunted,
For oh, the more of them you ate
   The more of them you wanted!

The years have dragged a weary pace
   Since last those joys I tasted,
And I have grown so wan of face
   And oh, so slender-waisted!
Yes, all is sadly changed, and yet
   If this eulogium reaches
A certain lady, I shall get
   A quick return in peaches.

May 15, 1893.

O'CONNOR'S ILOQUINT SPACHE

'T wuz whin O'Connor shpoke the crowd
   Grew pathriotic truly;
For him O'Dooley hit O'Dowd
   And Healy shtruck O'Dooley;
And Redmond give Muldoon a swat,
   And all wint well, begorry,
And there was Home Rule on that shpot,
Till to his fate O'Connor got,
An' sez, sez he: "For sayin' phwat
   Oi did," sez he, "Oi 'm sorry!"

July 29, 1893.

DOCTOR RABELAIS

Once—it was many years ago,
   In early wedded life,
Ere yet my loved one had become
   A very knowing wife,

She came to me and said: "My dear,
  I think (and do not you?)
That we should have about the house
  A doctor's book or two.

"Our little ones have sundry ills
  Which I should understand
And cure myself, if I but had
  A doctor's book at hand.
Why not economize, my dear,
  In point of doctor's bills
By purchasing the means to treat
  Our little household ills?"

Dear, honest, patient little wife!
  She did not even guess
She offered me the very prize
  I hankered to possess.
"You argue wisely, wife," quoth I.
  "Proceed without delay
To find and comprehend the works
  Of Doctor Rabelais."

I wrote the title out for her
  (She 'd never heard the name),
And presently she bought those books,
  And home she lugged the same;
I clearly read this taunting boast
  On her triumphant brow:
"Aha, ye venal doctors all,
  Ye are outwitted now!"

Those volumes stood upon the shelf
  A month or two unread,
Save as such times by night I conned
  Their precious wit in bed;
But once—it was a wintry time—
  I heard my loved one say:
"This child is croupy; I 'll consult
  My doctor, Rabelais!"

Soon from her delusive dream
  My beauteous bride awoke.
Too soon she grasped the fulness of
  My bibliomaniac joke.
There came a sudden, shocking change,
  As you may well suppose,
And with her reprehensive voice
  The temperature arose.

But that was many years ago,
  In early wedded life,
And that dear lady has become
  A very knowing wife;
For she hath learned from Rabelais
  What elsewhere is agreed:
The plague of bibliomania is
  A cureless ill indeed.

And still at night, when all the rest
  Are hushed in sweet repose,
O'er those two interdicted tomes
  I laugh and nod and doze.
From worldly ills and business cares
  My weary mind is lured,
And by that doctor's magic art
  My ailments all are cured.

So my dear, knowing little wife
  Is glad that it is so,
And with a smile recalls the trick
  I played her years ago;
And whensoe'er dyspeptic pangs
  Compel me to their sway,
The saucy girl bids me consult
  My Doctor Rabelais!
November 22, 1894.

SONG

WHY do the bells of Christmas ring?
Why do little children sing?

Once a lovely shining star,
Seen by shepherds from afar,
Gently moved until its light
Made a manger's cradle bright.

There a darling baby lay,
Pillowed soft upon the hay;
And its mother sung and smiled:
"This is Christ, the holy Child!"

Therefore bells for Christmas ring,
Therefore little children sing.
December 12, 1894.

TO WARD H. LAMON, ASLEEP ON HIS LIBRARY FLOOR

As you, dear Lamon, soundly slept,
  With books around you on the floor,
Into this pleasant nook I crept,
  To hear the music of your snore.

A man who sleeps as now you sleep,
  Who pipes as music'ly as you,
Who sinks all care in slumbers deep,
  As you, O happy man, now do,

Must have a conscience fully free
  Of troublous pangs and vain ado:
So ever may your slumbers be,
  So ever be your conscience, too!

And when the last sweet sleep of all
  Shall smooth the wrinkles from your brow,
Oh, may God's eyes as kindly fall
  Upon your sleep as mine do now!
February 13, 1891.

THE SNAKES

THESE are the snakes that Rowdy saw:
  Some were green and some were white,
  Some were black as the spawn of night;
    Some were yellow;
    And one big fellow
  Had monstrous blotches of angry red,
  And a scarlet welt on his slimy head;
And other snakes that Rowdy saw
    Were of every hue
    From pink to blue,
  And the longer he looked the bigger they grew!

An old he-snake with a frowsy head
Was one of the snakes that Rowdy saw.
  This old he-snake he grinned and leered
  When he saw that Rowdy was afeard;
  And he ran out his tongue in frightful wise
  As he batted his fireless dead-fish eyes;
    And he lashed his tail
    In the moonlight pale,
And he tickled his jaw with his left hind paw—
Did this old he-snake that Rowdy saw!

These hideous snakes that Rowdy saw
    Wriggled and twisted
    Wherever they listed,
    Straightway glided
    Or ambled one-sided.
  There were some of those things
  That had fiery wings—

Yes, some of the snakes that Rowdy saw
    Hummed round in the air
    With their eyeballs aglare
    And their whiskers aflare;
And they hissed their approval of Rowdy's despair!

And some of the snakes that Rowdy saw
    Had talons like bats,
And looked like a cross between buzzards and rats!
They crawled from his boots, and they sprawled on the floor;
They sat on the mantel, and perched on the door,
And grinned all the fiercer the louder he swore!

    Out, out of his boots
    Came the damnable brutes—
These murdersome snakes that Rowdy saw!
    Strange cries they uttered,
    And poison they sputtered
    As they crawled or they fluttered.
    This way and that
    Their venom they spat,
Till Rowdy had doubts as to where he was at.

They twined round his legs, and encircled his waist;
His arms and his neck and his breast they embraced;
They hissed in his ears, and they spat in his eyes,
And with their foul breaths interrupted his cries.
    Blue serpents and green,
    Red, yellow, and black,
    Of as hideous mien
    As ever was seen,
    Girt him round, fore and back,
    And higgling
    And wiggling,
With their slimy and grinny preponderance they bore
Rowdy down to the floor. He remembers no more.

The sequel is this: The snakes that he saw
    Were such hideous snakes, were such torturesome things,
    With their poison-tipped fangs and their devil-claw wings,

That he speaks of them now with a meaningful awe;
    And when in the bar-room the bottle goes round,
    And wassail and laughter and "boodle" abound,
Poor Rowdy he turns down his glass with a sigh.
"Come, Rowdy, drink hearty!" the aldermen cry.
His palate is yearning, his fauces are dry,
    The bottle appeals to his gullet and eye;
    But he thinks of the snakes, and he—lets it go by.

January 4, 1895.

THE BOY

    Down through the snow-drifts in the street
        With blustering joy he steers;
    His rubber boots are full of feet
        And his tippet full of ears.

January 15, 1895.

THE BUGABOO

    There was a wonderful bugaboo
        Lived in a drear Egyptian clime,
    And with a base intent he flew
        Up northward once upon a time.
    Where little Quincy Browning slept,
        This boogy flew without delay,
    And down the chimney-flue he crept
        To steal that pretty child away.

    Awakened in the dead of night
        By him a-crawling down the flue,
    Imagine little Quincy's fright
        To see the dreadful bugaboo.
    He wept with all his might and main
        Till all his tears were nearly spent,
    But his remonstrances were vain—
        The bugaboo would not relent.

"Be quiet," hissed the bugaboo,
  And then he scratched the infant sore,
And from his little crib he drew
  The screaming child upon the floor.
But all for nothing were his pains,
  For as he flew to Egypt wild
In rushed the good old Gran'ma Haines
  To see what ailed her precious child.

"Go, leave my pretty dear alone,
  And never dare again intrude!"
Cried gran'ma, in a savage tone
  And with a threatening attitude.
He dropped his screaming, struggling prey,
  And scuttled up the chimney-flue;
And back to Egypt far away
  Escaped the dreadful bugaboo.

January 28, 1885.

A VALENTINE

TO THE EVER-ADORABLE AND EVER-GRACIOUS MISSES ANNA DELLA
    AND ELIZABETH WINSLOW, AGED TEN AND SEVEN YEARS
    RESPECTIVELY

IF I were Eric Ericsson, with flowing flaxen hair,
Perhaps Miss Anna Della would not scoff at my despair.
Perhaps my sweet Elizabeth would bless me with a smile
If I were Patrick Miles O'Dowd—a lord from Erin's isle.
Alas, I am not Eric, and alas, I am not Pat!
I simply am a Yankee boy, and a tough old one at that.
Yet do I love these beauteous maids whom I have named above,
And send them both this valentine to tell them of my love—
A paltry, graceless thing, yet with a thousand kisses sealed,
And autographed (as you observe) by poor old   FIELD.

February 14, 1895.

THE TIN BANK

SPEAKING of the banks, I 'm bound to say
  That a bank of tin is far the best,
And I know of one that has stood for years
  In a pleasant home away out West;
It had stood for years on the mantelpiece,
  Between the clock and the Wedgwood plate—
A wonderful bank, as you 'll concede
  When you 've heard the things I 'll now relate.

This bank was made of McKinley tin,
  Well soldered up at sides and back;
But it didn't resemble tin at all,
  For they 'd painted it over an iron-black.
And that it really was a bank
  'T was an easy thing to see and say,
For above the door in gorgeous red
  Appeared the letters B–A–N–K.

This bank had been so well devised
  And wrought so cunningly that when
You put your money in that hole
  It couldn't get out of that hole again!
Somewhere about that stanch, snug thing
  A secret spring was hid away,
But where it was, or how it worked—
  Excuse me, please, but I will not say.

Thither, with dimpled cheeks aglow
  Came pretty children oftentimes,
And, standing upon a stool or chair,
  Put in their divers pence and dimes.
Once Uncle Hank came home from town,
  After a cycle of grand events,
And put in a round blue ivory thing
  He said was good for fifty cents!

The bank went clinkety-clinkety-clink,
　　And larger grew the precious sum,
Which grandma said she hoped would prove
　　A gracious boon to heathendom!
But there were those—I call no names—
　　Who did not fancy any plan
That did not in some wise involve
　　The candy and banana man.

Listen: Once when the wind went "Y-o-o-o-o-o!"
　　When with a wail the screech-owl flew
Out of her lair in the haunted barn—
　　There came three burglars down the road,
Three burglars skilled in arts of sin,
　　And they cried: "What's this? Aha! Oho!"

They burgled from half-past ten P. M.
　　Till the village bell struck four o'clock;
They hunted and searched and guessed and tried—
　　But the little tin bank would not unlock!
They couldn't discover the secret spring!
　　So when the barn-yard rooster crowed,
They up with their tools and stole away,
　　With the bitter remark that they'd be blowed!

Next morning came a sweet-faced child,
　　And reached her dimpled hand to take
A nickel to send to the heathen poor
　　And a nickel to spend for her stomach's sake;
She pressed the hidden secret spring,
　　And lo! the bank flew open then
With a cheery creek that seemed to say
　　"I am glad to see you come again!"

If you were I, and if I were you,
　　What would we keep our money in?
In a down-town bank of British steel
　　Or an at home bank of McKinley tin?

Some want silver and some want gold,
  But the little tin bank that wants the two
And is run on the double-standard plan—
  Why, that is the bank for me and you!

June 22, 1895.

————

MY SABINE FARM

AT last I have a Sabine farm
  Abloom with shrubs and flowers;
And garlands gay I weave by day
  Amid those fragrant bowers;
And yet, O fortune hideous,
I have no blooming Lydias;
And what, ah, what's a Sabine farm to us without its Lydias?

Within my cottage is a room
  Where I would fain be merry;
Come one and all unto that hall,
  Where you 'll be welcome, very!
I 've a butler who 's Hibernian—
But no, I 've no Falernian!
And what, ah, what 's a Sabine farm to you without Falernian?

Upon this cosey Sabine farm
  What breeds my melancholy?
Why is my Muse down with the blues
  Instead of up and jolly?
A secret this between us:
I 'm shy of a Mæcenas!
And what 's, oh, what 's a Sabine farm to me without Mæcenas!

August 1, 1895.

THE VINEYARD

INTO the vineyard I went with Bill,
  Blithe as youth can be,
As the sun declined beyond the hill
  And drowsed in the western sea;
And under the arching vines we sat,
And we sampled this and we sampled that
Till we didn't know where we were at,
  Nor the devil a bit cared we.

Out of the vineyard I came with Bill,
  Just in time to see
The sun peep over an eastern hill
  And grin at Bill and me.
And Bill remarked: "We quit too soon;
Let us sit in the light of that silvery moon
And list to the nightingale's plaintive tune!"
  So back to the vineyard went we.

September 7, 1895.

FOR THE CHARMING MISS I. F.'S ALBUM

IF you loved me as I love you,
No knife could cut our love in two!
Not even though that envious blade
Of rare Toledo stuff was made,
Not though its handle lay within
The grasp of mighty Saladin;
I should not heed; its feeble shock
Would fall as on a flinty rock,
And its attack would simply be
A trifling incident to me;
It could not cut our love in two
If you loved me as I love you!

Nor could the mighty cyclone's wrath,
That levels cities in its path,
Uproots whole forests, mows the grain,
And furrows up the stubborn plain,
It could not cause me to repine
If only your true love were mine!
I'd bid the boisterous breezes blow—
Knowing as only I should know
They could not rend our love in two
If you loved me as I love you!

And if a Herr Professor came
(I hint no hint, I name no name!)—
What if he came from oversea,
And fiddled, as can only he,
Antique sonatas by the score,
Études and opuses galore,
And other tunes from foreign lands
One likes, but seldom understands—
The tweedledees and tweedledums
We always get when Thomas comes;
We'd let him fiddle—all his art
Could never fiddle us apart,
Could never charm our love in two
If you loved me as I love you!

If—ah, that "if" stands in the way,
And so I've nothing more to say;
I'll to your father; he'll insure
A speedy menticulture cure
For him who would not wail "boo-hoo"
If you loved me as I love you!

October 16, 1895.

INDEX TO FIRST LINES

Printed in the United States .
145467LV00004B/28/P

9 781434 463128